CONSUMER BUYING GUIDE

CONTENTS_____

CONTENTS

CONTENTS

INTRODUCTION

Are you finally ready to buy that full-size stereo system with a CD player? Do you know what the difference is between a carousel and magazine disc changer? Is a five-disc changer better than a four? Looking to replace your aging television set with a feature laden new one? Are you sure you know what "cable ready" means?

In short, do you know how to determine what features you'll want in a product? Then, do you know how to get the most features for your money?

It takes experience and expert knowledge to spend your hard-earned dollars wisely in every facet of today's marketplace. Intelligent choices become more difficult when you consider rapid advances in technology and shifts in the world's economy. These factors can quickly change prices, availability, and long-term usefulness, making your buying decisions very confusing.

That's where we at CONSUMER GUIDE® can help. We recognize the challenge in picking a Best Buy, a product that meets your high standards of quality, performance, and value. Our experts in the major product fields have taken the guesswork and confusion out of making major purchases. CONSUMER GUIDE® has no affiliation with any manufacturers or retailers, we accept no advertising, and we are not interested in selling products. Our sole purpose is to provide you—the consumer—with the information needed to make informed, intelligent decisions.

In this publication, we have tried to review a wide variety of products to address diverse consumer needs. The products reviewed range from small personal items, such as irons, telephones, and automatic-drip coffeemakers, to major purchases, such as televisions, refrigerators, computers, and stereo systems. We have not limited the choices to lower-end products or top-of-the-line merchandise. We know that a product is only a Best Buy if it meets your needs and budget. Keeping this in mind, we have selected products in a variety of sizes and prices to match the requirements of different shoppers. In fact, this year we have attempted to meet the needs of more consumers than ever.

INTRODUCTION

Many consumers will find they benefit from exercising patience. When a new product first hits the market, it generally commands a premium price. However, if you wait, instead of rushing right out to make the purchase, you will probably observe that not only does the price come down, but changes and improvements will have been incorporated into the product. Prime examples include products such as CD players, personal cassette players, computers, and food processors. These items are much less expensive today than they were when they first came on the market, and the progression of refinements has been steady.

To get the most out of this book, first review the introductory material at the beginning of each chapter. This introduction contains important information about the product category, describes product features, and explains the terminology you need to know when you shop. Determine what features will be most useful to you or those using the item. Once you are acquainted with the criteria we use to select products, go on to our product reviews. Items rated as Best Buys were chosen for their usefulness, high quality, and overall value. A Best Buy isn't necessarily the least expensive model; it's the highest-quality product available at a reasonable price. Recommended selections are also good products, but for one reason or another, they do not measure up to our Best Buy standards. Such a product may carry a high price tag, it may have limited appeal, or it could be so new on the market that we haven't been able to accurately test its performance and durability over a period of time.

When you shop, compare prices and models. We provide an Approximate Low Price to serve as your price guide. If a dealer quotes a price close to the Approximate Low Price in this publication, then you know that you are getting first-rate value for your money. **All the prices listed are accurate at the time of printing but are subject to manufacturers' changes.** In some cases, products are so new that prices were not yet available. All products were checked to make sure that they would be available to consumers in 1997, but product manufacture and distribution is beyond our control. Occasionally, a product may get discontinued with little warning or notice.

TELEVISIONS AND TV-VCR COMBINATIONS

The American public's voracious appetite for color televisions led to the sale of almost 25 million sets last year. Many people seem to want a set in every room—including the bathroom. Some viewers have also fallen in love with bigger and bigger screens (larger than 27 inches). Sales of large-screen TVs and projection TVs are exploding as consumers buy the biggest sets and the best picture quality they can afford. The old adage that "a picture is worth a thousand words" could be revised today to "a picture is worth at least a thousand bucks." Clearly, price is no longer a barrier to the pursuit of the best possible picture.

In the past few years, closed-caption decoding has been introduced on all sets above 13 inches, and dark tint picture tubes now dominate virtually all sets 13 inches and above. Dark tint screens offer the higher contrast and brighter colors that most people look for in their TV sets. Other features are also desirable, but brightness and contrast rank highest.

When TVs were a novelty, a diagonal measurement was introduced as the standard designation of screen size. This was done to make round picture tubes seem larger, even though a fair number of round tubes were masked and didn't offer a useful picture. Flat, square TV screens have made the diagonal measurement more honest. Flatter tubes also reduce glare and provide less distortion at the corners of the set. Initially introduced a few years ago in 27-inch sets, FSTs (flat, square tube) now come in sets up to 36 inches and offer reduced curvature screens, thereby providing more viewing area with less reflection from room light.

An aspect ratio of 4:3 (meaning that the width of the screen is 4 units and the height is 3 units) is standard for a square TV screen. In the last few years, wide-screen TVs have appeared on the market using either 16:9 or Pioneer's 16:10.7 aspect ratios. The 16:9 aspect ratio offers a rectangular screen that mimics the shape of your local cinema's screen. RCA (and its Proscan brand line) offers the 16:9 aspect ratio in direct-view in 34-inch-wide configurations, and JVC, Pioneer, and Toshiba offer it in projection sets. These sets are the harbingers of things to come; a quasi-HDTV (High Definition Television) front-projection TV, which requires an HDTV decoder box, is already on the market from Zenith (the PRO900). A limited supply of the first true consumer HDTV sets may appear on the 1997/98 market and should become more readily available by the year 2000. Those sets will offer wide-screen aspect ratios. Projection TV provides more flexibility in dealing with the considerable variety of aspect ratios, since there is no absolute standard for wide-screen images.

Stereo sound is a significant feature in TVs today. Many sets offer digital sound processing, Dolby Surround Sound decoding, or other sound enhancement options. More than a third of all TVs sold are now stereo models, and all sets 27 inches and larger include stereo sound as a feature. Clearly, smaller-screen sets do not require stereo sound, although it's a pleasant option on 19-inch and 20-inch models. Some of these models use acoustic effects like XS stereo to create a more spacious sound on these small sets.

The fastest-growing TV/video category is the TV-VCR combination. Initially conceived as a business product, the TV-VCR combination has definitely found its niche in the home, with sales topping two million units in 1995. Although they are offered in screen sizes from 2 inches to 35 inches, the 13-inch and 20-inch sets are the most popular. They are equipped with either a two-head or four-head VCR and are great for the bedroom, den, or children's room. The 1996 models include a stereo TV and hi-fi VCR. You may not save any money by purchasing a combo, but you gain convenience by not having to deal with cables and wires.

Home theater is no longer a buzzword. It is becoming a way of life for many people in the 1990s. As more and more people prefer to spend time with family and friends at home, they naturally turn to the television for entertainment. Home theater can be anything you want it to be as long as you enhance your television with better audio (such as your stereo system). Many people get into home theater by purchasing a large-screen TV (either direct-view or projection). To get the full benefit from home theater, however, you need various other components. First, you need a hi-fi VCR. Movies today are hi-fi and are encoded with Dolby Surround Sound. Second, if you are in the market for a new stereo receiver, opt for an A/V receiver that includes Dolby Pro Logic decoding and five built-in amplifiers. Third, you will need to add center-channel and rear-channel speakers to your existing setup. For good audio choices, see the Stereo Components chapter. If you want the best possible picture quality, a laser disc player or a DVD player will round out the package. You can buy each component separately to gradually enhance your listening and viewing experience.

Projection TVs

Projection TVs come in two basic types: front and rear. Though neither type provided good pictures initially, picture quality today is often exceptional for both types. They offer different advantages for the end user. Projection TVs have become a mainstream product, selling close to a million units in 1996.

Rear-projection models come in sizes up to 70 inches, lines of resolution up to 1,000, and brightness topping 500 footlamberts for many models. They use cathode ray tubes (CRTs), mirrors, and complex lens systems to project an image onto a translucent screen for viewing. These sets are so bright that they can be viewed in normal room light without appreciable loss of picture quality. Many models have a tinted transparent plastic screen, which offers contrast as well as protection for the lenticular lens. Models are not as large as they used to be; some are only 20 inches deep. Thanks to casters, these sets are easy to move around the room. While woodtone cabinetry is still found on many models, black cabinets have become the norm because black blends into the decor of most rooms.

Front-projection TVs project the image from a CRT onto a screen. They need to be viewed in a dark room, which creates what some people feel is a true home theater experience. Units can be either ceiling-mounted or floor-standing. Some floor-standing models are housed in coffee tables. Besides the purchase of the TV itself, a screen is also required, which can add up to $2,000 to the set's purchase price. Front projectors range in screen size from 20 inches to 300 inches, in various aspect ratios. To improve picture quality even more, line doublers and line quadruplers are available from the major brands to enhance the visual element. These can add another $10,000 to $15,000 to the package.

LCD sets have become somewhat sophisticated and are now an attractive option. These are front projectors that use an LCD wafer and a powerful projector bulb to project an image onto an external surface. The higher the pixel (picture element) count, the better the LCD image that appears on the screen. LCD projectors are available from only a few brands. They can rival their tube counterparts in quality and high resolution, but they need to be viewed in a darkened room.

Satellite Television

Satellite broadcasting fell out of vogue several years ago because of the need for large dishes and the practice of descrambling by HBO and the other pay services. But it has made a strong comeback recently thanks in part to many people's dissatisfaction with local cable service and to the availability of smaller dishes. The introduction of direct-to-home (DTH) satellite broadcasting, championed by Hughes's DSS (Digital Satellite System), is revolutionizing the satellite industry. You can now receive the best possible television signals via satellite.

DSS is characterized by its small, 18-inch dish, superior picture quality, and CD-like sound. Initially marketed to rural areas and secondary cities, it is now taking many suburban neighborhoods by storm. In the span of one year, RCA has sold more than one million DSSs. Since the system is digital, updates and improvements in the system are done at the broadcast center, not through a set-top box, so that your current receiver will not become obsolete. The small dish can be attached unobtrusively anywhere on a dwelling. It requires a southern exposure free of tall trees to receive signals directly from the satellite 22,000 miles high in the sky. DSS can currently receive up to 175 channels from two programming providers, DirecTV and USSB, at a monthly cost comparable to that of cable. The DSS equipment can be purchased from several companies, including RCA, Sony, Toshiba, and Panasonic. (As of this writing, 12 brands are expected to offer DSS products.) The differences among the brands will come down to onscreen graphics, remotes, and accessories. Picture quality from all brands will be virtually identical, so shoppers will have to focus on price and features.

In any event, we can look to satellite television to come on strong during the second half of the 1990s. Satellite television has the potential to deliver the highest quality signals and sounds. HDTV, when broadcast, will initially come from satellite signals. Movies in different aspect ratios will be beamed by satellite as well. In fact, some cable channels, such as all the Turner channels, are already broadcasting letterboxed movies to retain the proper aspect ratio, as are three channels of pay-per-view (PPV) on DSS. The lure of DSS will also be enhanced when it comes combined with a television set. Note that RCA, Sony, and Toshiba—companies that offer DSS equipment—are also major television manufacturers and providers of all types of video equipment. By next year, we will see TV/DSS combo units making their debut in the marketplace.

Evaluating a Television Set

The obvious criteria in evaluating a television set are picture quality, brightness, contrast, detail, and lack of signal or video noise. Other factors to consider are good sound, a user-friendly remote, and connection options appropriate for your level of use. The colors should be pure and lifelike but not lurid. Whenever possible, evaluate a set by looking at programs that offer images you are familiar with for comparison. Black-and-white images will reveal the quality of the contrast and brightness of the set's picture. Dealers often have laser disc players hooked up to various television sets. A laser disc that displays the THX logo has been mastered and duplicated to the highest standards as set by Lucasfilm, Ltd., and will provide you with an excellent vehicle to evaluate picture quality. Ask your dealer to play one of these discs so that you can evaluate the set you are thinking about buying.

Since differences in major-brand televisions are slight, manufacturers have added all sorts of special features to their sets in an attempt to differentiate them. Deciding which television to buy is a matter of matching a set's features with your needs. For example, many TVs now offer a feature called either Parental Block or Channel Block. This option allows parents to program the set so their small children can't tune in certain stations, such as cable channels that offer adult programming. If you don't have children, you will have little use for a set with this feature.

TVs are becoming more automated. Most sets now offer auto-programming in which you indicate whether your system is attached to an antenna or to a cable system. At the flick of a button, it will automatically tune in all viewable channels. Most sets also include a sleep-timer function that lets you nod off to late-night television knowing that the set will automatically shut itself off at a preselected time. Other sets can be programmed to turn themselves on at preselected times to wake you up, as a security measure, or to be sure that you don't miss your favorite show. Many sets now include onscreen help for explanation of features.

Screen size is a matter of personal preference and budget. Ideally, you should view a TV image from a distance roughly twice as far from the screen as the screen is high. Sets with screen sizes of 2 to 5 inches are portable televisions designed to be carried around. The 9-inch to 13-inch sets are sometimes called decorator models and may come in several colors, with white being the most popular. These sets are often found in the kitchen and sometimes even in the bathroom. Sets in the 13- to 20-inch range are frequently used in bedrooms, dens, and children's rooms. The primary sets in most homes are now 25 inches or larger.

The majority of sets sold are monitor/receiver or tabletop models. Big floor-standing consoles are quickly diminishing in number, but upright consoles now comprise most of this market. Upright consoles take up about the same floor space as a tabletop model and offer built-in storage for a VCR and videotapes. While 27-inch TVs are very popular for the living room or family room, direct-view sets with screen sizes from 30 to 40 inches are selling in record numbers.

Features and Terminology

Remote control units come in one of the following types: basic, standard, unified, universal, or learning. A few models have a combination universal-learning remote. A basic remote manages primary functions such as volume or channel up/down and power on/off. A standard remote is an enhanced basic model with a keypad for direct access that also allows you to use onscreen menus and displays. Universal remotes come with preprogrammed codes for both VCRs and cable boxes. Some brands offer ergonomically designed models with keys of different shapes, colors, and sizes. On top of that, a handful of brands include devices with illuminated keys—a nice touch when you're trying to read those buttons in a dimly lit room. Learning remotes can be "taught" codes from other types of components, such as an A/V receiver. If you are trying to tie all your components together, a learning remote sounds attractive, but, at best, they can learn only the primary functions of each component. A learning remote from an A/V receiver or an after-market universal-learning unit might be a better bet for tying all your components together.

Dual antenna inputs can accommodate two antenna sources, such as the master antenna and cable box, or a master antenna/cable box and DSS decoder. You can then switch easily between antenna sources without using switching devices. Using a signal splitter, available from your cable company or electronics store, you can also split the cable signal before it goes into the cable box so that all unscrambled, basic programming is available on one antenna and the scrambled, premium programming is on the other. This enables your television set's universal remote to control your cable box so that you do not need to rent your cable company's remote.

Horizontal resolution refers to the number of horizontal lines that the TV set can display. Theoretically, the more lines that can be displayed, the better the picture, but this is limited by the picture's source. Broadcast television is 330 lines, VHS tapes use about 240 lines, S-VHS tapes use about 400 from a prerecorded video (330 from broadcast), and laser discs have about 425 lines. On the other hand, when sources with greater resolution, such as DSS, become available, a set with high horizontal resolution would be able to receive an enhanced signal.

Comb filter improves resolution and picture quality and reduces objectionable color patterns. Low-end to mid-line TV sets use a glass comb filter. High-end sets use a CCD, or digital comb filter, which greatly enhances resolution.

Special picture tubes improve picture quality. A recent innovation has taken the industry by storm: the inclusion of either dark tint or dark glass picture tubes. By darkening the face plate (of the tube), the picture tube provides greater contrast between black and white. However, those brands that include darkened picture tubes have had to increase brightness levels so that pictures do not appear too dark; most consumers prefer brightness over color accuracy. Other advancements include flat screens or flattened picture tubes, which offer less distortion on the outer edges of the picture. Some manufacturers use special coatings to help cut down on glare and dust buildup, giving the appearance of a richer picture. Some manufacturers use a combination of techniques to capture the highest performance from their picture tubes. These sets, while costly, offer the viewer a picture with the highest resolution and provide the most lifelike image.

Invar shadow mask, considered a premium feature, gives the picture more brightness and punch. When sets are very bright, a side effect called "blooming" occurs. To counteract this bleeding of colors, some manufacturers include the invar shadow mask.

PIP (picture-in-picture) allows you to view an image from a second video source in a box in one corner of the screen. Advanced PIP allows you to display multiple channels on the screen (all are frozen except the channel currently being scrolled through) and switch back and forth between main and PIP image. A handful of high-end models include a second tuner for PIP, thereby eliminating the need to use the VCR tuner as the second video source.

Scan velocity modulation adjusts the rate of horizontal movement of the beam as it "draws" the scan lines, which gives black-and-white picture transitions more punch. This results in a sharper picture.

Notch filter helps remove a small part of the signal that contains excess color information. By doing so, it helps eliminate some objectionable color effects from undesirable signals. However, a slight loss in picture resolution results.

Stereo television sets include an MTS (multichannel television sound) decoder, which receives and decodes all stereo signals broadcast by the networks or cable channels.

Surround sound uses a computer chip to decode Dolby Surround Sound signals. However, many manufacturers include matrix surround sound or other psychoacoustic effects to enhance the audio. This is sometimes called ambiance or extended stereo effects. More and more sets now include Dolby Pro Logic, which greatly improves the audio quality. You must add rear speakers to obtain the desired effect, however. Many of these sets do not have the power to produce this much sound on their own, but virtually all sets in this category include variable audio outs for connection to an A/V receiver. Some sets also include a center-channel input, which allows you to use the TV's internal speakers for the center channel.

Audio and video inputs/outputs are outlets for devices you can connect to the set. Normally there are more audio outputs than video ones. However, having more video outputs allows you more versatility in signal-switching between multiple VCRs and laser disc players. Depending on how you decide to hook up your A/V system, either the TV or your A/V receiver can be used for video switching. Hooking up a VCR with audio and video input jacks will provide better audio and video quality than putting the signal through your RF connector.

S-video jacks are now included on many components besides S-VHS VCRs. S-video separates the luminance (brightness) and chrominance (color), increasing resolution and improving color reproduction when the S-video jack is used.

Front A/V jacks (usually hidden under a panel) are handy for hooking up a camcorder or a video game.

External speaker jacks allow you to attach separate speakers directly to a TV for improved sound quality or to attach rear speakers for surround sound.

Parental lock-out or channel block prevents access to specific channels or disables them from being used for a specified time of day or period of hours.

Best Buys '97

Our Best Buy, Recommended, and Budget Buy television sets and TV-VCR combos follow. The unit we consider the best of the Best Buys is first, followed by our second choice, and so on. At the end of several categories, you will find one or more units listed as Budget Buys. These models may not have all the features of a Best Buy or Recommended product, but they offer a solid value in terms of performance, features, and price.

While features and styling differ from model to model, TV technology is often carried through a company's entire line. This means that many of the TVs from the same manufacturer offer the same picture quality, but the combination of features in addition to the price of the set is the basis for our choice of one TV over another as a Best Buy. For this reason, the Best Buy, Recommended, and Budget Buy designations apply only to the model listed and not necessarily to other models from the same manufacturer or to an entire product line.

35- TO 41-INCH TV SETS

PANASONIC CT-35XF53   ✓ BEST BUY

The Panasonic CT-35XF53 is one of the best sets in this 35-inch color TV category. Several years ago Panasonic revolutionized the industry by introducing SuperFlat Date Grade picture tubes that feature a black screen with an invar shadow mask. Into the mix, Panasonic added a digital comb filter, wideband video amplifier, color noise reduction, luminance noise reduction, velocity scan modulation, and horizontal edge correction. The manufacturer brought all these circuits together and added Artificial Intelligence control, a fuzzy logic computer chip with a selection of ideal pictures in memory. The resulting picture quality is excellent with little or no background video noise; edges are crisp; and colors are true and lifelike with no bleeding. The picture itself is very bright, and the set can display 800 lines of resolution. A color temperature control lets you adjust color tones from warm to cool. On the audio side, the set features Panasonic's 7-watts-per-channel dome sound system, which ports the speaker sound from the back of the set. To enhance the sound further, the CT-35XF53 includes matrix surround and Artificial Intelligence sound with auto-equalizer for more aural spaciousness, and XBS (extra bass system) to give its built-in subwoofer a boost. To make the set more versatile, a Dolby center-channel input is included. Essentially, you can transform the set's internal speakers into one center-channel speaker for your home theater. This TV is capable of receiving 181 channels. Of its several convenience features, one of the most striking is the two-tuner PIP, which allows you to watch two programs simultaneously without using your VCR's tuner. The CT-35XF53 also includes the StarSight electronic program guide, which offers up-to-date television listings and costs $5.00 per month for a subscription. The set also features dual antenna inputs with a built-in splitter for your cable box, three A/V inputs (including one S-video), and a fixed/variable audio output. Finally, the set includes a superb 50-button illuminated universal remote (including 12 dedicated StarSight keys found on the bottom), which will control a total of eight components. As you touch the keypad, the appropriate component key lights up to show what mode you're in. The set offers icon-based onscreen menus and easy-to-use displays. To complement the set's all-black cabinet, an optional stand with glass doors is available for convenient component storage.

Specifications: height, 29.3"; width, 37"; depth, 23.6"; weight, 176 lb. **Warranty:** 90 days, labor; 1 year, parts; 2 years, parts for tube.

Manufacturer's Suggested Retail Price: $2,300

Approximate Low Price: $2,035

SONY KV-35V35

`Recommended`

The KV-35V35 is Sony's new, first-ever 35-inch color TV. Housed in a sleek and stylish black cabinet with side-firing speakers, the KV-35V35 uses a hi-black Trinitron picture tube with a deep black, vertically flat screen to produce clear, clean images. Reduced-curvature screens help reduce in-room glare and minimize picture distortion. This TV has a comb filter along with scan velocity modulation to sharpen definition detail and reduce dot crawl. Other video enhancements include accurate focusing from corner-to-corner, accurate light-to-dark values, auto-white balance, minimal noise and distortion, and a broadened tuner bandwidth for improved signals. This package includes a light sensor that adjusts picture levels according to room light, an advanced dual-tuner PIP, bilingual (English/Spanish) onscreen displays and menus, parental control to block out two preset channels, and XDS (extended data service) reception. XDS provides information services (if they are broadcast in your area) that register correct time, station call letters, and program information. The KV-35V35 also features three Program Palette presets (standard, movie, and sports) that adjust brightness, tone, sharpness levels, and picture settings according to the type of program you're watching. Program Palette can memorize particular settings matched to specific video sources, which you can label as, for example, VHS or laser disc. Audio is piped though four side-mounted dynamic acoustic chamber (DAC) speakers rated at 10 watts per channel each. Audio enhancements include simulated surround sound and SRS, which helps provide realistic surround sound without adding extra speakers. SRS works well with either the set's internal speakers or another attached audio system. A universal remote that also controls a VCR/LD player and a cable box or DSS rounds out the package. This feature doesn't just control channels, it also offers access to the DSS's onscreen guide and menus. The KV-35V35 set comes with dual antenna inputs, two

A/V inputs (one S-video), front A/V jacks behind a drop-down door, and three outputs: one audio (fixed/variable) and two video (including monitor). Sony's new S-Link circuitry allows connections with other Sony equipment that has an S-Link output and offers one-button access. For example, if you press the play button on a Sony VCR, it will turn on the Sony TV, change the video input to its proper setting, and start to play.

Specifications: height, 29⅞"; width, 37⅝"; depth, 26¼"; weight, 198 lb. 7 oz. **Warranty:** 90 days, labor; 1 year, parts.

Manufacturer's Suggested Retail Price: $1,800

Approximate Low Price: $1,616

MITSUBISHI CS-40707

Recommended

The Mitsubishi CS-40707 is a 40-inch direct-view TV, the largest of its kind on the market. Part of a family of four 40-inch sets, this model offers exceptional picture quality and features. The fine picture quality is produced by the CS-40707's black tint, black matrix cathode ray tube (CRT), which features an invar shadow mask, and by its digital dynamic comb filter that has the capability of displaying 700 lines of horizontal resolution from its 181-channel FS tuner. Video circuitry includes dynamic aperture control, dynamic beam forming, dynamic black level expansion, scan velocity modulation, gamma compensation, and skin color compensation. Several of this year's Mitsubishi models offer color temperature control, which allows you to adjust color temperature from cool to warm to hot according to your particular preference. The built-in audio amplifier provides 7 watts per channel from its two front-firing speakers, and the set also includes external speaker jacks so you can hook up your own speakers. This TV's features also include an active subwoofer system, three audio and three video (with S-video) inputs, plus one video and one audio output. A pair of front A/V jacks are provided for video game or camcorder attachment, and dual antenna inputs are also included. The remote will also control both a VCR and a cable box. Convenience features include two-tuner advanced PIP, a new 3-D graphic ViewPoint onscreen menu system, parental control and lock, and XDS with automatic clock set. The set is housed in a very attractive black/gray cabinet with a Corian top.

Specifications: height, 32"; width, 39¹⁹⁄₃₂"; depth, 26³⁄₁₆"; weight, 243 lb. **Warranty:** 1 year, parts and labor; 2 years, tube.

Manufacturer's Suggested Retail Price: $3,799

Approximate Low Price: $3,633

RCA F35760MB

Recommended

The RCA F35760MB provides fine picture quality at an excellent price, making it a good choice for your budding home theater. Outfitted with RCA's new flatter, darker picture tube (FDT) with an invar shadow mask, the set can display up to 830 lines of horizontal resolution and receive 181 channels. The FDT tube produces a very clean picture, free of video noise, and is housed in a black cabinet with front-firing speakers. Audio performance is rated at 5 watts per channel, utilizing SRS to increase the spatial presence of sound. A 16-jack panel on the back of the set provides two A/V inputs (with one S-video) and one A/V output (fixed and variable). This set also includes front A/V jacks for the attachment of a camcorder or video game via a special plug. Two RF inputs allow the attachment of a TV antenna and cable/DSS satellite to the TV. The F35760MB comes with an ergonomically designed 46-button universal remote with color-coded keys for VCR and cable-box control.

Specifications: height, 32⅝"; width, 34⅞"; depth, 23⅝"; weight, 200 lb. **Warranty:** 90 days, labor; 1 year, parts.

Manufacturer's Suggested Retail Price: $1,999

Approximate Low Price: $1,721

31- TO 32-INCH TV SETS

MAGNAVOX TP3273C

✓ BEST BUY

The Magnavox TP3273C is a 32-inch tabletop monitor/receiver color TV that offers an excellent combination of features at a very reasonable price. The true 32-inch flat, square picture tube features dark glass for improved contrast, and an invar shadow mask that reduces blooming. Thanks in part to the analog comb filter, picture quality is good to very good on any of the receivable 181 channels. The set features an advanced one-tuner PIP. Automatic clock set is standard on this TV as well, which means the clock is set as soon as the TV is plugged in and a signal is received. Magnavox has given this TV a lot of "smart" features including Smart Sound, which tones down loud commercials and boosts weak audio signals; Smart Window, which displays picture-in-picture; and Smart Surf, which "memorizes" your four favorite channels. Like many other sets today, it offers menus and displays in three languages: English, French, and Spanish. You move about the menus via cursor/navigation keys situated at the top of the remote. Capable of controlling the TV, VCR, and cable box, the universal remote uses three AA batteries. If you misplace the remote, simply press the power button on the TV and the remote locator function will cause the remote to beep until it's found. Then you can silence the beep by touching any button on the remote. The TP3273C's audio is piped though two front-firing 5-inch speakers, each rated at 5 watts per channel. External speaker jacks are provided for surround speakers, and the set features one A/V input (including one S-Video jack) and one variable audio output to pipe sound into your A/V receiver for that home theater experience. As a matter of fact, this is a perfect TV component to include in your basic home theater system because it gives you useful features at a reasonable price.

Specifications: height, 27.1"; width, 30.6"; depth, 20.75"; weight, 114 lb. **Warranty:** 3 months, labor; 1 year, parts.

Manufacturer's Suggested Retail Price: $850

Approximate Low Price: $697

HITACHI 32UX8B

Recommended

The Hitachi 32UX8B is a 32-inch color TV housed in a black cabinet. Featuring Hitachi's dynamic focus picture tube, the face plate has a dark (almost black) tint.

Because of the dark tint, contrast and brightness levels are greatly increased, which produces a very good picture. This set receives 181 channels and can display up to 700 lines of resolution. Video noise and blooming are minimal thanks to built-in video noise reduction and advanced scan modulation circuitry. A digital three-line comb filter is included to improve picture quality. To enhance whatever you are watching, the set includes three home theater modes for movies, sports, and TV that adjust brightness, contrast, and other presets to optimum levels. Convenience features include PIP with a quick-freeze capability, which allows you to freeze whatever picture is on the screen; a stereo set with two speakers located at the sides of the screen; and external speaker jacks for the attachment of separate speakers or rear speakers. Because of the built-in circuitry Hitachi provides, you can also purchase wireless speakers for use as rear speakers. To enhance the audio package, an SES (spatially equalized sound) system is included along with a built-in Dolby surround decoder to give you true surround sound. The 32UX8B features three sets of A/V jacks (one front and two rear), one S-video rear jack, and one variable audio output jack for hookup to an external audio source. This TV also comes with a 33-key illuminated universal remote that can control both VCRs and cable boxes. The trilingual onscreen guide and the lock-out option for parents are welcome additions to this set's list of features, as is this year's new feature: volume correction circuitry that automatically lowers the volume of especially loud TV stations or channels.

Specifications: height, 26⁵⁄₁₆″; width, 31¹⁄₁₆″; depth, 22¼″; weight, 130 lb. **Warranty:** 1 year, parts and labor; 2 years, tube.

Manufacturer's Suggested Retail Price: $1,100

Approximate Low Price: $1,074

SONY KV-32XBR85

Recommended

The Sony KV-32XBR85, a 32-inch upright color TV, comes with its own stand integrated into a one-piece design so that it looks like a tabletop TV with its own table. The KV-32XBR85 comes in a black cabinet with maple trim at the base. This TV features top-mounted controls for easy access to set functions, and the base module contains two shelves for component storage plus a bottom-mounted 11-watt subwoofer covered by a glass door. Utilizing a Trinitron picture tube with a deep black screen and the Bi-CMOS video processor, the set produces clean, bright images, free of background video noise. The KV-32XBR85 has a digital comb filter that uses digital circuitry for the best picture with minimum distortion along with scan velocity modulation that sharpens definition detail; it also has a dual-tuner PIP for added convenience. Audio is piped through two side-mounted dynamic acoustic chamber speakers and an 11-watt subwoofer. The stand-up universal remote requires only one AA battery and controls four video products (including DSS) via a side-mounted switch. The set also features three A/V inputs (one S-video) and audio/video outputs.

Specifications: height, 45⅛"; width, 33½"; depth, 27⅛"; weight, 199 lb. 3 oz. **Warranty:** 1 year, parts and labor.

Manufacturer's Suggested Retail Price: $2,200

Approximate Low Price: $1,933

RCA F32730SB

Budget Buy

The RCA F32730SB provides very good picture quality at an excellent price. Outfitted with RCA's optimum contrast screen (OCS) tube, the set includes several upscale video features including a comb filter, a wideband video amplifier, video noise reduction, and scan velocity modulation. These video features give this set the capability of displaying up to 770 lines of horizontal resolution. It receives 181 channels with advanced auto-programming. The VHP tube creates a picture that's free of video noise and artifacts. The set is housed in a black cabinet with front-firing speakers. Audio performance is rated at 5 watts per channel utilizing SRS and matrix surround sound. SRS is employed to increase the sound's spatial presence and is especially noticeable when using the set's internal speakers. If you pipe the audio out via its variable output to a separate stereo system, however, the presence of SRS will be even more pronounced and the sound far more realistic and enveloping. A 16-jack panel on the set provides two rear and one front A/V inputs with one S-video output and one A/V fixed/variable output on back. To attach a camcorder or video game to the front A/V jacks, you'll need the special plug adapter that comes with the set. Convenience features include twin-tuner PIP, which works without an external source such as your VCR, and parental control. The F32730SB includes an ergonomically designed 46-button universal remote with color-coded keys for DSS or cable box, VCR, VCR/LD, and audio (RCA only) components. An optional stand is available for VCR/component storage.

Specifications: height, 29″; width, 30⅛″; depth, 22½″; weight, 120 lb. **Warranty:** 90 days, labor; 1 year, parts.

Manufacturer's Suggested Retail Price: $1,149

Approximate Low Price: $883

27-INCH TV SETS

JVC AV-27790

✔ **BEST BUY**

The JVC AV-27790 is a fully-loaded 27-inch stereo TV that includes TV Guide Plus+ as a standard feature. Equipped with a 181-channel tuner, this model features dual antenna inputs and dual-tuner PIP. This means that the set itself (without a VCR's tuner) can display two different programs simultaneously. Its bilingual (English/French) onscreen menus and displays are very easy to use. This set also includes onscreen help in case the manual isn't handy. Picture quality is very good, producing approximately 600 lines of resolution from its comb filter. Colors are natural and lifelike. You can change TV settings via the Video Status Memory menu, which features three different presets for brightness and sharpness: standard (factory preset), theater (NTSC standard), and choice (your own preference settings). The AV-27790 offers 3 watts per channel of stereo power from two side-firing speakers and hyper-surround sound. The onscreen menu allows you to shut off the internal speakers so that the variable audio output jack can be utilized or so external speakers can be attached. The set includes two A/V inputs, including a front jack. An S-video input for improved picture quality from equipped video sources is also provided. The fixed/variable audio output can be switched via the remote. You control this set with a 43-button illuminated universal remote that can also control your VCR and cable box. The remote is well designed, with the color-coded TV Guide Plus+ keys situated at the bottom along with the "light" key. TV Guide Plus+ is a free onscreen programming service, which is easily accessed by using the four color-coded keys (red, green, blue, yellow) found on the remote. You can then scroll up or down through every channel that you receive. A description of each channel's programming is displayed in the upper right-hand side of the screen. On the upper left-hand corner of the screen, the actual channel is displayed in the PIP-like window. You use the red key to indicate a particular time of day and the listings for that time will appear. The system allows you to sort by type of programming, such as movies, dramas, comedies, or variety shows, and see when that type of show will be aired in the next 7 days. If you see a program that you want to record, simply press the REC button on the remote, which will then store the information. All you have to do is be sure that your VCR is properly set up and has a blank tape in place. TV Guide Plus+ is easy to use and very helpful. All in all, the AV-27790 is definitely a solid performer.

Specifications: height, 23⅛"; width, 25¾"; depth, 20½"; weight, 80.1 lb. **Warranty:** 1 year, parts and labor; 2 years, tube.

Manufacturer's Suggested Retail Price: $650

Approximate Low Price: $594

MITSUBISHI CS-27407

Recommended

The Mitsubishi CS-27407 is a full-featured 27-inch stereo color TV. Utilizing a black tint and a black matrix cathode ray tube with a comb filter, it offers excellent picture quality. Images are sharp and clean, with minimal video noise, and the set can display 560 lines of resolution. Colors are natural and lifelike. Scan velocity modulation, dynamic black level expansion, and peak white with ACL are employed to improve overall picture quality. The color temperature control allows you to set your color tone preferences on a range from warm (whites are redder) to cool (whites are bluer). The CS-27407 is equipped with many desirable features, including advanced picture-in-picture; A/V memory by input, which permits adjustments to video 1 or video 2 to optimize viewing of VCRs and laser disc players; and a 181-channel tuner with auto-programming. Mitsubishi continues to provide its TVs and VCRs with trilingual (English/French/Spanish) onscreen displays and menus. The CS-27407's sound comes from two front-firing speakers rated at 3 watts per channel, enhanced by built-in matrix surround circuitry. The set features dual antenna inputs, two A/V inputs (including one S-video input), and a variable audio output for hookup to your hi-fi system. Front A/V jacks are also included for video games or camcorder attachment. The illuminated, multibrand remote controls a VCR, DSS, and a cable box. Other features include a one-week/one-event program timer, parental lock, and XDS with automatic clock set.

Specifications: height, 23$\frac{9}{16}$"; width, 26$\frac{9}{32}$"; depth, 19$\frac{1}{32}$"; weight, 86 lb. **Warranty:** 1 year, parts and labor; 2 years, tube.

Manufacturer's Suggested Retail Price: $949

Approximate Low Price: $899

TOSHIBA CX27F60

`Recommended`

The Toshiba CX27F60 is an excellent example of an upscale 27-inch color TV that offers superb picture quality. Using the FST black picture tube, a glass comb filter, and a black level expander, Toshiba equips this set to display 650 lines of horizontal resolution. Images are sharp and clear, and flesh tones are natural-looking. The tuner can receive up to 181 channels, audio is rated at 5 watts per channel from bottom-mounted front-firing speakers, and SBS (sub-bass system) can be employed to give the sound more depth. Inputs include two RF antennas, one S-video and two audio/video jacks, and there is one variable audio output. The 42-button universal remote can control the TV, a VCR, and a cable box. The CX27F60 also comes with a dual-tuner PIP, so you do not have to attach a VCR in order to activate the PIP function. You can move the smaller image to any of the four corners of the screen, freeze it, change its size, or swap images to watch two channels at once. The remote control keys that control your PIP functions also control VCR transport. Convenience features on this set include an 180-minute sleep timer and a parental lock that will lock out up to four channels. The trilingual onscreen graphics and menus are easy to use.

Specifications: height, 24⅝₆₄″; width, 28³⁹⁄₆₄″; depth, 19¹⁷⁄₃₂″; weight, 86.6 lb. **Warranty:** 1 year, parts and labor; 2 years, parts for tube.

Manufacturer's Suggested Retail Price: $750
Approximate Low Price: $547

HITACHI 27CX7B

Budget Buy

The Hitachi 27CX7B is a value-priced 27-inch color TV that combines a solid set of features with a very good picture. The set features a dark tint picture tube and a two-line digital comb filter to display up to 600 lines of resolution. The set includes a 181-channel tuner with auto-programming capability; two front-firing speakers rated at 3 watts per channel; loudness circuitry to boost bass sounds; volume-correction circuitry that lowers the volume of loud commercials or stations; advanced PIP with quick freeze; a message center that delivers an onscreen message to family members at a specified time; a child lock that shuts out selected channels from children; TV TimeOut, which shuts down the TV at specified times; on/off timers; trilingual onscreen menus; onscreen help, including a color graphic guide; and a 3-hour sleep timer. The 27CX7B comes with three A/V inputs with S-video capability, one variable audio output, and a 39-button universal remote with illuminated keys on the bottom half of the unit. The remote can also control a VCR and a cable box. Hitachi packages this Budget Buy in a sleek black cabinet.

Specifications: height, 23″; width, 26³⁹⁄₆₄″; depth, 20¹⁵⁄₃₂″; weight, 93 lb. **Warranty:** 1 year, parts and labor; 2 years, tube.

Manufacturer's Suggested Retail Price: $500

Approximate Low Price: $475

20-INCH TV SETS

PANASONIC CT-20G21

✔ **BEST BUY**

If you're looking for a color TV for the bedroom, the Panasonic CT-20G21 20-inch stereo TV is a good choice. This solid performer's picture tube provides excellent contrast and also features a notch filter and SAW (surface acoustic wave) filter that improve picture quality, allowing the set to display up to 500 lines of resolution. Equipped with a 181-channel tuner, auto-programming, and channel logos for up to 30 channels, the CT-20G21 is set in a black cabinet with a small base. The front-firing stereo speakers are located under the screen, and an MTS decoder sends the sound through a 1.5-watt-per-channel internal amplifier. A separate audio program feature is also included. To improve its aural quality, the CT-20G21 incorporates Artificial Intelligence sound, and sound can also be piped to your hi-fi or mini-system via the TV's variable audio outputs (a set of audio/video inputs is included as well). This package offers a trilingual (English/Spanish/French) onscreen icon menu; a game guard, which prevents video games from remaining on the screen too long; and a 32-button universal remote. Separate VCR power and transport keys are situated at the bottom of the remote, and you can operate your TV and your VCR simultaneously.

Specifications: height, 18.2"; width, 20.0"; depth, 19.0"; weight, 46.3 lb. **Warranty:** 90 days, labor for set and tube; 1 year, parts for set; 2 years, parts for tube.

Manufacturer's Suggested Retail Price: $350

Approximate Low Price: $283

MAGNAVOX PS1963C

Recommended

The Magnavox PS1963C is a better-than-average 19-inch stereo color TV that combines desirable features with a very reasonable price. Like virtually all TVs today, this set is capable of receiving 181 channels, and its Dark Tint/ Contrast 52 tube delivers a good picture. Smart Picture, one of the many features on this set, offers four factory presets—sports, movie, weak signal, and video game—for brightness, contrast, tint, color, and sharpness. These presets don't boost the signal at all; they simply adjust to optimum settings for the type of images you are watching. Smart Sound keeps volume levels constant even during loud commercials and also boosts weak audio signals. On the back of the set, you'll find one audio and video input jack and one audio output jack. Onscreen menus and displays are clear and easy to use and include an onscreen clock. The tapered, 24-button universal remote controls the TV, a VCR, and a cable box. The MTS/SAP stereo sound system with DBX noise reduction is rated at 2.5 watts per channel, and sound is piped through two 3-inch speakers.

Specifications: height, 18.7"; width, 19.9"; depth, 18.1"; weight, 42 lb. **Warranty:** 3 months, parts; 1 year, labor.

Manufacturer's Suggested Retail Price: $280

Approximate Low Price: Not available

RCA F20640BC

The RCA F20640BC is a 20-inch stereo color **Recommended** TV housed in an attractive black cabinet with rounded top edges. This set features a dark glass optimum contrast picture tube and includes a 181-channel tuner. Its trilingual (English/French/Spanish) onscreen menus and displays are clear and easy to use. The F20640BC also features an onscreen clock, a sleep and alarm timer, and a headphone jack. Picture quality is very good for a set in this size category. Audio, enhanced by XS Stereo circuitry (a psychoacoustic feature that enhances the sound imaging), is piped through two front-firing speakers. The F20640BC is equipped with one set of A/V input jacks and one pair of audio output jacks. New this year is a 36-button unified remote that will also control RCA VCRs. This remote has illuminated keys, and the channel up/down and volume up/down controls can be backlighted with the touch of a button on the side of the remote—a helpful feature in a setting with little or no lighting.

Specifications: height, 19⅛"; width, 20¼"; depth, 18⅞"; weight, 54 lb. **Warranty:** 90 days, labor; 1 year, parts.

Manufacturer's Suggested Retail Price: $319

Approximate Low Price: $266

PORTABLE TV SETS

RCA EO9310WH   ✓BEST BUY

The RCA EO9310WH is a 9-inch color TV designed to be mounted under a kitchen cabinet (mounting bracket hardware is included) or placed on a countertop. This TV, in a white cabinet, contains a built-in FM radio with a weather band channel. Picture quality is very good for a set of this screen size, boasting a resolution of about 270 lines. Other features include a 181-channel tuner with auto-programming, multilanguage onscreen displays, and an earphone jack. The set also features an onscreen clock, sleep and alarm timers, and commercial skip, which allows you to surf other channels for a predetermined time before jumping back to the channel where you started. No A/V inputs or outputs are included on this set. The front membrane panel and the numeric keypad remote control are easy to keep clean, and the set comes with a hook for hanging up the remote.

Specifications: height, 10⅛"; width, 11½"; depth, 13"; weight, 19 lb. **Warranty:** 90 days, labor; 1 year, parts.

Manufacturer's Suggested Retail Price: $279

Approximate Low Price: $225

GOLDSTAR GCT-1356M   Budget Buy

The Goldstar GCT-1356M is a portable 13-inch color TV set that features a high-contrast dark glass picture tube; its black tinting keeps images bright and bold. Housed in a stylish black cabinet, the GCT-1356M is a fine choice for the kitchen or the bedroom. The set includes a 181-

channel tuner, a bilingual (English/Spanish) onscreen menu and display, an onscreen clock, a 240-minute sleep timer, and channel recall that allows you to jump back and forth between two channels via the 23-button standard remote. Mono audio is piped through a single oval front-firing speaker located beneath the screen on the right side. This set has no A/V inputs or outputs. For portability, versatility, and price, it's a good Budget Buy.

Specifications: height, 15.1"; width, 15.0"; depth, 14.5"; weight, 21.4 lb. **Warranty:** 1 year, parts and labor.

Manufacturer's Suggested Retail Price: $190

Approximate Low Price: Not available

LCD MINI-TV SETS

SONY FDL-22 WATCHMAN

✔**BEST BUY**

The Sony FDL-22 WatchMan is a 2.2-inch LCD mini-TV that houses an innovative antenna in its carrying strap. A clip on the strap doubles as a stand. Equipped with a full 69-channel tuner, it receives all VHF and UHF stations. Channels can be changed via a rocker switch located on the right-hand side of the unit, and on/off, volume, and brightness controls are located on the left side. This triangular TV is located on top of a small speaker and is equipped for the attachment of optional stereo or mono headphones. Designed for easy portability, the WatchMan is powered by four AA alkaline batteries (for about 3½ hours of power) or an optional AC adapter. Like all LCD TVs, this one must be kept out of direct sunlight since direct sun will wash out the picture entirely. If you're carrying the FDL-22 WatchMan around your neck, the reception quality should be good since the human body acts as its own antenna.

Specifications: height, 6⅛"; width, 3¼"; depth, 1¾"; weight, 10.6 oz. **Warranty:** 90 days, parts and labor.

Manufacturer's Suggested Retail Price: $150

Approximate Low Price: $127

CASIO EV-2500

Recommended

The Casio EV-2500 portable color TV features a 2.5-inch LCD active matrix color screen that displays 61,380 pixels. It comes in a gray cabinet with purple trim and can sit easily on your desk or even in your hand. This TV features a 69-channel tuner that receives both UHF and VHF signals. A simple black knob changes channels, and the channel display itself is located across the top of the LCD screen. This model also contains an AM/FM radio with an earphone jack for private listening. The EV-2500 can be powered by an optional AC adapter or by three D batteries, which provide about 11 hours of power. Because it has a high pixel count, this TV offers good picture quality for its size. Like other LCD TVs, this one cannot be watched in direct sunlight, and no sunscreen is available. Better-than-average picture quality and its several convenience features make the EV-2500 a solid purchase.

Specifications: height, 4½"; width, 4⅜"; depth, 2⅖"; weight, 12.7 oz. **Warranty:** 1 year, parts and labor.

Manufacturer's Suggested Retail Price: $299

Approximate Low Price: $247

REAR-PROJECTION TV SETS

TOSHIBA TP50F90

✓BEST BUY

The Toshiba TP50F90 is a 50-inch rear-projection TV that features a high-contrast dark tint screen and includes three 7-inch CRTs. Utilizing a digital comb filter, the set has the capability of displaying 800 lines of horizontal resolution and a brightness level of 600 foot-lamberts. To keep its 181 channels in focus, the set includes digital convergence, so you don't have to line up the red and blue cross-hairs. The digital comb filter keeps images clear and bright, eliminating dot crawl and color interference. The set also offers velocity scan modulation, color detail enhancement, black level expander, picture preference for flesh-tone correction, video noise reduction, and adjustable color temperature. Of course, the better the source, the better the picture. The TP50F90 comes with dual antenna inputs, three A/V inputs (including one front and one rear S-video), front A/V jacks, and an A/V output. The set includes built-in StarSight capability, which provides a complete onscreen program guide with descriptions of all programs. This model sports a newly designed, illuminated 52-button remote for controlling the TV, a VCR, a cable box, DSS or any other auxiliary, and StarSight. As long as your VCR is properly attached, the remote gives you one-button recording ability. In addition, this remote has learning capabilities, so it can even control other DSS brands. Audio power is rated at 14 watts per channel for the front speakers, 10 watts per channel for the center speakers, and 10 watts per channel for the rear speakers—a total audio output of 68 watts. The set includes a built-in Dolby Pro Logic decoder along with a four-channel digital sound processor (DSP). Bass sounds are improved via a sub-bass system (SBS) that enhances bass sounds without muffling or distorting them. Separate rear speakers round out the audio package. Besides the rear speaker jacks, external speaker jacks are provided so that you can attach other speakers. Convenience features include parental channel lock and a 180-minute sleep timer. The new onscreen icon menus and displays are slick and easy to use. The TP50F90 offers underscreen storage behind glass doors for two side-by-side components, and it has in-wall capability if you prefer the "built-in" look for your TV set.

Specifications: height, 57⁹⁄₃₂"; width, 42¾"; depth, 21⁷⁄₆₄"; weight, 309 lb. **Warranty:** 1 year, parts and labor; 2 years, parts for tube.

Manufacturer's Suggested Retail Price: $3,400

Approximate Low Price: $2,732

MAGNAVOX MX5470C

Recommended

The Magnavox MX5470C, the company's top-of-the-line 54-inch rear-projection TV, comes in a sleek charcoal-colored cabinet. The set displays 700 lines of resolution via a digital comb filter, a brightness level of 550 foot-lamberts, and a viewing angle of 160 degrees. A tinted protective screen is permanently attached to the set's Delta 77/78 short focal length lenses for increased contrast. Besides its appealing and easy-to-use onscreen menus and graphics, this TV offers several interesting features, including built-in ghost-cancelling circuitry. If a network or cable company in your area sends out the ghost-cancelling signal, your picture should be improved. The circuit will help reduce or eliminate double images or ghosts, replace loss of color, and tone down excessive color. The MX5470C also comes with TV Guide Plus+, which works in conjunction with VCR Plus+. This free over-the-air onscreen program guide gives you a full 7 days of television programming information. This set also has an instant replay feature: At the touch of a button on the remote, you can freeze a given scene and then replay it at normal or slow speed for 8 seconds—and this doesn't even require the attachment of a VCR! This projection TV receives 181 channels, and its audio is rated at 25 watts per channel via six internal speakers. Magnavox equips this TV with center-channel input jacks so you can use the set's internal speakers as one center-channel speaker in a Dolby Pro Logic setup. A 35-button illuminated universal remote controls VCRs and cable boxes. This model also includes several "smart" features: Smart Sound tones down loud commercials and boosts weak audio signals, Smart Picture has four preset settings (sports, movies, weak signals, and video games), and Smart Surf remembers your favorite channels. The MX5470C includes parental control that can lock out specific channels or time periods. There are three audio and video inputs, and the outputs include one video and two audio. One S-video input jack is provided for the attachment of either an S-VHS VCR, a laser disc player, or a DVD player. Finally, the MX5470C comes with a remote locator. Simply touch the power button on the TV and the remote will beep until you find it. Then press any button to silence the beep. Beep codes are changeable.

Specifications: height, 59.62"; width, 49.56"; depth, 24.87"; weight, 200 lb. **Warranty:** 1 year, parts and labor.

Manufacturer's Suggested Retail Price: $2,799

Approximate Low Price: $2,449

MITSUBISHI TS-5545

`Recommended`

Mitsubishi claims that the TS-5545 is the world's only 55-inch tabletop rear-projection TV. It's packaged in a slim black cabinet and weighs only 153 pounds! This set is available with an optional base for component storage, and you also have the option of purchasing furniture that is specifically designed for this type of TV. The picture quality benefits from the manufacturer's six-element, high-speed, multicoated hybrid lens system with 7-inch CRTs and a dynamic digital comb filter. The TS-5545 can display up to 850 lines of resolution, and its brightness level is 320 foot-lamberts. To further improve contrast and brightness, the set utilizes a black tint, black matrix lenticular screen with a thin Fresnel lens and an integrated screen shield. The TS-5545 also includes a three-mode color temperature control that allows you to adjust color tones from cool to warm to hot according to your viewing preference. Sound emanates from two front-firing, 10-watt-per-channel speakers mounted under the screen, and matrix surround sound is available for increased ambiance. The TS-5545 features multilingual onscreen displays, two antenna inputs, three A/V inputs with S-video on the front and rear panels, front A/V jacks, fixed and variable audio outputs, and a tuner/monitor output. The redesigned illuminated universal remote will control the TV, a VCR, and a cable box. Mitsubishi has outfitted this set with parental control to lock out specific times or channels. XDS (extended data service) automatically sets the TV's clock and gives station call letters and program descriptions at the touch of a button.

Specifications: height, $47^{17}/_{32}$"; width, $46^{25}/_{32}$"; depth, $25^{5}/_{8}$"; weight, 153 lb. **Warranty:** 1 year, parts and labor (in-home service); 2 years, tube.

Manufacturer's Suggested Retail Price: $3,199

Approximate Low Price: $3,066

RCA P56740BG

`Recommended`

The RCA P56740BG is a new 56-inch rear-projection TV that couples very good picture quality with many desirable features. Using high-output, liquid-cooled cathode ray tubes, the set comes with an integrated antiglare protective screen that mimics a direct-view set, keeps fingerprints off the screen, and helps improve contrast. Video features include a comb filter, scan velocity modulation, auto color control, a wideband video amplifier, video noise reduction, edge replacement, dynamic gamma correction, dynamic focus, and adjustable color tone. The set displays 930 lines of resolution with a brightness level of 320 foot-lamberts and a maximum viewing angle of 160 degrees. The P56740BG's advanced auto-programming function will tune all 181 channels in just a few minutes. With a built-in 20-watt amplifier, each of the four speakers pumps 5 watts per channel. Sound is further enhanced by SRS and matrix surround sound. Two pairs of external speakers can be attached to heighten the surround sound experience, and sound can be piped to an A/V receiver. A/V jacks include three inputs—two rear, with one S-video, and one front—and one rear A/V output. The set also sports dual RF or antenna inputs. The 46-button universal remote can control an RCA DSS, two VCRs, laser disc or digital video players, and one RCA audio product. Convenience features include two-tuner PIP, which works without a second external source, and parental control. Because of RCA's slim cabinet projection technology, the P56740BG's simple black cabinet takes up very little floor space.

Specifications: height, 57⅛"; width, 48¹³⁄₁₆"; depth, 26½"; weight, 293 lb. **Warranty:** 90 days, labor; 1 year, parts.

Manufacturer's Suggested Retail Price: $2,799

Approximate Low Price: $2,454

FRONT-PROJECTION TV SETS

RUNCO CINEMAPRO 760A
✔ **BEST BUY**

The Runco CinemaPro 760A front-projection television can display images from 60 inches to 250 inches in size for PAL, SECAM, and NTSC TV formats. Housed in a black cabinet that can be mounted on a ceiling or placed on a table-top, it holds three 7-inch tubes—one each for red, green, and blue. To complete this package, screens are available from Runco or from other screen manufacturers. The 760A features three lens assemblies with high-definition, color-corrected mul-tilayer coatings, and hybrid lenses that produce strikingly clear images with very natural color. Thanks in part to its digital comb filter, the 760A can display 650 lines of resolution from a TV signal, 800 lines from a video source using an S-video jack, or 1,000 lines using the RGB input. Its brightness level is rated at 800 lumens or foot-lamberts. The 760A can properly display wide-aspect ratio movies in either 4:3 images (1.33:1) or 16:9 images (1.85:1). More severely letterboxed images at 2.35:1 will have small black bars at the top and bottom of the screen. The unit includes one composite video, an S-video, and one RGB video input and comes with a 35-button programmable remote control for accessing key controls. This front-projection TV set is clearly designed for anyone wanting a real home theater experience.

Specifications: height, 9⅞"; width, 22¼"; depth, 28⅛"; weight, 77 lb. **Warranty:** 1 year, parts; 2 years, labor.

Manufacturer's Suggested Retail Price: $7,995

Approximate Low Price: $7,995

SHARPVISION XV-S95U

The SharpVision XV-S95U is a front LCD **Recommended** projector that can project 25-inch to 200-inch images onto any white surface. In addition to displaying standard 4:3 images, the XV-S95U provides for variable imaging masking and can display 4:3, 16:9, or 21:9 modes for optimal viewing of even severely letterboxed movies. Viewers can change the aspect ratios via the remote or the front panel. Using three LCD pan-els, each rated at 309,120 pixels, this set displays more than 500 lines of resolution. This model LCD front-projector TV has the sharpest and brightest picture. It uses a 350-watt metal halide bulb, and the picture's brightness is rated at 4,000 lux lumi-nance. The XV-S95U can be placed on a tabletop, rear projected, or ceiling mounted. The ten-button remote is illuminated for ease of use. The projector does not have a built-in tuner; to watch regular TV or cable, you employ the tuner from your VCR or A/V receiver. The unit comes with two A/V inputs, including one S-video, and one A/V output. The XV-S95U features onscreen menus and displays and has a built-in 3-watt amplifier and one speaker. It can be attached to high-quality audio equipment for an even better home theater experience.

Specifications: height, $9\frac{1}{16}''$; width, $21\frac{15}{32}''$; depth, $17\frac{23}{32}''$; weight, 35 lb. **Warranty:** 90 days, projection lamp; 1 year, parts and labor (in-home service).

Manufacturer's Suggested Retail Price: $9,995

Approximate Low Price: $9,995

VIDIKRON VPF 40 SEL

`Recommended`

The Vidikron VPF 40 SEL front-projection TV can project images from 5 feet to 15 feet on any video system. It features six-element, high-resolution, multicoated, dual-focus hybrid lenses for each of its three (one each for red, blue, and green) cathode ray tubes. To complete this package, Vidikron offers screens priced from $199 to $2,640, depending on matte and grain. This TV is equipped with a chroma decoder to bring images closer to big-screen quality, a glass comb filter, a color transit circuit to eliminate color bleeding, advanced variable luminance to diminish color "ghosting," and aperture correction, which increases definition at the edges of larger areas. The unit can be floor- or ceiling-mounted. The VPF 40 SEL comes with two A/V inputs, one S-video input, two RGB (TTL and analog) inputs, two audio outputs, a 20-watt audio amplifier output for the attachment of speakers, and a 19-function remote control.

Specifications: height, 9"; width, 22.5"; depth, 29"; weight, 78 lb. **Warranty:** 1 year, parts and labor.

Manufacturer's Suggested Retail Price: $8,995

Approximate Low Price: $8,995

TV-VCR COMBINATIONS

PANASONIC PV-M2776

✓**BEST BUY**

The PV-M2776 combines a 27-inch stereo color TV and a four-head hi-fi VHS VCR. With its black level expansion circuitry, which improves and enhances contrast, this set offers fine picture quality. In the VCR category, Panasonic has always been a solid performer, and this VCR allows for double-fine, slow-motion, high-speed search, and double-speed playback. The set's tuner is capable of receiving 181 channels and can be programmed to record eight events over a 1-month period. The unit includes an automatic clock set feature that keeps the correct time (and even adjusts to daylight saving time) by means of a time signal continuously broadcast by your local PBS station and received via an extended data service (EDS) chip. Even after a power failure, the VCR will reset itself to the right time. A backup program memory is also included, and the unit is VCR Plus+ ready. The stereo portion of the TV is rated at 2 watts per channel from front-firing speakers. Audio is enhanced by internal spatializer circuitry that adds depth and ambiance to the sound. On the back of the set, audio output jacks permit attachment to an A/V receiver. Besides controlling both the TV and VCR, the 42-button universal remote can control most cable boxes. The PV-M2776 features a real-time counter; on/off sleep timer; bilingual onscreen icon displays and menus; a 1-minute backup for programs; commercial skip, which advances the tape up to 3 minutes; an earphone jack; a front A/V input; and a VCR lock that locks out the VCR functions to children. Another handy feature is a warning beeper that lets you know you have programmed the set incorrectly; following the beep is a display identifying the problem.

Specifications: height, 26"; width, 27⅜"; depth, 21⅛"; weight, 85.8 lb. **Warranty:** 90 days, labor for set and tube; 1 year, parts; 2 years, parts for tube.

Manufacturer's Suggested Retail Price: $900

Approximate Low Price: $726

TOSHIBA CV32F68

✔BEST BUY

The Toshiba CV32F68 is the company's first 32-inch stereo TV-VCR combination. Its exceptional picture is due to Toshiba's FST black picture tube with a black level expander—this helps keep the black areas of the picture truly black—and a glass comb filter providing 700 lines of resolution. It's coupled with a four-head hi-fi VCR and outfitted with two tuners so that you can tape one program while watching another. The two tuners also allow you to use PIP without an additional video source. The 181-channel tuner allows preset programming of six events over a 1-month period. The CV32F68 offers a unique onscreen analog clock system for programming through the remote control, though conventional onscreen programming is also available. The 46-button remote manages all functions of the combo. The unit has a rear A/V input for the attachment of another video component. It also features trilingual onscreen menus and displays, bass/treble/balance controls for its 10 watts of audio power, automatic head cleaner, and a 180-minute sleep timer. The CV32F68 is also equipped with parental channel lock.

Specifications: height, 30⁵⁄₁₆″; width, 31¹⁷⁄₆₄″; depth, 23¹⁄₃₂″; weight, 118.8 lb. **Warranty:** 1 year, parts and labor.

Manufacturer's Suggested Retail Price: $1,499

Approximate Low Price: Not available

MAGNAVOX CCU194AT

Recommended

The Magnavox CCU194AT combines a 19-inch color TV and a four-head VHS VCR. With its dark glass picture tube for improved contrast, its picture quality is quite good. The 181-channel tuner features auto-programming. The VCR portion uses four video heads, allowing for slow motion and frame advance, and you can record eight events over a 365-day period via the onscreen programmer. The VCR portion, housed with the TV in a black cabinet, is clearly an integral part of the set, not just an afterthought. The CCU194AT comes with front A/V inputs for easy attachment of a camcorder or a video game system and VCR Plus+ with a cable-box control to make recording easier. Another handy feature is Smart Sound, which lowers noisy commercials to preset levels and boosts weak audio signals. A remote locator makes the remote beep until you find it. The auto-clock function automatically sets the clock and calendar, adjusting for daylight saving time, and resets itself following a power failure. Onscreen displays and menus are easy to use, and programming the VCR is simple. Once you turn off the TV, the timer is set automatically. The long, black, 43-button full-featured universal remote controls all functions on the VCR, the TV, and your cable box.

Specifications: height, 19.7"; width, 19.4"; depth, 18.0"; weight, 46.2 lb. **Warranty:** 3 months, labor; 1 year, parts.

Manufacturer's Suggested Retail Price: $500

Approximate Low Price: $393

SHARP 25VT-H200

Recommended

The Sharp 25VT-H200 is a new breed of TV-VCR combinations, joining together a 25-inch color TV and a four-head mono VCR. Somewhat larger than the standard 20-inch TV-VCR combination, this set offers very good picture quality thanks to its high-focus, dark-tint picture tube and the 19-micron video heads of the VCR. The 19-micron heads improve the picture quality of videos recorded at the slowest speed. The 25VT-H200's 181-channel tuner features auto-programming, and you can record five events over a 1-month period via its onscreen programmer. This set, in its black cabinet, includes front A/V jacks for the attachment of a camcorder or video game system. The 42-button universal remote will control all TV and VCR functions, plus your cable box. This four-head VCR offers slow motion and frame advance along with other features, including an automatic head cleaner, digital auto-tracking, auto-repeat, a quick-start mechanism, timer backup, and trilingual onscreen displays (English/French/Spanish). The auto-clock feature sets the clock as soon as the 25VT-H200 is plugged in and receives a signal. This TV-VCR also features a parental control/tamperproof mechanism that locks out channels and limits time access for children. Two front-firing mono speakers rated at 1.5 watts each are situated under the screen. Sharp's EquiSound feature moderates the sound on loud commercials to preset levels.

Specifications: height, 25"; width, 20³⁄₃₂"; depth, 20³⁄₃₂"; weight, 73.4 lb. **Warranty:** 90 days, labor; 1 year, parts; 2 years, tube.

Manufacturer's Suggested Retail Price: $829

Approximate Low Price: $624

RCA T13070WH

Recommended

The RCA T13070WH is a smartly styled 13-inch TV-VCR combination housed in a white cabinet. Prepackaged with its own cookbook and cooking video, it can double as an instructional tool for whipping up new dishes, tape soap operas, or bring you the evening news from one of its 181 channels. The two-head mono VHS deck has an automatic head cleaner and can be preset to tape eight events over a 1-year period. Resolution is about 270 lines for the TV and 230 for the VCR. Like the set itself, the 30-button white membrane remote is ergonomically designed with color-coded keys in different shapes. The set also features trilingual displays, an onscreen clock, a sleep timer, and an alarm timer, plus both front and rear A/V jacks. The T13070WH includes an integrated low-to-the-counter "lazy susan" swivel base for easy movement.

Specifications: height, 15¾"; width, 14½"; depth, 15"; weight, 35 lb. **Warranty:** 90 days, labor; 1 year, parts.

Manufacturer's Suggested Retail Price: $479

Approximate Low Price: $399

ACCESSORIES

Digital Satellite Systems (DSS)

RCA DS4430RA

✓ **BEST BUY**

The RCA DS4430RA DSS system is the company's mid-end model, and may be the most popular second generation DSS model available. DSS consists of an 18-inch satellite dish and an all-digital receiver/decoder. The receiver unit has two antenna inputs—one for the satellite and one for either cable or a rooftop antenna. The DS4430RA's outputs include two audio, two video, one S-video, and one RF. To receive the best picture possible, you must plug the S-video output into your TV, which must have an S-video input. The system has been designed to output its signals to a television and a VCR and is capable of controlling two receivers. Depending on your TV, DSS can offer superb picture quality, displaying close to 500 lines of resolution for a seamless picture. The 39-button universal remote comes with an ergonomically designed, color-coded keypad and allows you to control the DSS, TV, VCR, cable box, and a laser disc player. The program guide lists every program broadcast and provides a description of each program at the top of the screen; you'll also find onscreen help with explanations of each aspect of the system. Using the cursor keys and a menu/select button, you can browse the system to select channels for viewing or buy movies to watch. You can set spending limits on pay-per-view and use your private code to lock out specific channels so that children may not watch them. The DS4430RA now offers a one-button record capability via StarSight. As long as you've properly attached your VCR, the DS4430RA can automatically record any receivable DSS channel. Just scroll over to the program name on the screen and press the record button. You never have to set the clock. Simply leave a blank tape in the turned-off machine—recording could not be easier. This DSS system also offers personal profiles; up to four users can program in their favorite channel and program lists, spending limits for PPV, and personal ID numbers along with parental control functions. Another convenient feature is the four-event scheduler, which programs the system to turn on, tune to a specified channel, and turn off at a preset time. It also allows these preset choices to be recorded on the VCR.

Specifications: height, 2.5"; width, 15.5"; depth, 14.25"; weight, 18.2 lb. **Warranty:** 90 days, labor; 1 year, parts.

Manufacturer's Suggested Retail Price: $749

Approximate Low Price: $654

SONY SAS-AD2

Recommended

The Sony SAS-AD2 DSS system, the company's top-of-the-line model, employs a 32-bit microprocessor. The SAS-AD2 is capable of controlling two receivers and comes prepackaged with its own 18-inch satellite dish and IRD receiver. Like the RCA unit, this receiver unit has two antenna inputs, one for the satellite and one for either cable or a rooftop antenna. The SAS-AD2 has seven outputs—three audio, two video, one S-video, and one RF digital audio. In the DSS category, features and onscreen graphics really differentiate the brands. The standard program guide features an express navigator with a direct tuning system that shows a list of channels, programs, and times along with a sports list, a station index, and a favorite station guide. The list's groupings for sports, movies, and other categories can be very helpful by presenting an alphabetical list in a left-hand column with show times across the top. This lets you scroll down to the film you want to see, then scroll out to the days and times when it will be shown. What really separates this DSS system from the others is its remote with the built-in trackball navigation system. This feature includes power and control keys on top, VCR function keys under a flip-up panel, a keypad with rubberized buttons in the middle, and the trackball/joystick with channel and volume up/down keys at the bottom. All menus and screens can be quickly and easily accessed with the joystick. This universal remote, with its 32-bit microprocessor, will control a TV, a VCR, and a cable box. The SAS-AD2 includes a built-in program timer that lets you tape DSS programs; simply program the receiver just as you would program your VCR, setting on/off timers, and channel number.

Specifications: height, 3¼"; width, 17"; depth, 10⅞"; weight, 6.4 lb. **Warranty:** 90 days labor; 1 year parts.

Manufacturer's Suggested Retail Price: $850

Approximate Low Price: $843

Universal Remotes

ONE FOR ALL URC-5061

✔ **BEST BUY**

The One For All 5 Device with Finder is an after-market universal remote that can control up to five audio and video components. What makes this universal remote special is that it includes a separate remote-finder transmitter. If you misplace this remote, just touch the button on the finder transmitter and it will send a signal to the remote to start beeping. What makes this remote a Best Buy is its ability to control a TV, a VCR/LD player, a CBL/SAT, an audio 1, and an audio 2 (for example, a TV, a VCR, a DSS satellite, a CD player, and an audio receiver/amp/tuner). If you prefer, the audio can be controlled via a separate audio power button. The raised keys of this remote are of different shapes and sizes so it's easy to use. The remote itself is bullet-shaped with the keys laid out in a logical fashion. The bean-shaped control keys are situated at the top with the sleep and menu keys directly below. With this remote, you can tap into the onscreen menus of various devices, such as the TV and VCR, so you do not need to go back to the original remote to program the VCR. Circular menu cursor keys are located in the center of this remote and control channel up/down and volume up/down. Just outside the ring of cursor keys are favorite channel and previous channel keys. The favorite channel button lets you preprogram up to ten favorite channels for exclusive scanning. Previous channel allows you to go back and forth between two channels. Directly below the ring is the raised numerical keypad for direct channel access followed by the VCR transport and record keys. As part of the package, this remote offers memory backup, which provides permanent memory retention of specific device codes—until you change them. The remote is powered by four AAA batteries, and the finder is powered by one 9-volt battery.

Specifications: length, 7.88"; width, 2.38"; depth, 1.25; weight, 4 oz. **Warranty:** 90 days.

Manufacturer's Suggested Retail Price: $25

Approximate Low Price: $25

RCA NITEGLO RCU4GLW

✔ BEST BUY

Ergonomically designed with raised clear keys that have black labels, this remote features 32 keys laid out in distinct sections. The RCU4GLW is capable of controlling four devices: a TV, VCR, cable box, and one auxiliary component. The function keys are situated across the top with VCR transport keys directly below, and the keypad is found in the middle of the remote. The bottom of the remote is shoehorn-shaped for easy resting in the palm of either a left- or right-handed person. The thumb, therefore, rests on both the circular channel and the volume up/down keys that are laid out as cursor keys. Below these you'll find the power button and, at the bottom, a light bulb key. The light bulb button activates the NiteGlo feature that illuminates all of the keys. Powered by four AAA batteries, the NiteGlo RCU4GLW makes it easy to program codes for the various components. This remote also introduces a new feature called the surf button; this lets you automatically scan through the channels on any of the devices it controls.

Specifications: height, 8.0"; width, 2.0"; depth, 0.75"; weight, 8 oz. **Warranty:** 90 days.

Manufacturer's Suggested Retail Price: $30

Approximate Low Price: $25

VCRS, LASER DISC PLAYERS, AND DVD PLAYERS

Twenty years ago, video cassette recorders (VCRs) were found in only a handful of consumer households. Today they can be found in more than 85 percent of all homes, and 13 million new VCRs are sold each year. Although other technologies are becoming common, VCRs still hold their position as the machine of choice, largely because they alone can record programs unattended.

Laser disc (LD) players, by comparison, offer the best picture and sound currently available for home video, but they do not record. The catalog of currently available discs is extensive, and virtually all films are now released on laser disc. Prices of discs are generally competitive with those of videotapes, though discs are far less subject to mechanical failure and wear than tapes. While a high-end laser disc player with dual-sided play and digital time base correction can cost around $700, excellent machines are available for less than $500. For someone who loves movies and doesn't do time-shift recording, a laser disc player could be a good alternative to a VCR.

A new disc format called DVD (Digital Video Disc) is scheduled for introduction this year. A DVD is a small, 5-inch, CD-like disc that can hold a 133-minute movie on one side of the disc. (Reportedly, 90 percent of all films released run 133 minutes or less). It will be dual-layered so that longer films can be continued on the lower layer, with no need to turn the discs over. According to the manufacturers, DVD players will start at $499 for a basic unit and range upward of $600 for full-featured models. Close to a dozen companies have announced DVD players for the coming year. The discs are currently estimated to cost about $20 each. According to the movie studios who are backing this format, we can expect an initial release of about 250 film titles concurrent with DVD's introduction.

Touted as the future of home video, DVD claims a far superior picture (500 lines of resolution or better) to DSS (approximately 480 lines of resolution), laser disc (425 lines of resolution), S-VHS (400 lines of resolution), or VHS (240 lines of resolution). Audio will be digital quality, on par with—or better than—the sound on current CDs. Viewers will be able to watch movies in multiple aspect ratios from pan-and-scan to letterbox, and they will be able to choose from several language and subtitled versions. These players will also offer parental control to delete questionable content from some films, making them suitable for children; in effect, parents will be able to turn an R-rated movie into a PG- or PG-13-version by eliminating specified footage.

Best Buys '97

Our Best Buy and Recommended VCRs, laser disc players, and DVD players follow. Within each category, items are listed by quality; the item we consider the best of the Best Buys is first, followed by our second choice, and so on. Remember that a Best Buy or Recommended designation applies only to the model listed; unless otherwise noted, it does not necessarily apply to other models made by the same manufacturer or to an entire product line.

VCRS

VCR Formats

The most common format for video cassette recorders is **VHS**, which uses ½-inch tape in a cassette shell roughly the size of a paperback book. **Hi-8mm** is a totally digital format that is technically dazzling and uses a much smaller cassette while producing markedly superior pictures and sound. Regular **8mm** tape offers digital images but does not match the technology of Hi-8mm decks. Only a handful of 8mm and Hi-8mm machines are available, because both formats are primarily used in camcorder applications. **Beta**, although in many ways superior to VHS, has virtually disappeared from the marketplace.

Sony continues to sell two consumer decks as replacements for its installed base of approximately nine million Betaphiles. **S-VHS** VCRs are VHS machines that separate luminance and chrominance signals to give a more detailed image with better definition. Due to the lack of prerecorded software, S-VHS never really caught on, so it represents only about one percent of total VCR sales. However, with the introduction of DSS (Digital Satellite System), we finally have a medium suitable for making S-VHS recordings. For the more than two million people who have already purchased DSS, an S-VHS deck makes a good choice for replacing an aging VCR—it will provide the best recorded image currently available.

Choosing Tapes

If you are going to record on a tape only once or twice and not play it back very often, standard-grade tapes are fine. However, if you plan to record and play back the same tape many times, it's worth the cost to purchase a high-grade tape. We also recommend that you use brand-name tapes rather than cheaper tapes from unknown manufacturers. Many of the less costly tapes are so poorly made that they can cause extensive and expensive damage to the heads of your VCR.

Most people buy T-120 tapes, which will record 2 hours at the fastest speed and 6 hours at the slowest speed. The longest tape currently available is a T-210 tape from JVC, which records 10½ hours at the slowest speed—perfect for recording a long miniseries.

Features and Terminology

Hi-Fi and Stereo Sound: Hi-fi is not the same thing as stereo sound. Stereo means that sound is recorded and played back through two channels, as opposed to monaural, one-channel sound. Hi-fi stands for high-fidelity, or high-quality, sound. If you want the best quality sound from your prerecorded movies or if you're thinking about putting together a home theater, you'll need a hi-fi VCR. All movies and videos are released with hi-fi soundtracks (encoded with Dolby Surround Sound). Prices for hi-fi VCRs range between $300 and $600.

Number of Video Heads: To record and play back a tape, you need only two video heads. Additional heads are used for special effects such as slow motion, freeze frame, and clear onscreen searching.

Programmability: If you are buying a VCR primarily to record television broadcasts, programmability is an important consideration. Except for VCPs (video cassette players), all VCRs can be programmed to record at least one program. The most rudimentary programming uses a built-in clock timer that you set to start and stop within the following 24 hours. More elaborate programming allows you to record several different programs on different channels for a period of 28 days or more. Other program operations let you record the same program every day or every week. Many VCRs are equipped with VCR Plus+, a simple method of programming by entering a number listed in television guides. Some VCR Plus+ models will also automatically switch channels on your cable box for recording. The newest program guide is TV Guide Plus+, which, if it's included in your VCR or TV package, will include free TV listings and one-button programming. One manufacturer outfits its models with Program Director, which allows quick programming via a remote. Simply move the remote's thumbwheel to the program you want, and press the thumbwheel. Most recently, some VCRs (and TVs) have come with StarSight programmers included. StarSight is an onscreen program guide available by subscription. It contains all the listings for your area and is updated daily. You simply scroll to the program you want to record on your onscreen guide and press record. The machine does the rest, since it knows the start and stop times and channel numbers in your area.

Tape Speeds: Virtually all VCRs let you choose two or three different recording speeds. The playback speed is automatically set, and even VCRs that record in only two speeds play back on all three speeds. The slow speeds allow more recording time on the videocassete, but the fast speed provides a better quality recording.

Quick Access/Quick Play: Many VCRs now provide quick play from the stop position. A number of VCRs provide quick access from fast-forward or fast-rewind to visual scanning and quick access from visual scanning to play.

Index Search: Many VCRs record an electronic index code at the beginning of each recording. To scan your recordings on a tape, you press index search. The VCR then stops at each index mark, and plays back a few seconds of the recording. Some VCRs even let you go directly to a specific index marker and start playback.

Jog/Shuttle Control: These special-effect tape-advance features allow you to precisely control the speed at which a tape is viewed. Shuttle control allows you to search forward or backward through a tape at a range of fast and slow speeds. Jog control allows you to move the tape forward or backward frame by frame.

Automatic Clock Set: This noteworthy feature was introduced by Sony 2 years ago and is now found on most brands of VCRs. These models set their own clock from a time signal sent by your local PBS station. This means that you never have to set the clock initially, change the time at the beginning and end of daylight saving time, or reset the clock after a blackout.

Commercial Advance: New decks by RCA/Proscan and a few others now include commercial-zapper circuitry that senses the beginning and end of commercials in a taped program. Upon playback, it will automatically fast-forward through the commercials (a blue screen appears during this interval) and go back into play mode when the program resumes.

Universal Remotes: Many step-up models feature preprogrammed universal remotes, which have the ability to control a TV and a cable box. A unified remote will control a TV that's the same brand as your VCR.

Editing Features: Unless you actually plan on editing your camcorder tapes and making dupes (duplicates) for family and friends, stay away from decks with sophisticated editing features, such as assemble editing, insert editing, and video dubbing. These features can add up to $100 to the cost of the model and will only make the machine more difficult and intimidating to use.

Hi-Fi VHS VCRs

TOSHIBA M782

✔ **BEST BUY**

The Toshiba M782 is a six-head hi-fi VCR that produces some of the finest video images available today. The M782 is a full-featured deck with two extra 19-micron heads to produce recorded images at its slowest speed (EP) that rival images recorded at its fastest speed (SP). In essence, the 19-micron heads provide steady, natural colors with fine edge detail. These new heads are coupled with the V3 chassis, which features a flying preamp that is integrated into the heads, providing less video noise at both playback speeds. To further improve picture quality, this VCR includes color signal enhancement (CSE). CSE makes colors more robust and distinct by reducing color bleed and eliminating multiphase processing. This model also offers DNR Perfect (digital noise reduction) circuitry to clean up taped images diminished by video noise, snow, and drop-outs. Equipped with a 181-channel tuner and programmable to record six events over a 1-month period, the M782 also sports a universal remote that controls your TV, DSS (all brands), and cable box. The remote goes one step further by giving you "Intel-A-Play II" keys, which act as macro keys that turn on the TV and the VCR and go to the proper video input with the touch of a single button. The macro key also rewinds tapes and turns off both the VCR and TV. To facilitate programming, the VCR includes new, easy-to-use onscreen graphics and VCR Plus+ with cable-box control. The VCR's circular transport keys become cursor keys for programming. Other features include a jog/shuttle dial on the unit, front and rear A/V jacks, auto-speed select, an automatic head cleaner, and a trilingual onscreen display. As with other hi-fi VCRs, the sound quality is excellent.

Specifications: height, 3⅝"; width, 16¹⁵⁄₁₆"; depth, 12½"; weight, 9.7 lb. **Warranty:** 1 year, parts and labor.

Manufacturer's Suggested Retail Price: $600

Approximate Low Price: Not available

PANASONIC PV-4662

The Panasonic PV-4662 is a four-head hi-fi **Recommended**
VCR. Its four heads, assisted by color noise reduction and
advanced noise reduction circuitry, produce high-quality
images with very little video noise at all three record and playback speeds (SP, LP, and SLP). This machine features a 181-
channel tuner programmable to record eight events over a 31-
day period. For programming ease, VCR Plus+ with cable-box
control is also included. The PV-4662 comes with its own program director. Originally, the director was a separate remote
control device, but it's now incorporated as a thumbwheel
located in the center of the remote. By rotating this thumbwheel forward or backward, you scroll through dates, times,
and channels until it reaches the show you want to tape; then
you press the thumbwheel, and the VCR is set to record. This
VCR also comes with a 42-button universal remote that will
control your TV and cable box. To simplify use, separate sections of the remote are dedicated to particular functions. The
PV-4662 includes digital spatializer circuitry, which gives the
sound added dimension or spaciousness. Other helpful features include the automatic clock set, front A/V jacks, a warning beeper (in case programming is disrupted), VCR lock, and
trilingual onscreen displays.

Specifications: height, 3½"; width, 15"; depth, 11¼"; weight, 8.6
lb. **Warranty:** 90 days, labor; 1 year, parts.

Manufacturer's Suggested Retail Price: $380

Approximate Low Price: $311

AIWA AV-X500

The Aiwa AV-X500 is a combination A/V **Recommended**
receiver and hi-fi VCR. The receiver includes a Dolby Pro Logic
decoder and is rated at 100 watts of power per channel (100
watts for left, center, and right, plus 100 watts for each rear
channel). Three A/V inputs and outputs give you added versatility by allowing you to attach your TV, laser disc or DVD
player, and CD player to the AV-X500. To improve sound quality from these different sources, a three-position BBE circuit is

included along with a three-position Super-T bass system. BBE enhances overall audio quality by giving added depth and breadth to sound. The Super-T bass system adds varying degrees of bass boost, depending on your preferences, and a digital signal processor offers four ambiance settings: dance, hall, live, and arena. The receiver also features a digital synthesizer AM/FM tuner with 32 station presets and a subwoofer output. This four-head VCR's 181-channel tuner offers programming of eight events over 365 days. VCR Plus+ with cable controller simplifies the programming process. An automatic head cleaner cleans your tape heads each time a tape is inserted or ejected, which is especially helpful if you play a lot of rental tapes. To complete the package, a learning remote comes with the unit. You can create a small home theater by hooking this VCR up to any of Aiwa's minisystems, and you can control the entire system with one remote.

Specifications: height, 10¼"; width, 14¼"; depth, 12½"; weight, 21.3 lb. **Warranty:** 90 days, limited on parts and labor.

Manufacturer's Suggested Retail Price: $650

Approximate Low Price: Not available

SONY SLV-960HF

`Recommended`

The Sony SLV-960HF four-head, hi-fi VCR produces fine video images at both the slowest and fastest record speeds. Images from prerecorded tapes are pristine, with very little video noise. Sony's heritage of technical expertise is represented in the SLV-960HF. Equipped with a 181-channel tuner and programming capability for eight programs over 31 days, the unit is a solid performer with numerous innovative features. Besides VCR Plus+ with cable-box control (via a cable mouse), this model has an automatic clock set feature that always displays the correct time. Cursor keys and an execute button found on top of the remote make the onscreen menus and setup easy to use. The included full-featured universal remote also controls your TV and DSS or cable box. Included on this 50-button universal remote is a recessed jog/shuttle ring, which makes it easy to move the tape forward or backward at varying speeds. It can all be accomplished with your thumb—whether you're left- or right-handed. This VCR unit also comes with an automatic head cleaner, commercial skip (it advances the tape 60 seconds each time you depress it), indexing, and adaptive picture control, which optimizes any tape placed into the VCR. Sony's new S-Link feature, when connected to a Sony TV, gives you complete control: If you put in a prerecorded tape and/or press the play button on the VCR, the TV will turn on, go to the proper video input, and start playing the tape. The SLV-960HF also offers exclusive VideoDirector Home PC software, which is attachable—via two supplied discs and cables—to your Sony camcorder, a VCR, and your computer. (You need Windows 3.1 or higher, 4Mb of RAM, and a free serial port on your computer.) This feature, with an easy-to-follow onscreen menu, lets you title, assemble, and edit tapes and raw videos on your computer, creating true home movies. The VCR's tape transport is housed under a door that can be locked from the remote to make it tamperproof.

Specifications: height, 4⅜"; width, 17"; depth, 12¼"; weight, 9 lb. 15 oz. **Warranty:** 90 days, labor; 1 year, parts.

Manufacturer's Suggested Retail Price: $599

Approximate Low Price: $449

RCA VR688HF

The RCA VR688HF four-head hi-fi VCR has **Recommended** the ability to zap out annoying commercials. Called Commercial Advance, this feature marks the beginnings and ends of commercial breaks as it records. When you play the tape back, the VCR senses those index marks and quickly fast-forwards through the commercial, displaying a blue screen in the interim. The VCR's 46-button illuminated universal remote control will also control a TV, a second VCR, a laser disc player, a DVD player, DSS, and an audio component. RCA's VR688HF features a 181-channel tuner capable of recording eight events over 365 days. Since it's DSS compatible, the tuner can record from any channel up to 999. A new feature found on this VCR is called ShowSaver Memory Protection. This function retains all your programming, even through a power failure. (In the past, if your electricity went out, your VCR's programming would be lost.) This VCR also comes with automatic clock set, VCR Plus+ with cable box, front A/V jacks for the attachment of a camcorder, an automatic head cleaner, and a child protection system.

Specifications: height, 3½"; width, 15½"; depth, 12½"; weight, 12.75 lb. **Warranty:** 90 days, labor; 1 year, parts.

Manufacturer's Suggested Retail Price: $449

Approximate Low Price: $353

8mm VCR

SAMSUNG SV2040U

Recommended

The Samsung SV2040U is a dual-deck 8mm/ VHS VCR that offers the luxury of recording, playing back, or dubbing tapes from one format to another. It also plays back and dubs Hi-8mm tapes onto VHS, so you can easily copy tapes, play tapes in sequence, and/or do sequence recording. The 8mm deck is on the left, and the VHS deck is on the right. Both decks are hi-fi, and because they share controls and features, editing is a breeze. The unit offers a 181-channel tuner and an eight-event/365-day programming capability. With this model, you can watch a tape on one deck and record a program on the other. It also allows you to record two different programs simultaneously—one on each deck (each with its own built-in TV tuner). The SV2040U comes with a synchro-edit feature to put the two decks into sync and an internal auto-assemble editor that allows you to put eight recorded scenes in a particular order. Other convenient features include audio-dubbing capability, audio insert, and a built-in titler, which lets you title your videos and add credits. The picture is very good in all formats, consistently displaying 240 lines or more of resolution, thanks to four video heads in VHS and two video heads in its 8mm mode. The 42-button remote controls both decks at the touch of a button, and the audio quality is excellent. A tape-remaining display tells you the amount of tape left, measured in hours, minutes, and seconds. The decks offer dual A/V inputs (front and rear) and dual outputs.

Specifications: height, 3¾"; width, 16⅞"; depth, 15½"; weight, 19½ lb. **Warranty:** 90 days, labor; 1 year, parts.

Manufacturer's Suggested Retail Price: $1,199

Approximate Low Price: $877

LASER DISC PLAYERS

A laser disc is an optical medium for playing video and digital audio recordings. Pits cut into the disc are read by a laser beam. Because information can be read from the discs without any physical contact, the acrylic-coated discs will last virtually forever. Laser discs also produce excellent image quality with ordinary hookups to your television set. When used with TVs that have S-video connections, they are capable of producing superb images with nearly twice the horizontal resolution of standard videotapes. Many laser discs are available in letter-boxed versions. Most laser disc players are combination players, meaning that they play multiple types of discs, from 5-inch CDs through 12-inch laser discs. Many models today provide a separate drawer for CD-only playback. These models utilize a CD-direct input that operates the drawer and disconnects the video circuitry for less interference.

Many laser disc players offer dual-sided play, which automatically turns the disc over. This process takes about 12 seconds. The unit will either display a blue screen or freeze the last frame of the video until the next scene starts. There are two types of laser discs: CAV (constant angular velocity) and CLV (constant linear velocity). CAV discs spin at a constant speed of 1,800 RPMs with a playing time of 30 minutes per side. All CAV discs can be played back with special effects. CLV discs spin at a speed ranging from 1,800 RPMs for the inner tracks to 600 RPMs for outer tracks. This permits a playing time of 60 minutes per side. Special effects with CLVs are possible only with players with digital frame memory.

Features and Terminology

Random Access: All laser disc players have the ability to provide random access, allowing you to quickly find a particular spot on the disc.

Chapter Numbers: These numbers are recorded on the discs and are used to indicate sections or chapters, almost like track numbers on CDs. A movie is divided into distinct sections. For example, in *Forrest Gump,* the sections might be Chapter 1, "Hello. My name is Forrest. Forrest Gump"; Chapter 2, "Through the Eyes of Forrest Gump"; Chapter 3, "Stupid Is as Stupid Does"; and so forth.

Digital Time Base Correction: Time base correction helps reduce jitter at the edges and corners of the picture.

Theater Mode: In this mode, several seconds are cut from the turnover time of a disc by skipping over side B's table of contents. It will also dim the laser disc's front panel illumination.

Digital Dolby AC-3: This means that the player has outputs for a new surround audio technique called Dolby Surround Digital—Dolby AC-3. Apparently the successor to Dolby Pro Logic, Dolby AC-3 sends discrete audio to all 5.1 channels of a home theater setup (left, right, center, right rear, left rear, and the subwoofer). In the AC-3 mode, distinct sound emanates from each speaker, as opposed to straight matrixed and steered Pro Logic sound. While there are other audio surround schemes out there, Dolby Surround Digital seems to be the *de facto* standard.

PIONEER CLD-D605

✓**BEST BUY**

The Pioneer CLD-D605 is part of a newer generation of Dolby Digital-ready laser disc players offering dual-sided play, direct CD, and digital time base correction. Picture quality is excellent due to the digital time base correction, which eliminates noise and jitter, allowing all 425 lines of resolution to come through. A picture control button further sharpens images, especially on older black-and-white movies. Direct CD, with its separate CD tray, disconnects all video circuitry for improved audio performance. The CLD-D605 comes with two A/V outputs, two S-video outputs, and one Dolby Digital output. Other features include a 40-button illuminated remote, Dolby Stereo Digital, and Quick Turn, which turns the disc over in approximately 10 seconds. This full-featured model even supplies digital echo, a microphone, and a sample karaoke disc. Theater Bass Surround enhances both the bass and surround sound. To fully realize Dolby Digital's power, you'll need either a stand-alone processor or a new breed of A/V receiver with a built-in Dolby Digital decoder.

Specifications: height, 5³⁄₁₆″; width, 16⁹⁄₁₆″; depth, 16⅛″; weight, 14 lb. 15 oz. **Warranty:** 1 year, parts and labor.

Manufacturer's Suggested Retail Price: $1,000

Approximate Low Price: $623

SONY MDP-650

Recommended

The Sony MDP-650 laser disc player is capable of displaying 425 lines of resolution, and it produces crisp images with very little video noise. This model employs what Sony calls tri-digital video processing, which consists of a digital time base corrector, a digital comb filter, a digital drop-out compensator, and a digital noise canceler. The auto-reverse feature automatically turns a disc over in about 8 seconds. Because of its eight-bit digital memory, the unit can conduct both freeze-frame and frame-by-frame advance searches for both CAV and CLV discs. The 26-key Sony remote that comes with the MDP-650 features phosphorescent illuminated basic function keys and a recessed jog/shuttle knob. The deck package includes two A/V outputs, two S-video outputs, and a fiber-optic cable output for attachment to a stand-alone D/A converter. Other features include theater mode, which lowers the picture's black level for improved contrast, and digital frame memory to retain images for display as a CD plays.

Specifications: height, 4⅝″; width, 17″; depth, 17⅛″; weight, 16 lb. 9 oz. **Warranty:** 90 days, labor; 1 year, parts.

Manufacturer's Suggested Retail Price: $899

Approximate Low Price: $676

DIGITAL VIDEO DISC (DVD) PLAYERS

TOSHIBA SD-3006

Recommended

The Toshiba SD-3006 is an excellent example of the new DVD techonolgy. In addition to playing movies off a 5-inch disc, it will also play all your CDs. DVD discs display 480 lines of resolution, compared to laser disc's 425 lines or Super VHS's 400 lines. The SD-3006 offers digital-quality audio and is capable of playing movies in the new Dolby Digital 5.1 surround format. DVD allows you to play back video in multiple aspect ratios: 16:9 format for a wide-screen TV, letterbox for a standard 4:3 set, and pan-and-scan. For foreign films, the disc can produce eight language tracks and 32 subtitle languages. DVD also allows you to view a scene from different camera angles, and each disc has multiple ratings so that, via parental control, you can change an R-rated movie to PG-13, directing the player to skip over unwanted scenes or dialogue. The SD-3006 comes with a preprogrammed universal remote that will also control a TV and cable box. This DVD player's outputs include one S-video, one composite video, one AC-3 digital audio, two pairs of analog audio, and one component video (color difference). All outputs are gold-plated for the best possible image fidelity.

Specifications: height, 3³⁄₁₆"; width, 16¹⁵⁄₁₆"; depth, 12¹⁄₈"; weight, 8.9 lb. **Warranty:** 1 year, parts and labor.

Manufacturer's Suggested Retail Price: $699

Approximate Low Price: Not available

RCA RC5500P

Recommended

The RCA RC5500P is an another fine product of the new DVD technology. It can play movies off a 5-inch disc, as well as all your CDs. DVD discs display 480 lines of resolution, and their picture quality is twice as good as that of standard VHS tapes. In addition, DVD offers digital-quality audio and the capability of playing movies in the new Dolby Digital 5.1 surround format. With DVD you can play back video in multiple aspect ratios: 16:9 format for a wide-screen TV, letterbox for a standard 4:3 set, and pan-and-scan. Depending on the movie you select, eight language tracks and 32 subtitle languages are available. If a scene has been specially programmed, DVD can show it from multiple camera angles. For parents, discs come with multiple ratings, meaning that you can skip over unwanted scenes or dialogue to change an R-rated movie to PG-13. The RC5500P comes with an ergonomically designed, preprogrammed, universal remote that will also control a TV, DSS, a VCR, an audio component, or a cable box. All keys are color-coded and divided into sections according to their functions. This model offers several outputs—one S-video, two composite video, one AC-3 digital audio, and two pairs of analog audio—plus a built-in AC-3 or Dolby Digital Surround decoder. Simply attach the VCR to an AC-3-ready A/V receiver or processor to enjoy the benefits of 5.1 audio. An AC-3-ready product will have inputs and outputs for left, right, center, left surround, right surround, and subwoofer.

Specifications: height, 2⅖"; width, 5½"; depth, 12½"; weight, 8.9 lb. **Warranty:** 90 days, labor; 1 year, parts.

Manufacturer's Suggested Retail Price: Not available

Approximate Low Price: Not available

CAMCORDERS

The camcorder is a combination video camera and video cassette recorder: It records live action on tape for near-instantaneous playback on any television.

Now that this product has matured, even the least expensive camcorders offer a variety of useful features with satisfactory performance. As the sales boom of the late 1980s faded, prices for basic models fell, reaching new lows in the 1990s in spite of the rising value of the Japanese yen. Sony, Panasonic, JVC, Sharp, and Hitachi manufacture nearly all camcorders on the market, no matter what the brand name is on the unit. This means you might be able to save a few dollars by comparing two similar (sometimes identical) models sold under different brand names.

Whereas picture quality varies only slightly among models in similar categories, the feel and the ease of operation can differ substantially. Shop for a camcorder as you would for a pair of shoes. Try it on for comfort, and try it out for ease of use. Many smaller models have diminutive buttons that are difficult for larger hands to manipulate. Be sure you're comfortable with the buttons and controls.

Camcorder Formats

The market share of the three camcorder formats has stabilized somewhat in the last couple of years, with 8mm and VHS-C in a dead heat at about 40 percent apiece. Figures vary from month to month and from manufacturer to manufacturer, but full-size VHS continues to lose its share and is down to about 15 percent of the market. Product offerings, naturally, reflect these trends.

VHS camcorders have the longest recording capacity of all formats. They can record up to 10 hours on a T-200 tape at extended play (EP) speed. However, picture and sound quality noticeably degrade at this slow speed. The bulky size of the VHS cassette, with its ½-inch-wide tape, requires a relatively large, often heavy, camcorder (though these have been downsized to about

4.5 lb.). Full-size VHS is the only format directly playable in home VHS VCRs. Camcorders without the hi-fi option record low-fidelity audio. An upgraded VHS format, Super VHS (S-VHS), uses a specially formulated, much more expensive tape and uses superior electronics. This tape records up to 400 lines of resolution—close to laser discs in video quality—and far outperforms conventional VHS (which has 240 lines of resolution). Super VHS also substantially improves the video quality of the slow EP tape speed, making it more acceptable for ordinary recording.

VHS-C (compact VHS), a variation of the VHS format, uses cassettes about a third of the size of regular VHS cassettes. The signals recorded on VHS-C are fully compatible with full-size VHS. This allows VHS-C cassettes to record and play back on any VHS VCR; you simply place the cassette in an adapter (supplied with nearly all VHS-C camcorders). VHS-C tapes record for a maximum of 40 minutes at the standard play (SP) speed and 2 hours at the lower quality extended play (EP) speed. This is twice the recording time of original VHS-C tapes. Like full-size-format camcorders, VHS-C camcorders without the hi-fi option record low-fidelity audio.

8mm cassettes are roughly the size of audiocassettes, though slightly thicker, and the tape itself is $\frac{1}{3}$-inch wide (narrower than the $\frac{1}{2}$-inch-wide VHS tape). By using metal tape to increase recording density, 8mm tapes reproduce an image comparable to VHS. Camcorders that use this format are compact and lightweight, with many models weighing less than $1\frac{1}{2}$ pounds. A standard 8mm camcorder records up to $2\frac{1}{2}$ hours on a single tape at SP speed.

Hi8 (Hi-Band 8mm) offers the same resolution as S-VHS (about 400 lines), but Hi8 records with slightly less color noise, making the picture quality slightly better than S-VHS's. Standard 8mm tapes will record and play back on Hi8 machines, but tapes recorded on Hi8 will not play back on conventional 8mm machines. Hi8 camcorders require special tape formulations: a premium metal evaporated tape (Hi8-ME) or an improved metal particle tape (Hi8-MP). Both are more expensive than standard VHS tapes. Hi8-ME offers superior performance, but it is difficult to manufacture, expensive, and can be difficult to find. The new Hi8-MP formulations narrow the performance gap and work well for everyday shooting. Hi8 camcorders, like S-VHS, include S-video jacks for maximum signal transfer quality to a TV or an S-VHS VCR. However, most of the Hi8 advantage can still be realized through ordinary cables.

The VHS and 8mm formats are electronically compatible. This allows you, for example, to connect your 8mm camcorder to your VHS VCR and copy your 8mm videos onto VHS tape. Front-panel input jacks for this purpose are becoming nearly standard on VHS decks, and input jacks have always been standard on the back panels. You can also connect your 8mm camcorder directly to your TV for viewing. In fact, many TVs also sport front AV jacks for this very purpose.

DV (Digital Video) camcorders, which were introduced last year, offer superior audio and video quality. With cassettes slightly larger than a matchbox, these camcorders record and process information digitally. This means that there is virtually no loss of picture quality when you dub to another format or to your computer. These camcorders use a $\frac{1}{3}$-inch, 570,000-pixel count CCD image sensor to create high-quality recordings. Their sound is equally superior thanks to PCM digital audio, which is several notches above VHS hi-fi. The standard DV cassette uses metal evaporated tape and records for 60 minutes.

Features and Terminology

Autofocus describes a feature that focuses the lens and keeps it focused even as the distance between the camcorder and the subject changes. Some camcorders also permit manual focusing. Each manufacturer uses a proprietary autofocus system, and these systems vary as to speed and accuracy. Although most companies employ some computerized through-the-lens (TTL) system, the simpler infrared system sometimes works better. Be sure to try out the autofocus when you evaluate a camcorder.

Aperture designation refers to the maximum opening of the iris—in other words, the greatest amount of light that can be admitted through the lens. The designation is given as an f-stop rating, such as f/1.6. The smaller the f-stop number, the larger the aperture and the more light passes through the lens. In all camcorders, the iris adjusts automatically, but some also offer manual adjustment.

An **imager (or imaging device)** is a solid-state device that collects light and transforms it into an electrical signal.

A **high-speed shutter** alters the camcorder's method of collecting light from its CCD imaging device, thereby allowing less light into the camcorder. A camcorder's high-speed shutter permits operation at speeds up to $1/40,000$ second. Unless you plan to shoot sporting events, this is probably not an essential feature. Most camcorders on the market today have a shutter range between $1/60$ second and $1/4,000$ second, which is adequate for most purposes.

Program autoexposure (or Program AE) offers different modes of preprogrammed exposures, depending on shooting and lighting conditions. The Program AE alters the shutter speed, iris, and white balance when the user selects different settings, such as snow, twilight, sepia, sports (high-speed shutter), or standard. The control for this feature is usually found on a dial at the side of the camcorder.

Lux is a unit of measurement that gauges the amount of light falling on a subject. Many camcorders have a low-light level rating of around 10 lux, which is the amount of light on a subject about 12 feet away from a single 60-watt light bulb. Although sensitive camcorders can deliver a picture at 1 lux, you are most likely to get a good image with 80 lux. For optimum color and depth of field, you need several hundred lux. For many years, manufacturers played a lux war game, with each claiming the lowest lux level, but there was no real standard for measuring lux. Now a standard is in place: It's called EIA-639, and it generally computes a slightly higher lux rating than the past lux measurements. Since this rating system has just recently been developed, most camcorders on the market now do not include this new standard; as of this writing, only RCA is measuring lux according to the EIA standard. The 1998 camcorder models are expected to include a lux rating "as measured by the EIA standard." Essentially, this means brand A's 3 lux will be equivalent to brand B's 3 lux, which will be very helpful to consumers.

Minimum illumination tells you the minimum amount of light, stated in lux, necessary to record a clear picture.

Automatic (or continuous) white balance keeps the color of the video image true to life under varying lighting conditions—outdoor or indoor, fluorescent or incandescent. An inaccurate white balance can produce a picture that is too pink or too blue.

Character generators allow you to add the time, the date, titles, and other written information to the images you record.

A **superimposer** is a digital memory function that can store images or titles. At the push of a button, you can superimpose the stored image over the picture currently being recorded.

Fade in/fade out automatically fades an image from or to a black (or white) screen.

CCD (charged-coupled device) is a solid-state imaging device that replaced the old pickup tube of earlier models. CCDs eliminate most image lag, which looks like a streaking highlight on a moving subject. CCDs function well under a broad range of lighting conditions and are rarely damaged by excessive light. The CCD system collects electrons and moves them through the imaging device. All of the CCDs used in camcorders are based on MOS (metal-oxide semiconductor) devices. The MOS is a type of light-sensitive transmitter that makes up the CCD. Reference to CCD or MOS in camcorder specifications is arbitrary and bears little relationship to the overall quality of the product.

A **flying erase head** is mounted on the spinning video head drum rather than set in a stationary position along the tape path. Because it spins with the other heads, a flying erase head allows you to make smooth transitions and eliminates noise bursts when you stop and start the tape between scenes, thereby improving the quality of your edited tapes.

Resolution is the ability to produce fine detail in a video picture. It is usually measured in horizontal lines. Vertical resolution, less frequently cited, is a more stringent measure. A good video monitor produces more than 500 lines. Television broadcasts have about 340 lines. Conventional VHS reproduces 240 lines, and 8mm yields slightly more.

A **pixel** (short for picture element) is one of the tiny points that make up a video image. A high pixel count produces a more detailed image, but because the size and type of imaging devices vary, comparing the pixel counts of different devices won't necessarily tell you which yields the most detailed image.

Image stabilization is a generic term for reducing unwanted camcorder motion, such as shakes and jitters. It has become a standard feature in recent years. Some manufacturers use a digital electronic system that fuzzes the picture slightly to reduce unwanted motion. Others compensate by rapidly moving the lens (they call this optical image stabilization). After reviewing a large number of camcorders with this feature, we question its overall benefit. The effectiveness of image stabilization does vary from brand to brand, so try a few camcorders with image stabilization to see which you prefer.

Microphones are built into all camcorders, and most can be connected to external mikes as well.

Best Buys '97

Our Best Buy, Recommended, and Budget Buy camcorders follow. They are presented in these categories: 8mm, compact VHS (VHS-C), full-size VHS, and digital video (DV). Within each category, camcorders are listed by quality; the item we consider the best of the Best Buys is first, followed by our second choice, and so on. A Budget Buy describes a less expensive product of respectable quality that perhaps sacrifices some of the performance and/or features of a Best Buy or Recommended model. Remember that a Best Buy, Recommended, or Budget Buy designation applies only to the model listed; it does not necessarily apply to other models made by the same manufacturer or to an entire product line.

8mm CAMCORDERS

SONY CCD-TR94

The Sony CCD-TR94 has one of the best combinations of features at the best price in the 8mm camcorder

✓ **BEST BUY**

category. Pushing the limits of 8mm technology, it uses a ⅓-inch, 470,000-pixel count CCD imager that is normally found only on Sony's Hi8mm models. The CCD-TR94 is equipped with the SteadyShot picture stabilization system, a 24-power digital zoom lens, and a variable-speed (4 to 12 seconds) 12-power optical zoom lens. The camcorder has the ability to shoot video down to 3 lux. To adapt to a variety of lighting situations, this model features a three-mode programmed auto-exposure: natural light, sports, and high-speed shutter (to ¼,₀₀₀ second). The CCD-TR94 uses an f/1.8 lens with a focal length of 64.8mm (f/5.4) and a 37mm filter. It also comes with a color viewfinder, a precision color LCD with 113,00 pixels, and Sony's Solar Window, which allows additional light into the LCD via a special top-mounted viewfinder window. The CCD-TR94's battery power has been improved by its use of "no memory effect" batteries, which retain a full charge even if you recharge them before they are completely dead. In addition, if you run out of standard battery power before you finish taping, you can use six AA batteries to give yourself up to 2 more hours of power. Like most of today's 8mm camcorders, this one lets you tape at two speeds: SP and LP. The integrated lens cover retracts when you turn the camcorder on, so you won't accidentally tape several minutes of nothing, and the quick-record feature lets you start recording almost instantly. With this camcorder, you can automatically record 5-second snippets for fast-paced videos. The built-in clock/calendar records date and time on your videos, and the character generator provides nine pre-programmed video titles. A nine-button remote is also included.

Specifications: height, 4"; width, 4⅓"; depth, 8"; weight, 1.5 lb. (without tape and battery). **Warranty:** 90 days, labor; 1 year, parts.

Manufacturer's Suggested Retail Price: $1,000

Approximate Low Price: $799

CANON ES900

The Canon ES900 is designed for the person ✔ **BEST BUY** who wants to edit his or her own videos. Its FlexiZone autofocus system allows perfect focus and exposure of your subject. FlexiZone's AF/AE keeps your subject in focus at all times, even if the subject moves to the left or right of center. The joystick-style controller on the back middle of the camcorder, within easy reach of your thumb, lets you center in on your subject. To activate FlexiZone, simply press the designated button on the top back of the camcorder. You can also use your thumb to flip the record switch to the right before you press the red record button underneath. This control arrangement is likely to be slightly different than what you are used to, but it's easy to manage. This camcorder's battery compartment is located on the bottom left-hand side to balance the weight of the unit. The ES900 uses a 20-power optical zoom featuring an f/1.6 lens with a focal length of 4 to 80mm, combined with optical image stabilization. The ¼-inch, 270,000-pixel CCD imager has a minimum light sensitivity of 3 lux. Canon's four-mode program autoexposure adjusts the camcorder for a variety of shooting conditions: portrait, sports, spotlight, and sand and snow. The 0.55-inch color viewfinder, with a solid 113,000 pixels, offers a fairly bright image, and the audio features hi-fi stereo sound. Two custom keys let you store up to 16 functions in memory for easy retrieval during taping. To edit your tapes, simply connect this camcorder to any VCR, then use its menu system via the ES900's remote. Through this menu, you can choose, for example, scene length or the sequence of scenes. When you've arranged the scene sequence from the tape inside the camcorder, press the execute button on the remote, and it will rearrange the scenes (according to the length and order you've selected) on the blank tape in the VCR. A built-in titler allows you to create your own titles as you film your video or in post-production. Titles are created from the character generator, which can also record one of three different data and time displays onto the tape. With a P6-150 tape, the maximum recording time is 2½ hours.

Specifications: height, 4³⁄₁₆"; width, 4⁵⁄₁₆"; depth, 7¼"; weight, 1 lb. 11 oz. (without tape and battery). **Warranty:** 1 year, parts and labor.

Manufacturer's Suggested Retail Price: $999

Approximate Low Price: $833

RCA PRO847   Recommended

The RCA PRO847, part of RCA's PRO8 line of 8mm camcorders, offers a dual-battery system so you can use either a standard NiCad battery or six AA batteries. Both types of batteries fit into the body of the camcorder. The NiCad, which charges inside the body of the camcorder so you don't need a charger stand, allows approximately 60 minutes of recording; the six AA batteries allow about 90 minutes. The ¼-inch, 250,000-pixel CCD imager is coupled with a 15-power zoom lens and includes an f/1.4 to 2.6 lens with a focal range of 4 to 60mm. The PRO847 features a 0.55-inch color viewfinder that displays date and time, tape remaining, battery life, and a zoom gauge. This camcorder comes with an 11-button miniremote, which is stored inside the battery compartment. The separate lens cap, tethered to the camcorder via a slender cord, will dangle if it isn't stored properly. The PRO847 also includes hi-fi sound, program autoexposure, and blank search.

Specifications: height, 4¾"; width, 4¼"; depth, 8⅜"; weight, 1.6 lb. (without tape and battery). **Warranty:** 90 days, labor; 1 year, parts.

Manufacturer's Suggested Retail Price: $699

Approximate Low Price: $600

HITACHI VM-H720A   Recommended

The Hitachi VM-H720A is one of the best examples of a Hi8mm camcorder at a reasonably affordable price. It's a handheld Hi8mm camcorder with a ¼-inch, 410,000-pixel count CCD imager, an f/1.6 lens, and a low-light sensitivity down to 2 lux. This model features two high-grade amorphous video heads and a flying erase head, which helps produce seamless edits free of video noise. It comes with both 12-power optical zoom and 24-power digital zoom lenses. The focal length of the optical zoom is 4 to 48mm, and an instant

1.5 zoom can be activated by pushing a button between the tele- and wide-zoom toggles. The VM-H720A's dual-battery system lets you use six AA batteries for about 45 minutes of additional power. Electronic image stabilization (EIS) keeps recorded images pretty solid. Hitachi equips this camcorder with a color viewfinder, hi-fi stereo with a stereo mike, and a wind filter for cutting down on recorded wind noise. The VM-H720A uses a $\frac{1}{60}$ to $\frac{1}{4,000}$ high-speed shutter along with autoexposure, automatic white balance, auto-iris, and auto-backlight. The universal miniremote lets you do both audio and video dubbing as well as insert edits. You can also control and synchro edit, which means that you can start/stop and record/play the camcorder and VCR simultaneously. This camcorder package includes a two-line, one-page titler with a character generator, and a hot shoe for the attachment of an optional color enhancement light. With this model, you can record in a 16:9 aspect ratio for playback on a wide-screen TV.

Specifications: height, 4¹²⁄₁₆"; width, 3¹¹⁄₁₆"; depth, 8⁵⁄₁₆"; weight, 1.9 lb. (without tape and battery). **Warranty:** 90 days, labor; 1 year, parts.

Manufacturer's Suggested Retail Price: $1,000

Approximate Low Price: $924

SAMSUNG SCX915

Budget Buy

A basic 8mm camcorder, the Samsung SCX915 comes with a color viewfinder (103,000 pixels), power zoom with a 12:1 zoom ratio, and a ⅓-inch, 270,000-pixel CCD imager. The SCX915 works with a minimum 2-lux illumination and uses an f/1.8 lens with a focal length of 64.8mm (f/5.4) and a 37mm filter. This model features a flying erase head and a four-mode (normal, portrait, sports, and high-speed shutter) Program AE that automatically sets focus, white balance, shutter speed, and iris. A built-in character generator allows you to superimpose a one-page, two-line, 32-character title onto your videos. Date- and time-set capabilities are held in a separate memory powered by a lithium battery, which lasts for approximately 1 year. Editing features include insert edit, which lets you lay down new audio and video over previously recorded material. The SCX915 also offers three levels of solarization digital special effects, which can add a surrealistic quality to your videos. The color viewfinder displays settings to show battery life, zoom meter, time elapsed, and calendar (day/date/time). If you add special effects to your shot or change the Program AE mode, the viewfinder also changes so that you see just what you are taping. A fade button on the front left-hand side of the camcorder helps make transitions from one scene to another. Edit search lets you watch, in the viewfinder, the last several seconds of a scene you've taped. The audio component of the SCX915 is standard hi-fi mono. This package even includes a 12-button, credit-card-size remote that plays back your videos or controls the camcorder (if you shoot from a tripod) to let you see the images you're taping on your TV screen. A 10-second self-timer and an interval timer for time-lapse recording come standard with this camcorder.

Specifications: height, 4⅛"; width, 4"; depth, 9⅝"; weight, 1⅝ lb. **Warranty:** 90 days, labor; 1 year, parts.

Manufacturer's Suggested Retail Price: $649

Approximate Low Price: $500

COMPACT VHS (VHS-C) CAMCORDERS

PANASONIC PV-A206

✔**BEST BUY**

Although the PV-A206 is at the low end of Panasonic's VHS-C Palmcorder IQ line, it performs just as well as the more expensive models. These compact Palmcorders all use the same kind of full-size video head cylinder found in a home VCR. The PV-A206 automatically sets recording parameters for optimum videos. The ⅓-inch, 270,000-pixel CCD image sensor has a low-light sensitivity of 1 lux. The 14-power autofocus zoom lens can be operated in four speeds (from 3 to 15 seconds) and the 0.5-inch color viewfinder offers 116,500 pixels. Not only will the PV-A206 date- and time-stamp your videos automatically, the clock will also reset itself from daylight saving to standard time and back again on the appropriate days. The clock comes preset for eastern standard time; if you live in a different time zone, you simply select your time zone from a menu in the viewfinder. The one-touch automatic fade is activated when you push the fade button once before starting or stopping a recording. A flying erase head virtually eliminates video noise when you start and stop recording, thus providing smoother edits. Graphical tape and battery gauges in the viewfinder show tape remaining and battery level, and the automatic lens cover opens when you turn on the camcorder. A built-in automatic titler comes with greetings for ten specific holidays. This model has an indicator light on the record button and a front tally lamp. The high-speed shutter has a range of $\frac{1}{100}$ to $\frac{1}{10,000}$ second.

Specifications: height, 4⅝"; width, 4⅛"; depth, 6⅞"; weight, 1.9 lb. (without tape and battery). **Warranty:** 90 days, labor; 1 year, parts.

Manufacturer's Suggested Retail Price: $900

Approximate Low Price: $583

JVC GR-AX710U

Recommended

This JVC VHS-C camcorder comes with a 0.55-inch color viewfinder (113,000 pixels), a power zoom with a ratio of 14:1, and a ⅓-inch, 270,000-pixel CCD imager. If the scene you're shooting becomes too dark, the built-in auto-light (rated at 5W) will turn on automatically. The GR-AX710U uses a fast f/1.2 lens with a focal length of 57.4mm (f/4.1). Its filter diameter is 46mm, and it comes with a flying erase head plus four other video heads. This model includes a seven-mode Program AE with special effects that automatically sets focus, white balance, shutter speed, and iris for particular taping conditions. The seven modes on the GR-AX71OU are sepia, twilight, fog filter, neutral density (NE) filter, sports, high-speed shutter for fast-moving objects, and automatic mode lock. This JVC camcorder also features a built-in character generator, which allows you to create messages of up to 18 characters or add instant titles from eight preset messages to your videos. The

CAMCORDERS

GR-AX710U has several editing functions: random assemble edit, which enables you to reorder scenes within the camcorder for transfer to another tape; animation; time lapse; insert editing; and audio dubbing. Besides the included 12-button miniremote, an optional, multibrand, credit-card-sized editing remote is also available. Within the viewfinder, there are displays for battery levels, zoom meter, time elapsed, special effects, and calendar (day/date/time), among others. If you add special effects to your composed scene or change the Program AE mode, the viewfinder automatically changes to show you exactly what you are taping. Intelligent function buttons (F1 or F2), located on the front left-hand side of the camcorder, allow you to preset different picture modes or effects so that you can access them easily while you are taping. This unit comes with mono sound, a self-timer, an automatic head cleaner, cinema mode (16:9) shooting capability, and a fader. Battery power will last approximately 60 minutes (less if you are shooting with the auto-light). A built-in lens cap rounds out the package.

Specifications: height, 5"; width, 4⁵⁄₁₆"; depth, 8¹⁵⁄₁₆"; weight, 1.6 lb. **Warranty:** 90 days, labor; 1 year, parts.

Manufacturer's Suggested Retail Price: $850

Approximate Low Price: $697

RCA CC636

Recommended

The RCA CC636 is a full-featured VHS-C camcorder. The CC636 has a ¼-inch, 250,000-pixel CCD imager with both a 14-power zoom lens and a 28-power digital zoom. This model utilizes a fast f/1.2 lens with a focal length of 57.4mm (f/4.1) along with a 0.55-inch, 113,000-pixel color viewfinder. The CC636 also features an electronic image stabilizer (EIS) and a 3-watt, three-setting (on, off, and auto) color-enhancement light on the front of the camcorder. The CC636 comes with a manually operated built-in lens cover. Programmed autoexposure, controlled via a dial on the left side of the camcorder, allows you eight modes, including auto, backlight, and frontlight. In addition to the autofocus mode, this camcorder has a focus lock feature that locks the focus on your subject. The CC636 also includes a one-page titler with eight separate titles, interval/time-lapse recording, audio/video dubbing, five digital fades, 16:9 recording capability, an 11-button remote, and mono audio. The VCR controls on this camcorder are hidden under a door flap.

Specifications: height, 4⅜"; width, 4½"; depth, 8½"; weight, 1.7 lb. (without tape and battery). **Warranty:** 90 days, labor; 1 year, parts.

Manufacturer's Suggested Retail Price: $899

Approximate Low Price: $800

FULL-SIZE VHS CAMCORDERS

PANASONIC PV-940

The Panasonic PV-940 full-size VHS camcorder ✓**BEST BUY** alleviates most of the awkwardness of the full-size format. The PV-940 has a handgrip centrally positioned below the lens and a viewfinder that flips from one side to the other to accommodate both left- and right-handed videographers. (This feature has given the camcorder the nickname "switch-hitter"). Its slim width makes it fit nicely into Panasonic's attaché-style carrying case. With its ⅓-inch, 270,000-pixel CCD coupled with a 14-power, dual-speed zoom lens, this model requires a minimum of 1 lux illumination. It offers fully automatic operation and a preset camcorder clock/calendar (just switch it to your time zone), which automatically switches to standard or daylight saving time on the correct days. Date and time can be automatically recorded on the tape. The bookmark search finds the end of the previous recording, eliminating gaps, and overlaps before new recordings—even if you remove and reinsert a tape. A flying erase head eliminates glitches when you stop and start recording, and a hot shoe located on top of the camcorder permits the attachment of a color-enhancement light.

Specifications: height, 8¼"; width, 3⅜"; depth, 15"; weight, 4.2 lb. (without tape and battery). **Warranty:** 90 days, labor; 1 year, parts.

Manufacturer's Suggested Retail Price: $700

Approximate Low Price: Not available

RCA CC431

Recommended

The RCA CC431 is a basic, full-size VHS camcorder that takes quality videos with a minimum of fuss and bother. The CC431 has a 12-power autofocus zoom lens coupled with a ¼-inch, 250,000-pixel CCD imager. Its full-sized video heads need as little as 2 lux (as measured by EIA standards) to record a picture. RCA has fully automated this camcorder, equipping it with programmed autoexposure and automatic white balance. The CC431 also comes with a two-line, one-page titler to record captions on your videos and a date and time recorder, which can also imprint on your videos. It offers a 0.55-inch color electric viewfinder that tilts and slides so you can position it more comfortably for either left- or right-eye viewing. Audio/video dubbing is included for replacing either the audio or video portion of a tape.

Specifications: height, 8⅛"; width, 4½"; depth, 13⅛"; weight, 4.4 lb. (without tape and battery). **Warranty:** 90 days, labor; 1 year, parts.

Manufacturer's Suggested Retail Price: $599

Approximate Low Price: $500

DIGITAL VIDEO (DV) CAMCORDER

JVC GR-DV1/RCA CC900D

Recommended

The JVC GR-DV1 and the RCA CC900D are the same digital video camcorder (DVC). You can attach this camcorder to a computer and manipulate images, store them on your hard drive/floppies, or send them out over the Internet. Besides shooting normal video, the GR-DV1/CC900D also allows you to take digital still pictures. In the snapshot mode, one 60-minute DV cassette will hold 5,400 stills, so it's like having two products in one. If you attach a color video printer, each snapshot can be processed and printed through the computer.

Digital enhancement extends the 10-power optical zoom to 20-power digital (2x digital) and 100-power digital (10x digital). At 20-power digital zoom, there is only a slight loss of picture quality; at 100-power digital zoom, the image becomes pixelized. Digital image stabilization is featured on both of these camcorders. The GR-DV1/CC900D utilizes a ⅓-inch, 570,000-pixel CCD image sensor. The digital stereo audio offers two digital audio recording modes (2-channel, 48kHz and 4-channel, 32kHz) plus a built-in, high-quality stereo microphone. The camcorder uses an f/1.6 lens with a focal length of 45mm (f/4.5) and a filter diameter of 27mm. The top-mounted 0.55-inch color viewfinder (113,000 pixels) slides backward, placing the camera in standby mode while also opening the lens cover to reveal the menu button hidden underneath. The GR-DV1/CC900D uses extensive onscreen menus and displays—all of which can be seen and accessed in the viewfinder or through an attached monitor. Twelve different effects can be utilized on the program autoexposure mode along with 18 different fades, wipes, and scene transitions. Up to five of these can be stored in memory for easy retrieval during taping. With the camcorder attached to its docking station for postproduction, you can add special effects and scene transitions after taping is completed. The built-in random assemble editor lets you assemble eight segments at one time, and with the 24-button multibrand remote, you can create your own home movies. The GR-DV1/CC900D attaches to its docking station for easy playback or for recharging of its lithium battery. (There is also a separate battery recharger.)

Specifications: height, 5¹³⁄₁₆"; width, 1¹¹⁄₁₆"; depth, 3½"; weight, 1 lb. **Warranty:** 90 days, labor; 1 year, parts.

Manufacturer's Suggested Retail Price: $3,000

Approximate Low Price: $1,994

STEREO COMPONENTS

Technology stampedes onward, while music remains eternal. Stereo components use technology to reproduce music, and, more recently, television and motion picture sound in the comfort of your home. The hobbyists who initiated the stereo industry in their basements and garages 50 years ago stand amazed at today's stereo equipment. No other consumer product provides as much value as home electronics. Among purists, music reproduction remains the sole purpose of stereo components. For the rest of us, today's audio and video components come tantalizingly close to recreating the movie theater experience in our homes. A good quality TV with a 27-inch or larger screen, combined with a Dolby Pro Logic equipped receiver and a quintet of speakers, can rival—even surpass—the local movie house in many ways. Technology improves as its costs fall, making a home theater a reality rather than a dream for increasing numbers of people. Manufacturers design stereo components with home theater in mind. Most receivers control the video as well as the audio signal, and many display their settings on your TV screen. Companies promote complete home theater packages with a receiver or five-channel amplifier and the five speakers necessary for Dolby Pro Logic Surround Sound. Pro Logic specifies the standard left and right front channels, plus a center front channel and a pair of rear (or surround) channels. Although there are two surrounds, they reproduce a mono signal. An optional subwoofer requiring a sixth channel of amplification adds realism to the lowest bass notes and special effects.

Last year Dolby debuted a digital upgrade for home theater sound called AC-3, which is now known as Dolby Digital. Rather than the analog Pro Logic, which is a technically awkward method of providing four channels, Dolby Digital provides five discrete channels, plus a special channel for the subwoofer. Initially, only laser discs contained Dolby Digital soundtracks, and only a handful of expensive receivers decoded Dolby Digital.

Next year Dolby Digital-equipped receivers will become more common. This year, the ultimate source for home theater sound arrives in the form of Digital Video Disc (DVD), on which Dolby Digital AC-3 Surround Sound is a standard feature. Other technologies warranting upgrading to a home theater system include the Digital Satellite System (DSS), digital video camcorders and VCRs, and Digital-VHS. These, along with CD (compact disc), justify a good stereo component system more than ever.

Most audio components mate easily with TVs, VCRs, and other video components that come equipped with audio output jacks. Avoid placing speakers too close to the TV unless they are specifically designed for this kind of placement. The magnetic field of regular speakers can distort the TV picture.

Buying stereo components instead of a prepackaged or all-in-one system lets you upgrade your equipment at any time without discarding the entire system. It also accepts new technologies as they come along. If you can't afford all the components you want or the quality of components you desire, begin with a good stereo receiver, a pair of speakers, and a budget CD player. This setup will provide a high-fidelity AM/FM stereo radio, play prerecorded music, and work with your TV and VCR as a basic home theater system. Later you can add a recording/reproducing system such as an analog cassette or digital tape. The major trends in stereo components today are the popularity of multi-disc CD changers and dual-transport cassette decks.

In the past five years various digital recording mediums vied for your attention. Digital Audio Tape (DAT) evolved into a professional medium; Digital Compact Cassette (DCC) proved a total market failure and vanished without a trace; and MiniDisc (MD), a promising recordable disc, barely survived. MD uses a 2½-inch disc encased in a protective caddy similar to a 3½-inch computer diskette. MD records and plays up to 74 minutes of sound. MD solves the portability problem that plagues the CD format by using memory chips that store 10 seconds of sound, so that if you jar the player, the sound will continue without a glitch. Many portable CD players now borrow this technology.

However, the circuitry in MD permits many novel recording and playback features unavailable on CD or tape. DAT and MD recorders sell for as little as $500, with some portable players costing slightly less. While DAT sounds identical to CD, there are subtle differences between MD and CD. Most listeners, however, notice little difference between the formats.

Over the past 30 years, technology continuously raised the performance level of audio components while lowering the prices. When CD players were introduced in 1982, they cost $1,000. Now, a far better sounding player than the first players can be had for about $150. With the dramatic exchange rate fluctuations between the dollar and the Japanese yen, Japanese companies managed to minimize price increases by increasing automation and by manufacturing off-shore in cheaper labor countries. Some manufacturing even returned to America. Rather than raising prices, some companies eliminated features and/or kept the same models in the line for two years rather than one. Even with these adaptations, components continue to offer better value in 1997 than ever before.

Best Buys '97

Our Best Buy, Recommended, and Budget Buy choices follow. Within each category, stereo components are listed by quality; the item we consider the best of the Best Buys is first, followed by our second choice, and so on. A Budget Buy describes a less-expensive product of respectable quality that perhaps sacrifices some of the performance and/or features of a Best Buy or Recommended product. Remember that a Best Buy, Recommended, or Budget Buy designation applies only to the model listed; it does not necessarily apply to other models made by the same manufacturer or to an entire product line.

LOUDSPEAKERS

Loudspeakers turn electrical impulses into sound. While other parts of the stereo system merely manipulate electrons, you directly hear the work of the speaker. This feat earns the speaker the primary position when choosing a stereo system. Speakers have much more effect on the personality of the system than the electronics do, and judging speaker quality becomes a sub-jective task. The choice of speaker also determines your choice of receiver, since some speakers require more power than oth-ers, and some receivers and speakers make a better match than others. Thus the advice of friends, magazine reviews, and the recommendations here should serve only as a starting point. Take great care in choosing your speakers by spending ample time listening.

More than 360 speaker companies flood the market with multiple models. Discerning differences between electronic components requires considerable concentration, but the dif-ferences between similarly priced speakers come through loud and clear. Insist on the right to return speakers that fail to meet your expectations. Speakers dramatically interact with room acoustics. What sounded splendid in the store may sound tinny, muddy, or boomy at home. The size of the speaker enclosure and the number of the individual speakers inside it (woofers, mid-ranges, and tweeters) do not always correlate with sound quality. We base our speaker ratings on the quality of con-struction, reputation, and listening tests.

Features and Terminology

Power Requirements: Different speakers take advantage of different physical properties to produce sound. High-efficiency ported systems, also known as ducted or reflex systems, are the most common among large speakers. Ported systems often require less power from the amplifier (or amplifier section of your receiver) to produce a given level of sound when com-pared to acoustic suspension speakers. They take advantage of the port's resonance to acoustically amplify the bass frequen-cies. Acoustic suspension speakers, sometimes referred to as air suspension speakers, are most common among bookshelf-size speakers. They seal the enclosure tightly and force the speaker to fight the air within. This causes them to be low in efficiency and less sensitive to power than ported speakers, therefore requiring more power from the amplifier to produce a given level of sound. A well-designed acoustic suspension system reproduces good, tightly controlled bass. Large floor-standing speakers can reproduce throbbing sound levels with as little as 20 watts of power, whereas compact bookshelf models often require twice that much power to reproduce the same sound level, if they can play that loudly.

Too much power can damage speakers, but speaker ratings and amplifier ratings don't always tell the whole story. Speakers rated at 100 watts maximum may safely be powered by a 300-watt amplifier, but if you force all 300 watts into the speaker, the sound will cause you pain and will damage the speakers. Too little power can also damage a speaker. If you try to play a low-powered amplifier too loudly it can distort the sound waves, and this distortion can destroy a speaker.

Speaker Impedance: Speaker impedances are commonly listed from 4 to 8 ohms, with some ranging from 2 to 16 ohms. This is a technical description of the amount of inductive resistance the speaker offers to the flow of electrical signals. Under normal circumstances, impedance bears no relation to sound quality, but many receivers need a minimum of 4 ohms to work properly. A good receiver may work with 2 ohms, but other receivers or amplifiers will automatically shut off or blow a fuse. If you intend to use two pairs of speakers in parallel from the same terminals, choose loudspeakers rated at least 8 ohms. Also note that speaker impedance ratings are nominal, meaning that a speaker may actually fall below its rated impedance at some frequencies.

Woofers, Tweeters, and Other Speaker Elements: The woofer is the largest speaker component. It reproduces bass notes and often the lower mid-range sounds as well. The tweeter is the smallest component and reproduces higher sounds. It is the most fragile component because of its very fine wires and is most prone to failure. Some speaker systems include one or more mid-range speaker components that reproduce the range of sound between the woofer and the tweeter—the range of the human voice. A mid-range component is not essential for good sound, although most larger systems include them. The point where the frequency range of an individual driver starts and finishes varies from one speaker to another.

The crossover network consists of resistors, capacitors, and coils that divide the incoming frequencies from the receiver, ensuring that the bass goes to the woofer and the treble to the tweeter. You cannot tell the actual sound or construction quality of a speaker system just by the size of its drivers and the material from which they are manufactured. An 8-inch woofer sometimes reproduces better bass than a 12-inch woofer, and paper sometimes surpasses plastics and metals in the quality of a speaker cone. The thickness, materials, and construction of the speaker enclosure, or cabinet, can influence the system's sound as much as the drivers. Look for a solid, rigid enclosure that shows minimal resonance when you rap your knuckles on it.

Home Theater Speakers: Five or six (counting a subwoofer) speakers are placed appropriately around the room for home theater. You can enjoy fairly small speakers when you include a subwoofer in the system to reproduce the deep bass. It's best to buy the entire theater system speakers from a single manufacturer. Ideally, the front three speakers should be a matched set and should be timbre-matched (each having the same sonic "color" and tonal balance). The surround speakers may be smaller, but should retain the same sonic characteristics as the rest of the system. One quick way to determine if the speakers are timbre-matched is to listen to the applause from a live recording. No one speaker should draw attention to itself with a different sound quality.

B&W CDM 2

The B&W CDM 2 bookshelf speakers pack a ✔**BEST BUY** punch from their small package. These high-tech speakers incorporate advances originally pioneered in B&W's expensive 800 series but at a much lower price. For example, the 6½-inch mid-range/woofer on this two-way system uses a woven Kevlar cone. Kevlar radiates sound waves with near-ideal stiffness for accuracy and low distortion. Similarly, the 1-inch tweeter uses a metal alloy formulated for accurate high-frequency reproduction without coloring the sound. Removing the stylish contoured grille, with its acoustically beneficial shape, reveals an unusually well-finished front baffle demonstrating conscientious workmanship. B&W surrounds the tweeter with eccentric diffraction rings that reduce the effect of the baffle on the high frequencies. This produces cleaner, more accurate sound. The gently beveled front baffle edges also reduce unwanted reflections from the speaker enclosure itself. Lifting the surprisingly heavy CDM 2 speakers quickly convinces you that these are no ordinary small speakers. The enclosure, covered in real wood veneer in black or red ash, is very dense. This nonresonant design reduces vibrations of the box, which muddy the sound. The quality of the sound, with substantial bass, clarity, and naturalness of voices, makes the speakers' small size almost irrelevant. You will need at least 30 watts per channel of amplifier power. The CDM 2 can be placed on a shelf or on a stand. Gold-plated, five-way binding posts simplify connections. These speakers are ideal for uncompromised sound in tight places for people whose budget is between modest and lavish.

Specifications: height, 12¼"; width, 8⅝"; depth, 9½"; weight, 16 lb. each. **Warranty:** 5 years, parts and labor.

Manufacturer's Suggested Retail Price: $800/pair

Approximate Low Price: $800/pair

MB QUART DOMAIN D45

✔ **BEST BUY**

The MB Quart Domain D45 loudspeaker proves that often a picture frame makes all the difference. A work of art needs a suitable frame to highlight the painting and to complement your decor. Designers at the German speaker company MB Quart figured this out when styling its new line of Domain loudspeakers. The D45 offers the option of ten different user-replaceable frames that attach to the front of the speakers like conventional grilles. You can choose from winter birch, driftwood, sunlit maple, mission oak, Jefferson cherry, midnight ash, high-gloss piano black, honey burl, tobacco burl, hurricane burl, and unfinished. There's also an attention to detail in the construction of both the frames and the speakers. The compact D45 columns stand about waist high. Quart finishes them in matte black, or as the company calls it "British

Suedette, Ebony Laminate." The D45 contains a 1-inch titanium-dome tweeter and a 6½-inch woofer. The D45 sounds impressive and offers good value for the money. The timpani and percussion not only exhibited a very natural timbre but full impact. When listening to pop vocals the voices sound full yet well defined. The D45 sounds exceptionally clean, almost as if it removes a whole layer of distortion from the listening experience. It reproduces a deep, natural stereo image so that voices and instruments on well-made recordings seem to materialize right where they should be in real life. Gold-plated, five-way binding posts simplify connections. It's the right size and price for many stereo systems. Quart makes sonically matched rear channel and center-channel speakers allowing these speakers to be used for a home theater system.

Specifications: height, 33½"; width, 8⅞"; depth, 14½"; weight, 42 lb. each. **Warranty:** 5 years, limited.

Manufacturer's Suggested Retail Price: $699/pair

Approximate Low Price: $633/pair

NHT SUPERONE

✔ BEST BUY

The NHT SuperOne is no misnomer. It ranks as the "mighty mouse" of speakers, producing a super sound from a compact size. NHT began by manufacturing small speakers, and though it now builds floor towers, it keeps returning to small speakers to see just how good it can make them. This two-way acoustic suspension speaker uses a 6½-inch woofer with a 1-inch, fluid-cooled, soft-dome tweeter. NHT magnetically shields the speaker for use near video equipment. While it won't reproduce the lowest organ notes, it does a surprisingly good job on the lowest piano notes as well as on the rest of the keyboard. Its natural tonal balance will please even the most critical listeners. Small speakers generally produce a good stereo image because of their small baffles. The SuperOnes excel in this important attribute. The voices and instruments sound as if they're playing not only between but in front of and behind the plane of these speakers. To achieve their impressive bass, the SuperOnes sacrifice some sensitivity, requiring a minimum of 25 watts; however, they'll accept plenty of high power. NHT offers the SuperOne loudspeakers in high-gloss black or white laminate. NHT also designed custom stands and custom wall-brackets for these speakers, although you can use any appropriate stand.

Specifications: height, 11⅜"; width, 7¼"; depth, 8½"; weight, 10 lb. each. **Warranty:** 5 years, parts and labor.

Manufacturer's Suggested Retail Price: $349/pair

Approximate Low Price: $346/pair

MISSION 735

Recommended

The Mission 735 loudspeakers make a statement by standing about 42 inches tall. In that space, Mission stacks three 7-inch woofer/mid-range polypropylene cone drivers and a 1-inch composite dome tweeter. Mission divides the cabinet internally into two subenclosures to reduce interference between the multiple drivers. The baffle, enhanced by high-tech manufacturing techniques, keeps the drivers rigidly in place while resisting vibration. The sound of the 735 makes the statement. The overall velvety sound hid no nuances in the recording. Once again, vocals sounded as if the vocalist shared the room. The 735 casts voices in the most pleasant light, without glossing over their flaws. The 735 virtually banishes ear fatigue. The stereo image teases and treats the ears. More than a wide horizontal sound stage, the 735 reproduces music with amazing depth. Instruments and voices seemingly came from behind and in front of the speakers and were even arrayed from the floor upwards. Few speakers display this depth of sound without compromises in other areas. The 735 pumps out plenty of bass. Mission rates it to 35 hertz, just above the lowest organ pipes. When the mallet hits the timpani, the whomp resounds deep, tight, and authentic. Bass quality and response will vary with your room's acoustics. We Recommend the 735 loudspeakers rather than listing them as a Best Buy mainly because of the high price tag.

Specifications: height, 41⁷⁄₁₀"; width, 8"; depth, 13"; weight, 45 lb. each. **Warranty:** 5 years, parts and labor.

Manufacturer's Suggested Retail Price: $1,099/pair
Approximate Low Price: $893/pair

DCM CX-11

`Recommended`

The small, robust DCM CX-11 proves to be a good all-around speaker, with a sensitivity that produces ample sound from low power but withstands high power and can produce big sound. A built-in circuit protects the speaker from damaging overload, a rarity among speakers at this price. The 6½-inch woofer and ¾-inch fluid-cooled and damped soft-dome tweeter are magnetically shielded, allowing these speakers to be used adjacent to video and computer monitors. The CX-11 reproduces a broad, wide, exceptionally smooth frequency response, including satisfying bass. DCM engineers a slight mid-bass boost to give the speakers both warmth and bass solidity. DCM also flips the placement of the woofer and tweeter, with the tweeter on the bottom to improve sound distribution. It sounds as if it works in this case. This probably contributes to the excellent stereo image, along with a fairly small baffle area. The spring-clip input jacks accept lugs and super heavy-gauge wires but not banana plugs and bare wires. DCM has always placed an emphasis on sound rather than appearance, but with the new CX-series loudspeakers, DCM created a stylish new look without cutting corners. The CX-11's seamless black woodgrain cabinet has a removable sculpted grille.

Specifications: height, 15.5"; width, 7.5"; depth, 7.5"; weight, 11 lb. each. **Warranty:** 5 years, parts and labor.

Manufacturer's Suggested Retail Price: $130/pair
Approximate Low Price: Not available

BOSE 201 SERIES IV

`Budget Buy`

The Bose 201 Series IV represents a further upgrade of the best-selling 201. Bose sells a lot of 201s, because, like Henry Ford, it perfected mass production without sacrificing quality. Bose sells the 201 Series IV in mirror-imaged pairs so that the 2-inch fluid-cooled tweeter angles from a corner of the enclosure to a broader listening area. This radiates high frequencies over a wider area and allows the good stereo image to be enjoyed over a wider area. This satisfies the Bose criteria of "direct/reflecting" sound. A 6½-inch woofer in the ported enclosure provides satisfying bass with as little as ten watts of power. The 201 Series IV reproduces appealing sound at a price nearly everyone can afford. The flared port reduces air noise. Injection molded polymer end caps, cloth grilles, and a black or rosewood vinyl finish provide a contemporary look.

Specifications: height, 9½"; width, 15⅛"; depth, 6¾"; weight, 9 lb. each. **Warranty:** 5 years, limited and transferable.

Manufacturer's Suggested Retail Price: $229/pair

Approximate Low Price: $199/pair

HOME THEATER SPEAKERS

ATLANTIC TECHNOLOGY SYSTEM 250.1 ✔BEST BUY

The Atlantic Technology System 250.1 represents an improved version of last year's System 250. The improvements include the ability to handle higher amounts of power, improved bass, full-range surround speakers (modeled after the company's far more expensive THX home theater system), and an increase in the power of the built-in subwoofer amplifier from 90 to 150 watts. The woofers weigh twice as much as those in the original 250, and the cabinet density and thickness have been increased fifty percent. Atlantic Technology raised the price of the System 250.1 only about $300 to cover these improvements, which make the speakers ready for the forthcoming Dolby Digital Surround Sound. The company conceived the six-piece system as a complete home theater system rather than just an assemblage of off-the-shelf parts. The three front speakers are timbre matched, although the tonal balances of the center speaker can be adjusted for position relative to the TV screen. The speakers are reasonably compact with small baffle areas for flexible placement and good imaging. The surround speakers are dipoles, which means they radiate in two directions. When the speakers are properly placed, this enhances realism. The subwoofer contains its own amplifier, since most Surround Sound receivers lack an amplified subwoofer channel. When used with a good receiver and properly installed, the System 250.1 reproduces smashing movie sound, better than that of many movie theaters. We like the well-conceived nature of the system, and while the individual parts may be purchased separately, it's the system as a whole that scores the high marks.

Warranty: 2 years, parts and labor.

Manufacturer's Suggested Retail Price: $1,736

Approximate Low Price: $1,466

DEFINITIVE TECHNOLOGY BP2000

`Recommended`

The Definitive BP2000 speakers create an astounding home theater experience. However, their high price excludes them from our Best Buy category, even though you receive a lot of equipment and sound for the money. The BP2000 stands about 4 feet tall, is enclosed in a dark charcoal grille cloth on all four sides, and has handsome endcaps finished in piano-lacquer black or lacquered solid cherry. The home theater system includes a substantial center channel speaker that works horizontally or vertically, and a pair of bipole rear-surround speakers. Definitive Technology uses a unique design for the BP2000 front channels. Speakers fire from both sides of the enclosure, three on each side, in a bipolar design. This means that each trio of speakers faces an opposite direction (two poles). When well executed, as it is in the case of the BP2000, bipolar design radiates a breathtakingly natural, open sound. Realizing that many music lovers might desire a high-quality speaker but might not be able to afford the appropriate electronics to power it, Definitive Technology builds amplified subwoofers into the BP2000. A 300-watt amplifier powers each of the massive 15-inch subwoofers. That allows you to use moderately powered, affordable electronics to power the rest of the system. Those big subwoofers surround you with all the bass you could desire. Controls on the rear of the speaker cabinets contour the bass to your taste and to room acoustics.

As theater speakers, the BP2000 system matches or exceeds anything in its class. When the train wrecks, the starship explodes, or the missile hits home, you'd better be wearing your seat belt. And there's no loss of dialog clarity or music quality for the benefit of boom. In fact, this system makes a first-rate stereo speaker system for music listening. There's a silky clarity to the sound, whether you're listening to music or movies.

Warranty: 3 years, parts and labor on electronics; 5 years, parts and labor.

Manufacturer's Suggested Retail Price: $4,548

Approximate Low Price: $4,516

CERWIN-VEGA SENSURROUND SYSTEM 6

Cerwin-Vega, best known for providing the [**Budget Buy**] most boom for the buck, succeeds admirably with its System 6. Movie soundtracks are most appropriate for systems with pronounced bass, and Cerwin-Vega provides the Sensurround system for movie theaters. Fortunately, Cerwin-Vega doesn't submerge the dialog in the bone-shaking bass. The System 6 contains the six standard surround components: left, right, and center front channels, two surround channels, and a subwoofer. The system saves money by using plain black woodgrain veneer enclosures without many frills. The identical left, right, and surround channels use 5-inch woofers and 1-inch dome tweeters. An electronic circuit protects the tweeters from overload. The subwoofer uses a 10-inch woofer. This is an ideal system for use with a Dolby Pro Logic receiver.

Warranty: 5 years, limited on parts and labor.

Manufacturer's Suggested Retail Price: $1,310

Approximate Low Price: $866

HEADPHONES

Like speakers, headphones are best judged according to how they sound. But unlike speakers, headphones are unaffected by room acoustics, and their sound quality needs to please no one but their owner. The general criteria for good headphone performance include a full bass response with accurate tonal definition and balance from the mid-range frequencies up to the highest frequencies.

A headset must also be comfortable. Weight and fit should be considered carefully. There are three basic designs for headphones. **Circumaural phones** cover your entire outer ear and block out all external sound. **Supra-aural phones** do not completely block out external sound. **Open-air phones** rest lightly against the outer ear and usually have a foam pad that separates the actual phone from your head. This allows almost all outside sounds to be heard while you're wearing them.

As a general rule, circumaural phones provide the best bass, whereas open-air phones usually provide the least bass. Another style of headphones inserts directly into the ear. These tend to be difficult to keep in the ear and are often uncomfortable.

GRADO LABS SR60

✔ **BEST BUY**

The Grado SR60 consistently scores praise from audio enthusiasts. It compares with headphones costing ten times as much. Its large foam pads sit on the ear without sealing out external sound. A wide, leatherette headband suspends the earcups. The main uncoiled cord is sturdier than most other phones. This 6-foot cord terminates in a gold-plated miniplug. Grado supplies a gold-plated standard ¼-inch plug adapter, so you can use them with a headphone stereo or home stereo components. Their high sensitivity works with even the lowest output headphone stereos and makes even weak portables sound their best. These phones sound exquisite with clear crisp treble, deep authoritative bass, and transparent vocals. Although larger and heavier than most phones and bare-bones in construction, they are fairly comfortable. These are the kind of headphones you wear by choice not necessity.

Specifications: weight, 7 oz. **Warranty:** 1 year, parts and labor.

Manufacturer's Suggested Retail Price: $69

Approximate Low Price: $66

SONY MDR-65

✔ **BEST BUY**

The lightweight, open-air-design Sony MDR-65 stereo headphones rest comfortably on the ear with their soft earpads on gimbal-mounted earcups. The wide, molded headband with its gentle cushion further adds to the comfort of these 2.5-ounce phones that feel like they're floating on your head. When it comes to sound, however, the MDR-65 is a heavyweight, with full, well-balanced sound from mid-sized diaphragms using powerful neodymium magnets. For convenience, a sturdy, nearly 7-foot-long, single cord (rather than the cumbersome yoke design) connects the phones to your stereo. That stereo can either be a personal one or consist of home components. The gold-plated miniplug comes with a screw-on adapter for standard ¼-inch jacks.

Specifications: weight, 2.5 oz. **Warranty:** 1 year, exchange.
Manufacturer's Suggested Retail Price: $40
Approximate Low Price: $37

KOSS PRO/4XTC

Recommended

The Koss PRO/4XTC stereo headphones depart noticeably from traditional Koss PRO/4 designs. At 10 ounces without the cord, they are lighter in weight, and they surround rather than clamp the ears. Instead of sealing out all external sound, the comfortable fabric cushions permit some sound to enter and escape. A well-padded headband and multiswivel earcups make the XTC extremely comfortable. These headphones sound as comfortable as they feel. A neodymium magnet reduces weight while increasing the power of the magnetic field for higher performance. Besides reproducing ample bass, they bring out crisp, clear treble without irritating emphasis. The slightly depressed mid-range frequencies do not muddy or obscure vocals, although they may sound a bit more distant. The sensitivity of the phones makes them suitable for many headphone stereos. A lightweight, 10-foot coiled cord tethers the XTC phones to your stereo. The cord ends in a right-angle, gold-plated miniplug with an integral snap-on, gold-plated, full-size ¼-inch adapter plug for regular stereo components. In reducing weight and bulk, Koss also made the XTC a little more fragile than the old PRO/4 design. This should cause little concern since Koss is the rare company offering a lifetime warranty, with free repairs or replacement (you pay only for shipping costs).

Specifications: weight, 10 oz. **Warranty:** lifetime.

Manufacturer's Suggested Retail Price: $80

Approximate Low Price: $80

AUDIO-TECHNICA ATH-P5   `Budget Buy`

The Audio-Technica ATH-P5 open-air phones sound great. They're fairly large for personal-style headphones, permitting a good-size diaphragm with neodymium magnets. Their foam cushions rest comfortably on the ear. The plastic headband is just wide enough and springy enough to avoid excessive pressure on your scalp. At 2.5 ounces without the cord, the ATH-P5 seems to virtually hover on your head. Unfortunately, not only do they come with an awkward Y-shaped yoke-style cord, but at only a bit over a yard long, it's too short. So even though Audio-Technica supplies a snap-on adapter for use with home gear, the cord is probably too short to take advantage of the adapter. That's the only thing that separates these terrific sounding phones from a Best Buy.

Specifications: weight, 2.5 oz. **Warranty:** 1 year, parts and labor.

Manufacturer's Suggested Retail Price: $30

Approximate Low Price: $28

STEREO RECEIVERS

Think of a stereo receiver as a convenient space saver. It combines what were once three separate components in a single compact package. In the early days of hi-fi, you needed a preamplifier and power amplifier for sound and a tuner for radio. The preamplifier served the dual role of boosting the weak signals from the phono cartridge to a high enough level to feed the power amplifier and adjusting the sound to your preference.

(This includes volume, tone controls, and listening source and taping source selection.) Many preamplifiers now leave out the phono amplification, as do most receivers. The power amplifiers provide the muscle that pumps up the sound to power the speakers.

A feature more common today in receivers is digital signal processing (DSP). DSP enables elaborate alteration of sound from sophisticated tone controls to simulate the sound of different listening environments, from jazz clubs to stadiums. We consider DSP a bit of overkill, but cost of the circuit has fallen so dramatically that it adds a minimal premium, usually less than $50, to the cost of the receiver.

Traditionally, receivers contained a pair of power amplifiers for the two stereo channels. Home theater systems now require four, five, or six channels of amplification. (On most receivers a single channel powers both of the surround speakers.) All but the most basic models include these extra channels. Premium two-channel receivers are becoming an endangered species.

For optimum effect, the power of each of the three front channels must be the same, and the rear channels should each have at least a quarter of the front-channel power. We suggest they have a third to a half of the front-channel power.

Video producers encode the surround channels on stereo hi-fi videotapes and laser discs. Surround Sound processors can also extract ambience from many music sources, such as CDs, which may pleasantly enhance the sound. Dolby Labs, the company that set the standard for noise reduction, also dictates Surround Sound decoding from video. Originally the system required four channels, but Dolby's improved Pro Logic system adds a fifth, front center channel for dialog reproduction from videos. This keeps the dialog centered on your TV screen for greater realism. With the advent of digital video system, such as DVD, Dolby upgraded Surround Sound with its AC-3 system (now called Dolby Digital). This provides five discrete channels, plus a subwoofer channel, as compared to the analog matrixed Pro Logic system. Retrieving four channels from two in the analog matrix requires considerable electronic skill, which can compromise sound quality, while the discrete Dolby Digital AC-3 system involves far fewer compromises. Pro Logic, virtually standard on receivers, adds only a few dollars in cost, plus the expense of the extra power amplifiers. Dolby Digital demands a substantial premium and is found only on receivers costing over $1,000.

Features and Terminology

Power output is stated in watts. The Federal Trade Commission (FTC) established a fair and concrete method for measuring power output and listing those measurements. The law states that manufacturers must specify levels of distortion, frequency response, impedance, and other factors when publishing or advertising power output. When you see advertisements featuring power output, be sure the wattage applies to each channel and not to the sum of both stereo channels. Most amplifiers and receivers deliver higher power when hooked up to 4-ohm speakers than they do when powering 8-ohm speakers. When you compare power claims, make sure they refer to the same speaker impedances. Incidentally, the FTC regulations apply only to home equipment that operates from AC power and not to battery-operated or car audio gear.

Stereo separation is the amount of separation between the left and right channels (or the difference between them). Separation figures vary between sources. Phonograph cartridges provide only 30 decibels of separation, whereas CD players often claim 90 dB of separation. The amplifier section of the receiver should have a channel of separation of at least 90 dB, and the tuner sections should be more than 30 dB.

Frequency response should be uniform, or "flat," over the entire range of human hearing, from 20 to 20,000 hertz.

Sensitivity is usually stated in microvolts or dBf. Excellent sensitivity figures of 2.0 microvolts or 10 to 12 dBf are typical. Sensitivity concerns you if you are attempting to receive weak radio stations or if you live in a fringe area.

Selectivity is the ability of a tuner to pick up and isolate stations that are close in frequency to each other. Selectivity is quoted in dB; the higher the number the better. Look for at least 60 dB.

Signal-to-noise ratio (S/N) is a measure of how much background noise is present compared with the desired signal. S/N is stated in decibels (dB); the higher the number the better. The stereo FM tuner S/N on a receiver should be about 75 dB; for CD the S/N should be over 100 dB.

Quieting (in dB, decibels) is the amount of signal that is needed at the antenna terminals to provide noise-free, acceptable reception. The lower the number, stated in microvolts (millionths of a volt) or dBf (femtowatts), the better.

Tape monitor (loop) is a set of output and input jacks that allow you to interpose an external audio component in the signal path of an amplifier to monitor recordings as you make them or to process the signal through a separate device.

Two-Channel Stereo Receivers

SONY STR-DE305

✔**BEST BUY**

The STR-DE305 continues a long line of value laden, high-performance receivers from Sony. This two-channel model produces 100 watts per channel. To maintain good sound quality, Sony uses discrete output transistors rather than integrated circuits and even powers the blue fluorescent display separately from the audio section. Sony designed the STR-DE305 as the centerpiece of a budget audio or audio/video system with a universal remote control that operates both audio and video components. There's still a phono input among the six inputs for people who value their LPS. A bass boost button compensates for lack of bass from small speakers, or for those who prefer hearty bass. The high-quality, digitally synthesized tuner in this model matches, in most respects, the tuners in Sony's most expensive receivers. Direct-access tuning makes tuning a snap on the STR-DE305. Just tap in the radio station's frequency on the numeric keypad of the supplied remote or on the front panel. Direct-access makes setting the 30 possible station presets quick work. The use of knobs, a giant one for volume and smaller ones for bass, treble, and balance, simplifies the operation of this receiver, which is elegant in its simplicity. The new styling features a subdued front panel with rounded edges.

Warranty: 1 year, parts and labor.

Manufacturer's Suggested Retail Price: $250

Approximate Low Price: $216

TECHNICS SA-EX100

The Technics SA-EX100 stereo receiver presents **✓BEST BUY** a quandary—it's so inexpensive it could be a Budget Buy, but its performance and features elevate it to a Best Buy. The SA-EX100 produces 100 watts per channel using Technics' proprietary, reliable Class H+ amplifier circuitry. Although rated at 100 watts, it keeps some extra power in reserve for musical peaks. This strictly audio receiver contains a VCR audio input, but it will not switch the video. There are a total of five inputs, including phono. Direct-access tuning makes for easy setting of the 30 possible radio station presets on the quartz-synthesized digital tuning system. Direct-access is available only from the 31-key supplied remote control. The blue fluorescent display with red highlights shows all you need to know about the operation of this receiver. A large volume control knob and small bass, treble, and balance knobs simplify operation. While the SA-EX100 is not loaded with frills, it is loaded with quality sound.

Warranty: 1 year, parts and labor.

Manufacturer's Suggested Retail Price: $180

Approximate Low Price: $179

ONKYO TX-8410

Recommended

The Onkyo TX-8410 stereo receiver not only produces 100 watts per channel at the standard 8-ohm rating, but it will also drive low-impedance speakers, producing up to 180 watts at 3 ohms. Onkyo uses this ability to differentiate its receivers from many competing models. Onkyo uses discrete transistors for the audio outputs for clean, low distortion sound.

This is a very versatile model with six audio and two audio-from-video inputs that also switch the video. The first-rate tuner automatically adjusts to reception conditions and has 30 presets. You can group these presets into three categories, such as rock, jazz, or classical, and then scan each category separately. Overall, this is a well-thought out, highly competent stereo receiver.

Warranty: 2 years, parts and labor.

Manufacturer's Suggested Retail Price: $350

Approximate Low Price: $332

YAMAHA RX-495

Recommended

The RX-495 stereo receiver produces 70 watts, with the ability to drive low-impedance speakers. This stable performer is conservatively rated and can handle most musical peaks without distortion. Yamaha uses discrete output transistors for optimum performance. The amplifier maintains tight control over the loudspeakers throughout the entire frequency spectrum—a benefit not engineered into all receivers. This receiver can power almost any speaker without overheating. You control most adjustments with easily grasped knobs, but source selection and radio tuning still require pushing buttons. If you prefer buttons all the way around, the RX-495 comes with a full-function wireless remote control. We particularly like the CD-direct button that allows the CD signal to bypass most of the preamplifier and tone control circuitry and travel directly to the power amplifier for the clearest possible sound. You can select 40 station presets on the very good digital tuner section, or the receiver will scan the dial and preset the 40 most powerful stations for you. This tuner is particularly good at separating stations on the crowded FM dial. We rate this receiver in the Recommended category because of its substantial price for its moderate wattage.

Warranty: 2 years, limited on parts and labor.

Manufacturer's Suggested Retail Price: $299

Approximate Low Price: $276

Multichannel Home Theater Receivers

TECHNICS SA-EX500

✓**BEST BUY**

The Technics SA-EX500 provides exceptional value and performance, surpassing last year's model in power while selling for less. The SA-EX500 produces 110 watts for each of the three front channels and splits 110 watts between the two surrounds (for 55 watts each). In two-channel stereo, each channel receives 120 watts. That's enough power for thrilling musical reproduction or a true theatrical experience. Technics' proprietary, highly advanced Class H+ amplifier circuitry makes extremely efficient use of power with high reliability. The front panel fluorescent and LED display shows not only the usual information, source, preset number, radio frequency, and so on but also a unique "help" function that alerts you when you've attempted an improper operation or forgotten where you or another member of the family have set the controls. Pushing the "help" button for 3 seconds returns all settings to normal and selects the FM radio. The SA-EX500 handles four audio sources and two video sources. To optimize home theater use, it includes a Dolby Pro Logic test mode as well as independent center and rear level controls. It also has different Dolby modes to match your installation if you cannot afford the speakers for a complete Pro Logic system. When you're not viewing movies, the surround circuitry can also create synthesized listening environments such as concert hall, club, live, and theater. You can preset 30 stations on the digitally synthesized tuner, with direct access via the 38-key audio/video universal remote control making the process easier.

Warranty: 1 year, parts and labor.

Manufacturer's Suggested Retail Price: $300

Approximate Low Price: $283

ONKYO TX-SV727

✓**BEST BUY**

The Onkyo TX-SV727 breaks new ground among home theater receivers by employing a custom-designed Motorola digital signal processing (DSP) chip. This DSP chip digitally processes the Dolby Pro Logic Surround Sound, as well as digitally synthesizing four acoustic environments—concert hall, live, and arena, plus a special setting called Pro Logic Theater. Processing the signal digitally within one integrated circuit chip accomplishes these tasks more effectively and accurately without adding to the cost. The TX-SV727 produces 80 watts each for the three front channels and 25 watts for each of the surround channels. In stereo, each of the two front channels produces 100 watts. Most important, the conservatively designed amplifiers can drive virtually any speaker without endangering either the amplifiers or the speakers. Even the massive multiway speaker binding posts instill confidence and provide convenience. The latter attribute is the key to the TX-SV727. Its easy operation makes home theater a pleasure. For example, when you turn on your TV, Onkyo's Intelligent Power Management System switches on the receiver and selects Video 1. The most important area of the programmable universal remote control glows so you can see which key you're pressing. This is especially useful with the lights dimmed while you're watching videos. This receiver also has multiroom and multisource capability, allowing it to serve as the center of a multiroom entertainment system. Multisource also allows taping one source while listening to another, or listening to different sources in different rooms. There are 30 radio station presets that you can organize into three groups that you name. In addition to the four video inputs and six audio inputs, front-panel jacks simplify connecting a camcorder. The TX-SV727 will even lull you to sleep with its sleep timer.

Warranty: 2 years, parts and labor.

Manufacturer's Suggested Retail Price: $800

Approximate Low Price: $697

YAMAHA RX-V490

Recommended

The Yamaha RX-V490 multichannel home theater receiver delivers very good sound, but its modest wattage and limited discounting drop it from Best Buy to Recommended status. The RX-V490 supplies 70 watts to each of the three front channels and 15 watts to each of the two surround channels. Fortunately, these are "honest" watts that will drive most speakers likely to be teamed with this receiver. It does a good job of taming difficult speakers and making them produce their best sound. In addition to Dolby Pro Logic, Yamaha includes its own surround-sound Cinema DSP for a more theater-like effect. The digital signal processing circuitry also emulates concert hall, rock concert, mono movies, and concert video environments. The RX-V490 incorporates the same outstanding AM/FM stereo tuner that's in Yamaha's more expensive models. You can preset 40 stations, or the receiver will automatically preset stations for you. The receiver comes with four audio inputs and two audio/video inputs. For proper Pro Logic balances, you can adjust the center and surround output levels. Yamaha supplies a remote control capable of operating other Yamaha components.

Warranty: 2 years, limited on parts and labor.

Manufacturer's Suggested Retail Price: $399

Approximate Low Price: $369

JVC RX-618VBK

The JVC RX-618VBK Dolby Pro Logic Sur- | Budget Buy |
round Sound receiver provides a good home theater experience and still leaves you money for popcorn. It produces 100 watts for each of the channels. In addition to Pro Logic, it also synthesizes a concert hall ambiance, for a "hall surround" sound. Two video inputs complement five audio inputs. JVC provides 40 AM/FM station presets on the tuner, which features a loudness switch. Besides the large master volume control knob, a unique clustered keypad is especially convenient for adjusting the center and surround levels. JVC also uses knobs for bass, treble, and balance. The blue fluorescent display with red highlights is fairly easy to see from across the room. JVC supplies a universal audio/video remote control with the system. The RX-618VBK offers all the features and power you really need to become involved with home theater. It also works fine as a conventional stereo receiver.

Warranty: 2 years, parts and labor.
Manufacturer's Suggested Retail Price: $330
Approximate Low Price: $300

COMPACT DISC PLAYERS

Compact discs (CDs) revolutionized sound reproduction, relegating the LP to a cult curiosity. Until the advent of CDs, all home audio equipment reproduced sound in analog form. The minute wiggles in the grooves of the vinyl record replicate actual sound vibrations; they are analogous to the original sound.

CDs, however, store sound as a string of numbers. A digital recorder samples the sound thousands of times each second and assigns each sample a numeric value based on a binary code of zero or one. These numbers represent electrical voltages than can be decoded back into sound by the computer chips in the CD player. The CD stores its digital information as a series of microscopic depressions, or pits, arranged in a continuous spiral pattern below the disc's clear plastic surface. The player reads the reflection of the laser beam that tracks these pits. Nothing but this beam of light actually touches the CD while it plays.

CDs usually surpass the sound quality of LPs and analog tapes in many ways. Besides having virtually inaudible distortion and flat (uniform) frequency response, CDs do not normally suffer from the annoying noise and hiss of analog recordings. When you hear hiss on a CD, you are actually hearing the hiss from the original analog master tape (some CDs originate from analog master recordings). CDs contribute no wow or flutter (distracting speed variations that cause a wavering of pitch) to the sound. And since CDs have no grooves that wear away, with proper care, they should last indefinitely.

During the past few years, CD changers have rapidly increased in popularity. The three-, five-, and six-disc carousel models allow you to easily add discs to and remove discs from a large platter, even as one disc plays. This style ideally suits most home situations. The magazine or cartridge changer holds six or ten discs, depending upon the manufacturer, and is most commonly used in automobiles. People with car CD changers benefit from being able to use the same magazine at home or on the road, providing their car changer is compatible with their home changer. The newest trend couples multiple magazines, or jukebox-style individual slots, for changers with 100 discs or more. Unfortunately the magazines are not standardized between manufacturers. In the meantime, the single-disc player becomes increasingly rare, except in the expensive audiophile category.

CD Programmability

CD players differ noticeably in programming capabilities. Programming is a machine's ability to store instructions in its electronic memory and execute them on command.

CDs are divided into tracks. A disc that offers a dozen songs will have 12 tracks, numbered 1 through 12. For classical music, such as a symphony, track numbers denote movements. For added convenience, some CDs further divide selections into index numbers within a given track. For example, index numbers in an opera recording can help you locate your favorite arias.

A programmable CD player can, at the very least, play specific tracks in ascending sequence, while many players also let you program the order in which the tracks will be heard. Some let you specify the tracks you don't want to hear, like telling the sandwich shop to hold the mayonnaise. A few CD players also let you program index numbers. Most machines can store at least a score of instructions in memory; others accept 32 or more.

Most CD players also offer repeat play. Pressing a button plays the disc, selected track, or sometimes even a selected portion of a track until you cancel the command. Most machines will also randomly shuffle the order in which they play tracks. A few players feature permanent programming memories of your favorite tracks on a disc. Players with this feature can store a few hundred selections.

Features and Terminology

Digital-to-Analog (D/A) Converters: These are integrated circuit chips that translate digital numbers back into an analog form. The CD uses 16 bits, meaning that all discs contain blocks of 16-bit information. However, manufacturers encountered great difficulty in producing large quantities of highly accurate 16-bit D/A chips. Thus, some use 18- and 20-bit chips to retrieve information from the disc. They cannot retrieve additional sound, but they do offer a greater margin of error from improved accuracy in the decoding process.

Engineers developed an alternative to the multibit converters. The one-bit system, sometimes known by one of its trade names, Bitstream, converts digital information to analog in a rapid stream of single bits. Each company proclaims a proprietary version of this technology, such as MASH, P.E.M., or PWM, along with a number-crunching technique called noise shaping, which shifts what would have been audible noise outside the range of human hearing. One-bit D/A conversion improves sound quality at a lower cost than other methods, a boon to low-cost CD players. However, even among one-bit conversion systems, there are differences in quality.

Error Correction and Tracking: Some manufacturers claim that a three-beam laser system surpasses a single-beam system. Both systems use only one laser, which is either split through the use of prisms and lenses into three beams or used as a single beam. Although either system can be effective, various CD players show differences in tracking accuracy and stability irrespective of how many beams are used.

If a CD player cannot read one or more numbers on a disc, an error may result, producing a clicking, or at worst, a crashing sound. Fortunately the CD player automatically mutes major errors to protect your speakers and ears. If several errors occur in a short time, the sound distorts. Developers incorporated error-correction systems in all CD players so that errors will be masked, and you many never hear them. These errors may be caused by a scratch or by dirty areas on the disc's surface.

You can best judge a CD player's tracking stability, in addition to its resistance to external vibration and shock, by tapping lightly on the top and sides of the player's cabinet with your hand. Those CD players with superior tracking ability will play through this type of test without skipping a beat.

Single-Play CD Players

SONY CDP-XA3ES

✔**BEST BUY**

The Sony CDP-XA3ES single-play CD player contains most of the same basic technology and features as Sony's top-of-the line player at one-fourth the price. The difference is that the CDP-XA3ES is not as ruggedly built and does not use the same hand-selected parts. While it's true that the CDP-XA3ES costs more than most single-disc players, we think people desiring a single-play machine are more interested in high performance than low price. The CDP-XA3ES represents a longer-term investment than players in the $200 to $450 range because of its significantly better construction quality. For example, the CDP-XA3ES uses an antiresonant frame-and-beam construction in a rather substantial chassis. Sony enhances this player with its most advanced technology, such as its proprietary 90-megahertz, single-bit, high-density, linear digital-to-analog converter with an 8x oversampling digital filter, and the equivalent of 20-bit resolution from standard 16-bit discs. This translates into crystal-clear, ultra-low distortion, ultra-low-noise sound. The player skips from tracks at one end of the disc to the other with blazing speed. Conveniences include Sony's Custom File memory system that memorizes your favorite tracks and listening level on up to 172 discs. It also has conventional programming of up to 32 tracks, easily accomplished from the supplied wireless remote control. The simple front panel layout—with large, basic function keys, large fluorescent display with a music calendar for selecting tracks, and direct track access from the remote—promotes simple operation.

Warranty: 3 years, limited on parts and labor.

Manufacturer's Suggested Retail Price: $700

Approximate Low Price: $683

ONKYO DX-7210

Recommended

The modest price of the Onkyo DX-7210 single-play compact disc player belies its wealth of sound and features. Onkyo's proprietary AccuPulse Quartz System single-bit digital-to-analog converter coupled with its Fine Pulse Conversion System, which includes an 8x oversampling filter, delivers natural sound without harshness. The 20-track music calendar on the blue fluorescent display simplifies the 36-track programming. The display offers a choice of elapsed track time, remaining track time, and disc time remaining. Direct track access on both the front panel and remote control facilitate listening to your favorite tracks. Once you press the keys, the player locates the tracks almost instantaneously. Onkyo designed the DX-7210 to make taping CDs easy. The time edit feature automatically calculates the combination of tracks that will best fill a cassette side, and peak-level search quickly locates the loudest portion of the disc for setting recording levels. Five different repeat modes, including random-shuffle play, offer plenty of listening flexibility. For private listening, there's a headphone jack with volume control.

Warranty: 1 year, parts and labor.

Manufacturer's Suggested Retail Price: $220

Approximate Low Price: $183

JVC XL-V182BK/XL-V282BK

Budget Buy

The twin JVC XL-V182BK and XL-V282BK single-play CD players differ only in that the latter comes with a wireless remote control. Single-play CD players can be found for less, but JVC maintains an impressive degree of quality with these players. JVC uses its proprietary Pulse Edge Modulation one-bit digital-to-analog converter with its advanced noise shaper and an 8x oversampling digital filter for clear, clean sound. You can program 32 tracks with assistance from the 15-track program chart on the fluorescent display and the direct track access buttons on the front panel (and on the remote). In addition to random play, you can set the machine to automatically repeat all tracks, single tracks, or programmed tracks.

When used with full-logic JVC cassette decks, it will automatically set recording levels and interact with the cassette deck. These players lack a headphone jack. The XL-V182/V282BK operates smoothly and reliably, reproducing satisfying sound in the process.

Warranty: 1 year, parts and carry-in labor.

Manufacturer's Suggested Retail Price: $170 (XL-V182BK); $190 (XL-V282BK)

Approximate Low Price: $139 (XL-V182BK); $154 (XL-V282BK)

Carousel CD Changers

TECHNICS SL-PD987

✓ BEST BUY

Technics offered carousel CD changers early, and the SL-PD987 represents generations of refinement and cost savings. An example is the SL-PD987's Quick Disc Rotation, which dramatically reduces the time required to change discs. It complements Technics' lightning-fast ability to skip from the first to last track on a disc. You can swap four discs while one plays. It even has a pitch adjustment, a rarity on CD players. An easy-to-read disc location display clearly shows discs loaded and which is playing. The disc selection buttons have two-color LED indicators. Technics provides a plethora of playing choices, including full random play, single-disc random play, or a spiral play that plays all the first tracks from each disc, followed by second, third, fourth, and so forth. You can even program the changer to delete tracks in the random mode. Similarly, the repeat mode can also repeat individual tracks, discs, or programmed sequences. The ID scan mode samples the loudest, and presumably most recognizable, portion of each track. Direct disc/track access keys, logically arrayed on the front panel, and the wireless remote make 32-track programming from any or all of the loaded discs easier. The Edit Guide feature computes optimum track arrangement for taping. Technics backs up all these features with good sound from its proprietary MASH single-bit digital-to-analog converters. Its advanced digital servo system accurately controls the laser pickup, optimizing it by scanning each disc before play and resisting minor shocks and vibration.

Warranty: 1 year, parts and labor.

Manufacturer's Suggested Retail Price: $250

Approximate Low Price: $208

SONY CDP-CE405 ✔BEST BUY

Leave it to the Sony CDP-CE405 five-disc carousel CD changer to change and spin discs with aplomb and agility. This changer uses Sony's new proprietary Hybrid Pulse digital-to-analog converter with an 8x oversampling digital filter on a single IC chip for shorter signal paths. Sony adds its Direct Digital Sync circuitry to minimize jitter, a digital phenomenon that subtly muddies sound. Antiresonant isolator feet reduce shelf vibrations that can indirectly affect tracking. Sony endowed this changer with several popular features—and then some. You can exchange four of the discs while one disc plays. Direct track and disc access, from the front panel or supplied remote control, make programming up to 32-tracks from any and all discs a cinch, with assistance from a 20-track music calendar on the blue fluorescent display. There are five play and three repeat modes. Time, program, and multi-disc program edit help fit CD choices on specific lengths of tape when recording. Peak search finds the loudest passage on the CD for setting record levels. Three different music scan modes aid in quickly finding the music you're looking for. The digital volume control lets you run the player directly into a power amplifier for the best possible sound.

Warranty: 1 year, parts and labor.

Manufacturer's Suggested Retail Price: $250

Approximate Low Price: $200

ONKYO DX-C530 ✔BEST BUY

Onkyo decided if five discs were good, then six discs were better, so the DX-C530 carousel changes six CDs. In the process, Onkyo's AccuPulse Quartz System single-bit digital-to-analog converters with Fine Pulse Conversion System 8x oversampling digital filters provide natural-sounding digital music. You can change three of the six discs while one plays. You can program 40 tracks from among the six discs, assisted by a 20-track music calendar on the fluorescent display. Or you can select one of the six repeat modes or random-shuffle play. Playing or programming tracks is easy with direct disc and track access buttons on the front panel and supplied remote. Not only will the peak-level search find the loudest portion of the disc for setting recording levels, but it will repeat the segment until you complete the level setting.

Warranty: 1 year, parts and labor.

Manufacturer's Suggested Retail Price: $350

Approximate Low Price: $316

MARANTZ CC-67

Recommended

The Marantz CC-67 five-disc carousel CD changer uses a recently developed one-bit Bitstream continuous calibration digital-to-analog converter that delivers the equivalent of 18-bit sound. Philips, the parent company of Marantz, invented the Bitstream converter and now has developed it to near perfection. The CC-67 also uses premium parts in its analog sections. To reduce noise, Marantz powers the analog and digital portions of this player separately and somewhat isolates the D/A converter. You can swap three discs while one plays on this unit. The laser mechanism quickly jumps between tracks. Features for taping include peak search for locating the loudest sound on a disc and tape edit for arranging the tracks optimally to fill a cassette side. The CC-65 allows programming of 30 tracks, which is made easier by direct disc and track access from the front panel and supplied remote control. This model also has random-shuffle play and three repeat modes. Although this player's features match most others in its class, we chose it for its fine sound quality. Because it costs significantly more than other players in its class, however, the CC-67 is Recommended rather than a Best Buy.

Warranty: 3 years, parts and labor.

Manufacturer's Suggested Retail Price: $400

Approximate Low Price: Not available

Magazine CD Changers

JVC XL-M218BK/XL-M318BK

✓**BEST BUY**

Electronically, the JVC XL-M218BK (without remote control) and the XL-M318BK (with remote) magazine CD changers strongly resemble the JVC single-play CD player we listed as a Budget Buy. The M218BK/M318BK twins use JVC's proprietary Pulse Edge Modulation one-bit digital-to-analog converter with JVC's advanced noise shaping technology and an 8x oversampling digital filter for good, clear sound. What we really like about this changer is the ability to load and play single CDs, even while the six-CD magazine remains loaded, for a total of seven CDs. It uses a separate loading tray just like a single disc player. You can program up to 32 tracks from these seven discs, with the aid of 20-track program chart on the blue fluorescent display. The front panel (and remote) offer direct disc access. These changers provide four-way repeat and random-shuffle play. You can turn off the player while playing, and it will resume at the track where it stopped. The remote-equipped XL-M318BK version also has a headphone jack with volume control.

Warranty: 1 year, parts and labor.

Manufacturer's Suggested Retail Price: $220 (XL-M218BK); $260 (XL-M318BK)

Approximate Low Price: $200 (XL-M218BK); $230 (XL-M318BK)

PIONEER PD-M403/PD-M423

Recommended

The PD-M403/PD-M423 six-disc magazine CD changers differ in that the PDM-423 comes with a remote control. The PD-M423 also has an additional programming fea-

111

ture—the ability to program by deleting tracks. The delete programming feature is a great convenience that justifies the $10 price difference between these two models. The changer uses Pioneer's proprietary one-bit Direct Linear Conversion digital-to-analog converter with noise shaping and an 8x oversampling digital filter. The magazine hi-lite scan feature lets you program the highlight, or identifying, section of each disc, or the first track of each disc, to ease the task of finding the song you want to hear. In addition to random-shuffle play mode, the unit offers six repeat modes. You can program 32 tracks, which is more easily done from the remote than from the front panel. Both the PD-M403 and PD-M423 are reliable, modestly featured changers that reproduce pleasing sound quality.

Warranty: 1 year, parts and labor.

Manufacturer's Suggested Retail Price: $235 (PDM-403); $245 (PDM-423)

Approximate Low Price: $160 (PDM-403); $180 (PDM-423)

SONY CDP-C910

Recommended

The Sony CDP-C910 offers an alternative to other magazine CD changers in that it changes ten discs, and its magazine is compatible with popular Sony automotive CD changers. This model's superb sound quality comes from Sony's High Density Linear Converter digital-to-analog converter with an 8x oversampling 45-bit digital filter and Sony's Direct Digital Sync circuit that reduces jitter. You can program 32 tracks with ease using the direct disc and track access keys on the front panel or the supplied remote control. The remote has 20-track keys rather than the usual ten. The 20-track music calendar on the high resolution fluorescent display aids in programming. The remote can also control the volume, which allows connecting the changer directly to a power amplifier or the power amp section of your receiver. This eliminates one stage of electronics, with the possible benefit of clearer sound. The custom file memory stores your favorite tracks on up to 184 discs and also lets you give each of those discs an eight-character name that's displayed on the front panel. The custom file program bank even remembers your custom-programmed sequences of songs. The CDP-C910 offers seven play modes, including random-shuffle play, and seven repeat modes. The changer will locate the peak levels on each disc in order to set recording levels and to set time, program, and link edit for the ultimate in recording ease, maximizing how much music you can store on each cassette. A three-mode music scan helps you quickly locate the song you want to hear. The changer includes a headphone jack with volume control and a timer switch in case you wish to connect an external timer so that the CDP-C910 works like a clock radio. We rate it Recommended rather than a Best Buy only because of its substantial price and incompatibility with other changers on the market. Otherwise, the CDP-C910 is one of the most impressive changers you'll find.

Warranty: 1 year, parts and labor.

Manufacturer's Suggested Retail Price: $600

Approximate Low Price: $400

Multiple CD Changers

PIONEER PD-F905

The Pioneer PD-F905 goes one disc beyond ✔**BEST BUY** most of its competitors—it's a 101-disc changer. For good sonic quality, it uses Pioneer's one-bit Pulseflow digital-to-analog converter—Pioneer's premier converter—with an 8x oversampling digital filter. The changer operates with Pioneer's Roulette Rack System behind a transparent door that opens and closes electronically; this makes loading single discs easy. Pioneer innovates a unique listening convenience feature called Automatic Digital Level Control (ADLC) that samples each CD and adjusts the volume so that each CD is played at roughly the same level. It also works when taping to optimize record levels. The PD-F905's previous disc scan feature samples 10 seconds of each of the last 20 discs you've played. Hi-lite scan plays back sections 60 to 70 seconds into each track. You can check each track on each disc, only the first track on each disc, just the discs and tracks you've selected in best selection memory, or tracks and discs you've defined in the custom filing function. The random-shuffle play function works on single discs, all discs, and discs you've programmed. You can program 32-tracks, and there are eight repeat modes.

Warranty: 1 year, parts and labor.

Manufacturer's Suggested Retail Price: $360

Approximate Low Price: $297

FISHER STUDIO 24 DAC-2406 [Recommended]

As its name implies, the Fisher Studio 24 DAC-2406 changes 24 discs using neither carousel nor magazine. Simply load the discs into a slot in the front of the player, and they are stored jukebox style. Fisher calls it a compact disc management system. The player comes with seven preset music categories to group CDs for playback, and you can program your own as well. This makes it easier to keep track of the discs you've loaded. Simply assign a new disc a category at the push of a button when loading. You can intermix play between categories or program the Studio 24 to play discs within a single category. It's amazingly versatile in its programming capabilities. The Studio 24 uses a one-bit D/A converter for good sound quality. Even though the player holds 24 discs, it still fits into a normal-size stereo component system.

Warranty: 1 year, parts and labor.

Manufacturer's Suggested Retail Price: $300

Approximate Low Price: $249

SONY CDP-CX90ES [Recommended]

The Sony CDP-CX90ES 200-CD changer sonically represents the top-of-the line of CD changers, but its substantial price rates it Recommended rather than a Best Buy. You can add a second changer unit for a whopping 400 discs. You load the discs vertically through a front panel door, which has a small window. Rather than relying strictly on its high-resolution blue fluorescent display, it displays menus, choices, titles, and tracks on your TV screen if you wire it to your TV and Sony receiver. You can also input disc information using any IBM-compatible personal computer keyboard. You can input categories for Sony's Custom File group file, which categorizes your discs by music type or family member, and Sony's Custom File disc memo, which allows you to assign a 13-character name to up to 400 discs. The custom file track memo permits assigning a 13-character name to individual tracks, and the custom file delete bank remembers to skip the songs you find boring on up to 200 discs. If you don't have a keyboard, the jog dial on the front panel and the remote somewhat ease the task of entering data. The CDP-CX90ES offers five play modes, three repeat modes, and 32-track programming from among 200 discs. A timer switch allows connecting an external timer to use the changer as a wake-up device instead of a clock radio. Sony incorporates its most advanced digital electronics including the Current Pulse High Density Linear analog-to-digital converter and its new Full Feed Forward 8x oversampling 45-bit digital filter with 20-bit outputs. This model is also equipped with Sony's Direct Digital Sync circuit to lessen digital jitter that can muddy the sound. Sony packs this changer with plenty of additional conveniences, making it a first-class changer well worth its high price.

Warranty: 3 years, parts and labor.

Manufacturer's Suggested Retail Price: $1,100

Approximate Low Price: $910

CASSETTE DECKS

The original cassette decks played and recorded on a single cassette tape. If you wanted to copy tapes, you needed two machines. More and more people wanted to copy tapes but didn't want to spend the money to buy two decks or fuss with interconnecting them. In the 1980s a single box was developed with two transports: the dual deck. This offered three advantages: one-button tape copying, double-speed copying, and lower cost than two separate decks. The dual transports of the double deck share many parts, reducing their cost to 30 to 50 percent of that of two separate decks of comparable quality. Initially only one deck of the dual-transport pair could record, so their main utility was copying. In this decade more and more dual-recording, dual-transport decks have appeared. This opens the possibilities of making two copies of an external source (such as a CD or an FM broadcast) simultaneously. It also enables making a virtually uninterrupted recording of nearly four hours if both transports auto-reverse, and most do. Dual recording adds between 15 and 20 percent to the price of a dual-transport cassette deck, depending on the manufacturer's marketing strategy. The ultimate quality cassette decks remain single-transport models. Below this ultimate quality level, single-transport models are disappearing in favor of the overwhelmingly popular dual-transport models.

Before you shop for a single- or dual-transport cassette deck for your stereo system, read through this brief explanation of the major specifications.

Frequency response, distortion, and signal-to-noise ratio are closely related. Frequency response is sometimes improved at the expense of distortion and signal-to-noise ratio. But achieving the true hi-fi range of 20 to 20,000 hertz may not mean the overall quality is better, since most humans (especially as they get older) cannot hear much above 15,000 hertz and few instruments other than a grand pipe organ produce tones that go much below 30 hertz. When comparing the frequency responses of two machines, be sure the response of each is accompanied by a tolerance, usually stated as plus or minus a certain number of decibels (dB); otherwise the frequency response statement is meaningless.

Distortion is quoted by tape deck manufacturers at a -20 dB recording level, lower than the level most people record at. (A few specs quote a more realistic 0 dB level.) Many manufacturers advise recording peaks as high as +5 dB. This specification depends on the type of tape, but it should be no higher than 1 percent.

Signal-to-noise ratios (S/N) often use the -20 dB recording level as a reference. Choose a deck with better than 60 dB S/N when the Dolby noise reduction is switched off. To enjoy the best sound from the tape deck you have selected, use the brand and type of tape recommended by the manufacturer, or have a technician adjust the machine for your favorite brand and type of tape. Avoid bargain-brand tapes; not only will they lower sound quality, they can potentially damage the machine.

Wow and flutter is a measurement of tape-speed fluctuation. It is usually listed as a percentage, followed by the acronym WRMS. For example, a wow-and-flutter specification might read 1/10 percent WRMS. Look for the lowest percentage available within your budget limitations.

Bias, equalization, and level-setting adjustments are not available on all cassette decks, but some tape decks offer fine-tuning controls that let you adjust for slight differences in the bias of recording tapes. Other decks control adjustments with microprocessor chips. These circuits test the tape and adjust for the optimum bias, equalization, and sensitivity to provide the best performance from a tape.

Three-head cassette decks have one head for erasing, another for recording, and a third for playback. This arrangement provides the same sort of rapid off-the-tape monitoring capability found on professional open-reel machines. Using a separate head for each function also improves performance by permitting the use of specialized heads for record and play.

Noise-Reduction Systems

Even with the very best cassette tape used in a superior cassette recorder, you will probably notice some tape hiss, or noise, when playing back your recordings. Hiss, which occurs where the human ear is most sensitive, in the upper mid-range and treble, is especially noticeable during playback of softer musical passages. Although several noise-reduction technologies competed during the cassette's early days, Dolby noise reduction proved the most viable. Different levels of noise reduction from Dolby Laboratories are now standard on all cassette decks. Dolby A is a very expensive professional noise-reduction system not used in consumer cassette decks.

Dolby B reduces high-frequency (treble) noise by 5 to 10 decibels; this is equivalent to perceiving about a 50 percent reduction in high-frequency noise. Tapes recorded in Dolby B can be played back on non-Dolby players with only a slight sonic aberration.

Dolby C reduces both mid-range and high-frequency noise by about 10 decibels, but it sounds as if it reduced noise twice as much as Dolby B. It also slightly lowers distortion on high-frequency peaks. While Dolby C-encoded tapes can be played back with some success using Dolby B, they sound unpleasant when played back on machines lacking any Dolby decoding.

Dolby S reduces noise throughout the audible range and as much as 20 decibels in the high frequencies. It also significantly reduces distortion. Dolby S is the consumer version of the Dolby SR professional noise-reduction system. Dolby requires a basic standard of quality for cassette decks equipped with Dolby S. Tapes recorded on these decks approach digital sound quality, with their dramatically low noise and distortion. Dolby S cannot eliminate speed variations such as wow and flutter. Dolby S tapes can be played back through Dolby B or C with reasonable success. Although its full benefits won't be realized, the sound quality is acceptable.

Dolby HX-Pro is a headroom expansion (HX) system that, unlike noise-reduction systems, is single-ended. That means it works only during recording and needs no decoding on playback. Dolby HX-Pro adjusts the recording current, or bias, to allow higher levels of high frequencies on the tape while lowering distortion. A by-product of this is a subtle reduction of noise. A cassette deck with HX-Pro will greatly assist your efforts to make superior tape recordings. It is now becoming standard on all but the least expensive models.

Single-Transport Cassette Decks

SONY TC-KE500S
We think the Sony TC-KE500S cassette deck   ✓**BEST BUY** admirably serves the serious home recordist who would choose a single-transport deck. High-performance is essential to the

single-transport category, and this deck rivals machines cost-ing twice its price. The three-head design allows monitoring directly from the tape while recording. It also permits opti-mization of the heads for optimum fidelity. Not only does the deck have the usual Dolby B and C noise reduction and HX-Pro for extended dynamic range, but it also has the newer Dolby S, which provides near digital dynamic range. Sony uses a very high-bias frequency to reduce tape distortion. You can manually adjust the bias for individual tapes for the utmost fidelity. The two-motor transport moves tape very rapidly and smoothly in the fast wind modes. Feather-touch full-logic controls simplify operation. A Sorbothane cassette stabilizer curbs vibrations that can muddy the sound. A linear time counter lets you know where you are on the tape in real-time minutes and seconds. A gold-plated headphone jack with vol-ume control permits private listening. This deck will record tapes that sound great at home, in the car, or on a headphone stereo.

Warranty: 1 year, parts and labor.

Manufacturer's Suggested Retail Price: $360

Approximate Low Price: $286

ONKYO TA-R410

Recommended

The Onkyo TA-R410 two-head cassette deck uses two motors for smooth, reasonably fast tape handling. Feather-touch, full-logic controls, which use a computer chip to operate the motors, contribute to smooth operation and tape motion. The TA-R410's quick auto-reverse functions with impressive speed. The deck includes Dolby B and C noise reduc-tion, plus HX-Pro. The large, dual-color fluorescent display with peak level indicators and four-digit electronic tape counter is easy to read, although we miss having a real-time tape counter. The manual Accubias system allows you to fine-tune the deck to specific tapes you plan to record on. If you have the time and patience to do this, you may noticeably improve recording quality. You can specify a section of tape you'd like to replay, and the deck will repeat the block up to eight times. The con-trols operate easily and are logically laid out.

Warranty: 1 year, parts and labor.

Manufacturer's Suggested Retail Price: $280

Approximate Low Price: $270

JVC TD-R272BK

> **Budget Buy**

The JVC TD-R272BK auto-reverse cassette deck makes good sounding tapes, using only Dolby B noise reduction. Full-logic control gently handles tape while simplifying operation. The deck automatically senses the type (normal/chrome/metal) of tape you insert. Unlike fancier decks, the TD-R272BK forgoes a fluorescent display for a two-color LED record level display and a mechanical tape counter. This deck uses two drive motors for tape motion and a third to operate the mechanism, such as opening and closing the loading door. While this unit lacks frills it does its job well, with the added convenience of auto-reverse.

Warranty: 1 year, parts and labor.

Manufacturer's Suggested Retail Price: $150

Approximate Low Price: $138

Double-Transport Cassette Decks

SONY TC-WE605S

> ✔ **BEST BUY**

The Sony TC-WE605S records only on one transport but otherwise equals the performance of two separate auto-reverse decks sharing the same chassis. Each has a two motor transport for fast, smooth tape handling, and both include Dolby B and C noise reduction as well as the newer and more effective Dolby S. The recording deck records with HX-Pro for maximum dynamic range. If you're not a knob twiddler, automatic record level sets the optimum recording levels, while automatic record calibration automatically matches the recording deck to the specific tape you insert. You can copy tapes at double speed with the high-speed dubbing feature, and a fader switch invokes automatic fade-ins and fade-outs for professional sounding copies. You can program the decks to play songs in any order, and the multiple track search on deck A lets you automatically skip up to nine tracks forward or back. The relay play feature plays both sides of the tape in deck A and then automatically plays both sides of the tapes in deck B for over 3 hours of uninterrupted music. The deck includes a headphone jack for private listening. The feather-touch, full-logic controls assure responsive, dependable operation.

Warranty: 1 year, parts and labor.

Manufacturer's Suggested Retail Price: $250

Approximate Low Price: $200

TECHNICS RS-TR575

✔**BEST BUY**

The Technics RS-TR575 stands out as an exceptional value among dual-transport cassette decks. All that's missing on this high-performance deck is a headphone jack. Its forte is sound quality, made possible not only by proper design but also by one of the most accurate automated tape-calibration circuits on the market. The RS-TR575 precisely adjusts its electronics for whatever individual tape you place in the machine. This noticeably improves fidelity. This deck plays and records on both transports, for parallel or serial recording. It loads tape automatically, like a VCR, and handles tape rapidly and smoothly. Each transport's dual-motor design contributes to making it one of the fastest winding decks on the market, at nearly twice the speed of many others. (Rewinding a C-60 takes 50 seconds.) The feather-touch, full-logic controls quickly translate your commands to accurate responses. The deck includes Dolby B and C noise reduction as well as HX-Pro. Sound quality and operation are exemplary for a deck in this price range.

Warranty: 1 year, parts and labor.

Manufacturer's Suggested Retail Price: $250

Approximate Low Price: $223

SONY TC-WA8ESA

Recommended

The Sony TC-WA8ESA dual auto-reverse, dual recording, dual-transport deck comes with all the features and performance to satisfy all but the most demanding home recordists. It also comes with a price that knocks it out of our Best Buy category. It comes with the expected retinue of features such as Dolby B, C, and S noise reduction as well as HX-Pro. The dual motors in each transport assure smooth, reliable operation. Since it's a dual record deck, you can record over 3 hours in the relay record mode as well as play for over 3 hours, or you can make two tapes of the same source simultaneously. You can copy a tape in half the time using the high-speed dubbing mode. The deck will automatically set record levels, and both decks automatically calibrate for the individual tapes on which you plan to record. This noticeably improves recording quality. You can program the deck to play songs in any order, or skip forward or back up to nine tracks to locate your favorite tune on deck A. A fader switch sets the decks to fade in and out of songs for professional results. Since this deck is in Sony's premium ES line, Sony even subtly modifies the electronics for improved performance with, for example, additional power supply circuitry to reduce noise. Feather-touch, full-logic controls provide simple, fail-safe operation. Sony tops it all off with a gold-plated headphone jack.

Warranty: 3 years, limited on parts and labor.

Manufacturer's Suggested Retail Price: $550

Approximate Low Price: $447

JVC TD-W218BK

Budget Buy

The JVC TD-W218BK offers a value superior in this double version deck to our Budget Buy single-deck TD-R272BK. On the TD-W218BK, only one transport records. Both decks auto-reverse, for over 3 hours of uninterrupted playing time. An even better value than the single deck, the TD-W218BK includes Dolby B and C noise reduction, and HX-Pro on the recording deck. The two decks each have three motors, one of which operates the mechanism, smoothly and automatically opening and closing doors. High-speed dubbing lets you copy tapes in half the normal time. A blue and red fluorescent display shows record levels, the numeric tape counter, and the operating mode. Full-logic controls provide simple, reliable operation. JVC even includes a headphone jack. This deck has the same performance specifications as JVC's most expensive double-deck; only the features are different.

Warranty: 1 year, parts and labor.

Manufacturer's Suggested Retail Price: $190

Approximate Low Price: $173

DIGITAL AUDIOTAPE (DAT) DECK

Digital audiotape (DAT) is to the analog cassette as CD is to the analog LP record. It records digitally using a system nearly identical to the CD system. DAT records using 16 data bits, but with a choice of sampling rates of 48,000 hertz for recordings originating on DAT, 44,100 hertz for copies from CD, and 32,000 hertz for long-play and special applications—at the cost of some fidelity. Because it is digital, DAT requires no noise-reduction system.

The record industry fought DAT's arrival because the system is capable of recording with fidelity virtually identical to the source material. Whereas each generation of copies of regular tapes loses a bit more fidelity, you can digitally copy from one DAT to another DAT to another, and so on, and the final copy will sound like the original. DAT decks can also make unrestricted copies with their analog inputs and outputs, but the results are not as perfect as when using digital inputs and outputs. This is because the signal must first go through a D/A converter and then back again through an A/D (analog-to-digital) converter.

The record industry and DAT manufacturers reached a compromise in 1989. Dutch electronics giant Philips—inventors of the analog compact cassette—developed a microchip that would limit digital copying without affecting sound quality. This chip, called Serial Copy Management System (SCMS), allows you to make a digital copy from a digital source. For example, you can copy a CD onto DAT, but you can't make digital copies of that copy. You can copy that same CD as many times as you like onto DAT. You can also copy DAT to DAT digitally one time. Analog sources such as LPs or radio broadcasts can be recorded on DAT and then digitally copied from DAT to DAT once only. DAT not only far surpasses the fidelity of conventional cassettes, it also offers superior tape handling. Any selection on a tape can be located within a minute by the touch of a button.

SONY DTC-60ES

Recommended

Because the DAT format met limited acceptance and the price of the Sony DTC-60ES DAT recorder is so substantial, we can give it only a Recommended listing, no matter how incredible its sound quality. There are less expensive DAT decks, but we think someone choosing this format desires ultimate sound quality, which the DTC-60ES provides. This deck can record and play with a quality equal or superior to most CDs. It uses a proprietary Sony technology called Super Bit Mapping (SBM) to provide the equivalent of a 20-bit digital system, an improvement over the 16-bit standard format. Yet the DTC-60ES remains compatible with all other DATs. The deck records and plays at all three DAT sampling frequencies, which includes the CD sampling frequency, simplifying digital dubs and pressing a CD from tapes recorded on this deck. In the long-play mode, you can record for 4 hours with a fidelity slightly better than that of FM radio. The deck uses single-bit analog-to-digital and digital-to-analog converters. The D/A converter is Sony's proprietary pulse converter. Three motors handle the fragile tape with assurance and suggest durability. Automatic and manual ID subcodes mark selections during or after recording for easy programming and recording. The Serial Copy Management System (SCMS) prevents serial copying of digital tapes, but it permits individual copies and serial copies from the deck's analog inputs/outputs. The DTC-60ES sounds better than any analog consumer recording system.

Warranty: 3 years, limited on parts and labor.

Manufacturer's Suggested Retail Price: $1,300

Approximate Low Price: $1,300

MINIDISC (MD) DECK

MD is a revolutionary digital recording system. It stores up to 74 minutes of sound on a 2½-inch disc encased in a caddy like a 3½-inch computer diskette. It compresses the digital data, using an algorithm to discard inaudible sound. Prerecorded MDs are pressed the same way as CDs and cost about the same; however, prerecorded MDs are few and far between. Like CDs, MDs are immune to wear.

The recordable/erasable MDs use a laser and a magnetic head similar to a tape head to record on the disc. Blank recordable/erasable MDs cost $12 to $14. MD matches CD in ease of use, with nearly instant access to desired tracks and programming capability. Recordable MDs offer the advantages of computer diskettes, permitting nonsequential recording on any blank space on the disc. You can also reorder selections on the MD without rerecording or programming.

MDs are nearly indestructible and resistant to heat. The caddy makes them less susceptible to damage than CDs. They fit easily into a shirt pocket.

All MD players incorporate a "shock-resistant memory." These memory computer chips store 10 seconds of sound. When the player is jarred or shaken, you hear no interruption of sound because of this memory. This makes MD a more effective portable medium than CD. Sony, the inventor of MD, intends it mostly as a portable/automotive format rather than home music format.

SONY MDS-JE500

Recommended

The Sony MDS-JE500 would rate a Best Buy if the MiniDisc technology were more widely accepted. It makes superb recordings on the 2.5-inch magneto-optical miniature discs, with versatility unavailable from any tape recording system. This MD deck brings the sound of MiniDisc within a hair of CD sound. The MDS-JE500 looks like a combination of a CD player and cassette tape deck, which is logical since it offers the best attributes of both. Sony's fourth generation ATRAC circuitry, which makes MD possible, subdues past criticisms of MD's fidelity. Sony's proprietary Hybrid Pulse digital-to-analog converter and an 8x oversampling 18-bit digital filter are the same as those used in the company's better CD players. The MDS-JE500 offers 25-track programming, aided by a 25-track music calendar on the fluorescent display, and simplified by the 25-key direct-track access on the supplied remote control. A jog dial on the front panel helps enter text for electronically labeling recordings. These electronic labels of disc title, track title, and artist name scroll across the fluorescent display. Because of its 4-second memory buffer and its use of a "table of contents," like that found on a computer floppy disk, you can combine, divide, reorder, move, and remove tracks on the disc without actually recording or rerecording. The deck offers many fascinating features available only in the MD format. It also comes with a headphone jack. The MDS-JE500 comes very close to last year's top-of-the-line model in performance at about half the price.

Warranty: 1 year, parts and labor.

Manufacturer's Suggested Retail Price: $600

Approximate Low Price: $467

STEREO SYSTEMS

Stereo systems, sometimes called rack systems, are audio components from a single manufacturer grouped together to offer optimum value and performance. Some companies also use this arrangement to optimize profit. A stereo system provides the assurance that the matched components will work well together and that little wiring will be required on your part.

Over the past few years, stereo systems have undergone an evolution. Mini- and microsystems have surpassed full-size systems in popularity. Many of these small systems reproduce sound faithfully, with output comparable to that of the bigger systems. An added attraction is that the mini- and microsystems often offer more features than larger systems, such as integral clock/timers.

When shopping for a stereo system, consider the components it includes. Just as compact disc players have replaced turntables in most systems available today, CD changers are replacing single-disc players. You may want to consider features such as a wireless remote control (which gives you full control of the system from across the room) and logic connections between the components. Logic connections work, for example, by turning off the CD player when you select the tuner, or vice versa. Most systems now interconnect the CD player and the tape deck to simplify tape copying.

In full-size systems, the weakest link is usually the speakers. Most electronics manufacturers do not make good loudspeakers. If possible, attempt to persuade the dealer to let you substitute different speakers for the ones supplied with the system. If that doesn't work, consider upgrading the speakers at a later date.

The stylish minisystems come with specially engineered small speakers that are important to the overall sound of the system. The amplifiers include special bass enhancement circuits, which allow the supplied speakers to reproduce impressive bass.

For additional information about stereo components, please refer to the preceding chapter.

Best Buys '97

Our Best Buy, Recommended, and Budget Buy stereo systems are classified into three categories: complete home theater systems, full-size systems, and compact stereo systems. In each category, systems are listed by quality, with the item we consider the best of the Best Buys listed first. A Budget Buy, which may be listed at the end of a category, is a less expensive product of respectable quality that sacrifices some performance level and/or features of a Best Buy or a Recommended product. Remember that the Best Buy, Recommended, or Budget Buy designation applies only to the model reviewed. It does not necessarily apply to other models by the same manufacturer or to an entire product line.

COMPLETE HOME THEATER SYSTEMS

BOSE LIFESTYLE 12

The Bose Lifestyle 12 home theater system is so ✓**BEST BUY** elegant, so easy to install, and so sonically pleasing that we list it as a Best Buy despite its high price. It includes a quality AM/FM stereo tuner, a CD player, a surround-sound decoder, five channels of amplification, and five pairs of cube speakers. The sleek, brushed-aluminum center is smaller than most coffee table books. A modest fluorescent display and a few buttons occupy a long oval cutout on the front left of the top. A hidden button raises the lid of the CD player. This Bose system is operated from a white, uncluttered, finger-friendly remote control. Because the Lifestyle remote works via radio waves rather than by the usual infrared light, you can conceal the music center or even control it from another room. To demonstrate this microsystem's big sound, Bose provides a super fidelity CD sampler. The Lifestyle's speakers are a refinement of a concept Bose pioneered a decade ago: The woofer (Bose calls it a bass module) uses Bose's Acoustimass design to draw thundering bass from a small enclosure. This bass module, about the size of a briefcase, contains all the power amplifiers and bass and treble controls for the system. The five pairs of speaker cubes can be placed on a shelf (the center channel on top of the TV) or, with their built-in threaded adapters, attached to stands or wall brackets. Each cube twists, so they can be aimed at right angles or even in opposite directions. Directing one cube toward you and the other cube at the wall will create a more spacious sound. Bose uses its own VideoStage surround decoding system and recently introduced an advanced version, the Lifestyle 20. This reduces the size of the speaker cubes by about 50 percent and replaces the single CD player with a six-disc changer, making the music center slightly larger.

Warranty: 1 year, parts and labor.

Manufacturer's Suggested Retail Price: $2,200

Approximate Low Price: $2,000

MAGNAVOX MX960AHT

Budget Buy

The Magnavox MX960AHT home theater system-in-a-box would be a Best Buy if it were better constructed. But if you team this unit up with any 27-inch (or larger) TV and a VHS hi-fi VCR, you'll have a real home theater. The sound is not the highest quality, but it's better than all but the very best surround systems that come with TV sets. Magnavox has incorporated Dolby Pro Logic sound and has placed a full-featured AM/FM stereo receiver at the heart of this system. The front panel's large backlighted crystal display is easily readable from across the room and even scrolls instructions for certain functions. Number keys allow direct-access tuning of radio stations by tapping into their frequencies. You can preset 48 stations or let the receiver automatically preset the strongest 16 AM and 32 FM stations. A spectrum analyzer on the receiver helps you work with the equalizer, which comes preset for rock, jazz, classical, and pop music. This model—priced the same as last year's receiver-only model—includes a seven-disc elevator-style CD changer with 50-track programming and five play modes. The amplifier produces 45 watts for each of the three front channels and 22.5 watts for each of the rear channels. The bookshelf-size unit, with magnetically shielded left and right speakers, fits nicely beside a

27-inch TV, and the center speaker can sit atop or below the TV. The unobtrusive surrounds come with eyeholes and screws for wall mounting, and the whole package includes front panel audio/video jacks, a headphone jack, and a remote control that also works with other Magnavox products.

Warranty: 1 year, carry-in parts and labor.

Manufacturer's Suggested Retail Price: $500

Approximate Low Price: Not available

FULL-SIZE STEREO SYSTEMS

SONY R-2600
✓**BEST BUY**

The Sony R-2600 full-size stereo rack system may be basic, but it delivers solid performance at a very attractive price. Sony packages a 100-watt-per-channel stereo amplifier with five inputs; a seven-band spectrum analyzer, which offers visual confirmation of bass and treble adjustments; a five-disc carousel CD changer; an AM/FM stereo tuner; and a dual-transport cassette deck in a modern black cabinet flanked by floor-standing speakers. The CD changer uses Sony's single-bit, pulse-type, digital-to-analog converter with an 8x oversampling digital filter. The changer offers direct disc access. With the help of the 20-track music calendar on the fluorescent display, you can program 32 tracks from any of the five discs. The changer offers three play modes, two repeat modes, and a custom edit mode for taping CDs. The cassette deck plays on both transports and records on one, using Dolby B noise reduction on both. Full-logic feather-touch controls make it easy to program up to 30 radio stations on the tuner, and Sony supplies a full-function remote control for the system. The two-way speakers each consist of a 10-inch woofer and a 3-inch tweeter and are finished in black to match the cabinet. The R-2600 gives you high-quality sound, without unnecessary frills.

Warranty: 1 year, parts and labor.

Manufacturer's Suggested Retail Price: $700

Approximate Low Price: $633

PIONEER D-2200 K/Q

`Recommended`

The D-2200 K/Q may be the simplest of Pioneer's full-size rack systems, but it sports several impressive features. The system includes the popular 25-disc CD changer, a 100-watt-per-channel amplifier, a five-band graphic equalizer with spectrum analyzer to display relative frequency levels, an AM/FM stereo tuner with 24 radio station presets, and a dual-transport cassette deck that records and plays on one transport and plays on the other (with Dolby B noise reduction on both). Unfortunately, it's the sound quality of the cassette deck that, at this price level, lowers this system to Recommended status. The 25-disc CD changer has Pioneer's Custom Mode: When you hear a track you really like, you simply press a button on the remote control, and the player will memorize up to 15 of these favorites for instant recall. The three-way speakers include 10-inch woofers, 2½-inch mid-ranges, and ¾-inch dome tweeters. You can add a fully automatic turntable for about $100 extra. Cabinet and speakers are available in black or vinyl oak.

Warranty: 1 year, parts and labor.

Manufacturer's Suggested Retail Price: $815

Approximate Low Price: $658

KENWOOD SPECTRUM 350

`Recommended`

The Kenwood Spectrum 350 full-size rack system places its emphasis on CDs rather than on tapes. It comes with a five-disc carousel CD changer and a dual-cassette deck with mechanical controls and LED recording-level meters. The receiver produces 100 watts per channel. The AM/FM quartz-synthesized stereo tuner has 30 radio station presets, and the CD changer uses dual one-bit digital-to-analog converters with an 8x oversampling digital filter with noise shaping. The 20-track music calendar on the fluorescent display helps you program up to 32 tracks, and you can exchange four discs while one is playing. The system allows random-shuffle play from all five discs, and the changer can automatically calculate the best track order for optimum recording. The speakers are as tall as the rack and include 10-inch woofers, 3-inch mid-ranges, and

1-inch tweeters. The speakers and rack come in a rich wood-grain finish.

Warranty: 1 year, parts and labor.

Manufacturer's Suggested Retail Price: $700

Approximate Low Price: Not available

COMPACT STEREO SYSTEMS

JVC UX-C30BK/UX-C30WT

The JVC UX-C30 is the kind of minisystem ✓**BEST BUY** you'd give to your best friend as a wedding present or to your mom for her birthday. It provides ample sound and plenty of flexibility in a very compact package—it's almost a microsystem. The system combines a three-disc CD changer, AM/FM stereo tuner, cassette deck, amplifiers, and matching speakers in a unit that fits easily on a kitchen counter. The CD changer loads each CD in a separate drawer for instant accessibility. It uses JVC's standard one-bit digital-to-analog converter with 8x oversampling. You can program 20 tracks from any or all of the discs, and the digitally synthesized tuner has 30 presets (15 AM/15 FM) that you can choose yourself or have the tuner set automatically. The single auto-reverse cassette deck has full-logic electronic controls and Dolby B noise reduction, and it works in conjunction with the CD changer to record CDs. The amplifier produces 12 watts per channel—a lot of power from such a small unit—and has preset equalizations for beat, pop, clear, and live. Other features include an auxiliary input for other components (such as a VCR), a fluorescent display with a clock/timer for automatic shutoff and wake-up, and a full-function remote control. The matched speakers produce impressive sound. This JVC system is available in two colors: black (UX-C30BK) and white (UX-C30WT).

Warranty: 1 year, parts and labor.

Manufacturer's Suggested Retail Price: $330

Approximate Low Price: $298

YAMAHA GX-50

✔**BEST BUY**

The Yamaha GX-50 compact stereo system features the most current technology from the company that gave this category sonic credibility almost a decade ago. The key to the impressive sound is Yamaha's "active servo technology" in which amplifiers and speakers work as a team, with the amplifier reacting to feedback from the speakers to correct errors in the sound. The result is unusually low distortion and a big sound from small speakers. The GX-50 system includes an AM/FM stereo receiver, a three-disc CD changer, and a dual-transport, auto-reverse cassette deck. The receiver incorporates Yamaha's Digital Super Surround (DSS), a derivative of the company's acclaimed digital-sound-field processing technology. Through the GX-50's two speakers, DSS synthesizes the ambiance of a concert hall, a disco, a church, a jazz club, and something it calls "relax" for New Age music. The receiver even custom tailors the sound if you switch from the speakers to the headphones. If all this isn't enough, the GX-50's disc changer lets you swap two discs while the third is playing, and the cassette deck records on one transport and plays on both with Dolby B and C noise reduction. This system also includes S-bit, one-bit digital-to-analog converters.

Warranty: 1 year, parts and labor.

Manufacturer's Suggested Retail Price: $499

Approximate Low Price: $499

PIONEER CCS-305

✔**BEST BUY**

The Pioneer CCS-305 compact stereo system takes a big step forward in convenience. It incorporates a 25-disc CD changer and still takes up no more space than most other compacts. The changer, with direct disc access, uses Pioneer's CD File System to categorize discs, by music type or family member, for example. The touch of a button on the front panel or the remote will tag your favorite 15 tracks, and the unit also has disc title memory. The player operates on Pioneer's standard one-bit, pulsed digital-to-analog converter. The dual-transport cassette deck records on one transport and plays on both with Dolby B for noise control. For taping, it offers high-speed copying and works with the CD changer to record. Full-logic controls keep operation simple. The CCS-305's amplifier produces a whopping 100 watts per channel through speakers with what Pioneer calls Super Extended Bass Drive with Side Spread Wing Duct—put simply, this means heavy bass from small speakers. The bass duct is on the side of the speaker, so you can place the system flush against a rear wall with minimal effect on the sound. You can also season the sound with Sound Field Control options labeled disco, hall, movie, and live. The AM/FM stereo tuner offers 24 radio station presets. As a bonus, Pioneer throws in a stand for 25 CD jewel boxes.

Warranty: 1 year, parts and labor.

Manufacturer's Suggested Retail Price: $630

Approximate Low Price: $500

SONY LBT-D270

The Sony LBT-D270 compact stereo system [Recommended] packs the essentials into an unusually user-friendly product. The amplifier produces 100 watts per channel and includes what Sony calls Matrix Surround Sound, which gives the illusion of a fuller sound using only two speakers. A five-band equalizer, with five preset settings and memory for five settings of your choice, can tailor tonal balances to your taste more precisely than simple bass and treble controls. The five-disc carousel CD changer features Sony's one-bit digital-to-analog converter and 8x oversampling. You can change four discs while the fifth is playing. The 20-track music calendar helps you program up to 32 tracks, and the three play modes include random-shuffle play. The dual-transport cassette deck records on one transport and plays on both, and Dolby B noise reduction is available on both. The frequency-synthesized tuner includes 30 station presets, a clock/timer for sleep shutoff and for waking up to music, a video input for a hi-fi VCR, and a phonograph input. Sony also includes super tweeters in the speakers and provides an ergonomic remote control.

Warranty: 1 year, parts and labor.

Manufacturer's Suggested Retail Price: $450
Approximate Low Price: $400

AIWA NSX-V2000

Budget Buy

By sacrificing some refinement, Aiwa builds a bargain into the NSX-V2000 minisystem. It combines a seven-disc elevator-style CD changer, a digitally synthesized AM/FM stereo tuner, and a dual-transport cassette deck, topped off with a remote control. The 10-watts-per-channel amplifier has a bass boost circuit and three electronic graphic equalization settings for rock, pop, and jazz. The settings may be based on slightly inaccurate musical stereotypes, but they do let you choose your tonal balance. The cassette deck lacks Dolby B, but offers high-speed dubbing, and it plays and records on both transports. Aiwa also includes a microphone input for anyone who wants to use the unit for karaoke. The CD changer offers 30-track programming, a 20-track music calendar, and three play modes. The NSX-V2000 has a solid sound and offers a lot of listening pleasure for the price.

Warranty: 1 year, parts and labor.

Manufacturer's Suggested Retail Price: $300

Approximate Low Price: $223

PERSONAL STEREOS

We live in motion these days, and personal stereos complement our increasingly kinetic lifestyles. The personal stereo revolutionized music listening. For the first time, people could enjoy their music anytime and anywhere with high-fidelity sound. The personal stereo forever altered the music industry—cassettes and FM radio achieved prominence over LPs and AM radio. Now personal stereos are forsaking cassettes for CDs; portable headphone CD players—along with personal DAT (digital audio tape) and MD (minidisc) players—are close to surpassing cassette players in sales. Sony invented the personal stereo category in 1979 and still offers the widest array of models. Sony's trademark name of Walkman has become almost a generic label for a category alternatively known as headphone stereos and personal portables.

Various portable models offer a variety of the following features: Dolby B and Dolby C noise reduction, auto-reverse, automatic music search (AMS), graphic equalizer for fine-tuning frequency response, bass booster, water resistance, and recording capability. Portables may also supply integral rechargeable batteries, solar power, TV sound (on units with radio tuners), and digitally synthesized tuning. Be aware that many of these features are marketing ploys rather than performance enhancements. However, you may find auto-reverse and digitally synthesized tuning with preset station buttons a great convenience.

Choosing a Portable

Most major brand-name portable stereos perform impressively under ideal conditions, but the true test of a portable is how it performs in motion. Listen for tape skewing (a varying amount of treble) and for wow and flutter (warbling or off-speed sound) while you shake and vibrate the unit to simulate jogging or cycling.

The critical test of FM reception occurs in big cities, where the unit may overload from nearby transmitters. This problem is often compounded by multipath distortion caused by signals bouncing between tall buildings. A stereo/mono switch or a local/distant switch helps in these situations. Some FM models use automatic stereo/mono blending to assist in smoothing out the rapid and distorting change between stereo and monaural sound that can occur in urban areas. The length of the headphone cord determines the quality of FM reception in units that use this cord as the FM antenna. A few inches of cord, more or less than the ideal 31 inches, make a great difference.

Best Buys '97

Our Best Buy, Recommended, and Budget Buy personal stereos follow. Within each category, systems are listed by quality; the item we consider the best of the Best Buys is first, followed by our second choice, and so on. At the end of some categories, you will find a Budget Buy. A Budget Buy is a less expensive product of respectable quality that may not offer all the performance and/or features of a Best Buy or Recommended product. Some categories may not have a Best Buy listed because the price, features, and specifications for the top items are not up to Best Buy standards; Recommended items are the best in those categories. Remember that a Best Buy, Recommended, or Budget Buy designation applies only to the model listed; it does not necessarily apply to other models made by the same manufacturer or to an entire product line.

PORTABLE CD PLAYERS

SONY D-245
                                                         ✔ **BEST BUY**

The Sony D-245 Discman plays for up to 12 hours, powered by a pair of AA alkaline batteries. Sony supplies it with an AC power adapter for plugging in and a line output for attaching it to your stereo system. Its sound quality comes from the one-bit digital-to-analog converter with an 8x oversampling digital filter. The D-245's most frequently used controls are on the top front of the lid (play/pause, stop, skip/scan, forward/back). A liquid crystal display (LCD) on the front lip shows tracks and timings. Although the Discman is constructed with some mechanical shock absorption, Sony also builds in 3 seconds of electronic shock protection (ESP). This stores sound in computer memory chips so that if the unit is bumped or jarred while playing and the laser mistracks, you'll probably hear little, if any, interruption of the music. (Be warned, however, that ESP shortens battery life by a third.) You can program 22 tracks and take advantage of ten playback modes. Sony provides comfortable, on-the-ear headphones with foam cushions connected by a plastic headband. The Mega Bass sound system ensures plenty of bass sound from the phones. A three-position automatic volume limiter on the unit protects your hearing. If you use nickel-cadmium batteries, the D-245 can recharge them within the unit.

Specifications: height, 1¼"; width, 5¼"; depth, 6"; weight, 9.7 oz. (without batteries). **Warranty:** 90 days, labor; 1 year, parts.

Manufacturer's Suggested Retail Price: $150

Approximate Low Price: $129

PANASONIC SL-S401C

Recommended

The Panasonic SL-S401C portable CD player, part of the company's Platinum Series, comes Recommended for its performance, construction, and price. Two AA alkaline batteries, which fit inside the unit's durable, heat-resistant polycarbonate body, power the SL-S401C for about 17 hours. (If you decide to buy rechargeable batteries instead, the player can recharge them internally.) When you press the eject button, the top lid opens and the disc pops out as if it were being handed to you. The lid contains most of the controls and a large, backlighted LCD for easy viewing of tracks and timings. The player uses Panasonic's MASH one-bit digital-to-analog converters for good sound and has a line output for connection to your stereo system. The unit's XBS headphones are excellent, and the headphone pads on the wide plastic headband rest comfortably on your ears. Panasonic supplies an AC power adapter and a power adapter for your car, along with a cassette adapter that can be inserted into your car's cassette player for listening on the road. You can program 24 tracks and enjoy five play modes, including random play. The SL-S401C has reasonably good mechanical shock absorption plus an additional 10 seconds of antishock memory. The antishock memory feature masks interruptions caused by bumps and bounces but also noticeably decreases battery life.

Specifications: height, 1¼"; width, 5⅛₆"; depth, 5⅜"; weight, 9.2 oz. (without batteries). **Warranty:** 1 year, parts and labor.

Manufacturer's Suggested Retail Price: $270

Approximate Low Price: $226

PANASONIC SL-S140

We thought long and hard about rating this `Budget Buy` Panasonic SL-S140 portable CD player, because there's a fine line between Budget Buy and Best Buy. Many budget-priced players eat up any savings in batteries but not the SL-S140: This unit plays for about 10 hours on one pair of AA alkaline batteries. At the touch of a button, the pop-up disc-ejection system opens the lid and virtually hands you the disc. The player uses Panasonic's MASH one-bit digital-to-analog converter with 32x sampling frequency noise shaping. It comes with comfortable, foam-padded, XBS on-the-ear headphones suspended from a wide plastic headband. A line-out jack permits connection to your stereo system. This portable system has two play (random and resume) and two repeat (repeat one and repeat all) modes, and you can program 24 tracks. Should you choose to buy the optional rechargeable batteries, they will recharge inside the unit. An LCD on the upper front edge shows tracks, timings, and battery life. Panasonic conveniently places the controls on either side of the display. The durable polycarbonate body resists heat. Panasonic includes an AC power adapter, making the SL-S140 CD player an exceptionally good Budget Buy.

Specifications: height, 1⅛"; width, 5⅛₆"; depth, 5½"; weight, 8 oz. (without batteries). **Warranty:** 90 days, labor; 1 year, parts.

Manufacturer's Suggested Retail Price: $90

Approximate Low Price: $80

PERSONAL RADIO-CASSETTE PLAYER-RECORDERS

AIWA HS-JS445

✓**BEST BUY**

Although Aiwa's HS-JS445 personal radio-cassette player-recorder is not the least expensive model of its type, it combines several desirable features at a reasonable price. It records in stereo on standard or high-bias tape from its tuner or from the supplied one-point stereo microphone. The digital tuner permits six AM and 12 FM radio presets. An LED registers the remaining life of the two AA batteries that power the unit. Aiwa supplies comfortable on-the-ear headphones supported by a wide plastic headband. The antirolling mechanism on the HS-JS445 reduces warbling tape distortion caused by motion. The multisound processor optimizes playback sound for different types of music such as classic, pop, rock, and jazz, although many listeners may prefer their music without the processor. The auto-reverse and Dolby B noise reduction features function only during the playback mode. A belt clip provides convenient on-the-go listening. In addition to its many features, the HS-JS445 sounds very good and operates reliably.

Specifications: height, $3\frac{1}{2}$"; width, $4\frac{11}{16}$"; depth, $1\frac{1}{2}$"; weight, 6.3 oz. (without batteries). **Warranty:** 90 days, parts and labor.

Manufacturer's Suggested Retail Price: $135

Approximate Low Price: $126

SONY WM-GX302

Recommended

The Sony WM-GX302 records as well as plays your tapes in stereo. It records from either the built-in AM/FM stereo tuner or the supplied one-point stereo microphone. The tape reverses automatically on playback, and in record mode it shuts off automatically at the end of each side. You can monitor tapes in mono from a small built-in monitor speaker or listen through the stereo headphones. Some people may find the narrow metal headband uncomfortable, but the earphones it supports carry good sound quality. Sony's Mega Bass pumps up the bass for listeners who can't get enough of it. The FM local/distant switch optimizes tuner reception conditions—an especially helpful feature when you're near the center of a big city. The Automatic Volume Limiter System adjusts dynamic range to protect your hearing. The WM-GX302 operates on a pair of AA batteries. The recording quality is adequate for school classes and business meetings and will do for live music in a pinch. The playback quality of this radio-cassette player-recorder is very good.

Specifications: height, 3⅜"; width, 4¾"; depth, 1⅜"; weight, 8 oz. (with batteries). **Warranty:** 90 days, labor; 1 year, parts.

Manufacturer's Suggested Retail Price: $90

Approximate Low Price: $90

PANASONIC RQ-A161

Budget Buy

The Panasonic RQ-A161 records in mono but plays tapes in stereo. It comes with a built-in, nondirectional microphone on the front of the unit. During recording the player automatically stops at the end of the side, and during playback it auto reverses. One-touch recording resume helps to quickly capture sounds. You tune the AM/FM radio manually using a slide-rule dial at the top front of the unit. A local/distant switch optimizes FM reception, which is an especially useful feature when you're near the center of a large city. Panasonic's shell-lock design seals the case tightly like a car-door lock, protecting the tape and the mechanism. Foam-covered earpieces suspended from a wide plastic headband rest gently on the ear, and, for bass lovers, the sound is augmented by Panasonic's XBS. This radio-cassette player-recorder operates on a pair of AA batteries, and it comes with a detachable belt clip for portability.

Specifications: height, 4¹³⁄₁₆"; width, 3¹¹⁄₁₆"; depth, 1¹¹⁄₁₆"; weight, 6.8 oz. (without batteries). **Warranty:** 1 year, parts and labor.

Manufacturer's Suggested Retail Price: $70

Approximate Low Price: $62

PERSONAL RADIO-CASSETTE PLAYERS

PANASONIC RQ-V201

✔**BEST BUY**

We rated the Panasonic RQ-V201 personal radio-cassette player as a Best Buy because of its ruggedness, value, and good performance. Panasonic's shell-lock case works like a car-door lock to keep the case tightly sealed, protecting the tape and the mechanism. Sturdy mechanical tape-function switches reduce the chance of accidental operation of the tape deck, but the radio can be turned on with a lighter touch. The digital synthesizer tuner includes a maximum of 20 presets, five AM and five FM, in two different banks, plus five direct preset keys spaced in a semicircle on the top of the case. An LCD shows radio frequency, preset number, and tape direction for the auto-reverse tape player, and an LED glows when stations are optimally tuned. The RQ-V201 features a local/distant switch that helps optimize FM reception. Panasonic supplies its comfortable XBS headphones with large foam earpads suspended from a wide plastic headband. The electronic Extra Bass System augments the bass in the headphones. The unit comes with a detachable belt clip and operates on a pair of AA batteries.

Specifications: height, 3⁷⁄₁₆"; width, 4½"; depth, 1½"; weight, 6.5 oz. (without batteries). **Warranty:** 1 year, parts and labor.

Manufacturer's Suggested Retail Price: $60

Approximate Low Price: $54

SONY WM-FX511

Recommended

The Sony WM-FX511, a deluxe personal radio-cassette player, is a good value largely because of its highly economical operation. On the power of one AA alkaline battery, you can play tapes for 15 hours or listen to the radio even longer. Sony endows this radio-cassette player with a host of desirable features, such as auto-reverse, Dolby B noise reduction (an increasing rarity among personal portables), an automatic music sensor that skips forward or back to as many as three songs, and even a one-song repeat. The digital synthesizer tuner has 24 station presets (8 AM/16 FM) but lacks direct access keys. Feather-touch controls operate the tape player and radio. Sony enhances the antirolling mechanism tape stabilizer in this unit, and the Automatic Volume Limiter System automatically adjusts music volume to protect your hearing. You can select between normal and chrome/metal settings for optimal tape tonal balance. Fast forward and rewind are faster (two and a half times) than on most other personal cassette players. An LCD in the center of the cover shows radio station frequency, preset number, and cassette operation. The tape automatically shuts off at the end of fast-wind and play modes. Sony's moderately large, foam-covered earpieces are suspended from a narrow metal headband, which some users may find uncomfortable. The entire unit is about the size of a cassette case, and it comes with its own nylon carrying case.

Specifications: height, 4⁵⁄₁₆"; width, 3⅛"; depth, ¹³⁄₁₆"; weight, 6 oz. (with battery). **Warranty:** 90 days, labor; 1 year, parts.

Manufacturer's Suggested Retail Price: $180

Approximate Low Price: $150

AIWA HS-TA133

Budget Buy

The Aiwa HS-TA133 personal radio-cassette player is so simple that there's not much we can say about it except that it works, it appears durable, and it sounds surprisingly good for the price. The manual tuning dial adequately pulls in stations. The cassette player shuts off at the end of a tape, and you have to flip the tape over manually. The headphones look and feel flimsy but produce satisfying sound. The HS-TA133 operates on a pair of AA batteries. This unit is just as small as—and actually lighter than—some of the more expensive models.

Specifications: height, 4⁹⁄₁₆"; width, 3⅝"; depth, 1⅜"; weight, 4.6 oz. (without batteries). **Warranty:** 90 days, labor; 1 year, parts.

Manufacturer's Suggested Retail Price: $25

Approximate Low Price: $25

PERSONAL CASSETTE PLAYERS

SONY WM-EX122

✓**BEST BUY**

The Sony WM-EX122 is one of the increasingly rare tape-only personal stereos. It's blissfully simple, with no frills and few features. For the consumer who wants economy and good performance, the WM-EX122 fits the bill. One very desirable feature is its 13-hour battery life, using a pair of AA batteries. The unit shuts off automatically at the end of a tape side. A selector switch optimizes the tonal balance for normal or chrome/metal tapes. The Automatic Volume Limiter System protects your hearing. The Mega Bass enhancement circuit pumps up the bass for bass lovers. This Sony model provides quality headphones with large foam earpads suspended from a thin metal headband.

Specifications: height, 4⅜"; width, 3½"; depth, ¹⁵⁄₁₆"; weight, 6.3 oz. (with batteries). **Warranty:** 90 days, labor; 1 year, parts.

Manufacturer's Suggested Retail Price: $27

Approximate Low Price: $24

AIWA HS-PX257

Recommended

The HS-PX257 tape-only personal stereo differs in several respects from the Sony WM-EX122. The HS-PX257's impressively elegant package is less than an inch thick and is operated by full-logic controls arrayed on a silvery bar on its face. A hold switch prevents accidental activation of these light-touch controls. The unit automatically reverses when it reaches the end of the tape. Dolby B ensures the proper reproduction of tapes encoded with the noise reduction system. Aiwa's Super Bass reinforces the already good bass response of the comfortable headphones, which have large foam earpads suspended from a wide plastic headband. The case closes firmly with a center lock mechanism. It operates on a pair of AAA batteries—a slight drawback because of their higher price than AAs.

Specifications: height, 3.10"; width, 4.33"; depth, 0.96"; weight, 4.94 oz. (without batteries). **Warranty:** 90 days, parts and labor.

Manufacturer's Suggested Retail Price: $115
Approximate Low Price: $96

PERSONAL HEADSET RADIOS

SONY SRF-H2

✔**BEST BUY**

The Sony SRF-H2 AM/FM stereo headset radio stays securely on your head because of its double headband. You won't mind the tenacity because it's extremely lightweight and has reasonably comfortable on-the-ear cushions. A flexible short-whip antenna resists breaking, and it pulls in stations loud and clear. The reflective yellow tip on the antenna is a safety feature that increases visibility, which is especially useful when jogging at night. The SRF-H2 has a local/distant switch for optimizing FM reception. Radio reception is quite good, although an overload is possible in the immediate vicinity of powerful transmitters. The unit operates for about 70 hours on a AAA alkaline battery (about 25 hours on a regular battery).

Specifications: weight, 4.2 oz. (with battery). **Warranty:** 90 days, labor; 1 year, parts.

Manufacturer's Suggested Retail Price: $35

Approximate Low Price: $32

PANASONIC RF-H7

Recommended

The Panasonic RF-H7 AM/FM stereo headset radio is equipped not only with a wide, flexible primary headband but also with a fully adjustable secondary headband that has a built-in antenna. The headband keeps the radio phones firmly and comfortably on your head. A light reflector is a safety feature that increases visibility, which is especially useful at night. The RF-H7 has a local/distant switch for optimizing FM reception, and a large window on one of the earcups shows the radio station frequencies for tuning. The two AA batteries required to power the unit also substantially increase the unit's weight. We rate this model below the Sony because of its notably greater weight.

Specifications: weight, 6.7 oz. (without batteries). **Warranty:** 1 year, parts and labor.

Manufacturer's Suggested Retail Price: $35

Approximate Low Price: $34

PERSONAL RADIOS

SONY SRF-85

✓**BEST BUY**

Although this sports model Sony SRF-85 personal radio carries a premium price for its bright yellow water-resistant case, we think it's convenient to own at least one all-purpose, nearly indestructible radio that brings in good reception. This AM/FM stereo model has a local/distant switch to optimize FM reception. It includes Sony's Automatic Volume Limiter System to protect your hearing and reduce noise distortion. For this radio, Sony's ultra-light, in-the-ear headphones make sense since they tend to stay put better than the over-the-ear kind when you're active. A belt clip and a swiveling armband/handgrip keep the SRF-85 glued to you whether you're relaxing or jogging. It operates on a single AA battery. We prefer the old-fashioned mechanical tuning of the SRF-85, because the feather-touch buttons of the digital models can accidentally activate when you put the radio in a pocket or purse.

Specifications: height, 3⅞"; width, 2⅝"; depth, 3½₂"; weight, 3.4 oz. (without battery). **Warranty:** 90 days, labor; 1 year, parts.

Manufacturer's Suggested Retail Price: $40

Approximate Low Price: $38

SONY SRF-39

Budget Buy

The Sony SRF-39 AM/FM personal radio brings in reasonably good reception under most conditions. Its large tuning wheel with slide-rule dial makes this model easy to use. A local/distant switch optimizes FM reception. The light, on-the-ear headphones are supported by a thin metal band. Sony supplies a belt clip, but this radio is easily pocketable. It operates on a single AA battery.

Specifications: height, 3⅝"; width, 2½"; depth, 1"; weight, 2⅓ oz. (without battery). **Warranty:** 90 days, labor; 1 year, parts.

Manufacturer's Suggested Retail Price: $20

Approximate Low Price: $20

PERSONAL MINIDISC PLAYER

SONY MZ-E40
Recommended

The Sony MZ-E40 MiniDisc (MD) personal player finally brings the cost of MD playback down from the stratosphere. This player offers nearly all of the benefits of MDs: 10-second, shock resistant memory for stable playback, nearly instant random access, and a small LCD that shows disc and song title, track number, battery life, and play mode. An MD player is extremely portable because of its small, robust discs that play for 74 minutes. All controls, including the volume, are touch buttons. The unit can play for 4 hours on a pair of AA batteries, and Sony offers an optional rechargeable battery that charges within the unit. The sound quality is better than a cassette portable's but no better than a CD portable's. This handsomely designed player offers comfortable on-the-ear headphones, an AC power adapter, and a carrying case.

Specifications: height, ¹⁵⁄₁₆"; width, 5"; depth, 3"; weight, 6 oz. (without batteries). **Warranty:** 90 days, parts; 1 year, labor.

Manufacturer's Suggested Retail Price: $200

Approximate Low Price: $199

BOOM BOXES

Boom Boxes with CDs

JVC PC-XC7
✔ BEST BUY

JVC introduces an enhanced, high-quality digital sound system with the PC-XC7. This full-featured portable stereo system comes with a three-disc CD changer tray and a single-cassette tape deck. The Hyper-Bass Pro sound system drives two 4-inch speakers and does a good job of eliminating the distortion that can occur in converting digital soundtracks. The three-disc CD changer tray lets users exchange two CDs while the third is playing. Each CD changer has continuous 20-track play/repeat/random options. The PC-XC7 has a one-touch button that powers up the unit by selecting either the CD player, the cassette deck, or the tuner (for AM/FM stereo reception). The tuner circuitry uses a built-in digital synthesizer for precise, drift-free station selection. Users can preset 15 AM and 15 FM stations. A wireless remote control device controls CD and tuner operations, power, volume, and bass. The cassette deck shuts off automatically at the end of a tape and has an automatic recording-level control. The unit also offers timer mode with sleep and wake-up functions. Eight D batteries power the PC-XC7.

Specifications: height, 10¾"; width, 26⅛"; depth, 13⅛"; weight, 17.2 lb. (without batteries). **Warranty:** 1 year, parts and labor.

Manufacturer's Suggested Retail Price: $220

Approximate Low Price: $210

RCA RP-9115

Recommended

The RCA RP-9115 is a mini home entertainment system with several features that will enhance your listening pleasure. Along with its two tape decks and drawer-load CD player, this model offers deep stereo sound on FM stations and tunes in standard AM bands as well. The RP-9115's sound production benefits from both a bass boost system and the Bass Reflex Speaker System. Controls allow you to repeat or shuffle play CDs. The controls for both tape decks are stop, pause, fast forward, rewind, play, and, for one deck, record. One of the best features on this model is the remote control. This battery-operated, hand-held device lets users power the unit on and off, raise and lower volume, and start and stop the tape decks. This quality boom box also comes with stereo headphones.

Specifications: height, 11¾"; width, 21"; depth, 8¼"; weight, 18.3 lb. (without batteries). **Warranty:** 1 year, limited.

Manufacturer's Suggested Retail Price: $170
Approximate Low Price: $136

PANASONIC RX-DT530

If excellent sound is a priority for you but a **Budget Buy** multiple CD changer isn't, then consider the Panasonic RX-DT530. Although this model has only one MASH CD player, its dual tape deck is loaded with features. Both tape decks play and one records, so you can conveniently make tape-to-tape transfers. High-speed dubbing cuts in half the time it takes to copy a tape. For CD-to-tape editing, the Synchro Editing feature begins the CD at the same time the record button is pressed. With Relay Playback, play on deck 2 begins automatically when the tape in deck 1 stops. This boom box has two detachable 5-inch speakers containing a pair of woofers and ¾-inch tweeters. The already powerful bass is enhanced by dual bass reflex ports on each cabinet, and the RX-DT530 has a four-band graphic equalizer. A large LCD display shows cassette and CD modes and serves as a CD counter. The unit is powered with an AC cord (included) or eight D batteries (not included).

Specifications: height, 9¹⁄₁₆"; width, 18"; depth, 8½"; weight, 10 lb. 3 oz. (without batteries). **Warranty:** 1 year, parts and labor.

Manufacturer's Suggested Retail Price: $160
Approximate Low Price: $150

Boom Boxes without CDs

PANASONIC RX-FS470

The Panasonic RX-FS470 is a compact portable **✓BEST BUY** stereo with big boom-box sound. The pleasing sound quality comes from the three-band graphic equalizer that permits users to custom-tailor the output. The two-way, four-speaker system has free edge woofers for great low-frequency range reproduction. This combination results in a clear sound of impressive clarity. Bass sounds are enhanced with the Extra Bass System's on/off switch and level control. This model features an FM stereo/mono mode selector, a built-in condenser microphone, and a headphone jack. The tape deck has one-touch recording and a soft-eject system. The unit is powered by six D batteries or an included AC power cord. There is no built-in CD player, but you can use the RX-FS470 as an amplifier system by plugging a mini CD player into the external CD jack.

Specifications: height, 5⅞"; width, 18⅛"; depth, 6"; weight, 5.5 lb. (without batteries). **Warranty:** 1 year.

Manufacturer's Suggested Retail Price: $80

Approximate Low Price: $70

RCA RP-7700

Budget Buy

The RCA RP-7700, a basic portable radio-cassette player, delivers good sound from AM/FM stations and its single cassette deck. The cassette deck also handles "off air" recording from any radio station received by the AM/FM tuner. The recording function captures sounds in the room through a built-in condenser microphone. The playback quality from the single 4-inch dynamic speaker is good enough for use at business or social gatherings. Whether it's playing back or recording, the tape deck will automatically shut off at the end of the cassette. This model's controls are situated across its top for easy tuning and adjustment of the slide volume control. The tape deck offers one-touch recording and a cassette carry door with cushion eject. It operates on a detachable AC power cord or four D batteries. If stereo music isn't a priority for you, this model is a fine choice.

Specifications: height, 5½"; width, 11½"; depth, 4"; weight, 4.4 lb. (without batteries). **Warranty:** 1 year, limited.

Manufacturer's Suggested Retail Price: $25

Approximate Low Price: $22

CAMERAS

Every year more than 60 billion pictures are taken, and the vast majority of them are on color negative film. This predominant use of color negative film is due in large part to the ready availability of rapid processing from minilabs, but may also be attributed to the easy operation of most modern cameras. You no longer have to study photography to operate a camera. Today most cameras will automatically focus the lens, measure the light, set the proper combination of lens aperture and shutter speed, and warn you when the light level is too low to take pictures without a flash. Some will even activate the flash automatically when it's needed. Some models offer you a choice between fully automatic and manual operation, which is a plus for buyers interested in pursuing the more artistic and creative aspects of photography.

Photographs can be a visual diary, captured moments of personal history, artistic expressions, or all of the above. Before buying a camera, you should determine what types of photos you want to take and how involved in the process you want to be. Then, shop for the camera that best meets your needs. Today even some of the less expensive cameras provide very sophisticated systems to automate your photography.

Types of Cameras

When you use a **single-lens reflex (SLR) camera,** you view the subject of your picture through the lens that takes the picture, so you see exactly what the camera sees. Single-lens reflex cameras come in two basic types. The first is the **interchangeable lens** type, which offers a wide variety of lens choices—wide angle, telephoto, zoom, macro—as secondary purchases to supplement the lens that comes with the camera. The second basic type of SLR camera is the **zoom-lens reflex,** which comes with a permanently attached zoom lens. While slightly less versatile, these cameras will fill all the needs of many photographers, and they are more compact and less expensive than a complete interchangeable-lens camera outfit.

When you look through the eyepiece of a **viewfinder camera,** you see the image you are going to photograph through a window—or viewfinder—in the camera's body. The view you see is close, but not identical, to the view the camera sees through its taking lens. The 35mm autofocus and compact cameras listed in this section are viewfinder cameras.

An **autofocus (AF) camera** focuses the lens automatically when you touch the shutter release button.

A **fixed-focus camera,** usually called a point-and-shoot camera, is a viewfinder camera with its focus fixed at a certain point. With this type of camera, everything from a specified minimum distance to infinity is in focus. Today these are found only among the lowest priced models.

A **rangefinder camera** uses manual focusing to converge a split image of the subject in the viewfinder. Today these are available only as very expensive professional models.

Instant-print cameras, now available only from Polaroid, have a relatively high per-print cost, but they offer the advantage of nearly instant access to the photographs. The quality of the photographs produced by the better models is quite good.

Features and Terminology

The **aperture,** or **f-stop,** is the ratio of the diameter of the lens opening to the focal length of the lens. All lenses are identified by their focal length and their largest aperture. A standard, or normal, lens for a 35mm camera is usually listed as a 50mm f/2 lens. (This lens produces a picture that approximates the perspective and degree of magnification seen by the human eye, excluding peripheral vision.) The f-stop is a function of the lens aperture setting. The standard series is f/1.4, f/2, f/2.8, f/4, f/5.6, f/8, f/11, f/16, f/22, and f/32. The smaller the number, the larger the aperture and the more light strikes the film: An f/1.4 aperture allows twice as much light to pass through the lens as does an f/2 aperture. Most lenses do not cover the full range of settings, but some lenses' settings extend even higher or lower than the standard series.

A **focal-plane shutter** uses curtains or blades that travel either vertically or horizontally across the film plane to make an expo-

CAMERAS

sure. Almost all 35mm SLR cameras use this shutter because it allows the camera to use interchangeable lenses.

A **leaf shutter** uses a series of blades arranged in a circle that opens and closes to make an exposure. Compact 35mm cameras with fixed lenses use leaf shutters.

Exposure value (EV) compensation is used to correct the automatic exposure of subjects that are either very light or very dark. One EV is equivalent to one full f-stop.

Viewfinder information is a visual display in the camera's viewfinder of the exposure information you need to take good pictures. All autofocus SLR cameras have signals that indicate when an image is in focus, and some also signal out-of-focus conditions. Most cameras provide flash signals that tell you when the flash is needed for a good exposure.

DX coding imparts information about the film directly to the camera. Metal strips on the 35mm film cassette make contact with pins in the camera and tell the camera the film speed, exposure latitude, and number of exposures on the roll. Most SLRs offer both DX coding and manual film-speed settings, but compact 35mm cameras offer only DX coding.

The **International Standards Organization**, or **ISO**, is a numerical system that indicates the film's relative speed, or sensitivity to light. The higher the ISO number, the faster the film is in recording the image and the less light it requires. To take photographs in low light, you use a high-speed film.

A **dedicated hot shoe** is a shoe, or clip, found on most 35mm SLR cameras. It interfaces accessories such as electronic flashes with the camera's electronics. Some dedicated systems provide through-the-lens-off-the-film (TTL-OTF) flash control.

A **self-timer,** found on most 35mm cameras, is a switch that delays the operation of the shutter for about 10 seconds, allowing the photographer to get into the picture.

Best Buys '97

Our Best Buy, Recommended, and Budget Buy cameras follow. They are presented in six categories: 35mm manual-focus SLR cameras, 35mm autofocus SLR cameras, 35mm autofocus cameras, 35mm compact cameras, 24mm Advanced Photo

System (APS) cameras, and instant-print cameras. Within each category, products are listed according to overall quality. The best of the Best Buys is first, followed by our second choice, and so on. At the end of each category, you may find one or more products listed as Budget Buys. These products may not have all the features of a Best Buy or a Recommended product, but they are still a good value. Remember that a Best Buy, Recommended, or Budget Buy rating applies only to the model listed and not to other models in the same product line or from the same manufacturer.

35mm MANUAL-FOCUS
SLR CAMERAS

The 35mm SLR (single-lens reflex) camera is probably the most widely used professional camera. Newspaper, combat, and sports photographers use 35mm SLRs, as do fashion and nature photographers, scientists, and doctors. Manual-focus SLR cameras are particularly suitable for amateur photographers who want to use focus and exposure controls to master the images they create. Our selections in this category all have built-in metering with both automatic and manual exposure controls.

MINOLTA X-370S
✔**BEST BUY**

The Minolta X-370S is a full-featured manual-focus SLR with both manual and automatic exposure operation. The camera features both aperture-priority autoexposure (AE) and fully manual exposure. Metering is activated by partial pressure on the shutter speed button. Correct exposure in manual mode is indicated by lighted indicators in the viewfinder. The light meter is a simple center-weighted type, which works well in most exposure situations. AE lock is offered for use in aperture-priority mode to hold the meter's settings while the photographer recomposes the image. The shutter-speed range in the aperture-priority automatic setting is from 4 seconds to $\frac{1}{1000}$ second. In manual mode this changes to from 1 second to $\frac{1}{1000}$ second. Flash synchronization is at $\frac{1}{60}$ second or slower.

Among our choices of manual focus SLR cameras, the Minolta X-370S is the only one with an optional accessory auto-winder and a motor drive. These features differ, essentially, in speed—the auto-winder allows up to two frames per second, and the motor drive allows up to 3.5 frames per second. ISO setting is manual, with a range from ISO-12 to ISO-3200. The focusing screen offers both a split-image rangefinder and a microprism ring for ease of focus. The range of lenses offered by Minolta is extensive, and Minolta also offers a useful range of accessories, including infrared remote control units.

Warranty: 1 year, parts and labor.

Manufacturer's Suggested Retail Price: $325

Approximate Low Price: $217

PENTAX K-1000 `Recommended`

The Pentax K-1000 was first introduced in 1977 and has continued in production—unchanged—for 20 years. The reason for this long production run is its popularity as the world's largest selling manual camera. The K-1000 is an all-metal camera of very strong construction. The shutter is a horizontal traveling silk focal plane. Film advance is manual, using the lever on the right, and rewind is also manual, using the crank on the left. ISO is set by lifting the shutter speed dial and turning it until the desired ISO is visible in the small window at the top of the dial. The ISO range runs from 32 to 3200. You set the shutter speed by turning the same dial without lifting. Shutter-speed range is from 1 second to $\frac{1}{1000}$ second with a B setting for timed exposures. The exposure is set by changing the shutter speed, the lens aperture, or both, to center a moving needle on the right of the viewfinder between a plus and a minus mark. The camera comes with a hot shoe and a PC socket but does not have a self-timer. The K-mount allows you to choose lenses from a wide variety of manufacturers.

Warranty: 1 year, parts and labor.

Manufacturer's Suggested Retail Price: $323

Approximate Low Price: $200

VIVITAR V3000S

Recommended

The V3000S is a sleek black camera with a cast-metal body and a lightweight polycarbonate top and bottom cover. It comes with a raised grip on the right side of the camera for taking both horizontal and vertical photos. Manual film advance works via a lever on the right side of the camera, and rewind works by means of a crank on the left. The large shutter-speed knob on top of the camera doubles as an ISO-setting control. To set the ISO, you pull up on this knob and turn it until the desired ISO is visible in the window. ISO range is from 1 second up to a surprising top speed of ½₀₀₀ second, and there is a B setting for timed exposures. The light-meter indicator is three LEDs to the right of the viewfinder's image area. The upper red plus sign indicates overexposure, the lower red minus sign indicates underexposure, and the green circle indicates correct exposure. The lens included with the camera is a 50mm f/1.7 Vivitar, but since the camera is equipped with a K-mount lens bayonet, lenses from many manufacturers will fit the V3000S. Film loading is completely manual, and the camera comes with a fitted carrying case, a neck strap, and a lens cap.

Warranty: 1 year.

Manufacturer's Suggested Retail Price: $318

Approximate Low Price: $185

KIEV 19M

Budget Buy

The no-nonsense Kiev 19M is a metal-bodied camera with a high-quality 50mm lens. Since the camera uses a Nikon F AI-type lens mount, however, both new and old lenses from many manufacturers will fit it. The manual film-advance lever is thumb-operated, and the manual rewind works via a crank at the top left of the camera. To focus through the viewfinder's glass prism, you can use either the split-image rangefinder in the center of the focusing screen or the microprism doughnut surrounding it. The metal-bladed shutter functions at speeds from ½ second to ¹⁄₅₀₀ second, and these settings appear in full-stop increments on a knob at the left front of the camera. There is also a B setting for timed exposures. Manual ISO settings are made on the dial that surrounds the rewind crank, and they range from ISO-25 to ISO-3200. The exposure is correct when two red LED dots to the left of the viewfinder's image light up. You adjust the shutter speed, lens aperture, or both until the two dots are illuminated. The 19M also comes with a hot shoe, a PC socket, a mechanical self-timer, a fitted cloth carrying case, a neck strap, and a lens cap.

Warranty: 90 days, parts and labor.

Manufacturer's Suggested Retail Price: $225

Approximate Low Price: $225

35mm AUTOFOCUS SLR CAMERAS

Automatic focusing makes photography much easier, for both the beginner and the advanced photographer. Today's autofocus (AF) SLR cameras offer highly advanced autofocus systems that are faster and more accurate than their predecessors. Autofocus SLR cameras are almost as easy to use as simple point-and-shoot cameras, but they offer far greater versatility. The biggest advantage of SLR design is that you are actually looking through the taking lens when you look into the viewfinder, so you and the camera are seeing essentially the same thing. Many modern AF SLR cameras feature small, built-in flash units that are adequate for general indoor photography and work well for fill flash outdoors. The built-in flashes extend into very dim light or even into total darkness on models with autofocus illuminators (which use infra-red or near-infra-red beams to assist in focusing). Most AF SLR cameras offer interchangeable lenses, letting the photographer choose from a wide variety of zoom and non-zoom options.

CANON EOS ELAN IIE

✓ BEST BUY

Canon had a winner in its original EOS Elan, and with this new model, it has only made a good camera better. In addition to totally new styling, which uses dials rather than buttons, this new Elan IIE has a very sophisticated autofocus system. When you look into the viewfinder, three autofocus areas are clearly outlined. The EOS Elan IIE actually tracks your eye movement to discern the autofocus area that you are looking at, and it doesn't matter whether you are holding the camera for horizontal or vertical photos. Depth-of-field preview is also eye-controlled and is activated when you look at a small diamond in the upper left of the viewfinder. This eye-control system can be switched off and the autofocus area selected manually by the photographer. The advanced, six-zone evaluative metering system is linked to the autofocus so that exposure emphasis is placed on the point of focus. The camera also offers partial (semi-spot) and center-weighted metering. Major settings are selected by turning the large command dial to the desired mode: portrait, landscape, close-up, sports, and full program (depicted by pictorial icons) or program, aperture priority, shutter priority, depth-of-field program, and manual (represented by letters). The exclusive Canon depth-of-field program lets the photographer choose the zone of sharpness in the photo. This model also includes manual film-speed setting, automatic exposure bracketing, exposure compensation, and multiple (up to nine) exposures. Its drive belts make the EOS Elan IIE one of the quietest cameras available. The built-in flash uses TTL exposure and has a red-eye reduction light. This model can be set from ISO-25 to ISO-5000 automatically with DX-coded film, or you can set it manually from ISO-6 to ISO-6400.

Warranty: 1 year, parts and labor.

Manufacturer's Suggested Retail Price: $800

Approximate Low Price: $590

CANON EOS REBEL G

✓ **BEST BUY**

The Canon EOS Rebel G, which offers many of the features of the Canon EOS Elan IIE, accepts all Canon EF lenses and most EOS accessories. By leaving out eye-control of the autofocus and custom functions and streamlining some other features, Canon is able to offer this camera at a very attractive price. The most important difference is that the Rebel G has a simpler, three-point autofocus sensor system that covers a broad area in the center of the viewfinder. The active sensor can be selected automatically by the camera or manually by the photographer. Other differences include a simplified light meter with six-segment metering and the use of a lightweight plastic prism—instead of glass—in the viewfinder system. Unlike other cameras using such hollow prisms, the viewfinder in the Rebel G is just as bright as in the Elan IIE. Using a hollow plastic prism reduces the camera's weight by almost 2 ounces, helping to make it the lightest AF SLR camera with flash. This camera also features partial (semi-spot) metering, automatic bracketing, an oversized LCD display located on top of the camera for easy reading, exposure compensation, a built-in flash, and a red-eye reduction light. The standard Canon hot shoe found on this model allows you to use any Canon-dedicated flash unit. Flash metering uses a three-zone system linked to the autofocusing sensors so that proper flash exposure favors the subject, and the Rebel G works with Canon's E-TTL flash metering when used with the appropriate Canon flash. The autofocus beeper may be switched off in all modes if desired. The exposure modes available include portrait, landscape, close-up, sports, fully automatic (accessed by turning the command dial to pictorial icons), shutter priority, aperture priority, program, depth-of-field program, and manual (accessed by setting the command dial to abbreviations). Along with the automatic DX system, which sets film speeds from ISO-25 to ISO-5000, the camera offers manual ISO setting from ISO-6 to ISO-6400.

Warranty: 1 year, parts and labor.

Manufacturer's Suggested Retail Price: $400 (body only); $610 (with 35 to 80mm zoom lens)

Approximate Low Price: Not available

OLYMPUS IS-3 ZOOM LENS REFLEX

Recommended

The Olympus IS-3 is an example of a rather new breed of camera—the true SLR with a permanently attached zoom lens. The unique shape of the IS-3 fits nicely in your hands; it's comfortable to hold and use for extended periods of time. While many photographers need an SLR with interchangeable lenses, many others will find that the focal length range of the 35 to 180mm f/4.5 to 5.6 lens on this camera is all they will ever need. Wide-angle (converts to 28mm wide angle), telephoto (converts to 300mm maximum), and macro (focuses down to half life-size) converters are available as accessories to make the lens more versatile. It focuses as close as 3.9 feet in normal mode and 2 feet in macro mode. The camera has four program modes: standard, sports, portrait, and night scene. It also offers aperture priority, shutter priority, and manual modes. The built-in flash features two flash tubes to provide proper flash exposure at a variety of distances, and red-eye reduction. Films from ISO-25 to ISO-5000 will automatically set the film speed by means of DX coding. While there is no manual ISO input (which is rarely needed these days), the exposure compensation's broad range of +4 to -4 EV somewhat makes up for this. The IS-3 also comes with motorized film advance (up to 2 frames per second) and rewind, double exposure, and power manual focus. Normally, the light meter uses the Olympus ESP fuzzy logic system to compute exposure, but center-weighted and spot metering are also easy to set if you need them. If the built-in flash isn't powerful enough, you can purchase an accessory G40 flash unit. The Olympus IS-3 is an unusual camera, combining ease of operation, convenient handling, and a high-quality zoom lens in a compact package.

Warranty: 1 year, parts and labor worldwide.

Manufacturer's Suggested Retail Price: $1,020

Approximate Low Price: $620

PENTAX ZX-5

Recommended

The Pentax ZX-5 is one of the lightest SLR cameras and has most of the features found on much more expensive professional cameras. The ZX-5's lighter weight is achieved through the use of polycarbonate in the body. This Pentax model sports a sleek and functional design. The camera offers fully programmed autoexposure, aperture priority, shutter priority, and full-manual operation. Three sensors in the viewfinder control autofocusing, but the user can manually select the central sensor when desired. Light metering is done by a six-segment evaluative metering system, but the camera also has spot metering and center-weighted metering for special applications. The built-in pop-up flash has red-eye reduction, and the motorized film advance lets you shoot at up to two frames per second. The DX system automatically senses and sets film speeds from ISO-25 to ISO-5000, and manual ISO setting is also possible on a range from ISO-6 to ISO-6400. All operating modes and other information are displayed on a large LCD panel on top of the camera. The camera has a 12-second self-timer and can accept an optional electronic remote cable.

Warranty: 1 year, parts and labor.

Manufacturer's Suggested Retail Price: $698

Approximate Low Price: $408

35mm AUTOFOCUS CAMERAS

The 35mm leaf-shutter autofocus (AF) camera is popular because it makes it easy to shoot with high-quality 35mm film. An AF camera does more than automatically focus the lens. It also loads the film, advances it after each exposure, and rewinds it at the end of the roll. Many AF cameras come with a sophisticated meter that activates a built-in flash in difficult lighting situations, such as backlighting, to produce a lighting balance between the subject and the background. Dual-lens cameras have both a normal and a moderate telephoto lens. Others have a zoom lens that gives you a variety of focal lengths. Many now have special red-eye reduction features. The ultracompact design trend has come to zoom cameras, and the panorama format has come to the autofocus field.

OLYMPUS INFINITY STYLUS ✔BEST BUY

The Olympus Infinity Stylus has two important advantages: It is very compact, and it takes quality pictures.

Olympus has always been successful in making its cameras small without sacrificing features or quality, and the company has applied all its experience to the Infinity Stylus. The lens is a 35mm f/3.5 lens that focuses to 14 inches for exceptional close-ups. Autofocus is active infrared, and the flash has two auto modes, with one featuring red-eye reduction. The flash can be switched off or kept on for fill flash in bright light. The sliding clamshell design of the protective cover shields the lens when you close it, but it also covers the viewfinder, the autofocus system, and the flash, providing full protection when the camera is pocketed. The Infinity Stylus has full DX capability and accepts films with ISO speeds from 50 to 3200. It also comes with a self-timer. Frame count, mode, and battery condition are displayed on the relatively large LCD panel on top. The chrome shutter release button is comfortable to use, and the camera is powered by one CR123A lithium cell.

Warranty: 1 year, parts and labor.

Manufacturer's Suggested Retail Price: $235

Approximate Low Price: $121

YASHICA T4 SUPER WEATHERPROOF
✔**BEST BUY**

In addition to building cameras under the Yashica name, Kyocera also builds expensive professional cameras under the Contax name in collaboration with Carl Zeiss of Germany, long renowned as one of the world's finest lens makers. The Yashica T4 Super Weatherproof, therefore, comes with a Carl Zeiss Tessar 35mm f/3.5 lens of extremely high-quality. The lens focuses very close (to almost 14 inches), and, combined with the autofocus system, it provides the user with sharp, clear photos. This Yashica model features a protective trapdoor to cover the lens when the camera is switched off, a built-in flash that can be switched off or left on (for outdoor fill flash), and a 10-second self-timer. For distant shots, the autofocus can be turned off, and the camera's focus set to infinity. Film loading, advance, and rewind are motorized and automatic. The weatherproof designation does not mean that this camera can be used underwater, but rain or a splash of water will not harm it. One unique feature of this camera is that it has two viewfinders: The standard one is on the upper back of the camera, and a second waist-level viewfinder is found on top of the camera. The second viewfinder is useful for taking pictures around corners or when holding the camera overhead to shoot above a crowd. This camera is powered by one C123A lithium cell. Overall, the Yashica T4 Super Weatherproof is a versatile, weather-resistant camera with a high-quality lens.

Warranty: 1 year, parts and labor.

Manufacturer's Suggested Retail Price: $352

Approximate Low Price: $203

PENTAX IQ ZOOM 160

Recommended

Pentax is known for the quality of its cameras and lenses, and this new model exemplifies that reputation. As of this writing, the 160mm telephoto capability of the zoom lens offers the greatest magnification of any point-and-shoot camera. The slightly wide 38mm focal length at the other end of the zoom range is adequate for users who do not need an ultrawide-angle lens, and its close focus of 2.6 feet is close enough for most users. The power-driven zoom lens is operated by a large, easily accessible rocker switch positioned conveniently under the right thumb. All operational modes are accessed via a control dial at the top left of the camera. Information is displayed on a large LCD panel on top of the camera, and the panel is automatically illuminated under low-light conditions. The IQ Zoom 160 has fully automatic exposure, plus a night exposure mode and a B setting for long exposures (with or without flash). The flash can be turned off, kept on for outdoor fill flash, or set to fire flash as needed. It also offers redeye reduction. There are three autofocus modes: standard multipoint AF for most applications, spot AF for more control, and an infinity setting for faraway subjects. A switch beside the viewfinder allows you to take panoramic exposures at any point throughout the roll of film, and there's an eyesight compensation dial to the left of the viewfinder. The camera is powered by a single CR123A lithium cell.

Warranty: 1 year, parts and labor.

Manufacturer's Suggested Retail Price: $612

Approximate Low Price: $403

MINOLTA FREEDOM ZOOM EXPLORER

Recommended

The Minolta Freedom Zoom Explorer has an unusual camera design with completely rounded contours. In spite of its unique appearance, this camera fits comfortably in the user's hands, and all controls are conveniently located. On its front, a round cover protects the lens when the camera is not in use. The lens is a 28 to 70mm zoom with autofocus from 1.6 feet to infinity. A close-up mode allows shooting as close as 1.3 feet. In landscape mode, the camera lens is set to infinity, for distance or for shooting through glass. The multibeam autofocus can focus on a subject, even if it is not centered in the viewfinder. The built-in pop-up flash is keyed to focusing distance to prevent overexposure, and the flash has red-eye reduction, fill flash, and flash-off for creative control. Shutter speed is automatically timed and goes to 8 seconds for very dim light. Slow shutter speed and flash can be combined in night mode. The motor drive allows shooting as fast as 1.2 frames per second for action shots. Film with ISO speeds from 25 to 3200 can be used, and DX coding sets film speed automatically. While the Minolta Freedom Zoom Explorer is a distinctively styled camera fitted with many advanced features, it is still easy to use and produces quality photos.

Warranty: 1 year, parts and labor.

Manufacturer's Suggested Retail Price: $308

Approximate Low Price: $217

CANON SURE SHOT Z135

Recommended

Photographers who do most of their pictures in the telephoto range will appreciate the Canon Z135, which is fitted with a 38 to 135 mm zoom lens (f/3.6 to 8.9) that provides a range from slightly wide to medium-telephoto in a very compact package. Although this camera can be set for fully automatic point-and-shoot operation, more advanced users will appreciate the seven different shooting modes it offers: close-up, action, portrait, silent (greatly reduced camera noise), spot (spot metering for backlighted scenes), night (combines red-eye reducing flash and slow shutter speeds), and automatic. You can set modes quickly by turning the large dial on the back of the camera. Autofocus uses three sensors so the subject does not have to be in the center of the frame for proper focus. Exposure compensation allows settings from +1.5 to -1.5 EV. Instead of prefiring the flash for red-eye reduction, this camera uses a bright krypton light that comes on just prior to flash exposure (this is a better method for preventing red-eye). The automatic daylight fill flash is switched on by the metering system as needed. All operating indications are shown on a large LCD panel on the back of the camera. An optional infrared remote control unit is included with this camera. The Z135 has a date-imprinting capability, and it can also imprint phrases such as "Thank You," "Happy Birthday," "Congratulations," or "Season's Greetings" on the photos for special occasions.

Warranty: 1 year, parts and labor.

Manufacturer's Suggested Retail Price: $500

Approximate Low Price: $315

VIVITAR A35 SPLASH PROOF

Budget Buy

The Vivitar A35 Splash Proof is a simple, compact camera with uncomplicated operation. It is well-sealed against water, so a splash of water will not damage it. Its 35mm f/5.6 lens is set for sharp photos from 4 feet to infinity, and it can use films with an ISO from 100 to 400. Film loading and advance are automatic, and the built-in flash features red-eye reduction. This Vivitar model is the ideal carry-around camera for inclement weather, the beach, boating, water sports, and other outdoor activities.

Warranty: 1 year, parts and labor.

Manufacturer's Suggested Retail Price: $100

Approximate Low Price: $58

35mm COMPACT CAMERAS

The 35mm compact is a relatively inexpensive camera with a fixed lens. Many 35mm compact cameras are point-and-shoot cameras with simple exposure systems designed for color negative film. Some compacts are more versatile and take high-quality photographs; these cameras demand more input from the photographer than point-and-shoot and autofocus compacts, but they produce excellent results.

KONICA U-MINI

✓BEST BUY

The Konica U-Mini camera is easily portable since it will conveniently slip into small pockets. The fixed focus lens produces sharp images from about 3 feet to infinity, so there is no need for autofocus. The lens is a Konica 28mm f/6.7, which covers a relatively wide angle. The U-Mini's built-in flash has red-eye reduction and is automatically switched on when the light level drops too low. With the camera's DX sensor, it can set itself for the proper ISO speed, but it is limited to film speeds of 100, 200, and 400. A switch under the lens closes the protective cover and turns the camera off. A small LCD panel on top shows the number of exposures taken, the flash-ready signal, and battery life. This camera comes in black and several other stylish colors and is powered by one CR123A lithium cell.

Warranty: 1 year, limited.

Manufacturer's Suggested Retail Price: $76

Approximate Low Price: $60

CANON SURE SHOT OWL

Recommended

The first thing that catches your attention about the Canon Sure Shot Owl is its big viewfinder. This viewfinder is about three times the size of those on most cameras, which makes it easier to use—especially for eyeglass wearers. This camera has three-step autofocus with close focus to 2.6 feet. Even though the fully programmed autoexposure is the

Owl's only exposure mode, it is suitable for most subjects. The built-in flash can be switched off when it's not in use, and it offers red-eye reduction. The flash is good up to 11.1 feet with ISO-100 and ISO-200 film and up to 22.3 feet with ISO-400 film. Film loading and film advance are automatic and very quiet. The protective lens cover also functions as the camera's on/off switch. The Canon Sure Shot Owl is an excellent, attractively priced small camera with an unusually good viewfinder.

Warranty: 1 year, parts and labor.

Manufacturer's Suggested Retail Price: $125

Approximate Low Price: $83

YASHICA EXPRESSION AF PLUS

Recommended

The Yashica Expression AF Plus is a basic, inexpensive point-and-shoot camera with a good-quality lens, an active infrared autofocus system, and motorized film advance and rewind. The camera uses film with ISO speeds of 100, 200, 400, and 1000. The built-in flash features red-eye reduction and can be manually turned on with a switch on the front of the camera whenever outdoor fill flash is desired. A sliding cover protects the lens when the camera is not in use and shuts the camera off when it is closed to prevent accidental exposures. The lens is a 34mm f/4.5 coated optical glass lens. The camera is powered by two AA alkaline cells. Focusing is as close as 4 feet. The camera is sold in a kit, which includes a carrying case, a strap, a roll of film, and batteries. While not loaded with features, the Expression AF Plus is still capable of taking very good photos.

Warranty: 1 year, parts and labor.

Manufacturer's Suggested Retail Price: $151

Approximate Low Price: $79

KODAK CAMEO MOTOR EX

Budget Buy

The Kodak Cameo Motor EX camera is a simple, focus-free compact camera suitable for general photography. The lens is factory adjusted to produce sharp photos from

4 feet to infinity. The built-in flash also acts as a protective lens cover when it is folded down. The camera has automatic DX film-speed sensing and can accept films of ISO 100, 200, 400, and 1000. Camera operation is powered by two AAA cells, which advance the film automatically after each photo. Flash range is from 4 feet up to a maximum of 35 feet with ISO-1000 film. The Cameo Motor EX also has an automatic fill flash mode and a 10-second self-timer. Mode, frame number, low battery, flash charging, and indicators for fill flash, self-timer, and midroll rewind are indicated on an LCD panel on top of the camera. Overall, the Cameo Motor EX is a nice, practical snapshot camera with an attractive price.

Warranty: 1 year, full.

Manufacturer's Suggested Retail Price: $80

Approximate Low Price: $52

24mm ADVANCED PHOTO SYSTEM (APS) CAMERAS

The Advanced Photo System (APS) is a new photographic system jointly developed by Kodak, Fuji, Canon, Nikon, and Minolta. The heart of this system is the new film and cassette. The new film is 24mm wide instead of the more common 35mm, and the new cassette is made completely of molded plastic. No film protrudes from the cassette, and it is thrust out by a camera mechanism when the film is loaded. This makes film loading easier and foolproof. The other trick up the APS sleeve is the fact that this new film communicates with both the camera and the processing machinery in two new ways. First of all, the film is completely coated with a transparent magnetic coating, and many APS cameras can write to this magnetic coating just like a tape recorder to store important information such as lighting conditions, desired print format, camera orientation (horizontal or vertical), number of prints desired from each frame, date and time, and more. Additionally, many simpler APS cameras use Fat Optical Bits (FOB), information recorded optically onto the film to provide input data to the processing machinery. This technology allows the printing machinery to automatically compensate for photographic conditions, as well as to retrieve information and print the desired print format (two standard sizes and panoramic) and number of prints. Date and time can be printed on the backs of the prints as well. Theoretically, this should allow APS to produce better photos than 35mm, but the smaller negative size somewhat counterbalances this. Most observers regard APS prints as equal to or not quite as good as 35mm prints. Some APS cameras allow Mid Roll Interchange (MRI) without the loss of any photos or danger of double exposure, so you can switch from one type of film to another at any time. Since APS is still very new and cameras are just becoming available, it is premature to judge the success of this system.

MINOLTA VECTIS S-1 SLR

✔ **BEST BUY**

The Minolta Vectis S-1 is a chunky little camera, smaller than any 35mm SLR and lacking the characteristic 35mm SLR "prism hump." The viewfinder eyepiece is set at the far left on the back of the camera, which is another variation on the usual SLR design. This camera takes its own set of lenses and does not accept lenses designed for Minolta's 35mm cameras. A built-in pop-up flash is on the top of the camera, and there's a Minolta-type hot shoe at the right side of the camera top for the new Vectis SF-1 flash, designed specifically for this camera. Pressing a large gray button under the viewfinder eyepiece turns the camera on and activates the large LCD panel on the back. The mode button then allows you to set the main modes: full-auto, aperture priority, shutter priority, and manual. A control dial on the back allows access to special subject modes: portrait, scenic, close-up, action, and night portrait. Spot metering, flash mode, and exposure compensation are available via controls on the back of the camera. The camera allows you to print date and time information on the front, back, or both sides of the photos as well as a selection of titles in 12 languages. Another added benefit of this model is that it is splashproof, allowing the user to shoot pictures in the rain or near water without damaging the camera. The lenses that are initially available include several zoom lenses (22 to 80mm, 28 to 56mm, 56 to 170mm, and 80 to 240mm) and a 50mm macro lens. The Vectis S-1 is a true system compact SLR camera with all the capabilities of a high-class 35mm SLR.

Warranty: 1 year, parts and labor.

Manufacturer's Suggested Retail Price: $590 (body only); $786 (full kit, including lens, film, and battery)

Approximate Low Price: $460

CANON ELPH

The Canon ELPH, with its stainless steel case **✔BEST BUY** and elegant design, looks as though it would be more at home in a jewelry case than a camera case. Underneath the striking exterior is a fully functional compact camera with a 24 to 48mm zoom lens—all in a body about the size of a pack of cigarettes. The ELPH features a pop-up electronic flash with red-eye reduction and several flash modes, including auto-flash, flash on/flash off, and slow synchro. This camera can be set to imprint the date or time on the photo's front or back or both, and it can also imprint one of five titles in any of six languages. Since date/time/title information is recorded magnetically rather than optically, the actual imprinting onto your photos depends on the capabilities of the processing lab you use. All camera settings are indicated on an LCD panel located on top of the camera. The settings can be adjusted using the small buttons next to the panel; a plastic pin attached to the camera strap is provided to help you press the small buttons. The camera has a self-timer, and it has a receiver on the front for use with the optional Canon RC-5 infrared remote control unit. Overall, the Canon ELPH is a stylish and remarkably small SLR camera with a full array of advanced features to produce quality photos.

Warranty: 1 year, parts and labor.

Manufacturer's Suggested Retail Price: $420

Approximate Low Price: $320

FUJI ENDEAVOR 300 ZOOM

Recommended

Among the models Fuji initially introduced, the Endeavor 300 Zoom is the company's top APS point-and-shoot camera. The Endeavor 300 Zoom features a 30 to 90mm zoom lens, which is approximately a normal to short telephoto equivalent in the APS format. This camera offers autofocus, fully programmed operation, and built-in flash with the red-eye reduction feature. It also offers a distant scenery (infinity focus) mode and a night mode for combining flash with long shutter speeds. Automatic fill flash is always provided when the camera senses the need, but this function can be shut off. Date and time information can be imprinted on the front of the photo, the back of the photo, or both. A sliding tab under the viewfinder eyepiece allows for setting the eyesight compensation. The Endeavor 300 Zoom is a versatile compact camera that can slip into most pockets for easy portability.

Warranty: 1 year, parts and labor.

Manufacturer's Suggested Retail Price: $540

Approximate Low Price: $363

KODAK ADVANTIX 3700IX

Budget Buy

The Kodak Advantix 3700ix is a good introductory camera for the APS system. It has a 24mm f/3.6 Kodak Ekton lens, which is a slightly wide angle on APS. The camera uses a 200-zone auto focus system to assure accuracy on a focusing range from 2 feet to infinity. Film with ISO speeds of 25, 50, 100, 200, 400, 800, and 1600 can be used with fully automatic film-speed setting. The built-in flash folds down to act as a protective cover for the lens and viewfinder. When this flash is folded down, the camera turns itself off automatically if it is not used within approximately 1 minute. Lifting this lens-cover/flash turns the camera on and charges the flash. The flash automatically fires when needed and will automatically provide outdoor fill flash when the camera detects the need for it. Manual setting of full-time fill flash and flash off is also possible. The flash has a range up to 16 feet with ISO-200 film. A self-timer is also included so the photographer can be included in the picture. Date and time imprinting on the back of the photos is featured on this model (subject to the capabilities of your film processing lab). The Advantix 3700ix is a simple camera with an advanced design, and it makes an excellent go-anywhere pocket camera.

Warranty: 1 year.

Manufacturer's Suggested Retail Price: $195

Approximate Low Price: $156

INSTANT-PRINT CAMERAS

Instant-print cameras are available only from Polaroid in the United States. Consumer models produce color prints that self-develop within a few minutes. Although the cost per print is higher than with 35mm and APS, these cameras offer the advantage of providing immediate gratification for those who can't wait to see the pictures they've taken.

POLAROID CAPTIVA SLR/CAPTIVA DATE+ ✔**BEST BUY**

The Polaroid Captiva SLR is an instant-picture camera with true SLR viewing, which means that you are actually looking through the taking lens when you look into the viewfinder. This allows more precise framing of your scene than you can manage with other Polaroid cameras. For carrying, the Captiva SLR also folds into a compact package. This camera uses only Captiva 95 film. As each photo is taken, the camera motor moves it into a picture storage compartment on the camera back, where it develops. A full pack of ten photos can be stored for removal later, so there is no concern about losing photos. The camera uses optical autofocus for accurate photos from 2 feet to infinity, and it produces photos with a $2\frac{7}{8} \times 2\frac{1}{8}$-inch image area. It also comes with a 12-second self-timer and a lighten/darken control for adjusting photos under unusual lighting conditions or just to suit your personal preferences. The built-in flash has a range of up to 10 feet. There are two versions of the Captiva SLR: the standard model and the Captiva Date+. The more expensive Captiva Date+ has a higher quality optical glass lens with a coated glass front element. It has the capability to record date and time information on the photos, and it has a cordless infrared remote control unit. Both models are easy to use and produce quality pictures.

Warranty: 1 year, parts and labor.

Manufacturer's Suggested Retail Price: $159 (Standard Captiva SLR); $209 (Captiva Date+)

Approximate Low Price: $93 (Standard Captiva SLR)

POLAROID SPECTRA AF

Recommended

The Polaroid Spectra AF is a versatile instant-print camera with many features that give you both image control and creative control. A three-element lens produces sharp, colorful prints with an image area that measures $3\frac{5}{8}\times2\frac{7}{8}$ inches. The Spectra AF is an autofocus camera with the capability to focus as close as 2 feet. The autofocus can be switched off for shooting photos at infinity or through windows at outdoor scenes. On the back of the camera you'll find the LCD information panel, system control buttons, and flash-status LEDs. Control buttons let you change modes, but with this camera most photos will be taken in the standard auto-flash mode. In this mode, the camera determines whether the flash is needed and automatically activates it if it is. Flash range is from 2 to 15 feet, and viewfinder indicators let you know when you are outside that range. Audible signals indicate focus confirmation, self-timer countdown, and an empty film pack. Overall, the Spectra AF is a fine instant-print camera for general use.

Warranty: 5 years.

Manufacturer's Suggested Retail Price: $166

Approximate Low Price: $100

POLAROID ONESTEP AUTOFOCUS/ ONESTEP TALKING CAMERA

Budget Buy

The Polaroid OneStep AutoFocus and the OneStep Talking Camera are almost identical except that the talking camera can record up to 8 seconds of sound segments and then play them back just before the picture is taken. This allows you to have the camera say, "Smile," "Say Cheese," or whatever photographic phrase you use to produce a smile from your photo subjects. While it doesn't take better pictures than the AutoFocus version, this camera is a lot of fun to use—particularly for children. Both models are simple instant-print cameras that use Polaroid 600 high-definition film. The Auto-Focus model has replaced the earlier fixed focus model for greater versatility and has automatic focus from 2 feet to infinity. The built-in flash has a range of 10 feet, which is adequate for most purposes. In normal operation, the flash always fires, but it can be switched off when desired. The OneStep Auto-Focus and OneStep Talking Camera are simple, low-priced models that make nice introductory cameras for beginning photographers.

Warranty: 1 year, parts and labor.

Manufacturer's Suggested Retail Price: $60 (AutoFocus); $50 (Talking)

Approximate Low Price: $57 (AutoFocus); $42 (Talking)

TELEPHONES AND ANSWERING MACHINES

Technological developments in the telephone industry continue to expand rapidly. Cellular advancements make carrying "cell" phones more convenient for everyday use. The number of features on basic and feature phones keeps growing as well: Mute buttons, speakerphones, call screening, last number redial, and phone-number memory have made cellular, portable, and feature models more attractive and easier to use. Answering machines, too, have improved greatly in the last year. Many models use digital technology so they can double as both a telephone and answering machine to provide what amounts to a communications center in your home. Many cellular phone companies duplicate these services so you can remain in touch from your car.

Technology isn't the only new development in the telephone industry. Last year, corporation officials split off AT&T's product division and folded its consumer computer division. The segment of AT&T that produced the telephone and answering machine products became known as Lucent Technologies. Lucent's products now carry a new label, but they are the same products previously marketed by AT&T. Some of these products are reviewed in this chapter.

Telephone Features

Automatic Last Number Redial: If the last number called was busy, the phone keeps redialing until a preset number of attempts is reached. The redial efforts continue every 45 or 60 seconds until a connection occurs.

Flash: This works like a switch hook and is used with customer-calling services like call waiting and conference calling. It sends a half-second signal through the line to activate these services.

Hearing-Aid Compatible: These telephones provide distortion-free conversation for people who wear hearing aids. Most telephones have this feature.

Last-Number Redial: The last number dialed is temporarily stored in the phone's memory so it can be redialed by pushing one or two buttons.

Mute: This is similar to a hold button. By pressing the mute button, you can have a conversation in the room without being heard by the person on the other end of the line.

Pause: This inserts a pause between numbers in the memory-dialing sequence to allow for switchboard delays encountered by long-distance phone equipment.

Speakerphone: A button on the base of the phone activates a microphone and speaker so you can make and receive calls without picking up the handset.

Speed-Dialing Memory: Phone numbers are stored so they can be dialed by pushing one or two buttons. Base models store ten or more numbers, while feature phones can keep up to 100 numbers.

Best Buys '97

Our Best Buy, Recommended, and Budget Buy choices follow. We have listed our reviews for telephones by category. Our answering machine reviews are found after the telephone reviews. Within each category the unit we consider the best of the Best Buys is listed first, followed by our second choice, and so on. Remember that a Best Buy, Recommended, or Budget Buy designation applies only to the model listed. It does not necessarily apply to other models made by the same manufacturer or to an entire product line.

FEATURE TELEPHONES

LUCENT TECHNOLOGIES 882

✔**BEST BUY**

The Lucent 882 is a full-featured, two-line telephone system that comes packed with features designed to serve an office rather than a household. Billed as a Personal

Information Center, or PIC, the 882 has a speakerphone and a large LCD display screen that shows eight lines by 24 characters. The unit combines the functions of a memory dialer and an electronic address book capable of storing up to 200 names and contact information with four separate telephone numbers, addresses, and birth dates for each entry. The 882 automatically alphabetizes names in up to eight separate directories with access reserved for multiple users. Numbers shown on the display screen can be auto dialed from the display. Users program their entries on a typewriter-style keyboard. A reminder directory has three main features: It records up to 50 active reminders, it provides visual and audible notes on calendar appointments, and it stores calendar notes for retrieval in any given month. The two-line phone allows for a distinctive ring capability, three-way conferencing, and caller ID for each line. It also lets users pick up an incoming call or make a call without pre-selecting an available line.

Warranty: 1 year, limited.

Manufacturer's Suggested Retail Price: $200

Approximate Low Price: $190

PANASONIC KX-T3175   ✔ BEST BUY

The Panasonic KX-T3175 is an ideal feature phone for busy households or a home office. A two-line speakerphone provides hands-free conversations. Each line has a separate ringer for fast line identification. A 12-digit LCD readout window displays a clock, the number dialed, the duration of the call, and the call's status. The KX-T3175 has 24 one-touch automatic-dialing stations for quick access to frequently called numbers. Other features include a hold button for each line and two line-selector buttons. This model also provides three-way conferencing capability by letting users link two separate lines together for conversations with all three parties.

Warranty: 1 year, parts and labor.

Manufacturer's Suggested Retail Price: $120

Approximate Low Price: $89

GENERAL ELECTRIC 2-9420
Recommended

The GE 2-9420 is a two-line phone with 12-number memory. This gives users three one-touch emergency dialing locations plus nine other speed-dial stations. Though not as feature heavy as other two-line telephones, this model delivers good audio quality and several useful features. This unit has a conference call function, dual ringer controls, line status lights, a hold button for each line, and pause and flash functions. The 2-9420 can be mounted on a wall or placed on a desk or table. This model works well in a home setting where users want one line for voice calls and a second line for occasional fax machine or modem use. It is also suitable for use in a small office where basic phone features are needed.

Warranty: 2 years, limited.

Manufacturer's Suggested Retail Price: $60

Approximate Low Price: $40

SOUTHWESTERN BELL FM855
Budget Buy

These days, features in most phones have become fairly standard. Still, the Southwestern Bell FM855 has an impressive list of qualities that make using the phone quick and easy. One of its most useful features is the speakerphone. With the push of a button, users can carry on a conversation without holding the handset. This convenient function comes in handy when the phone is used in the kitchen or in a small office. Pressing the speakerphone button again shuts off the speaker and diverts the incoming call to the handset earpiece. The FM855 has three priority speed-dial settings and ten-number storage. Both the ringer and the speaker have volume controls. Other features include a last-number redial, flash (for call waiting), and a hold button to shut off the microphone or the mouthpiece temporarily. This model is also hearing-aid compatible and can be mounted on a desk or wall.

Warranty: 1 year, limited.

Manufacturer's Suggested Retail Price: $35

Approximate Low Price: $35

CORDLESS TELEPHONES

Think of cordless phones as portable extension phones. They keep you from missing calls when you are outside or away from an extension phone. In addition to mobility, today's cordless phones offer more features than ever before. They use a special radio for transmissions between base and handset, and the latest technology has produced excellent sound quality. Multichannel scanning lets your phone send and receive on various frequencies so your conversations are clearer. Some models even let you select high or low channels to improve performance as you move about the house. New noise reduction features help lessen interference and improve reception. Recently, the Federal Communications Commission authorized the use of 25 different channels in the frequency range used by cordless phones. (Previously, the maximum number of channels was ten.) This is a vast improvement over earlier models because more channels mean clearer reception.

When shopping for a cordless phone, be sure to consider other options besides voice clarity. Check how long battery charges last. A cordless phone that has to be frequently recharged isn't much of a convenience. Two other important features to consider are intercom and paging. Intercom allows you to speak between the base and the handset, while paging lets you send a tone signal between base and handset. The paging function comes in handy when you have to locate a misplaced handset.

SHARP CL-355   ✓**BEST BUY**

The Sharp CL-355 is a 25-channel cordless phone. It sports dual speakerphones and dual keypads so the handset and the base unit can each be used as separate phones serving the same number. Of course, the speakerphone in the base unit allows for hands-free talking. But that functionality is extended to the handset as well with the second speakerphone. This combination also gives users a powerful hands-free intercom system. A feature absent from most cordless phones but included on the CL-355 is an illuminated keypad. This provides easy dialing in low-level lighting for both the handset and the base unit. Another top-line feature is the three-way mounting capability. The base unit can be mounted on a wall or placed on a tabletop. With either mounting option, the handset sits securely with the keypad facing either up or down as well as standing vertically and independent of the base unit. The battery can be fully charged in 3 hours and has a 14-day standby battery life. The CL-355 holds up to ten auto-dial numbers in memory.

Warranty: 1 year, parts and labor.

Manufacturer's Suggested Retail Price: $209

Approximate Low Price: $130

LUCENT TECHNOLOGIES 5860

Recommended

The Lucent Technologies 5860 is one of the first 25-channel cordless phones to use the expanded frequencies permitted by the federal government. The sound quality is as good as a corded phone's. This is partly due to the expanded frequency range that eliminates much of the static and interference often found in ten-channel models. This model automatically selects a free and clear channel every time a call is initiated or received. Both the antenna and the battery can be easily replaced. The 5860 has a 20-number dialing memory for storing frequently called phone numbers. It also has a digital security system that helps prevent unauthorized access. This model has a two-way intercom feature that lets users operate the base and handheld units as pagers or intercoms at varying distances, depending on the surroundings. The 5860 has a multifunction LCD display in the handset to show the phone number being dialed and to view the phone numbers stored in memory.

Warranty: 1 year, limited.

Manufacturer's Suggested Retail Price: $130

Approximate Low Price: $107

SONY SPP-Q110

Recommended

The Sony SPP-Q110 is a cordless 25-channel phone with extras that make it an excellent choice for home or office use. The unit automatically scans for a clear channel, but this is only one tool responsible for clear, static-free conversations. A noise reduction system automatically filters out background noise. Several other features make the SPP-Q110 a superior product. Its 21-day battery standby time allows for longer intervals between charging, and a battery strength indicator shows when the battery power is running low. A related feature saves battery consumption when the handheld unit is off the charger but not in use. A signal strength indicator also warns users when the handset is out of usable range from the base unit. This model has a paging feature that sends a beep from the base unit to the handset to signal another person, but there is no intercom function. The SPP-Q110 turns on when any button is pressed and redials the last number called with a single touch. It also has ten speed-dialing locations. This model can be placed on a flat surface or mounted on a wall.

Warranty: 1 year, parts and labor.

Manufacturer's Suggested Retail Price: $90

Approximate Low Price: $62

LUCENT TECHNOLOGIES 5830

Recommended

The Lucent Technologies 5830 25-channel cordless phone is almost identical to the Lucent 5860, except it does not have the multifunction LCD screen and the two-way page and intercom features. The sound quality is as good as the 5860, and the unit automatically selects a free and clear channel every time a call is initiated or received. Both the antenna and the battery can be easily replaced. The 5830 also has a 20-number dialing memory for storing frequently called phone numbers. Although the 5860's LCD is a nice feature, users can easily live without it if price is an issue. Instead of scrolling through a directory of stored numbers on the screen, users enter the one- or two-digit number on the keypad for the desired speed-dial number. The 5830 also has a digital security system that helps prevent unauthorized access. Other features include a handset locator, mute button, and lighted dial.

Warranty: 1 year, limited.

Manufacturer's Suggested Retail Price: $100

Approximate Low Price: $90

CELLULAR TELEPHONES

Cellular phones have become enormously popular since their introduction in 1983. Once a status symbol for business executives and professionals, cellular phones are now the personal communication device of busy family members, allowing them to stay in touch while commuting or traveling. Cellular phones are so popular that they have invaded American homes at a faster pace than any other consumer electronic product, including color TVs and VCRs. There are more than ten million users in the United States, and the cellular-phone market continues to grow by thousands every day.

Pricing varies widely. Near major cities, consumers often have a choice of carrier. The Federal Communications Commission, which regulates cellular services, allocates cellular licenses to two carriers in each major metro area. As competition expands, you will probably find an independent carrier and cellular service provided by your regional phone company. Approximate retail and low prices have not been included in this section because, as it so often happens, pricing depends on available service. Many cellular companies offer a number of free calling hours and other discounts. Fees are billed monthly. A typical service fee includes the company's service charge plus toll calls. You will pay for air time on calls you originate as well as on ones you receive.

One of the biggest concerns about using cellular phones is the issue of security. Eavesdropping can occur because radio-frequency scanners can pick up your conversations. Cellular-phone users should be careful about giving out information—credit card and phone numbers, addresses, and details about long absences from home could fall into the wrong hands. To improve security, consider buying a digital phone, which makes it impossible for scanner operators to listen in. The drawback here is that digital phone technology is relatively new, making digital models costlier than analog units.

A word to the wise: There's potential danger in using any cellular phone while driving a motor vehicle. It's easy to become distracted while engaged in a phone conversation.

MITSUBISHI AH-5000

✔ **BEST BUY**

The Mitsubishi AH-5000 is one of the smallest, lightest cellular phones available. It weighs 6.5 ounces with its slimline battery and 7.7 ounces with the extended-life battery. Only 6.1 inches long and 2 inches wide, it's barely an inch longer than a flip phone and tiny enough to fit in a pocket. The slimline battery version gives 60 minutes of talk time and 12 hours of reserve time; the extended battery provides 130 minutes of talk time with 28 hours of reserve time. It has a 20-character LCD display with an electronic function menu. Memory features include 99 speed-dial locations, a one-touch dialing button, and ten private memory locations. A handy feature is the ability to program the user's home area code to stored seven-digit numbers for easier dialing from roam areas. An automatic answer feature beeps and saves numbers that the caller keys in. The AH-5000 also offers call timing, voice mute button, selectable ring tone, and a pager mode with time stamp.

Warranty: 3 years, limited.

MOTOROLA MC480

✔ **BEST BUY**

The Motorola MC480 is a classic mobile or car phone, weighing 3.1 pounds (without the battery). It has large buttons for safe, easy operation while driving. Its large, seven-character LCD display is plainly visible from the front seat or the dashboard. Operating this panel is made even easier with the menu system, which presents features in a list on the display screen. Another use for the large display is the ability to attach a seven-character name to a phone number. This lets users locate and dial a number by scrolling through a list of names. The MC480 gives one-touch handling with eight speed-dial locations and 102 memory locations. With the hands-free feature, simply hang up the handset and speak into the microphone. The automatic answer feature answers the phone after two rings. This model has several other features designed for efficient, safe operation while driving.

Warranty: 3 years.

MITSUBISHI AT-1000

Recommended

The AT-1000 by Mitsubishi delivers a clear signal and high-quality portability. This small-size phone weighs only 2.06 pounds (including the lightweight battery), making it easy to carry around. The slim handset holds the backlit keypad in a special design that keeps hands from accidentally pressing keys during use. The LCD is part of the handset and displays two 14-digit lines. To eliminate a separate, bulky battery pack, the AT-1000 has an optional battery pack that fits into the handset. This model has 114 total memory locations including 99 alphanumeric memory locations, two one-touch dial locations, and ten private locations. The battery pack provides 60 minutes of talk time and 8 hours of standby time. Convenience features include automatic and any-key answer, escalating ringer, voice muting, and a call timer. The AT-1000 lets users conserve battery power by selecting the power output. In strong reception areas, users can operate the phone at 0.6 watts. In less favorable reception areas, users can select 1.2 watts. When connected to the car battery via an optional cigarette lighter adapter, the unit operates at 3 watts and recharges the batteries.

Warranty: 3 years, limited.

ERICSSON AH-320

Recommended

Ericsson makes cellular phones under its own name and also for the General Electric cellular phone line. The Ericsson AH-320 is a featherweight model that you can easily carry in a pocket or purse. The flip design contributes to the phone's compact size; the mouthpiece portion of the phone folds closed over the number pad. With the slimline battery, talk time is 45 minutes with up to 14 hours of standby time. The medium-capacity battery provides 110 minutes of talk time and has up to 27 hours of standby time. The AH-320 weighs 8.7 ounces with this standard battery. The high-capacity battery provides 120 minutes of talk time with up to 28 hours of standby time. With this battery, the unit weight increases to 9.4 ounces. The display window shows 20 characters. The memory holds 109 speed-dialing numbers with a ten-number secured memory and memory-scrolling features. Other convenient features on the Ericsson AH-320 include a five-number scratchpad, four call timers, an easy-to-use menu, and alphanumeric name tagging.

Warranty: 1 year, manufacturer defects.

MITSUBISHI AH-129

Recommended

The Mitsubishi AH-129 is a new, slim 8.3-ounce portable telephone. Its simple operation makes it a good choice for first-time cellular phone buyers, and it has a built-in user's manual that provides step-by-step directions on all advanced features. It has a large, two-line 14-digit LCD backlit display and oversized send and end keys. An optional hands-free headset makes the AH-129 a good alternative to standard mobile phones for safe use while driving. This model's battery offers 105 minutes of talk time with 14 hours of standby time. It comes with a built-in rapid recharger that works with the AC adapter or optional cigarette lighter adapter to charge the battery in 2 hours or less. The AH-129 also has an advanced fraud prevention circuit built in. This feature automatically verifies that the phone is legitimate and has not been cloned. Plus, there are four function levels to restrict use of the phone. There are 39 alphanumeric speed-dial memory numbers for frequently called numbers, including nine one-touch dialing locations and 11-character name tags for phone numbers. The AH-129 also has an automatic answer function that answers a call after 10 seconds.

Warranty: 1 year, limited.

SONY CM-H333

The Sony CM-H333 is a lightweight trans- **Recommended**
portable cellular telephone that is dependable and easy to use.
A slide-up ear piece serves as a send/end key and extends the
phone's length. When in the end or off position, the earpiece
closes over the keypad and prevents the user from accidentally
hitting the on/off button. The keypad lights, and pressing any
key answers an incoming call. An optional hands-free kit automatically answers the phone after two rings. The CM-H333 has
two one-touch dialing keys and nine speed-dial memory settings. The standard battery provides 90 minutes of talk time or
24 hours of standby time. It takes 10 hours to fully charge the
battery or 1.5 hours of rapid charging. The LCD window displays the signal strength, the phone's own telephone number,
and the battery level.

Warranty: 90 days.

ANSWERING MACHINES

Answering machines are more of a necessity than a luxury
these days. In the home, they provide a simple and inexpensive way to screen calls, and they also keep family and friends
in touch. Although the business world is increasingly relying on
computerized voice mail, answering machines are still preferred
by many home and small businesses.

Some answering machines use digital technology to record
messages on a voice chip, but others continue to rely on one
or two audio tapes to record outgoing and incoming messages. One major drawback to machines with digital storage
is the recording time: Voice chips allow fewer and shorter
messages.

Consider your needs in selecting an answering machine.
Smaller and cheaper machines designed for a low volume of
calls put outgoing and incoming messages on a single audio
tape. This tape must be changed occasionally, as wear and tear
can hurt voice quality. Integrated answering machines do double duty as telephones and message centers. These units are

equipped with a handset and are ideal when phone jacks are in short supply.

Features and Terminology

Announce Only: You set the machine to deliver an outgoing message only. This setting does not allow recording of incoming messages. It's useful for a business wishing to announce hours of operation or directions.

Autodisconnect: This lets you pick up the telephone and automatically stop the answering machine. On some models, this feature works with any extension phone.

Beeperless Remote: This allows you to call in for messages from any push-button phone. The answering machine is accessed by a personal security code.

Memo: You put a message on your machine for someone who is expected to arrive after you leave.

Remote Turn-On: This lets you turn on your machine when you are away from home.

Room Monitor: You can monitor sounds in a room while you are away via beeperless remote.

Time/Day Stamp: The machine indicates the time and day a message was received.

Toll-Saver: This is a money-saving feature. The machine rings four times before answering the first call but only rings once to answer subsequent calls. Thus, you can call your number and know by the second ring that there are no messages, then hang up to avoid a toll charge.

VOX: This allows incoming calls of any length, up to the tape's capacity. The machine records as long as the person continues to speak, deactivating within a few seconds after the caller hangs up.

Basic Answering Machines

SOUTHWESTERN BELL FA990   ✔**BEST BUY**

The Southwestern Bell FA990 has a cylindrical shape and simple-to-use design that will enhance any desk or

CONSUMER GUIDE®

countertop. The digital circuitry provides tapeless recording of incoming and outgoing messages. All controls resemble a tape recorder's with play, skip, and repeat buttons clearly marked with words and arrows. Time check and announcement buttons complete the controls along the top front edge of the answering machine. The sound knob is on the left side, and other function buttons line along the back edge. A display window shows the number of messages waiting, answer on, and low battery indicators. A voice message added to each recorded message announces the date and time of the call. Users can leave voice memos to others and retrieve messages by calling their phone number. The FA990 has an automatic answering function that can be set for two or four rings. The toll-saver feature found on this model delays answering so users can hang up without paying a toll charge when calling to check on waiting messages.

Warranty: 1 year, limited.

Manufacturer's Suggested Retail Price: $50

Approximate Low Price: $50

GENERAL ELECTRIC 2-9815
Recommended

The GE 2-9815 uses a single microcassette to handle incoming and outgoing messages. It offers a feature not found in other answering machines—music that plays during message shuttling. Operating this model couldn't be easier because of its one-touch control. All functions are activated with a multiposition selector switch. The 2-9815 records a voice stamp for the time and date of each message. An LED indicator blinks to alert users of waiting messages. Users can set up to ten push-button remote access options on this answering machine. The GE 2-9815 won't serve a business office well, but it will handle the basic needs of a college dormitory room or small household.

Warranty: 1 year, limited.

Manufacturer's Suggested Retail Price: $50

Approximate Low Price: $31

Integrated Answering Machines

PANASONIC KX-T4550

✓BEST BUY

The Panasonic KX-T4550 combines cordless phone convenience and digital messaging flexibility. This merger of technologies makes the KX-T4550 a handy upgrade for users of conventional cordless telephones. Both incoming and outgoing messages are recorded on voice chips so there are no cassette tapes to snarl, break, or wear out. The digital recording system records 23 minutes of incoming messages. This model has four voice mailboxes to separate business calls, calls for roommates, or calls for a home office from household calls. Each mailbox is protected by pass codes so family members or employees can maintain privacy. A pager-compatible feature makes staying in touch very easy. When a message is received, the answering machine signals a preset pager to announce that a call is waiting. This is an important option for someone who doesn't carry a cellular phone or who wants to restrict a mobile number. A great feature of the KX-T4550's cordless phone is a digital microphone in the charging base unit that lets users use the phone "hands free." The phone also has a ten-station speed-dialing feature. An auto-scan feature constantly sets the operating frequency to one of ten channels for interference-free conversations.

Warranty: 1 year, limited on parts and labor.

Manufacturer's Suggested Retail Price: $180

Approximate Low Price: $175

SONY IT-A200

Recommended

The Sony IT-A200 is a reliable tabletop corded phone and answering machine that is well-suited for household or home office use. It has a digital voice chip with a prerecorded message that can be recorded over to leave a personal greeting. The maximum outgoing message length is 19 seconds. Incoming messages are recorded on an MC-30 microcassette. An announce-only mode answers calls without taking messages. A built-in voice guide helps users set up and operate all the features. Remote access lets users change outgoing messages and other features without being at the answering machine. The IT-A200's memory holds ten speed-dialing numbers and three one-touch dialing locations for frequently-called numbers. Other features include memo recording of messages directly into the incoming message tape, auto interrupt of outgoing message when an extension phone is answered, and 60-second room monitoring where the phone is located. One microcassette and a wall-mounting bracket are included.

Warranty: 1 year, parts and labor.

Manufacturer's Suggested Retail Price: $110

Approximate Low Price: $90

COMPUTERS

Buying your first computer or upgrading your current system can be an overwhelming experience—even for veteran computer users—because of the wealth of products on today's market. To make the process easier, we've compared dozens of computers and peripherals and then chosen the best values. In this section you'll find detailed reviews for a variety of products, such as high-powered computers and data storage devices. We've also determined approximately how much you can expect to pay for each product. Although prices vary according to market conditions, our price information will help you to budget your computer investment.

The Ratings

At the end of each review, you'll find ratings based on a scale of 1 (worst) to 10 (best).

The **overall value** rating compares the product's price to its performance, ease of use, and features. Accordingly, an overpriced item won't have a high overall value rating, even if it is an excellent product.

The **performance** rating tells how well the product performs its various functions. Keep in mind that the performance ratings of different items can't always be fairly compared unless the products are similar.

The **expandability** rating (for computer systems) is determined by the availability of and capacity for add-ons or peripherals. Portable computers (also called laptops and notebooks) are given an expandability rating because most of them have provisions for adding more memory, a fax/modem, networking interfaces, and other peripherals. Most have a parallel port for connecting a printer, tape backup drive, or other expansion device.

The **ease of use** rating (for peripherals) is based on the efficiency of set up and operation of the product.

The **documentation** rating judges whether or not the manuals and online help are effective and well organized.

Understanding Computer Terminology

Although computers have become much easier to use over the years, a basic understanding of computer terms is useful.

The computer's "brain" is the **central processing unit,** or **CPU;** an equivalent term is **microprocessor.** Like car engines, CPUs run at different speeds, usually measured in **megahertz** (MHz). The CPU and the computer's software-based operating system regulate the flow of data between the computer's internal components, as well as between the computer and its printer, monitor, and other peripherals.

The CPU usually receives data from an input device such as the disk drive or keyboard; sometimes data will come from a mouse or trackball. A **mouse** is a small device that you move around on a desktop or pad to move the cursor, or onscreen pointer. The button or buttons on a mouse let you access onscreen functions. **Trackballs** also have buttons, but instead of moving the mouse on a level surface, you merely spin the trackball in its socket to position the cursor.

The CPU manipulates data and software programs in **random-access memory** (RAM). **Read-only memory** (ROM) might store an operating system, a utility program, or an application like a word processing program, so it can be sent into RAM. When the computer is turned off, RAM usually loses its contents; ROM retains its memory. RAM changes constantly; in most cases, ROM never changes. Printers use internal RAM buffers to store data received from the computer. Because such data are received much faster than they can be printed, without a buffer the computer would be unusable until printing is completed.

RAM and ROM are measured in bytes, which are made up of bits. A **bit** (binary digit) is the smallest unit of data. Its value is either one or zero (yes or no). A **byte** is a group of bits, usually eight, that stands for one character (it could be a letter, number, or symbol) and is treated as a unit of data. A **kilobyte** (Kb) is roughly a thousand bytes, while a **megabyte** (Mb) is about a million bytes. A **gigabyte** (Gb) equals 1,000Mb. With more RAM, a computer can run powerful programs faster. You can increase the amount of RAM by adding chips or expansion cards.

Programs and data can be saved to magnetic disks. Floppy disks are circular, 5.25 inches in diameter, and flexible, although they are packaged in square, stiff housings. Compared to floppy disks, the more popular **microfloppies** are smaller (3.5 inches in diameter), have sturdier plastic housings, and are more durable. Hard disks are normally fixed in place, holding much more data than floppies, sometimes a hundred times more. **Hard disks** work at high speeds, so they can load software into RAM more quickly and make programs run much faster than floppies can.

High-density disks are the most common; they hold between 1.2 and 1.44Mb of data. When shopping for disks, avoid the inexpensive, no-name variety. Considering the amount of input that could be lost if a disk fails, buying poorly made disks saves you very little money—and could end up costing you a lot of time and anguish in the long run. For the same reasons, most people use a second disk to make backup copies of important information.

A **disk drive** transfers data and programs back and forth between a disk and RAM. There are different sizes of floppy drives and hard-disk drives. The disk drives differ in diameter (usually 5.25 and 3.5 inches) and height (there are full-height, half-height, and even third-height drives). Disk drives also differ in the average speed at which they randomly access data from the disk. This access time is measured in milliseconds (ms). A good hard drive should have an access speed of between 10ms and 18ms.

An operating system that stores data on a disk is called a **disk operating system** (DOS). The most common is Microsoft's DOS, or MS-DOS, and its IBM version, PC-DOS. IBM personal computers, or PCs, are copied by other firms more than any other system. These IBM-compatible computers can use most peripherals and software designed for IBM-type computers. Other operating systems include IBM's OS/2, introduced in 1987, and the highly popular Microsoft Windows, which employs a graphical user interface, or GUI (pronounced "gooey"), that involves selecting onscreen icons with a mouse instead of typing lengthy text commands.

When the CPU finishes its work, it sends data to an output device, such as a disk drive, monitor, printer, or modem. A modem, in turn, sends data over telephone lines to another computer. The CPU, RAM, ROM, connecting circuits, and other parts are found on the main circuit board, called the motherboard. This board often has slots for expansion cards, which are circuit boards that increase a computer's functions, speed, or memory.

The number and type of ports (connectors) and the kind of operating system employed by a computer often limit the peripherals and programs it can use. Application software (such as a spreadsheet or database program) is commonly sold for only one operating system. Similarly, an RS-232C port can communicate only with devices that have RS-232C interfaces (software and hardware that permit the transfer of data). The application software must also be able to use that port.

Prices

We have tried to provide accurate prices in this chapter. However, the release of new products, the withdrawal of older models that are thought to be outdated, and strong competition in certain markets cause prices to change constantly. Manufacturers occasionally offer special prices or add "free" items to their packages. Prices also vary across the nation. To complicate matters further, the availability of dynamic RAM (DRAM) chips (the kind supplied with computers, peripherals, and electronic devices) often varies, which might cause prices to change. Finally, the fluctuating U.S. dollar produces price changes as well.

All this means that the retail and low prices in this buying guide might differ from what you find at your local store. Be sure to contact several dealers and compare their prices. Also, check newspaper and magazine ads for sales. Low profit margins or a lack of direct competition might make discounts hard to find on some items.

Best Buys '97

Our Best Buy and Recommended choices follow. They are broken down into the following categories: home and small-business computers, high-powered computers, portable computers, and peripherals. Personal digital assistants (PDAs) are covered in the Home Office chapter. The unit we consider to be the best of the Best Buys is listed first, followed by our second choice, and so on. Remember that a Best Buy or Recommended designation applies only to the model listed. It does not necessarily apply to other models by the same manufacturer.

HOME AND SMALL-BUSINESS COMPUTERS

APPLE PERFORMA 6230 CD

Recommended

On the surface, Apple's Performa 6230 CD might not seem all that competitive against Pentium 166 powerhouses. But if you're intimidated by the Windows operating system and hardware that goes with it, the Performa is a user-friendly alternative.

Where the power home machines we see elsewhere in this chapter are mostly in tower or mini-tower cases, the Performa comes in an attractive slimline case. The case doesn't afford much upgrade ability, but the system is already pretty well stocked. Plus, you can always add peripherals on the outside.

Under the hood, the Performa is equipped with a PowerPC 603 75MHz processor and 8Mb of RAM. You can upgrade the memory to 64Mb, but you'll probably need to take it to an Apple dealer to do so. There's also a quad-speed CD-ROM drive, an 850Mb hard disk drive, a 14.4 Global Village TelePort Gold IIv modem, and full audio circuitry that delivers stereo sound through the bundled monitor's internal speakers. If you're into video editing, the Performa has a video-in slot for an optional full-motion video card and a port for an internal TV tuner card.

Although it's difficult to compare a Macintosh's performance with that of an Intel-based system, the Performa delivers average overall performance. By the time you read this, Apple will likely offer a faster model for the same price.

Apple offers you a choice of operating systems: System 7.5, the standard Macintosh interface, or Apple At Ease, a novice-oriented interface that employs tabbed folders. Other preloaded software includes ClarisWorks, MegaPhone, and Expresso.

The Performa 6230 CD is not Apple's flagship Macintosh, but it's a good all-around choice for a home system.

Specifications: operating system, Mac OS Version 7.5; RAM (base/tested/max.), 8Mb/8Mb/64Mb; CPU/MHz, PowerPC 603/75MHz; hard drive/speed, 1Gb/12ms; storage bays, 3 drive bays; expansion slots, 1 LC PDS slot; ports, 2 serial, ADB, SCSI, monitor, IR Port; monitor, 15-inch standard. **Warranty:** 1 year, parts and labor. **Ratings:** overall value, 9; performance, 7; expandability, 8; documentation, 8.

Manufacturer's Suggested Retail Price: $2,499

Approximate Low Price: Not available

HEWLETT-PACKARD PAVILION 7170

Recommended

In case you missed it, there's a new player in the home PC market: Hewlett-Packard. The number one printer manufacturer has created a top-flight system for the home or small office. We tested one of the first versions of HP's Pavilion 7170—the higher end of the Pavilion product spectrum. Though a little on the pricey side, it offers a 166MHz Pentium processor, 16Mb of EDO RAM, and an upgradable 256K cache. Its hard disk spans 2Gb of space and works well with the 6X CD-ROM drive.

Like most other home players, the Pavilion aims to be more than just a PC. Not only is it attractively styled to fit in with home decor, it also makes itself useful as a communications center. The Pavilion offers a 28.8 fax/modem, easy Internet access, and speakerphone and answering machine capabilities.

Out of the box, this machine is a dream to set up. HP's Welcome Mat provides clear graphical instructions; a clever organizer tray lets you keep track of all those small items that can get lost during installation (screws, tools, plugs, etc.); and color- and icon-coded plugs are provided for easy, "no-brainer" connections. The 17-inch monitor we reviewed was truly awesome. Capable of 1,280×1,024 resolution, this display also supports vertical scan rates up to 100Hz.

The company's 1-year warranty is acceptable but not outstanding. And while HP offers toll-free support for first-time setup and configuration problems, you may be charged for later support service. On the other hand, you will be able to speak with someone 24 hours a day, 7 days a week. With its attractive styling and attention to detail, the HP Pavilion is a solid choice for the home or office.

Specifications: operating system, Windows 95; RAM (std./max.), 16Mb/128Mb; CPU/MHz, Pentium/ 166MHz; floppy drives, single 1.44Mb 3.5-inch; hard drive/speed, 2.0Gb/12ms; storage bays, two 5.25-inch, five 3.5-inch; expansion slots, 2 PCI, 5 ISA; ports, 2 hi-speed serial, 1 hi-speed parallel, keyboard, mouse; monitor, optional (tested 17-inch HP Pavilion Multimedia). **Warranty:** 1 year, limited; 1 year, on-site free. **Ratings:** overall value, 8; performance, 9; expandability, 8; documentation, 7.

Manufacturer's Suggested Retail Price: $3,748 (as tested)

Approximate Low Price: $2,550

HIGH-POWERED COMPUTERS

DIGITAL EQUIPMENT CORPORATION
CELEBRIS GL 5166 ST

✓BEST BUY

Digital is one of those companies that many novice or even intermediate PC buyers tend to avoid. But if you're in the market for an extremely solid and well-engineered desktop workstation, Digital is a company you should consider. We checked out one of Digital's Celebris GL series of Pentium 166MHz-based workstations. Not only is it affordable, but the whole system features careful, painstaking engineering aimed solely at providing the most for your money.

Inside the Celebris, everything is neatly arranged and easy to access for upgrades. We found 32Mb of EDO-based RAM (expandable to 128Mb) and 256K of pipeline-burst secondary cache memory (expandable to 512K). The Celebris's MGA Millennium PCI video accelerator card delivers first-rate video performance, especially when it's connected to Digital's 17-inch VR17-HA monitor. The VR17-HA may have a clumsy name, but its display quality is wonderfully even and clear, with a complete set of digital front-mounted image controls.

Returning to the inside of the Celebris's case, we find the hard drive. This is a 2.0Gb SCSI affair, wired to a motherboard-mounted SCSI controller chip that's the same as those found on Adaptec's AHA-2940 controller cards. For those purchasing a number of workstations for use in a networked environment, the Celebris's ship features an integrated network interface, and both 10Base-T and AUI Ethernet ports. There's also built-in support for DMI (Desktop Management Interface).

The Celebris's motherboard-integrated sound chip delivers 16-bit stereo audio. The CD-ROM drive is a quad-speed; this is good for fast loading of new business applications or accessing a large CD-based text database, but not good for playing games.

From its advanced, 64-bit memory architecture to its high-quality components and careful network-oriented design, the Celebris GL 5166 ST is a well-designed machine that sells for a sensible price.

Specifications: operating system, Windows 95 or Windows NT Workstation (NT tested); RAM (std./tested/max.), 16Mb/32Mb/128Mb EDO; CPU/MHz, Pentium/166MHz; floppy drives, single 1.44Mb 3.5-inch; hard drive/speed, 2.0Gb/12ms; storage bays, three 5.25-inch, four 3.5-inch; expansion slots, 1 PCI, 3 ISA, 1 ISA/PCI; ports, 2 hi-speed serial, 1 hi-speed parallel, keyboard, mouse; monitor, 17-inch VR17-HA. **Warranty:** 3 years, parts and labor; first year on-site. **Ratings:** overall value, 9; performance, 9; expandability, 9; documentation, 9.

Manufacturer's Suggested Retail Price: $4,169 (base)

Approximate Low Price: $3,889

ACER ASPIRE SOHO EDITION

✔ BEST BUY

True to its name, the Acer Aspire Soho Edition is a PC designed for small offices and home offices. Like other Aspire models, the Soho sports an attractive charcoal-gray tower case with sleek, futuristic lines. Fortunately, the Aspire isn't merely form without substance. The inside of the machine is just as impressive as its exterior.

Our Aspire shipped with a Pentium 166MHz CPU, 16Mb of RAM, a 2.5Gb hard disk, and a state-of-the-art 8X CD-ROM drive. We particularly liked the fast PCI-based video accelerator, which included hardware-based MPEG video support.

Acer's 17-inch monitor is exceptional, not only because it can support up to 1,280×1,024 pixels at a rock solid 100Hz refresh rate, but also because it's attractively designed and incorporates 6-watt stereo speakers and a unidirectional microphone. The monitor, sold separately, lists for $799—a great deal for a display of this caliber.

The Aspire features some admirable telephone-type features. The unit's 28.8kbps V.34 fax/modem works with the sound hardware to serve as a speakerphone and includes software that can turn the PC into a full-featured voice-mail center.

Software also distinguishes the Soho Aspire from other models. Acer includes Lotus SmartSuite 96, a powerful compilation of business applications including spreadsheet, word processing, contact management and presentation graphics. Softkey's Multimedia MBA provides a complete reference guide to starting and maintaining a small business. Other bundled applications include Quicken SE and PhoneDisc, plus a wealth of communication software.

Acer's 3-year warranty rounds out a fine machine that would be an asset to anyone running a small business. The Acer Aspire Soho Edition is a well-built, powerful computer at a great price.

Specifications: operating system, Windows 95; RAM (std./tested/max.), 16Mb/16Mb/128Mb EDO; CPU/MHz, Pentium/166MHz; floppy drives, single 1.44Mb 3.5-inch; hard drive/speed, 2.5Gb/12ms; storage bays, two 5.25-inch, three 3.5-inch; expansion slots, 3 PCI, 4 ISA, 1 ISA/PCI; ports, 2 hi-speed serial, 1 hi-speed parallel, keyboard, mouse; monitor, optional ($799 for our tested version). **Warranty:** 3 years, parts and labor; first year on-site free. **Ratings:** overall value, 9; performance, 8; expandability, 8; documentation, 7.

Manufacturer's Suggested Retail Price: $2,899 (as tested)
Approximate Low Price: $2,416

DELL DIMENSION XPS P166C

✓**BEST BUY**

While it doesn't sport a Pentium Pro or come bundled with Windows NT, the Dell Dimension XPS P166c is still a solid workstation PC. It's designed for business use yet priced for the mainstream, and we were impressed by the Dimension's solid construction, high-quality bundled hardware, and even the thought that went into its packaging.

The Dimension's medium-size tower case has room for growth. In addition to the drive bays occupied by the 2Gb hard disk, 6X CD-ROM drive, and 3.5-inch disk drive, there were still two open 5.25-inch bays and one unused 3.5-incher. All the Dimension's drive bays are mounted up front in an easy-to-reach rack mount.

The rest of the system is built for performance. Dell includes 32Mb of speedy EDO RAM and a large 512K pipeline-burst processor cache. Video display is exceptionally strong, based around the Number 9 FX Motion Graphics Accelerator that is wired to Dell's 17LS monitor. The 17LS is a nice piece of work, with front-mounted digital controls and decent image quality.

Serious office users may be surprised to find a high-quality sound card in the Dimension, but the included SoundBlaster AWE32 and Altec Lansing speakers are not there for game playing. With office applications like voice and video conferencing as well as computer-based training becoming very popular, these devices have become a staple of the corporate personal computer. A 28.8 US Robotics Courier internal modem is an available option ($149) for those requiring an online service or Internet access.

While our test system was fairly expensive for a Pentium 166MHz configuration, we think Dell's engineering, quality assurance, fine warranty, and attention to detail make the whole unit a great buy.

Specifications: operating system, Windows 95; RAM (std./tested/max.), 16Mb/32Mb/128Mb EDO; CPU/MHz, Pentium/166MHz; floppy drives, single 1.44Mb 3.5-inch; hard drive/speed, 2.0Gb/12ms; storage bays, four 5.25-inch, two 3.5-inch; expansion slots, 3 PCI, 3 ISA, 1 ISA/PCI; ports, 2 hi-speed serial, 1 hi-speed parallel, keyboard, mouse; monitor, Dell 17LS, included. **Warranty:** 3 years; first year on-site. **Ratings:** overall value, 8; performance, 9; expandability, 8; documentation, 9.

Manufacturer's Suggested Retail Price: $4,298 (as tested)

Approximate Low Price: $2,570

HEWLETT-PACKARD VECTRA XU 6/150 `Recommended`

When it comes to high-end corporate level computing equipment, Hewlett-Packard has always been a player. We reviewed one of the latest generations of HP's much respected Vectra line of power workstation PCs, and it was impressive. Based around an HP-designed motherboard carrying the latest Intel Pentium Pro 150MHz processor, this machine is almost difficult to describe as a desktop system.

The Vectra XU 6/150 is filled with high-end components, including 32Mb of RAM, a 2.1Gb Seagate Barracuda hard drive, and an MGA Millenium video card from Matrox. SoundBlaster audio hardware is integrated onto the system motherboard, as is an Ultra SCSIFast 20 hard-disk controller. Clearly, this system is built for speed.

As for the rest of the Vectra's bundled components, they're top quality. HP's 17-inch Ultra VGA monitor offers a clean, crisp display and front-mounted digital image controls. Networking hardware comes in the form of a PCI 10BaseT/100VG AnyLAN interface card. If necessary, you can swap the network adapter for one that will fit in better with your network.

In such a high-end system, we expected a CD-ROM drive faster than the included Sony 4X. HP may substitute something faster by the time you read this, but we were disappointed with this shortcoming. Compensation comes in the form of HP's 3-year warranty, which includes 1 year of on-site service.

If one day you need more power from the Vectra, a simple—but expensive—upgrade option is available. For about $1,400 you can install a second Pentium processor. This isn't a replacement but an add-on. The result is a super powerful dual-processor system—one that will handle even the most demanding computing tasks. If it's within your budget, the HP Vectra XU 6/150 is worth considering.

Specifications: operating system, Windows NT; RAM (std./max.), 16Mb/256Mb ECC; CPU/MHz, Pentium Pro/150Mhz (dual optional); floppy drives, single 1.44Mb 3.5-inch; hard drive/speed, 2.0Gb/10ms; storage bays, 7; expansion slots, 3 PCI, 2 ISA, 1 PCI/ISA shared; ports, 2 hi-speed serial, 1 hi-speed parallel, 1 external high-density SCSI, 1 Ethernet, keyboard, mouse, joystick, audio-in and audio-out; monitor, 17-inch HP Ultra VGA. **Warranty:** 3 years, limited; first year on-site free. **Ratings:** overall value, 6; performance, 7; expandability, 7; documentation, 8.

Manufacturer's Suggested Retail Price: $6,500

Approximate Low Price: $4,846

PORTABLE COMPUTERS

TOSHIBA PORTÉGÉ 610CT

The Toshiba Portégé is a comfortable little computer. It's small but solid, with a nice screen and keyboard and great battery life. It's about as good as sub-notebooks can be.

✔**BEST BUY**

Under the Portégé's hood lies a 90MHz Pentium processor, 8Mb of RAM, and a 686Mb hard drive. The latter is a bit small for our taste, and we recommend upgrading to 16Mb of RAM if you plan to run high-end business applications. The Portégé lacks a CD-ROM drive but offers 16-bit audio.

The unit's 9.5-inch active-matrix color screen is small by today's standards, but we expect Toshiba will be offering a larger display at the same price by the time you read this. At its current size, the screen was bright and very clear.

As always, Toshiba includes a terrific keyboard. A raised ridge supports the palms, and rounded edges make long bouts of typing very comfortable. Two fold-out feet make for a comfortable typing angle.

The Portégé could be called "portrait" size, measuring about 8×10×2 inches. At under 5 pounds, it's pretty easy to tote along, and the separate floppy drive and power supply don't add much weight. The floppy drive attaches easily by a short cable to the right side of the computer, and it may be connected without rebooting.

The back port cover slides into the unit—a clever design. It covers 9-pin serial and 25-pin parallel ports, and a video/docking port. The PC Card slot on the side of the Portégé accepts two Type II cards or one Type III.

The Portégé is a bit expensive in comparison with other models, but its small form-factor and rugged design make it an excellent traveling companion.

Specifications: operating system, Windows 95; RAM (std./max.), 8Mb/40Mb EDO; CPU/MHZ, SL-enhanced Pentium (2.9v/3.3v)/90MHz; floppy drives, plug-in 1.44Mb 3.5-inch; hard drive, 686Mb; storage bays, none; expansion slots, two type II and one Type III PC Card slot; ports, 25-pin ECP parallel, 9-pin serial, external floppy, 72-pin replicator port (provides SVGA output with replicator option); monitor, 9.5-inch diagonal active matrix 640×480×256 internal, external supports 1024×768×256. **Warranty:** 3 years, limited on parts and labor. **Ratings:** overall value, 9; performance, 9; expandability, 9; documentation, 10.

Manufacturer's Suggested Retail Price: $3,199

Approximate Low Price: $2,716

WINBOOK XP5 PENTIUM 75

Recommended

The WinBook XP5 notebook delivers almost unparalleled bang for the buck. Powered by a business-class 75MHz Pentium processor, the XP5 also features 16Mb of RAM, an 810Mb hard drive, and an active-matrix color display. And at just over 6 pounds, the XP5 is easy to carry around. Few other notebook manufacturers offer such a sweet setup for such an affordable price.

A particularly appealing aspect of the XP5 is that it comes with your choice of pointing devices. The unit comes standard with a built-in eraser-tip pointer, but for a few dollars more you can opt for a trackball or touchpad. As for the keyboard, it has a solid feel, but we disliked the scattered layout of the cursor-control keys.

The XP5's 10.4-inch active matrix screen is bright and sharp, and capable of simultaneous display with an external monitor. The lithium-ion battery survived 3 hours and 25 minutes on our toughest battery test. With a full range of power-saving options, including suspend-to-disk, the XP5 helps you get the most out of the battery.

SoundBlaster-compatible audio is optional on the XP5, but at $79.95 it's a must-have. Stereo speakers and a microphone are already in place. Also built-in is a 14.4 fax/modem, which gives you instant access to online services (although only fax and communication software is included).

The one item you won't find in the XP5 is a CD-ROM drive. Should you wish to turn this notebook into a full-blown multimedia workstation, you can purchase WinBook's $399 docking station that provides additional expansion ports and a quad-speed CD-ROM drive. If you need a powerful portable at an affordable price, the WinBook XP5 is just the ticket.

Specifications: operating system, Windows 95; RAM (std./max.), 16Mb (base 8Mb expandable to 16Mb)/32Mb; CPU/MHz, 75MHz, 256K L2 cache; floppy drives, 1.44Mb 3.5-inch; hard drive, 810Mb (540Mb/1.2Gb also available); storage bays, none; expansion slots, two Type II and one Type III PC Card, port for $399 docking station with 4X CD-ROM; ports, 9-pin serial, 25-pin parallel, PS/2 keyboard/mouse with Y-adapter included, SVGA; monitor, 10.4-inch active matrix 1Mb VRAM, 640×480×256 internal, 1024×768×256 external. **Warranty:** 30 days for full refund; 1 year, limited on parts and labor. **Ratings:** overall value, 10; performance, 9; expandability, 9; documentation, 10.

Manufacturer's Suggested Retail Price: $2,799 (75MHz, 16Mb RAM, 810Mb HD); $2,999 (100MHz); $3,199 (120MHz, 810Mb HD); $3,599 (133MHz)

Approximate Low Price: $2,099 (75MHz); $2,399 (100MHz); $2,699 (120MHz); $2,999 (133MHz)

PERIPHERALS

A computer is the sum of its parts. Just as a car comprises an engine, a chassis, a steering wheel, and four tires, a computer is made up of various components. These components, known as peripherals, include the hard drive, monitor, modem, CD-ROM drive, and even the printer. Because better peripherals ultimately add up to a better overall computer, we're going to introduce you to some of the best peripherals on the market. Whether you choose to incorporate them into a new PC or buy them as replacement parts, you'll enjoy the benefits of each.

Data storage devices are the receptacles for computer information. Hard drives are the most popular of these, and with good reason: They are fast, inexpensive, and able to store large quantities of data. However, because they're one of a computer's few mechanical devices, they're also fallible. That's why you need a tape backup drive—to keep your data safe and sound even if your hard drive hits a brick wall. Of course, the real excitement these days revolves around removable-storage drives, which afford virtually unlimited storage capacity.

When you're looking for a monitor, think twice before you settle for a small screen. Your eyes will be happier gazing at a 15- or 17-inch monitor, and your productivity will improve as a result. Although bigger screens do cost more, they provide an almost unbeatable return on the investment.

The venerable modem is your ticket to e-mail, faxing, and the much-ballyhooed Internet. Some models also afford voice-mail services and simultaneous speech during data transmissions. If you're not "surfing the Net," you're missing out on the biggest thing since fax machines.

Few peripherals play as big a role in daily computing as the printer. The right model can help a small business look big, or simply provide color copies of the kids' computer-created drawings. The latest crop of printers, which include low-cost lasers and color inkjets, offers something to fit every budget.

Multimedia hardware consists of a peripheral triple-play: the CD-ROM drive, sound card, and speakers. Multiple-disc CD changers are hot property these days, as are 3D-enhanced sound cards and speakers. Isn't it time you upgraded your first-generation multimedia equipment?

Data Storage Devices

QUANTUM BIGFOOT 2.5 AT

A 5.25-inch hard drive? Aren't those relics of the ancient PC XT, when 10Mb was a lot of storage? If Quantum has its way, the bigger 5.25-inch hard drives will be making a comeback. The Quantum Bigfoot may be big in the physical sense, but it's low in cost and high in storage capacity. The initial models store 1.2Gb and 2.5Gb, respectively.

✓**BEST BUY**

Most modern PCs have at least one free 5.25-inch drive bay, while almost all the hard drives currently on the market are of the smaller 3.5-inch form factor. The smaller drives can be installed in the larger bays using adapters, but by building a larger drive, Quantum was able to make a higher capacity unit at a lower price.

We examined the 2.5Gb model, the Bigfoot 2.5 AT. The drive has the length and width of a CD-ROM drive, but only about half the height. It should be possible to fit two of these drives in a single half-height bay. The drive sports a 14.5ms average seek time and a data transfer rate of up to 16.6Mb per second. Overall, we found the performance comparable to a Western Digital 3.5-inch 1.6Gb drive installed in the same system.

Installation is a snap if your PC is equipped with an EIDE interface—just plug it in and partition the drive. (Because MS-DOS and Windows 95 can only handle drive partitions as large as 2.1Gb, you'll need to split the drive into two partitions unless you're running OS/2 or Windows NT.) If your PC has the older-style standard IDE interface, you'll need to use software such as Disk Manager (included) to configure the drive.

With its huge storage capacity, ample speed, and easy installation, the Bigfoot 2.5 is an ideal upgrade if your PC is cramped for space.

Available for: IBM PCs and compatibles. **Ratings:** overall value, 10; performance, 9; ease of use, 10; documentation, 10.

Manufacturer's Suggested Retail Price: $370 (2.5Gb); $225 (1.2Gb)

Approximate Low Price: $297 (2.5Gb); $188 (1.2Gb)

IOMEGA ZIP DRIVE

✔**BEST BUY**

Iomega invented a whole new category of peripherals last year when it released the Zip Drive, an external storage device for PCs and Macs. This little blue drive—about the size of an external floppy drive—stores 100Mb of data on small cartridges that resemble thick floppy disks.

Three models of the Zip Drive are now available: an external version that attaches to a PC's parallel port, and internal and external SCSI versions that can be used with both PCs and Macs. The SCSI versions are the fastest and most versatile, since they can be used with PCs, Macs, and even lesser-known computers such as Amigas. The disadvantage, though, is that they require an SCSI interface card when used with PCs. Since most PCs don't include SCSI as a built-in option, you won't be able to just pop it on any PC in your home or office. That's where the parallel-port version comes in. Although it's about half the speed of the SCSI model, it is wonderfully portable. Just attach it to the printer port of any IBM-compatible PC or notebook, pop in a utility disk, and install one driver. There is no need to modify your system-configuration files, so the Zip is a snap to install for novices and experts alike.

Once connected, the Zip Drive can be used as a second hard drive. You can copy files from Zip disks to free space on your primary hard drive, or use Zip disks to transport large files that won't fit on floppies. Versatile and portable, the Zip is a great choice if you're starved for storage space.

Available for: IBM PCs and compatibles; Macintoshes; any computer with an SCSI interface. **Ratings:** overall value, 10; performance, 9; ease of use, 10; documentation, 7.

Manufacturer's Suggested Retail Price: $199

Approximate Low Price: $199

Monitors

MAG INNOVISION DX1795

✔**BEST BUY**

The MAG Innovision DX1795 is an outstanding monitor for the home office. When used with the Windows 95 operating system, the monitor supports plug-and-play compatibility. That means that you can pull it out of the box and plug it in, and your computer will automatically recognize the new monitor and configure itself accordingly.

Image quality is excellent overall. The DX1795 boasts a .26mm dot pitch, which translates to slightly sharper images than you'll see from a .28mm display. Better still, the DX1795 offers a larger viewing area than most 17-inch monitors. (Often, the plastic bezel surrounding the tube obscures some of the display.)

Environmentally and ergonomically, the DX1795 shines. It conforms to the MPR II standard for low electromagnetic field emissions, making it theoretically safer to use. The unit also supports the EPA's Energy Star guidelines, which means you can program the monitor to power down after a period of inactivity. That can save you a few dollars in operating costs over the course of a year, and it conserves energy as well. Color distribution is clear and well-balanced across the spectrum, from one side of the monitor to the next and from top to bottom. There is no curving of the image from side to side. Antiglare treatment by means of etch treatment keeps the picture crisp and dispels ambient light.

MAG backs its monitor with a 3-year limited warranty. Because a monitor is one of the most expensive computer components, such a lengthy policy is admirable indeed. And with its rock-bottom price, the DX1795 is an excellent choice for anyone in need of a 17-inch monitor.

Available for: IBM PCs and compatibles; Macintoshes. **Warranty:** 3 years, limited. **Ratings:** overall value, 9; performance, 10; ease of use, 10; documentation, 7.

Manufacturer's Suggested Retail Price: $729

Approximate Low Price: $661

NEC MULTISYNC XV17+

✓ BEST BUY

Walk into any computer superstore or office-supply warehouse and you'll see NEC monitors stacked to the ceiling. After viewing the spacious screen and rich colors of NEC's 17-inch MultiSync XV17+, we're not surprised by the popularity of these monitors.

The XV17+'s rounded back and recessed cable connections keep cord clutter to a minimum. In front, the monitors glare is reduced for a sharp picture and clear text characters. Like any good monitor, the XV17+ follows the MPR II specifications for reduced electromagnetic emissions. An optional MultiSync Monitor Lens can reduce emissions even further, keeping in line with the more stringent European TCO '92 specifications. However, the XV17+'s display looks great even without the extra lens.

The screen provides a 15.6-inch viewable area; other 17-inch monitors offer a bit more room. Comfort on the eyes comes with a dot pitch of .28mm, perfectly suitable for long periods of use. Flat-square CRT engineering reduces the glare from ambient light and keeps image distortion at a minimum. The Invar Shadow Mask, a thin sheet of metal directly behind the glass that directs the electron beams for each color, helps supply better focus, brightness, and better overall contrast.

All parts of the picture can be easily adjusted with push-button controls at the front of the monitor. Using a display that appears on the screen at the user's request, one can make simple adjustments to balance the depth of color or make more complex corrections to straighten the display geometry.

Another benefit to the NEC monitor is the manufacturer's limited warranty, which covers parts and labor for 3 years. When more than a third of the price of your new PC is wrapped up in the monitor, that's true peace of mind.

Available for: IBM PCs and compatibles; Macintoshes.
Warranty: 3 years, limited. **Ratings:** overall value, 9; performance, 10; ease of use, 10; documentation, 9.
Manufacturer's Suggested Retail Price: $849
Approximate Low Price: $809

CONSUMER GUIDE®

Modems

CARDINAL MVP288XV2 28.8

✔ BEST BUY

Cardinal has been making inexpensive, high-quality components for many years, and the MVP288XV2 external modem continues the tradition. A plug-and-play device, the MVP supports Caller ID and provides distinctive ring detection. Updates to the modem can be made easily, since the MVP uses Flash ROM for its firmware. The MVP is not only a good value, it's a fine modem.

The MVP has some common-sense features like a front-mounted on/off/volume switch and a speaker that's plenty loud. The sturdy plastic case lets the modem sit upright or flat. A rear-mounted jack lets you add a powered speaker to screen calls. The package includes a phone cord but no data cable. As for front-panel lights, they're neither as visible nor as numerous as we'd like.

The MVP supports the expected standards, including V.34 28.8 kbps, V.42 and MNP2-4, V.42bis and MNP5 for throughput of up to 115.2 kbps, MNP10 and MNP10EC (for connecting with cellular modems), and Class 1 and 2 fax. The modem uses a Rockwell AT#V command chipset.

The modem includes FaxWorks Voice 3.0 voice-mail, fax, and terminal software—a good product, but designed for Windows 3.1. FaxWorks automatically detects whether an incoming call is voice or fax and routes it accordingly. It provides up to 1,000 voice-mail boxes and has fax-on-demand capability. You can retrieve voice and fax messages via touch-tone phone and receive automatic pager notification if you wish. You may create your own greetings or use the ones included. Using the supplied voice software, we found the sound quality acceptable but not excellent.

The MVP also offers VoiceView 1.0 capability, a technology that lets you send data while talking on the phone (to a person using another VoiceView-capable modem). The unit's documentation is good, providing a list of modem commands and suggestions for successful connections to major online services.

Available for: IBM PCs and compatibles with 386SX or better; DOS 5/Windows 3.1 or higher, including Windows 95. **Warranty:** Lifetime, limited. **Ratings:** overall value, 9; performance, 9; ease of use, 10; documentation, 9.

Manufacturer's Suggested Retail Price: $189 (external); $169 (internal)

Approximate Low Price: $160 (external); $141 (internal)

US ROBOTICS SPORTSTER VOICE   `Recommended`
The Sportster Voice is a small, lightweight voice/fax/data modem capable of communicating at up to 33.6 kbps with compatible devices. Supporting V.34 with V.42/MNP 2-4 and V.42bis/MNP 5 (for throughput up to 115.2 kbps), the Sportster acts as a Class 1 and 2 fax/modem at up to 14.4 kbps, and it supports Caller ID and distinctive ring.

True to its name, the Sportster Voice has voice-mail capabilities and can serve as a full-duplex speakerphone (if you have powered speakers). Callers should find the sound clear, and the incoming sound is excellent. However, the sound is occasionally distorted when conversation volumes peak.

The Sportster automatically detects and directs fax and voice calls with the Windows 3.1 QuickLink Message Center voice/fax/data software. QuickLink lets you quickly and easily set up voice mail and supports remote message retrieval, fax-on-demand, and pager notification. Unfortunately, the software is designed for Windows 3.1—although it will work under Windows 95.

The Sportster's lightweight plastic case can lay flat or stand upright and has eight bright status indicator lights on the front. The modem has a built-in microphone, volume control, and power switch.

The documentation for the Sportster is helpful in most respects, but we wanted more specific help with modem setup strings, and Windows 95 support was lacking. The manual mentions ways of downloading a more thorough manual, but we found this to be a poor solution. If your modem isn't working, it's hard to download a file or get a fax back.

Data communications performance was great, but we occasionally had problems connecting and staying connected to America Online. Technical support was helpful and, after some experimenting, we found a setup that worked well. If you want to turn your PC into a state-of-the-art communications center, the Sportster is an excellent choice.

Available for: IBM PCs and compatibles with Windows 3.1 or higher. **Warranty:** 5 years, limited. **Ratings:** overall value, 9; performance, 9; ease of use, 8; documentation, 8.

Manufacturer's Suggested Retail Price: $129

Approximate Low Price: $98

Printers

CANON BJC-4100

✓**BEST BUY**

There's a lot to like about the Canon BJC-4100 printer. For starters, it's smaller than most inkjets. Measuring just 7.8×14.4×8.8 inches (HWD), the BJC-4100 is tall but not deep. Its 100-sheet document feeder holds paper upright (adding to its overall height) and delivers pages to a retractable front tray. If your desk space is at a minimum, you'll appreciate this printer's diminutive stature.

The BJC-4100 is also quick, churning out text pages at nearly four per minute. Color printing speeds vary depending on the contents of the page. Because the printer employs two ink cartridges simultaneously, you don't have to swap cartridges when you want to switch between black and color printing.

Setting up the BJC-4100 is an exceptionally simple process: Install the ink cartridges, insert paper, and load the Windows software. Canon's handy quick-start guide and superb documentation further simplify setup.

On plain paper, the BJC-4100 can produce both color and black output at 360×360 dots per inch (dpi). If you buy special glossy paper, you can take advantage of a 720×360 dpi high-quality mode, which produces even sharper images and text.

Although the BJC-4100 produced just about the best text we've ever seen from an inkjet printer, the colors in our sample PhotoCD image were noticeably faded. One of the printer's strongest assets is the software Canon bundles with it. Dubbed Canon Creative, this CD-ROM includes programs for creating everything from greeting cards and stationery to stickers and cross-stitch patterns. All this great software means you can put the BJC-4100 to use right out of the box.

Canon backs the unit with a generous 2-year warranty and toll-free technical support that's available 7 days a week. Attractively styled, reasonably priced, and quick on the draw, the BJC-4100 is a fine choice for the home office or small business.

Available for: IBM PCs and compatibles. **Warranty:** 2 years. **Ratings:** overall value, 9; performance, 8; ease of use, 10; documentation, 10.

Manufacturer's Suggested Retail Price: $299

Approximate Low Price: $260

HEWLETT-PACKARD LASERJET 5L

✔ BEST BUY

It wasn't long ago that a laser printer capable of 600-dpi output cost upwards of $1,000. Today, Hewlett-Packard's LaserJet 5L costs half that and sacrifices next to nothing for the discount. Designed for home or small-office use, the LaserJet 5L combines outstanding print quality with a small footprint and flexible paper handling.

Successor to HP's popular LaserJet 4L, the 5L sports a totally redesigned look and some valuable new features. Most significant among the latter is higher-resolution printing. The results are readily visible: exceptionally sharp text, perfectly contrasted photos, and smooth gray scales. Part of the acclaim goes to HP's Resolution Enhancement technology, which, among other print-enhancing functions, delivers up to 210 levels of gray. Few other laser printers can match the 5L's splendid print quality.

The trade-off is speed. Many lasers in the same price range can produce up to six pages per minute, but the 5L tops out at four. That can make a big difference if you need to do a high volume of printing.

Unlike the 4L, which used a slide-out paper tray, the 5L employs a vertical tray that holds paper upright. Printed sheets are deposited in a second upright bin; the flip of a switch can redirect them to a trayless front chute. The latter approach creates a straight-through paper path, ideal for printing envelopes and heavier paper stocks. A single-sheet slot allows you to feed envelopes or specialty paper without disrupting the main paper supply.

While the 5L's paper handling is very effective, it makes for a somewhat tall printer. With paper loaded into the 100-sheet tray, the unit stands over 13 inches high.

As usual, HP includes excellent documentation with the printer. The box-to-desktop experience is quick and painless. If you're looking for a top-quality printer for the home or office, look no further than the HP LaserJet 5L.

Available for: IBM PCs and compatibles. **Warranty:** 1 year. **Ratings:** overall value, 9; performance, 8; ease of use, 10; documentation, 10.

Manufacturer's Suggested Retail Price: $586

Approximate Low Price: $472

Multimedia Hardware

NEC MULTISPIN 4×4
✔**BEST BUY**

Just as the makers of CD players invented multidisc changers to accommodate ever-growing music libraries, so have CD-ROM manufacturers begun to produce similar products for expanding software collections. Think of it: You could stock your CD-ROM drive with an encyclopedia, a favorite game, an audio disc, and still have a spot open for another disc.

Such is the allure behind NEC's MultiSpin 4×4, the latest and greatest of this new breed. The aptly named four-disc changer spins CDs at four times the speed of original drives. Its convenience and low price make it an extremely attractive upgrade.

The 4×4 is an internal drive, meaning it needs a home in an empty drive bay inside your PC. If you're replacing an existing single-disc drive, the 4×4 can occupy that same bay. Installing the 4×4 is a simple endeavor, thanks to a large illustrated poster that outlines the procedure and an included video that demonstrates it. The drive requires an Enhanced IDE (EIDE) interface. Most newer systems already have one, and NEC includes an EIDE card for those that don't.

The 4×4 includes software drivers for both Windows 3.1 and Windows 95. In either operating system, you can configure the 4×4 in one of two operating modes: one drive letter for all four disc slots, or a different drive letter for each slot. The problem with the latter approach is that you may have to reconfigure some previously installed software, which won't know where to look for relocated CDs.

The drive itself uses neither a slide-out tray nor a disc caddy. Rather, discs slide into the drive like videocassettes into a VCR. Four buttons on the front of the drive determine into which slot each disc will go.

Available for: IBM PCs and compatibles. **Warranty:** 1 year. **Ratings:** overall value, 10; performance, 8; ease of use, 9; documentation, 10.

Manufacturer's Suggested Retail Price: $279

Approximate Low Price: $99

HOME OFFICE

Small Office/Home Office consumers comprise a major new industry known as the SOHO product line. This office equipment is designed and priced for home business owners, students, job seekers, and employees who spend part of their week working at home.

Americans today are buying home office products in record numbers. These products are capable of delivering the reliability, productivity, and many of the same features as their high-priced counterparts in commercial offices. However, products made for use at home are often not designed for the heavy use that commercial office equipment must endure.

Best Buys '97

Our Best Buy, Recommended, and Budget Buy home office products follow. They are categorized into word processors, desktop copiers, scanners, desktop fax machines, electronic organizers, and personal digital assistants. Within each category the product we consider to be the best of the Best Buys is listed first, followed by our second choice, and so on. At the end of certain categories, we list some products as Budget Buys. These are products that may not have all the features of a Best Buy or Recommended product, but they offer a solid value in terms of performance, features, and price. Remember that a Best Buy, Recommended, or Budget Buy designation applies only to the model listed. It does not necessarily apply to other models made by the same manufacturer.

WORD PROCESSORS

A word processor is a specialized computer designed primarily for creating and printing professional-looking reports, manuscripts, letters, and other documents. Some word processors can also produce spreadsheets and perform other functions typically done with a personal computer. Some models interface with computers and printers.

Most home office word processors are portable and produce letter-quality (high-quality, professional-looking print) documents. When shopping for word processors, consider the storage capacity of the floppy disks designed for various models. Some models still use 3.5-inch diskettes that can only store up to 720Kb. This is an older standard that has become obsolete. Newer technology relies on high-density diskettes of the same size that store up to 1.4 Mb, nearly twice the capacity. If the word processor has a read-out screen, check the number of lines or parts of documents it displays. Another feature worth considering is the merge function; this allows you to automatically generate individual letters to names on a mailing list. Also look for features borrowed from computers, such as address books, spreadsheet programs, and information management programs.

CANON STARWRITER JET 300

✓ BEST BUY

The StarWriter Jet 300 is a new entry into the word processing lineup, which combines versatile paper handling, graphics, and word processing functions. One of its most impressive features is the built-in 30-page automatic paper feeder. Being able to store an ample paper supply in the word processor makes printing multiple page reports much more convenient. Add to this the high-quality bubble-jet printer, and you have a personal publishing system that rivals high-end desktop computers. The StarWriter Jet 300 prints documents fast, at 360×360 dpi (dots per inch), producing near laser-quality resolution. Plus, a built-in clip art feature offers some 75 images to enhance documents and presentations. Data is stored on a 1.44Mb floppy disk that is compatible with personal computers using built-in conversion software. Other features include label printing capabilities, 60 graphics symbols, text characters in 21 languages, and more than 700 print style variations.

Specifications: height, 2.9"; width, 12.6"; depth, 15.3"; weight, 7 lb. **Warranty:** 1 year, limited on parts and labor.

Manufacturer's Suggested Retail Price: $299

Approximate Low Price: $296

BROTHER WP-330MDS

`Recommended`

The Brother WP-330MDS is a new, improved version of the WP5600MDS. The only difference from the previous model is the inclusion of a game disk that contains three action games and three card games. Like the model it replaces, the WP-330MDS has a high-density 3.5-inch 1.44Mb floppy disk drive. The data saved on floppy disks can be used on a PC if you convert the files using included software. The WP-330MDS has a 14-inch monitor that shows 20 lines by 90 characters. The printing carriage is 12.8 inches and has a 9-inch typing width. The address book has data merge for printing individually addressed letters from a master document. Other functions include a dual screen feature, the abbreviated phrase memory, and a spreadsheet program. The spreadsheet feature allows for conversion of Lotus files between the WP-330MDS and a PC. This word processor has a 95,000-word dictionary spell checker, a 45,000-word thesaurus, and a punctuation checker. This model uses interchangeable cassette daisy wheels to print various type styles on a built-in impact, or typewriter-style, printer.

Specifications: height, 5.4"; width, 16.4"; depth, 17.2"; weight, 12.3 lb. (monitor excluded). **Warranty:** 90 days, labor; 1 year, parts.

Manufacturer's Suggested Retail Price: $600

Approximate Low Price: $312

DESKTOP COPIERS

Desktop photocopy machines used to be considered a luxury item in the home office. Today, improved design and affordable pricing have made copy machines an indispensable home office tool. One of the best features of desktop copiers is a user-friendly design that makes them easy for the owner to service. New models are built to take up very little space. They are also time- and cost-effective when compared to the inconvenience and expense of using a print shop or coin-operated copier. Before you buy any copier, test a floor model in the store to ensure it produces clear copies. The major upkeep on photo-copy machines is related to the toner, a powdery substance used to re-create the image being copied. Some models require replacement of a toner cartridge; others have a refillable toner reservoir. Toner cartridges vary in price depending on the manufacturer and the suppliers. A few companies recycle empty cartridges, making their replacement a bit less costly.

SHARP Z-85III

✔**BEST BUY**

If desktop space in your home office is limited, the Sharp Z-85III may be the solution. Its size and price tag, plus a great combination of features, make this model well-suited for home and small office use. The Z-85III maximizes space by combining a stationary platen with an internal 100-sheet paper cassette. It makes ten copies per minute and has a manual-feed bypass feature, which lets users insert letterhead and other special stationery without refilling the paper cassette. Plus, its clamshell design makes clearing misfed copy paper quick and easy. In addition, most copiers need a warm-up period of up to 3 minutes before they accept copying orders. The Z-85III's auto-start feature permits users to enter copying orders as soon as they turn on the unit; the copier gets right to work as soon as it is warmed up. There are four preset reduction and enlargement settings; these provide flexibility for making flyers, pamphlets, newsletters, brochures, menus, greeting cards, and graphic presentations. Optional color toner cartridges enhance printing through five-color single tone copying in black, red, blue, brown, or green.

Specifications: height, $11\frac{5}{8}$"; width, $19\frac{15}{16}$"; depth, $17\frac{15}{16}$"; weight, 48.5 lb. **Warranty:** 1 year, parts and labor.

Manufacturer's Suggested Retail Price: $1,000

Approximate Low Price: $765

CANON PC720

Recommended

The PC720 is one of Canon's newest additions and has the latest energy-efficient features. As with all Canon copiers, the PC720 has the optional single-cartridge system, which contains everything that can run or wear out. This puts the drum, development unit, and toner in one easy-to-replace cartridge. Printing is a bit slower than competing brands at eight copies per minute. The unit makes up to 100 multiple copies per session and has a 250-sheet front-loading cassette and a single sheet bypass tray for special paper sizes. The PC720 provides instant warm-up, so there's no waiting time. Auto-shutoff is a built-in energy-saving feature designed to automatically shut off the copier after 5 minutes of inactivity. The PC720 prints in black, red, blue, brown, or green, depending on the type of cartridge loaded.

Specifications: height, 11¼"; width, 19⅛"; depth, 17¼"; weight, 41.9 lb. **Warranty:** 1 year, limited on parts and labor.

Manufacturer's Suggested Retail Price: $1,295

Approximate Low Price: $682

XEROX XC580

The Xerox XC580 Personal Copier is a good | Budget Buy | choice for small-office use where copy needs are light to moderate. It will handle about 500 copies a month. The XC580 is smaller and lighter than most home office models, making it easy to squeeze into cramped working areas. The start-up feature allows you to set your copy job immediately, so that it begins automatically when warm-up is complete. The XC580 takes about 18 seconds to warm up and makes about five copies per minute. The multi-copy feature automatically makes up to 20 copies in one session. The paper tray holds 100 sheets of paper, and the XC580 copies up to legal-size documents. The first drum cartridge is included, but replacement cartridges and toner cartridges are sold separately. A power-saver feature cuts power consumption in half during periods of inactivity.

Specifications: height, 4.9"; width, 17.2"; depth, 17.2"; weight, 26.4 lb. **Warranty:** 3 years, parts and labor.

Manufacturer's Suggested Retail Price: $479

Approximate Low Price: $479

SCANNERS

A scanner is a personal computer input device that lets you transfer printed text to the computer without rekeying the material. It also lets you transfer graphics directly into the computer. There are three types of scanners. Two traditional types are the hand-held and the flatbed scanners. Flatbed scanners are often more convenient because they capture an entire page more easily, but they are much more costly. Hand-held scanners have software that seams several passes together to make a completed page. The newest type of scanner, a page scanner, resembles a portable printer. It passes a piece of paper around a cylinder and delivers the paper's contents to the computer screen. Its main disadvantage is the inability to scan pages from a book or a magazine without first tearing out the page.

In shopping for a scanner, be sure to select one that is designed to work with the operating system of your computer—DOS, Windows, Windows 95, or Macintosh. (If you have Windows 95, be aware that you may have to order special software drivers from the scanner's manufacturer before it will work with your computer.) Some manufacturers offer an optional optical character recognition (OCR) software package for scanning text. Retailers may offer a variety of OCR software at a variety of prices as part of a scanner package. Scanners require lots of memory, so be sure your computer has enough for the scanner's needs. Scanners come in two basic types—gray scale and color. Color models are more expensive.

HEWLETT-PACKARD SCANJET 4s ✔BEST BUY

Hewlett-Packard's ScanJet 4s personal desktop scanner is the newest item in scanning hardware. It lets users scan, file, share, fax, e-mail, and edit paper documents electronically without having to type an original copy into the computer. Compact and usable, it fits between the keyboard and monitor and plugs into any available serial port without installing a special card in the computer. It scans documents from business cards to 8½×30-inch pages. The 4s turns on and off automatically as a document passes through the feeder. The scanned image appears instantly on the monitor, and included OCR software sends scanned text directly to the user's word processor. Its auto-launch software moves documents into some 60 different applications with a single mouse click. Scanned pages are reproduced at 400 or 200 dpi. The Scanjet 4s is compatible with Windows 3.1, Windows for Workgroups, Windows 95, and Macintosh 7.0 and up. The Scanjet 4s produces quick results with a typical page scanning in less than 10 seconds.

Specifications: height, 3.5"; width, 3.0"; depth, 12.5"; weight, 2.5 lb. **Warranty:** 1 year, parts and labor.

Manufacturer's Suggested Retail Price: $369

Approximate Low Price: $252

BROTHER IMAGECENTER 150ocr

Recommended

The Brother ImageCenter 150ocr is a document scanner that can also fax, print, and copy if used with a separate computer fax modem and printer. Unlike other Brother fax and scanning machine combos, this model comes with the Xerox Textbridge OCR software so scanned text can instantly be edited in word processing programs. An extra software package permits business cards to be scanned into an electronic database. Scanner features include a 20-page automatic document feeder, image resolution of 400×400 dpi, 64 gray scale shades, and a scanning rate of four pages per minute. Scanned images can be saved in TIF, BMP, and EPS file formats. The ImageCenter connects to a computer through the parallel connector to the printer. The ImageCenter's 4Mb of random access memory (RAM) allows fast copies of up to 20 original documents sent directly to a printer without first scanning the page into the computer.

Specifications: height, 5.1"; width, 12.7"; depth, 7.3"; weight, 4.4 lb. **Warranty:** 1 year, parts and labor.

Manufacturer's Suggested Retail Price: $199

Approximate Low Price: $199

DESKTOP FAX MACHINES

Fax is the commonly used term for facsimile machine or the electronic facsimile transmission of documents. It is now considered a must-have item in the home office. In fact, many families are bringing them home for personal use. Fax machines today are easily affordable: Low-end models with basic features cost only a few hundred dollars.

Most models now include an attached phone so the fax machine can double as an extension phone in the household or home office. Other useful features include built-in answering machines and the ability to make copies of single-sheet documents. Many models also have a small LCD (liquid crystal display) screen for programming features. Some fax machines use heat-sensitive paper to print transmissions and copies of personal documents. More expensive models use plain paper (like desktop copiers). This type of fax machine requires large ink cartridges for printing, which adds to the overall cost. Fax machines transmit and receive over ordinary telephone lines, and no special skills are needed to hook up a fax machine. It is not necessary to have a separate phone number, although it is often more convenient and productive to have a dedicated fax line if the machine is used in a home office.

Some high-end models are actually multipurpose machines that combine faxing and desktop copying. One of the newest features in these models lets you connect the fax machine to a computer to work as a page scanner as well as a printer.

PANASONIC KX-F1200
✔ **BEST BUY**

Two of the most popular features on a fax machine are plain-paper capability and two-line operation. The Panasonic KX-F1200 offers both features plus digital answering machines on both phone lines and a built-in copier. This combination of features makes the KX-F1200 a handy alternative to buying multiple office machines, giving users double the machine for the price of one. It sends and receives faxes on either line, acts as a two-line speakerphone, answers voice calls on either line, and makes plain-paper copies. The KX-F1200 handles multiple tasks simultaneously and can distinguish between incoming fax and voice calls. The paper supply tray holds 250 sheets of letter- or legal-size paper and has a 15-page document feeder. A special feature, when activated, lets users block junk faxes by requiring callers to enter a four-digit code before sending a fax. The answering machine accepts messages to three separate voice mailboxes, and each can have a separate password. A total of 84 auto-dialing stations are available for phone and fax. The KX-F1200's transmission speed is 15 seconds per page.

Specifications: height, 9⅝₆"; width, 16⅝"; depth, 15¼"; weight, 19.4 lb. **Warranty:** 1 year, parts and labor.

Manufacturer's Suggested Retail Price: $600

Approximate Low Price: $543

BROTHER MFC-1750

Recommended

For consumers who need to pack a lot of features into one fax machine, the Brother MFC-1750 can be almost all the office machinery a small operation needs. The MFC-1750 combines the latest in fax features with those of a copier, PC scanner, and PC fax machine. The fax machine features include plain-paper faxing and 256Kb of memory to store up to ten pages for broadcasting. This memory also holds faxes that arrive while the fax machine is out of paper. The paper tray holds 200 sheets, while the document feeder holds 20. The copier features include multicopying (up to 99 copies), copy sorting, and enlargement/reduction from 50 percent to 150 percent. The MFC-1750 connects to a Windows-based PC and uses optional software to scan in text, line art, logos, and photos. It also sends and receives faxes directly to computers without having a separate modem installed on the PC. The fax modem built into the MFC-1750 is a high-speed 14.4bps device. The fax machine prints two pages per minute.

Specifications: height, 8.4"; width, 14.8"; depth, 15.9"; weight, 14.6 lb. **Warranty:** 90 days, on-site; 1 year, replacement on parts and labor.

Manufacturer's Suggested Retail Price: $799

Approximate Low Price: $430

HEWLETT-PACKARD FAX-700

Recommended

The advantage of using the Hewlett-Packard Fax-700 is the superior printing quality produced by the inkjet system. Hewlett-Packard perfected inkjet technology and uses that same printing engine in its fax machines. Coupled with plain paper, faxes printed on the Fax-700 look like they came from a laser printer. This method is actually more economical than the ink film cartridges used in other fax machines, since the replacement inkjet cartridge costs less than ink film cartridges. This model stores 100 sheets of paper and accepts up to 20 pages in the document feeder. Onboard memory of 256Kb allows for unprinted faxes to be stored in memory. The Fax-700 is ideal for home and small office use where there is only one phone line because the unit has a built-in phone/fax switch, which automatically recognizes the type of incoming call. Among its other features are the ability to broadcast to 50 locations and the capacity to store up to 50 phone numbers in autodial mode. The Fax-700 is economical to use, sending one full page in 9 seconds.

Specifications: height, 8.6"; width, 13.6"; depth, 13.0"; weight, 19 lb. **Warranty:** 1 year, HP express exchange.

Manufacturer's Suggested Retail Price: $599

Approximate Low Price: $490

SHARP UX-206

Recommended

The Sharp UX-206 incorporates some of the hottest new features for home office and small office users. While this model doesn't use plain paper, it can accommodate a super-size 164-foot roll of thermal paper. The automatic document cutter and anticurl mechanism make this model more convenient than a plain-paper model for printing incoming faxes and making copies. A benefit of photosensitive continuous paper is that the fax machine will never run out of ink.

Printing is clean and clear with regular and super-fine resolution settings. The printing mechanism reproduces 64-level halftone images to ensure flawless photographs and illustrations. The automatic document feeder holds up to 20 sheets of paper. The LCD display works as part of the caller ID-ready feature so users can see the name and number of the person dialing in. The all-digital answering machine has a 12-minute recording time capacity with four voice mailboxes so users can separate messages for either business or home use. A flash memory feature retains voice messages or fax receptions during power failure without the need of battery backup. The distinctive ring pattern feature allows up to four telephone numbers to be shared over a single phone line, which eliminates the need for a dedicated phone line.

Specifications: height, 5.1"; width, 13.9"; depth, 11.6"; weight, 7.7 lb. **Warranty:** 90 days, parts and labor.

Manufacturer's Suggested Retail Price: $470

Approximate Low Price: $270

ELECTRONIC ORGANIZERS

Electronic organizers are quickly becoming the preferred way for busy executives and students to keep track of schedules and information. These devices resemble computers but are so small they fit in a purse or pocket. They typically have an LCD screen and special programs that help you keep track of important phone numbers, appointments, and bank account numbers. Electronic organizers usually have date and time displays, calculator functions, and time alarms. Some models have enough memory to include calendars and to-do lists. Some electronic organizers come with software and cables so you can move data between a desktop computer and the electronic organizer.

PSION SERIES 3a (512K)

✓ **BEST BUY**

The Psion Series 3a is a combination pocket organizer and laptop computer that fits in a purse or pocket for easy transport. This model comes with 512Kb of internal memory. The clamshell design opens so the keyboard rests on any flat surface and the screen fills the top half. The small size makes five-finger typing difficult, but the raised keys and uniform spacing let users enter data at a comfortable pace using one or two fingers on the standard letter placement (Q-W-E-R-T-Y) keyboard. The black and white LCD provides clear images. Usually, screens on pocket organizers are tiny and square; on the 3a, the screen is long and displays up to 80 characters by 17 lines. Users can take the 3a on the road and have the same convenience available from an office computer. It works much like a PC with menus and windows. The 3a has a full-featured word processor, spreadsheet, database, and organizer programs that are fully compatible with a PC or a Macintosh computer, using optional software to transfer files. Programs are accessed by pressing buttons below the LCD. There are buttons for system features, data management, word processing, the agenda organizer, spreadsheet, time/alarm functions, calculator, and world clock. Two AA batteries provide 2 to 4 months of typical usage. A separate backup battery protects data when the two AA batteries wear down or are replaced. If you're looking for larger memory capacity, 1Mb and 2Mb models are also available in the Series 3a. Both cost more than the 512k model and come with a built-in spell checker and thesaurus.

Specifications: height, 0.87"; width, 6.5"; depth, 3.35"; weight, 9.68 oz. **Warranty:** 1 year, parts and labor.

Manufacturer's Suggested Retail Price: $349

Approximate Low Price: $333

SHARP OZ-5600

Recommended

The Sharp OZ-5600 is a compact, reliable pocket organizer with lots of storage power. It comes with 512Kb of memory and a backlighted screen for easy viewing in all conditions. This unit gives you a big advantage over a full-size PDA (see next section) but sacrifices little. It comes with a variety of powerful time and data management features. A calculator function lets users perform traditional business calculations such as cost/sell/margin and markup. Built-in templates make it easy to get organized. Optional link software and a wireless adapter let users transfer or back up stored information to a PC or Macintosh computer. An optional wireless adapter lets users print information to a standard PC printer. Its other features include all the expected organizer tools: a calendar, appointment scheduler, to-do list, phone book, world clock, memo/notebook, and outliner. The OZ-5600 also comes with a powerful financial program that lets users manage their checking, savings, cash, and credit transactions.

Specifications: height, 0.72"; width, 6.3"; depth, 3.5"; weight, 9.3 oz. **Warranty:** 1 year, parts and labor.

Manufacturer's Suggested Retail Price: $370

Approximate Low Price: $277

PERSONAL DIGITAL ASSISTANTS

Personal Digital Assistants (PDAs) are hand-held computers used to write notes, track appointments, and help you computerize other daily chores to keep your life in order. When selecting a PDA, consider the screen size, memory expansion capabilities, and availability of add-on programs through plug-in cards. With the array of built-in programs and other features, PDAs can be a good alternative to lugging around a larger, heavier laptop computer—and they cost at least 50 percent less.

SHARP ZAURUS ZR-5800FX
✔**BEST BUY**

The ZR-5800FX is an ultramodern personal digital assistant with an enhanced keyboard. It is the ideal companion to your desktop computer when you are away from your desk. From this one palmtop computer you get expanded access to information in your PC, to other Zaurus users, and to online data and Internet sources. The screen is very readable thanks to improved backlighting; this makes it much easier to use in low-light locations. The unit packs 2Mb of memory and comes loaded with enhanced programs that are easily transferred to desktop computers. The spreadsheet program works

HOME OFFICE

with both the pen and the keyboard, and data can be copied or moved easily with drag and drop operations. Text documents created in the ZR-5800FX are saved in rich text format (RTF) for easy conversion to a computer, eliminating the need to reformat Zaurus word processing documents; all drawings, graphics, and text are retained in the transfer.

Specifications: height, 1.0"; width, 6.7"; depth, 3.9"; weight, 13.6 oz. **Warranty:** 1 year, parts and labor.

Manufacturer's Suggested Retail Price: $800

Approximate Low Price: $660

PANASONIC NEOFILE CF-CR100   Recommended

The NeoFile is a business card scanner and personal assistant rolled into one. It scans in and stores memory information from business cards and performs the functions of a scheduler, reservation book, notebook, world clock, and calculator. All of the information created in these functions, except the calculator data, can be revised and edited on a PC in an organizer format. NeoFile can link to any software that accepts comma separated value (CSV) files, though this requires the purchase of a special interface kit (the CF-CAA10 for $125). This interface kit includes transfer software, a cable to link with a PC's serial port, and an instruction manual. With the special interface, users can edit business card information on a PC and send it back to NeoFile. All files can be printed on a standard printer. Business card lists can be arranged horizontally or vertically, and users can generate lists of just names, phone numbers, company names, or any combination thereof.

Specifications: height, 1.0"; width, 6.8"; depth, 3.7"; weight, 0.07 lb. (without batteries). **Warranty:** 1 year, parts and labor.

Manufacturer's Suggested Retail Price: $400

Approximate Low Price: $399

HOME FITNESS

Twenty years ago, few people were concerned with fitness. Now almost everyone is. Gyms, fitness clubs, and spas can be found all across America, even in small towns. A vast selection of fitness or workout clothing is available, including sneakers designed for aerobics and cross-training. Add to this the wide variety of foods, vitamin supplements, and high-energy drinks on the market and you'll quickly get the picture: Millions of people are concerned about fitness, exercise, eating right, and looking healthy.

We all lead busy lives, and it can be very difficult to find several free hours a week to work out at a gym. In fact, you can maintain health and fitness simply by cutting down on fat intake and participating in a regular exercise program, such as walking. Unfortunately, time constraints, bad weather, and dangerous neighborhoods can get in the way of regular outdoor exercise. One obvious solution is to buy home exercise equipment. Many professionals and experts suggest you buy the best aerobic exercise equipment you can afford, plus a set of basic weight-lifting equipment. Others recommend purchasing a machine that you enjoy using—one that will get your heart rate up.

It is important to shop wisely for home exercise equipment that you will use on a regular basis. Avoid trendy, popular, new, or cute equipment. Choose a machine that you will use daily or at least several times a week. If the machine is uncomfortable to sit on or difficult to use, it will just become an expensive clothing rack.

Best Buys '97

Our Best Buy, Recommended, and Budget Buy home fitness equipment products follow. In each category, the item we consider to be the best of the Best Buys is listed first, followed by our second choice, and so on. Remember that a Best Buy, Recommended, or Budget Buy rating applies only to the model listed; it does not necessarily apply to an entire product line or to other models made by the same manufacturer.

EXERCISE CYCLES

Exercise bikes are popular for home use. There are many on the market, so try several before making your purchase. Find a unit that is comfortable to sit on and to pedal, and one that other family members can also use. A number of optional features are available, but they do increase your cost, so select those that best meet your needs.

Standard upright cycles are still available, and several of them also offer upper-body workouts. The latest designs, however, feature recumbent seating that supports your lower back with a lounge-chair-style seat and leaves your hands and arms free to use weights for upper-body exercise while you pedal. Make sure you test the seat for comfort before buying.

LIFE FITNESS LIFECYCLE 5500

✓ **BEST BUY**

The Lifecycle 5500 is the home version of the health club exercise bike. This unit has an adjustable seat, pedal straps, closed-cell urethane handle grips, and small front casters for easy transport around your home. A battery-powered electronic console displays continuous feedback, time elapsed, total calories expended, calories burned per hour, total miles ridden, and pedal speed, in addition to a workout summary. The Lifecycle 5500 comes with five workout programs: hill profile, which simulates a sequence of hills and valleys; random, which includes a series of over one million different workout combinations; manual, which provides a constant, steadily paced workout with fixed resistance; 12-speed race, which incorporates the simulated action of a 12-speed racing bike; and fit test, which features an estimate of your cardiovascular fitness during exercise.

Specifications: height, 55"; width, 23"; length, 41"; weight, 78 lb.
Warranty: 3 years, limited on mechanical and electrical components.

Manufacturer's Suggested Retail Price: $1,099

Approximate Low Price: $1,000

CYBEX SEMI

The Semi from Cybex is a well-made, full- **Recommended** featured recumbent exercise cycle. Its comfortable seat is easy to adjust for different leg lengths and can be positioned so that you use all of your lower body muscles—not just the quadriceps. Six preset workout programs offer 15 levels of difficulty, including manual mode in which you race against a computer, and modes that test both aerobic and anaerobic fitness. The Semi features an optional heart rate transmitter that allows you to key your workout to your desired heart rate. Electronic readouts display work rate in calories per hour, watts, or kilograms; speed in mph, kph, or rpm; distance in miles or kilometers traveled; calories consumed; and heart rate (optional). The pedals on the Semi move smoothly and have the realistic feel of a large chain and gear-driven flywheel, providing you with an energetic workout.

Specifications: height, 51"; width, 22"; length, 59"; weight, 215 lb. **Warranty:** 90 days, seat, friction belt, handle grips, and pedal straps; 2 years, all other parts and labor.

Manufacturer's Suggested Retail Price: $2,690

Approximate Low Price: $2,690

TUNTURI ECB F570

The Tunturi ECB F570 recumbent stationary **Recommended** exercise bike uses eddy current, or magnetic resistance, to vary the load and is completely silent in operation. Easily adjustable, the front flywheel unit is connected to the seat with a large metal tube that collapses to accommodate users of any height. The seat holds you in an upright position, fostering a posture that engages most prime mover muscles. An electronic control panel includes simple controls for selecting various programs or a manual operation mode. Program mode offers you a choice of five preset programs of varying duration. The level of difficulty can be adjusted on the console. Resistance is easy to set via buttons on the display console. The ECB F570's sound construction is made up of a 3-inch-thick, rust-resistant, tubular steel frame.

Specifications: height, 32⅖"; width, 23"; length, 69¹⁄₁₀"; weight, not available. **Warranty:** 1 year, labor (at recommended service center); 2 years, parts (except frame); 10 years, frame.

Manufacturer's Suggested Retail Price: $699

Approximate Low Price: $631

SCHWINN AIRDYNE EVOLUTION PRO   Recommended

The Schwinn Airdyne Evolution Pro is an updated version of one of the first at-home exercise cycles. This unit offers a patented synchronized arm-and-leg action that provides total body fitness by simulating natural bike-riding movement. The Airdyne Evolution Pro has two steel handlebars with PVC grips that move back and forth as you pedal the bike. A fully enclosed fan provides resistance as well as a cooling effect for the user. A battery display terminal comes with a high-contrast LCD screen that displays time, distance, calories, levels, rpm, and watts. The display unit shuts off after 5 minutes if not in use. The Airdyne Evolution Pro offers four programs—hills, intervals, summit, and manual—plus a 14-position adjustable seat, footrests, and transport wheels.

Specifications: height, 48"; width, 23½ "; length, 52"; weight, 90 lb. **Warranty:** 2 years, electronics; lifetime, mechanical (original owner only).

Manufacturer's Suggested Retail Price: $700

Approximate Low Price: $699

GRAVITY BIKES

Gravity bikes, also known as riders, offer both upper body and lower body aerobic workouts, and—because you actually use your body as part of the equipment—they are less expensive than many other exercise machines. To use a gravity bike, you push with both feet as you pull on the handlebars. You provide resistance by adjusting a shock-absorber-like cylinder, adding weights, repositioning your feet to higher foot pegs, or adjusting the height of the handlebars.

All gravity bikes are similar in principle but different in design and construction. Try several units before you make a choice. Worthwhile features to look for include a monitor with a variety of functions, an adjustable seat, and accessories to increase the versatility of the unit.

EXERHEALTH HEALTHRIDER

✔**BEST BUY**

The Exerhealth HealthRider is a top-of-the-line gravity bike that's easy to assemble and fun to use. The seat adjusts for users of almost any size, and the foam-padded rotating handlebar has two basic height positions. To increase resistance during your workout, the elevation panel can be set to one of three higher positions. Move the handlebar to the secondary position, just in front of the seat, to direct the workout to your back and lower body muscles. Optional weights can be added to a bar under the seat for additional resistance. Both the upper and lower foot pegs have wide pedals; you can use the upper pedals to increase the intensity of your upper body workout. A small but easy to read LCD panel registers elapsed time, number of repetitions, and average reps per minute. The monitor has an auto on/off feature. Optional accessories include a padded seat cover, weights, and a heart rate monitor. This model also comes with two additional 5-pound weights.

Specifications: height, 39"; width, 19½"; depth, 40½"; weight, 73 lb. **Warranty:** 5 years, parts; lifetime, frame.

Manufacturer's Suggested Retail Price: $500

Approximate Low Price: $500

WESLO CARDIOGLIDE

Recommended

The low-priced Weslo CardioGlide is well made and easy to use. A shock-absorber-like cylinder, mounted under the seat, provides resistance and is adjusted by rotating its collar. There are nine resistance levels: 1 to 3 for fat burning, 4 to 6 for aerobic training, and 7 to 9 for strength training. The powder-coated handlebar is looped and nonadjustable. The lower foot pegs have self-leveling pedals that rotate with the user's foot (the upper pegs do not). The comfortable seat is well padded but not adjustable. The small monitor registers speed achieved, time elapsed, total repetitions, and calories burned. A scan mode displays all functions for 5 seconds each.

Specifications: height, 46"; width, 22"; depth, 42"; weight, 55 lb. **Warranty:** 10 years, limited.

Manufacturer's Suggested Retail Price: $199

Approximate Low Price: $194

ROWING MACHINES

At one time, rowing machines were the most popular home exercise devices on the market. As new and more advanced types of home exercise equipment were introduced, rowing machines declined in popularity. Better models accurately reproduce the catch and pull of rowing to provide a true total body exercise. The action is weight-supported and zero-impact. Rowing's motion is fluid, and the lengthy stroke works both the abdominals and back.

When you shop for a rowing machine, look for a smooth-gliding seat and a sturdy glide rail that is the right length for your legs. A well-made unit should be able to accommodate both tall and short rowers. Electronic features such as a heart rate monitor and silent magnetic resistance add to the cost but may be worth it if you prefer a quieter workout.

CONCEPT II INDOOR ROWER MODEL C ✓BEST BUY

The Concept II Indoor Rower Model C, a fly-wheel/fan-type rowing machine, can provide a lifetime of rowing exercise for the whole family. Its wide, comfortable seat slides easily on a strong aluminum I-beam. The footrests flex naturally and are adjustable to a wide range of foot sizes, and the footstraps hold your feet firmly in place. The oar is a solid maple handle covered with molded rubber grips. The electronic monitor—mounted on a movable arm—is centrally located and easy to read. It registers time for 500 meters, approximate calories per hour, duration of workout, average stroke rate, heart rate (optional), approximate total calories, on/off, and memory recall. You can choose from three levels of operation: automatic, preset workout, and recall. There are extra functions for advanced users. The unit folds for easy storage and has built-in casters. A heart rate interface is available at an extra cost.

Specifications: height, 35"; width, 24"; length, 95"; weight, 61 lb.
Warranty: 2 years, select moving parts; 5 years, frame.

Manufacturer's Suggested Retail Price: $725

Approximate Low Price: $725

TUNTURI R701

Recommended

Similar in appearance to the Concept II rower, the Tunturi R701 also has the advantage of a folding design. Folded, the unit can easily slide into a closet. Its fan, covered by a fine mesh screen, provides air resistance for smooth, fluid motion. The seat is stable and glides smoothly on the glide rail. This unit has pivoting foot plates with adjustable straps, and the rowing handle is large and well padded. It comes with a small LCD readout monitor that indicates track load, tempo, calories, calories per minute, strokes, and time. Controls are simple: on/off, start/stop, reset, and mode. This rowing machine has a 100-percent carbon steel frame. Overall, this model is a safe and well-designed machine that will fulfill the needs of most exercisers.

Specifications: height, 25½"; width, 19½"; length, 93"; weight, 72 lb. **Warranty:** 1 year, labor (at recommended service centers); 2 years, parts (except frame); 10 years, frame.

Manufacturer's Suggested Retail Price: $799

Approximate Low Price: $622

TREADMILLS

Treadmills are popular, at least in part, because they offer an indoor opportunity to walk or run. Basically, a treadmill consists of a wide belt stretched over a bed and around two or more rollers. Some units are powered by their users, but others are motor-driven. AC motors usually run at one continuous speed and rely on a transmission to regulate speed. DC motors use variable voltage to regulate the speed at which the belt turns. For running, it's advisable to choose a treadmill with at least a 1½-horsepower motor.

When shopping for a treadmill, consider service history and look for these basic features: a monitor that indicates belt speed and other factors such as heart rate, mph, and distance covered; adjustable incline; handrails or levers; and easy-to-reach controls. Choose a model with a wide belt that is long enough for your stride. Better units will offer some type of cushioning between the belt and the bed, a valuable feature if you jog or run on the machine.

PACEMASTER PRO PLUS H.R.
✔**BEST BUY**

The PaceMaster Pro Plus H.R. is a top-of-the-line treadmill with an attractive price tag. Its 2.3-horsepower motor turns the belt at a speed between 0.7 and 11 mph, and the grade can be adjusted from flat to 15 percent in 0.5 percent increments. A "softstep" deck cushions each step on the 18×54-inch walking surface to reduce stress on ankles, feet, and back. This quiet, smooth-running treadmill features four preset programs—endurance, interval, cardiovascular, and fat burn—and up to four custom programs can be created and memorized by the computer. The monitor registers calorie burn, aerobic points, and distance for any combination of time, speed, and incline. Users can add an automatic warm-up and/or cooldown to any workout. A heart rate control function (included) varies the intensity of the workout to keep the user in his or her target training zone.

Specifications: height, 50"; width, 28½"; length, 68"; weight, 165 lb. **Warranty:** 1 year, labor; 2 years, limited overall; 3 years, motor; lifetime, frame.

Manufacturer's Suggested Retail Price: $1,895

Approximate Low Price: $1,895

PRECOR M9.25

Recommended

The Precor M9.25 electric treadmill is a quiet, smooth-running unit with a 1.7-horsepower motor. You can adjust its grade from 0 to 15 percent. The "floating" platform softens foot strike. Precor's "Ground Effects" elastomeric suspension system cushions the bed, and the integrated footplant increases stability by minutely reducing belt speed as your foot hits the belt. This model comes with the Precor cardiologic system to monitor heart rate and adjust speed accordingly. The M9.25 can recognize up to four users and retains information such as weight and preferred work level for each. The control console includes a manual control, custom programs, and five preprogrammed courses, including three interval courses—heart rate fitness test, weight loss, and quick start, which jumps to the last program used or to manual mode.

Specifications: height, 46"; width, 32" (at handrail); length, 68"; weight, 192 lb. **Warranty:** 1 year, labor; 3 years, parts; lifetime, frame.

Manufacturer's Suggested Retail Price: $3,000

Approximate Low Price: $2,898

STAR TRAC TR900

Recommended

Star Trac has been supplying treadmills to fitness clubs for a long time and, for several years, has offered the reliable Star Trac TR900 for home use. A foam-rubber cushion on the deck diminishes foot-strike stress. The speed of the 2-horsepower motor is monitored at a rate of 430,000 times per minute for precise control. A heart rate monitor can keep you in your training range by automatically adjusting speed and incline. The monitor displays an oval track on which small triangles indicate your position and progress while other indicators show your progress in variable-effort programs. Electronic readouts register speed, distance, elapsed time, total calories, laps, pace, and heart rate. Other controls offer scan, stop/start, speed change, elevation change, heart rate, and program selection. The 15 program options include eight hill settings, manual, weight loss, cardio plus, custom, 5K, 10K, and varied. A built-in emergency stop clip-on brings the treadmill to a safe stop as soon as it's removed. The TR900 also comes with a new "cool down" feature that allows the user to end a workout by pressing the designated key. The unit then automatically goes into a 2-minute cooling down period instead of coming to an abrupt stop.

Specifications: height, 52"; width, 28¼"; length, 69"; weight, 200 lb. **Warranty:** 1 year, labor; 2 years, parts; lifetime, frame.

Manufacturer's Suggested Retail Price: $2,995

Approximate Low Price: $2,448

STAIR CLIMBERS

Stair climbers are excellent machines for burning calories and for exercising the large major muscle groups of the lower body. Add-on accessories for the upper body can provide a total body workout. An all-out workout on a stair climber can consume as much energy as you are capable of producing.

The best stair climbers keep your feet on an even plane with the floor at all times, allowing totally natural foot articulation. Some machines, however, prevent extreme foot flexion without keeping their steps completely horizontal. When you shop for a stair climber, look for sturdy, padded handrails to aid balance; electronic programs to keep you interested; and easy-to-set resistance settings. A sturdy steel or aluminum frame is a must.

TECTRIX PERSONAL CLIMBER   ✔**BEST BUY**

The Tectrix Personal Climber utilizes a patented cable drive system for smooth, quiet operation. A patented friction brake system allows consistent and precise speed control across a wide range of climbing speeds—from 10 to 150 feet per minute. This unit features five programs: manual, custom, race, peak, and interval. The self-leveling pedals operate independently, staying horizontal throughout all phases of the workout. The large surface of the pedals provides stable support. The monitor's large LED display is easy to read and shows both progress and level of difficulty. The monitor registers the number of feet climbed per minute, program in use, distance traveled, calories burned per hour, heart rate (with the optional transmitter accessory), and time remaining/elapsed or intervals.

Specifications: height, 58"; width, 31"; depth, 42"; weight, 152 lb. **Warranty:** 1 year, labor; 3 years, parts.

Manufacturer's Suggested Retail Price: $2,295

Approximate Low Price: $2,200

STAIRMASTER 4000 PT

Stairmaster popularized stair climbers, so **Recommended** you'll find its 4000 PT model in health clubs and homes everywhere. This climber features four-bar linkage on the pedal arms to keep the pedals parallel to the ground throughout the stroke; comfortable, sloping, padded handrails; an electromagnetic brake that precisely controls pedal descent, from 26 to 138 steps per minute; and a monitor that charts elapsed time, step rate, cumulative work output, and instant/average power—it also produces a progress report. Eight preprogrammed courses and ten customizable programs are available in addition to the 14 manual control settings. This climber offers ten levels of difficulty as well as exercise periods from 1 to 45 minutes in duration. The Stairmaster 4000 PT is a rugged and dependable machine.

Specifications: height, 58"; width, 32"; depth, 40½"; weight, 150 lb. **Warranty:** 1 year, parts.

Manufacturer's Suggested Retail Price: $2,195

Approximate Low Price: $2,195

TUNTURI C416i

The Tunturi C416i, a low-priced stair climber, **Budget Buy** features independent foot action, easily adjustable resistance cylinders, and padded handlebars. The 12 preset resistance levels are adjusted by turning a dial. This unit has a carbon steel frame and a wide base for stability. A monitor registers elapsed time, steps, steps per minute, calories per minute, and total calories burned. The padded handlebars are conveniently positioned. The C416i basic climber is suitable for beginners but does not offer the advanced features and smoothness of the higher priced machines.

Specifications: height, 47½"; width, 23½"; depth, 33½"; weight, 60 lb. **Warranty:** 2 years, parts; 10 years, structural components.

Manufacturer's Suggested Retail Price: $199

Approximate Low Price: $199

SKI SIMULATORS

Ski machines offer all the benefits of cross-country skiing, which some experts consider the best all-around form of exercise. Cross-country skiing provides total body fitness. The poling motion builds upper body strength, the leg motion builds leg and lower-back strength, and the combined motions add up to a cardiovascular workout. In addition, cross-country skiing is a nonimpact exercise that doesn't pressure knees, ankles, or other joints.

NordicTrack introduced the first ski simulators in the mid-70s, and now many other companies also offer ski machines in their lines of home (and health club) equipment. There are two basic types of ski machines: independent leg motion and dependent leg motion. The former is harder to master but offers a better workout. Dependent models commonly cost more. Worthwhile features on ski machines include an easy-to-use LCD (liquid crystal display) monitor that performs a number of functions, a variable incline feature to increase front thigh workout, and preset resistance settings. Most ski machines fold for easy storage, and some have wheels for easy movement. Try several machines before you make a final choice.

NORDICTRACK PRO　　　　　　　　　　✓**BEST BUY**

The NordicTrack Pro, the most popular ski simulator from the company that started it all, is widely available via mail order and in shopping malls everywhere. It requires some effort to learn to use this machine properly. Coordinating arm and leg movements is challenging because the unit resists only during the push phase (in imitation of actual cross-country skiing), but the rewards are great once you master the technique. The front of this machine elevates to six different positions (from 0 to 10 degrees) to simulate climbing uphill, which effectively isolates and tones the quadriceps, hamstrings, and buttocks. Upper and lower resistance are set separately, and the vinyl hip-support pad can be adjusted for different users. The frame is made from chrome-plated steel, the base is oak, and the skis are oak laminate. The skis glide easily and quietly on hard rubber rollers. The nonprogrammable AccuTrack Workout monitor registers time elapsed, distance traveled, speed attained, and calories burned. An optional pulse indicator and book rack are also available. The unit folds for convenient storage and can be easily moved on its own set of rear wheels.

Specifications: height, adjustable (maximum height, 88"); width, 36"; depth, 96"; weight, 53 lb. **Warranty:** 2 years, limited on parts and labor.

Manufacturer's Suggested Retail Price: $600

Approximate Low Price: $600

TUNTURI XC560 SKIFIT

Tunturi's XC560 SkiFit provides a smooth `Recommended` glide by means of magnetic resistance. Two ski poles with molded grips add to the sensation of skiing and also pump air to increase resistance. Arm and foot movements are totally independent. Angled foot skates (instead of skis) keep feet from slipping out of position. These operate independently, and their large toe pockets can accommodate any size shoe. The display console keeps track of time, speed, distance, and calories. Hand grips on either side of the display are helpful for beginners who are not yet ready to use the poles. The display mast can be adjusted to the user's height and can be folded down for storage.

Specifications: height, 44" to 52"; width, 25"; depth, 68"; weight, 82 lb. **Warranty:** 2 years, parts (except structural parts); 10 years, structural parts.

Manufacturer's Suggested Retail Price: $249

Approximate Low Price: $224

STRIDERS

Striders are an offshoot of the ski-simulator category. On these exercisers, the legs move in a scissor-like motion, but the similarity to skiing ends there. As a rule, striders tend to work on the lower part of the body and do little for the upper part. Hands grasp a stationary rail while feet and legs go through the exercise motions. Nevertheless, striders do provide a zero-impact aerobic workout and can burn off calories when used on a regular basis.

FITNESS MASTER FM 220

✔ **BEST BUY**

The FM 220 strider is a low-cost, entry-level home machine for zero-impact aerobic exercise. The user grasps the handlebar for balance while the lower body works out. A comfortable walking stride for most people is about 24 inches, but the FM 220 can be set for strides up to 41 inches long. The machine offers no resistance, so the pace at which you exercise governs how many calories are burned. Because its hard plastic wheels roll on a plastic track, this strider tends to be noisy, so it would be difficult to listen to a TV or radio while exercising. A small display indicates elapsed time, speed attained, distance traveled, and calories burned and can also be set to count down for a specified workout period. A pacer beeps to keep you at a preset tempo, but this feature can be muted if you prefer to set your own pace. The handlebar folds down for storage.

Specifications: height, 52"; width, 20"; length, 57"; weight, 30 lb. **Warranty:** 1 year, electronics; 2 years, parts.

Manufacturer's Suggested Retail Price: $299

Approximate Low Price: $290

HOME GYMS

Home gyms have made enormous strides in recent years; now they are more advanced than ever before. Some units offer rowing, leg curls, leg extensions, inner and outer thigh exercises, ab crunches, and pulldowns, to name only a few exercise options. Knowing in advance what types of regular exercise you prefer will enable you to choose the best equipment.

Quality construction in a home gym is easy to spot: The tube frame should be at least 2 inches square, cables should be aircraft-grade and coated, pulleys should be heavy duty, and weight stacks should be easy to adjust (usually by setting a pin). Size is also an important consideration. Before you go shopping, know the measurements of the room where you will place the unit. Most of these machines can fit easily in a 10×10-foot space, but you should allow for walking-around room.

TUFF STUFF CARDIO-GYM
✔ **BEST BUY**

The Cardio-Gym is Tuff Stuff's newest model. It offers a wide variety of toning and conditioning exercises in one machine. This three-station unit (main, low pulley, and leg press) is designed to fit into the corner of a room at a 45 degree angle, so it takes up less space than some other home gyms. A unique flyarm design allows you to perform more than 20 exercises in a complete range-of-motion manner. The Cardio-Gym has two independent, 75-pound weight stacks in 5-pound increments. The frame is made from 2-inch square, 11-gauge, 120-wall tubular steel. Pulleys are heavy duty, 4½-inch, solid nylon wheels with sealed roller bearings for smooth operation. Cables are nylon coated, and stress is rated at 2,200 pounds.

Specifications: height, 74"; width, 77"; depth 61½"; weight, 480 lb. **Warranty:** 1 year, upholstery, cables, and pulleys; lifetime, limited on welded frame.

Manufacturer's Suggested Retail Price: $1,995

Approximate Low Price: $1,898

VECTRA FITNESS ON-LINE 1800   `Recommended`

The Vectra On-Line 1800 is a multistation
home gym with many features of the machines found in clubs.
Its stations include: press, butterfly (pec-dec), high pulley,
abdominal, and leg extension/leg curl. The weight stack is 210
pounds in 10-pound increments. The press station offers quick-
lock press with ball bearings. The basic 235-pound plates are
expandable to 285 pounds. All pulleys are 4½-inch nylon with
ball bearing hubs. The ⅛-inch aircraft-quality cables are internally lubricated and nylon coated, with 7-by-19-strand construction and a tensile strength rated at 2,000 pounds. Standard
accessories include a lat bar, a curl bar, padded ankle straps, a
D-handle, a padded ab strap, a squat attachment with calf
block, and a lat hold-down attachment. Optional equipment
is also available: cable-adapter clips, an accessory rack, a custom handle kit, and a 260-pound weight stack (instead of the
standard 210-lb.). This unit's high price puts it in the Recommended rather than the Best Buy category, but if you have the
space and the money, this home gym is worth considering.

Specifications: height, 83"; width, 132"; depth, 72"; weight,
677 lb. **Warranty:** 1 year, cables and upholstery; 5 years, weight
stack and pulleys; 10 years, frame.

Manufacturer's Suggested Retail Price: $3,995

Approximate Low Price: $3,995

SOLOFLEX   `Recommended`

The Soloflex has been around for about 18
years and may be the best-known home gym in the world. It
offers anaerobic and aerobic exercises. Instead of actual weights,
this home gym utilizes weightstraps, which resemble large rubber bands, in 2.5-, 5-, 10-, 25-, 50-, and 100-pound sizes. The
user increases resistance simply by adding more weightstraps.
The straight weight bar has no grips, so it offers unlimited hand
spacing, much like a free-weight barbell. Iron plates, which are
sold separately, can be added to the basic weightstraps—up to
a 900-pound limit (400 pounds in straps, 500 pounds in plates).
The barbell arm is designed to float so that it overloads your

weaker side to give that side more exercise; this develops the weaker side faster until both sides are equal. A leg extension attachment and a butterfly attachment are available options.

Specifications: height, 72"; width, 48"; depth, 48"; weight, 170 lb. **Warranty:** 5 years, limited.

Manufacturer's Suggested Retail Price: $995

Approximate Low Price: $895

TOTAL BODY CONDITIONING MACHINES

Total body conditioning machines are a new concept in fitness. They allow you to perform a number of exercises at the same time, thereby burning calories and toning muscles in a no-impact workout. While most fitness machines work one major muscle group at a time, total body conditioning machines work several simultaneously.

CROSS CONDITIONING SYSTEMS
BODY MILL

✓ **BEST BUY**

The Cross Conditioning Systems Body Mill is a total body workout machine designed to be used by all family members of all abilities. The unit resembles a ski machine in that there are poles for both hands, and the feet slide in a skiing motion. A padded waist belt holds the user from behind, and a computer-controlled electromagnetic brake provides resistance. The frame and towers are welded, high-tensile-strength, aluminum extrusions, and the tower supports are welded structural steel. All bearings are factory lubricated and sealed, so they do not require periodic maintenance. This machine comes with eight preprogrammed exercise courses, from "walk in the park" to "Himalayan trek." Up to five custom profiles can be created and stored in memory. The Body Mill tones muscles in the chest, arms, back, hips, legs, and glutes. A vacuum fluorescent display (VFD) monitor registers goal speed, actual speed, total distance, time remaining (or elapsed), energy expenditure (in calories per hour, watts, or mets), total calories, and heart rate. Displays and VFD instructions are available in English, German, Japanese, and Spanish.

Specifications: height, 60"; length, 85"; width, 29"; weight, 305 lb. **Warranty:** 2 years, limited on parts and labor.

Manufacturer's Suggested Retail Price: $4,995

Approximate Low Price: $4,395

CROSS CONDITIONING SYSTEMS
BODY TREK

✔ **BEST BUY**

Like the Body Mill, the Body Trek is a total body workout machine designed for use by all family members, regardless of ability level. This model resembles a walking or jogging machine in that the user's feet move in a natural elliptical motion, providing a no-impact workout for less stress on joints. As you walk, your hands grasp poles that move in conjunction with your leg motion. The result is smooth, fluid movement that tones arms, chest, back, hips, legs, and glutes. The unit, which can move either forward or in reverse, is constructed of welded structural steel and requires no lubrication. Its eight preprogrammed exercise courses include Vail pass, steady climb, and competition. The easy-to-read display shows calories burned, calories per hour, distance traveled, speed attained, and time remaining or elapsed. An optional heart rate monitor is also available.

Specifications: height, 64¼"; length, 65"; width, 29"; weight, 290 lb. **Warranty:** 2 years, limited on parts and labor.

Manufacturer's Suggested Retail Price: $3,595

Approximate Low Price: $3,595

HOME IMPROVEMENT

Maintaining a home, whether it be a house, condo, or apartment, can be a time-consuming and expensive task. First and foremost, a home must be kept safe from such threats as fire and carbon monoxide fumes. Also important is keeping up with repairs and maintenance. The products in this chapter can help you do both.

SAFETY EQUIPMENT

The relative cost of smoke alarms, carbon monoxide (CO) detectors, and fire extinguishers is small compared to the lethal danger of carbon monoxide or the damage incurred during a home fire. Smoke alarms can warn you relatively early that a fire has started in the home, and the proper use of a reliable fire extinguisher can save you thousands of dollars in damage. Additionally, a reliable CO detector can warn you and your family early if this deadly gas is present in the home.

Fire extinguishers are rated by Underwriter's Laboratories, Inc. according to the types of fire they are designed to put out. There are three classes of fires. Class A fires involve paper, wood, cloth, rubber, and some plastics. Class B fires involve flammable liquids such as grease, motor oil, paint thinner, and gasoline. Class C fires involve electrical equipment. Generally, fire extinguishers rated A, B, *and* C are best for home use.

All fire extinguishers receive a numeric rating, which indicates the size of the fire they are capable of fighting. For example, a 4-A rating means that the unit will put out twice as much Class A fire as a unit with a 2-A rating. There are no numeric ratings for C class (electrical) fires, because the C rating simply means that the extinguishing agent in the unit is not electrically conductive.

You should check your extinguishers on a monthly basis. Extinguishers with a dial-type gauge are easiest to check. A needle indicates whether the unit is operable or in need of recharging. The unit should be recharged by qualified professionals after every use, no matter how brief. Look in the Yellow Pages under "Fire Extinguishers."

All fire extinguishers come with mounting brackets. The most common are simple hooks or brackets that can be screwed into a wall stud. Marine brackets are also available, but they are best used in cases where knocking the unit out of the bracket is a possibility. Hang fire extinguishers where they will be handy but not in the way.

Smoke alarms can be found in almost every home in America. They are relatively inexpensive and almost foolproof. Smoke alarms go off when smoke is detected in the home. A smoke alarm is useless if it does not work, and estimates suggest that about one-third of all smoke detectors in use today are inoperable due to dead batteries. Manufacturers and firefighters recommend that you check all smoke alarms in your home weekly.

Most smoke detectors are operated by a 9-volt battery. Some units are hard-wired into the electrical circuits of homes and then use a 9-volt battery in the event of a power failure. More and more, this type of unit is being required by state and local building codes in newly constructed buildings. The hearing impaired should consider a smoke detector that has a strobe light as well as an alarm.

Check your smoke alarm annually to make certain that dust does not clog the vents on the case. Never paint smoke alarms to match ceiling or wall colors as this could hinder operation.

Smoke detectors generally operate by one of two methods: ionization or photoelectricity. Some of the high-end units use both methods of smoke detection. Ionization involves the use of a small, harmless amount of radioactive material to make the air in an internal chamber conduct electricity. When smoke passes into this chamber, the flow of electricity is interrupted, and the alarm is sounded. Ionization alarms are widely sold and inexpensive (usually under $20). They pose no threat to your health or the environment.

Photoelectric smoke detectors, like all photoelectric systems, shine a tiny beam of light toward a sensor. When smoke passes through the beam, it breaks the stream and the alarm is sounded.

All models reviewed in this section have a test button so you can check the condition of the battery to make sure the unit is working. One of the units can be checked by shining a flashlight at the button, a handy feature if the unit is to be mounted on a high ceiling. For those units that have both ionization and photoelectric sensors, there are two buttons for checking both systems. All units chirp when the battery is low on power. Do not ignore this sound or remove the battery to stop it—replace the battery immediately. To test units in stairwells or on high ceilings, use a broom handle.

Carbon monoxide (CO) is a colorless, odorless, deadly gas that can be present in the home as a result of incomplete combustion in any fuel-burning appliance. Exposure to low levels of CO can cause flu-like symptoms, such as headache, dizziness, fatigue, nausea, confusion, and irritability. Prolonged exposure to higher levels of CO causes fainting and, in extreme cases, can lead to coma, brain damage, or death.

The best way to protect yourself and your family from the dangers of CO is to make certain that all appliances are running properly, including the furnace, clothes dryer, water heater, wood-burning stove, fireplace, and space heaters. Check your home for proper ventilation. Also keep in mind that automobile exhaust contains carbon monoxide and can enter a home if a car is left running in an attached garage. A well-vented home with properly operating appliances should have minimum accumulations of CO. If your home is tightly sealed against the weather, which is common during the winter months, the danger of CO accumulation increases.

The Consumer Product Safety Commission (CPSC) recommends installing at least one carbon monoxide detector with an audible alarm near the sleeping area of a home. Most CO detectors resemble smoke alarms in appearance. Some units plug into an electrical outlet in the home and have battery backup as well. Others are operated by a 9-volt battery.

Best Buys '97

   The fire extinguishers, smoke detectors, and CO detectors
that follow have been rated as Best Buys because we believe
they offer good value for the price you'll pay. If you want additional information on safety and effectiveness for these or any
other units you may consider purchasing, you can consult public safety organizations such as the National Safety Council.
Remember that a Best Buy designation applies only to the
model listed. It does not apply to other models made by the
same manufacturer.

Fire Extinguishers

KIDDE FIRE EXTINGUISHER FA340HD   ✔**BEST BUY**

   As a multipurpose fire extinguisher for the
home, the Kidde FA340HD is a good choice. While the unit is
rated for fighting all classes of fires, it is especially useful for
Class B and C fires. The unit has plastic handles, a plastic break-
away pull ring, and a dial-type gauge for checking the charge
condition. It comes with a plastic, U-shaped wall-mounting
bracket, which holds the unit just below the handles. Mounting screws were not included with the unit we tested.

Specifications: height, 16"; diameter, 7"; weight, 9 lb.
UL Rating: 3-A, 40-B, C. **Warranty:** 6 years, limited.

Manufacturer's Suggested Retail Price: $64

Approximate Low Price: $24

FIRST ALERT FIRE EXTINGUISHER FE2A10   ✔**BEST BUY**

   The First Alert FE2A10 fire extinguisher is a
dependable, multipurpose unit for fighting small fires around
the home. At a filled weight of 10 pounds, the unit may prove
to be too heavy for some users, but it is powerful enough to
douse all classes of fires in the home. The unit has metal handles and a pull ring, with a tamper-proof plastic security seal
and a metal hose-retainer clip. A dial-type gauge shows the
condition of the charge at a glance. The unit is rechargeable. A

metal ring is located on the back for wall mounting on the supplied hook.

Specifications: height, 14¾"; diameter, 5¼"; weight, 10 lb. **UL Rating:** 2-A, 10-B, C. **Warranty:** 5 years, limited.

Manufacturer's Suggested Retail Price: $32

Approximate Low Price: $31

Smoke Detectors

FIRST ALERT 10 YEAR LITHIUM POWER SA10YR

✓**BEST BUY**

This is a top-of-the-line ionization smoke detector with an 85dB alarm horn. It has a clear plastic button for testing the unit and a blue plastic button that will silence the unit for about 10 minutes if the alarm goes off because of nuisance smoke (for example, cooking smoke in the kitchen). The unit has a special activation switch, which must be turned on before use by turning a screw on the back. This smoke detector will beep once a minute when it requires replacement. Batteries are permanently installed and cannot be replaced. You must buy a new unit when the 10-year battery dies. It comes with a plastic mounting bracket, mounting screws, and screw anchors.

Specifications: length, 5⅝"; width, 2½"; depth, 8⅝"; weight, 9 oz. **Warranty:** 10 years, limited.

Manufacturer's Suggested Retail Price: $30

Approximate Low Price: $30

FIRST ALERT DOUBLE SYSTEM SA301

✓**BEST BUY**

The First Alert Double System is a high-quality, dual ionization and photoelectric smoke and fire detector. The unit has two test buttons and an 85dB alarm horn. One of the test buttons is clear plastic and flashes red several times a minute to let you know the unit is working. The alarm will beep once a minute for about 30 days when the battery requires replacement. The battery is installed through the back of the unit. It comes with a 9-volt battery, metal mounting bracket, mounting screws, and screw anchors. An informative booklet is also included.

Specifications: length, 5½"; width, 2½"; weight, 11 oz. **Warranty:** 5 years, limited.

Manufacturer's Suggested Retail Price: $30

Approximate Low Price: $26

FYRNETICS 1275H   ✓BEST BUY

The Fyrnetics 1275H is a 120-volt, hard-wired unit that can be connected in series to other smoke alarms in the home—up to 24 smoke detectors total. The unit should be connected to the household current by a licensed electrician. This unit utilizes the ionization method of smoke detection, and it has a 9-volt battery backup to keep it operating during a power failure. A test button flashes red every 40 seconds to indicate that the unit is operating. A distinctive chirp can be heard when the battery needs replacing or if the unit is not receiving household current. A hush button, located next to the test button, can be used to silence the alarm if it goes off because of nuisance smoke. It has an 85dB alarm horn. The unit is supplied with a 9-volt battery, a 120-volt wiring harness, a plastic mounting bracket, a tamper-resistant locking pin, and an informative booklet.

Specifications: height, 1½"; diameter, 5"; weight, 0.58 lb. with battery. **Warranty:** 5 years, limited.

Manufacturer's Suggested Retail Price: $30

Approximate Low Price: $21

FIRST ALERT HALL & STAIRWAY SA150LTD   ✓BEST BUY

The SA150LTD makes an effective smoke detector for halls and stairways. It utilizes the ionization method of smoke detection. This unit has a built-in escape light, which is activated at the same time as the alarm, and the bulb is replaceable. It has a gold-colored test button that can be activated by pressing on it or by shining any D-cell flashlight on it (from up to 15 feet away). The alarm will beep once a minute for about 30 days when the battery requires replacement. The alarm horn sounds at 85 dB. This unit requires two 9-volt batteries, which are included. The batteries are installed in the base of the unit after opening the hinged cover. The unit comes supplied with a plastic mounting base, mounting screws, and screw anchors. An informative booklet is also included.

Specifications: height, 1¾"; diameter, 5½"; weight, 8 oz. **Warranty:** 5 years, limited.

Manufacturer's Suggested Retail Price: $20

Approximate Low Price: $18

Carbon Monoxide Detectors

FIRST ALERT FCD1

✔**BEST BUY**

The First Alert FCD1 is a top-of-the-line detector with a replaceable sensor module. This patented module, called SensorPack, contains two discs that simulate the body's response to carbon monoxide exposure over time. The module also contains a sealed, long-life battery. To activate this unit, the module is installed in the side of the detector, and the unit is then mounted in a suitable location. A test button flashes once every 45 seconds to indicate the unit is operating. This button can also be used to silence the alarm. The unit will chirp when the module needs replacing, which, according to the manufacturer, is after 2 to 3 years. The alarm horn sounds at 85 dB. This detector will sound an alarm within 60 minutes for CO levels of 100 PPM, within 25 minutes for CO levels of 200 PPM, and within 10 minutes for CO levels of 400 PPM. This unit is supplied with a plastic mounting base, mounting screws, and screw anchors. An informative booklet is also included.

Specifications: height, 2.16"; diameter, 5.66"; weight, 0.71 lb. **Warranty:** 1 year, full; 2 years on SensorPack module; 5 years, limited.

Manufacturer's Suggested Retail Price: $50

Approximate Low Price: $38

FYRNETICS LIFESAVER FYCO 5N

✓**BEST BUY**

The Fyrnetics Lifesaver FYCO 5N carbon monoxide detector is a plug-in unit with a 9-volt battery backup. The unit's CO sensor has a 10-year life span. It monitors CO levels every 2½ minutes, and the alarm horn sounds at 85 dB. A test/reset button can be used to silence the alarm. A green LED indicates that the unit is operating properly. If the green LED blinks and the alarm chirps, replace the battery. This same LED will blink red when CO levels reach 60 PPM, at which time you will also hear a low-level beep. Fyrnetics refers to this as its low-level warning feature. This detector will sound its 85dB alarm within 90 minutes for a CO level of 100 PPM, within 35 minutes for a level of 200 PPM, and within 15 minutes for a level of 400 PPM. A 9-volt battery and an instruction booklet come with this unit.

Specifications: height, 3½"; diameter, 5⅝"; weight, 1.3 lb. with battery. **Warranty:** 5 years, limited.

Manufacturer's Suggested Retail Price: $70

Approximate Low Price: $50

ENZONE AIR ZONE II

✓**BEST BUY**

The Enzone Air Zone II carbon monoxide detector is a plug-in unit with battery backup (six AA batteries are required). It has an 8-foot-long power cord so the unit can be mounted at eye level—a location the manufacturer feels is more suitable for detecting CO levels than at the standard outlet height. When carbon monoxide is created, it is hot and therefore lighter than cold air, causing it to rise. Thus, concentrations of CO will be greater near the ceiling. The unit is equipped with a test/reset button, a green power-on light, a yellow warning light for CO levels of less than 100 PPM, and a red alarm light. The red light will blink and the alarm will chirp every 5 seconds when batteries need to be changed. This detector will sound its 85dB alarm horn within 90 minutes for a CO level of 100 PPM, within 35 minutes for a level of 200 PPM, and within 15 minutes for a level of 400 PPM. The unit is supplied with an AC adapter, an 8-foot cord, and an instruction book.

Specifications: height, 7.35"; width, 3.75"; depth, 1.55"; weight, 1.75 lb. with transformer. **Warranty:** 2 years, limited.

Manufacturer's Suggested Retail Price: $40

Approximate Low Price: $40

GARAGE DOOR OPENERS

Garage door openers allow you to open a garage door with the push of a button from the safety and convenience of your automobile. Another push of the button closes and locks the door. Garage door openers are widely available in home centers, and most units can be installed by the do-it-yourselfer with common hand and power tools. Complete installation takes about a day, though an extra pair of hands will make part of the work easier to accomplish. Retail prices range from $130 to $350. Some units come complete with a rail while others require that the rail be purchased separately (an additional $80 to $90).

All new garage door openers are required to have several safety features to prevent injury. Since 1982, all openers have been required to include a mechanism that automatically reverses the door within 2 seconds after coming into contact with anything in its path. In addition, most openers now have an electric eye, which is mounted on the door jamb about 12 inches from the floor. This convenient feature reverses the door if anything gets in its path.

All garage door openers come with at least one remote control and a doorbell-like button for operating the door from inside the garage. Some manufacturers offer a remote control with codes that can be set by the user. More advanced units are offered by many manufacturers in an effort to foil burglars. Genie, for example, offers a remote controller that selects a new access code from 4.3 billion combinations each time the unit is used.

Additional features on many garage door openers include an exterior keypad for opening the door without a remote controller, a lighted wall button on the interior of the garage, a key chain-size remote controller, and a controller that turns on exterior lights and opens the garage door.

Best Buys '97

Our Best Buy, Recommended, and Budget Buy choices follow for garage door openers. Remember that a particular designation applies only to the model listed, not to other models made by the same manufacturer.

GENIE IS550-2

✓ BEST BUY

The dependable Genie IS550-2 is a screw-drive garage door opener with a ½-horsepower motor. One of the features that make this unit a Best Buy is a system that automatically reverses the closing garage door when objects pass through its infrared beam. This same system is also self-diagnostic, emitting a code via red and green LED indicators to help homeowners easily identify problems and their possible solutions. This Genie unit also uses a sensitivity system to open and close a garage door with minimum force. During installation, the homeowner simply presets the level of force with the opener's separate opening and closing sensitivity adjustments. Each time the system opens or closes the door, it refers to these settings and never exceeds the amount of force preset. Also featured on new Genie openers and remote controllers is a security system. This system prevents thieves from entering the garage by eliminating access code duplication. Each time the system is activated, it automatically selects a new access code from 4.3 billion combinations. The Genie IS550-2 is supplied with two remote controllers, a lighted wall button, an installation manual, and a toll-free telephone number for installation assistance.

Warranty: 2 years, limited on parts.

Manufacturer's Suggested Retail Price: $190

Approximate Low Price: $181

STANLEY SL 700

✓ BEST BUY

The SL 700 is a top-of-the-line chain-drive unit that uses a ½-horsepower motor for a little extra power to lift garage doors up to 8 feet in height. This unit has several effective safety systems and features. Among the most significant is an electronic instant reverse system, which automatically opens the door if it is obstructed during the closing cycle. Also useful is a safety monitor that electronically controls the force-resistance of a door's closing cycle. When the force exceeds a safe limit, this system causes the door to reverse and open. An infrared reversing system stops and reverses a closing door when the infrared beam detects something in the threshold. Another safety system opens the door if it hasn't closed completely in 23 seconds, while yet another system flashes lights when a safety feature has been activated. Finally, there is a feature that will allow the opener to accept the closing signal only from the wall button, and that button must be held down for the entire closing cycle or the door will automatically open. There is also a 4½ minute light delay. This unit comes with one hand-held two-button transmitter and a lighted wall-mounted push-button opener. An informative installation booklet is enclosed.

Warranty: Lifetime limited on the motor; 1 year, parts.

Manufacturer's Suggested Retail Price: $199

Approximate Low Price: $195

SEARS CRAFTSMAN 53491 ✔BEST BUY

A screw-drive unit, the Sears Craftsman 53491 garage door opener is as dependable as the 53535 chain/cable-driven unit (reviewed later in this section). This ½-horsepower model features an isolation system that reduces motor vibration, resulting in fairly quiet operation. The timing belt, which controls the speed at which the door is closed, is made of high-strength fiberglass wrapped in rubber for durability. Standard safety features include an infrared safety reversing sensor, a safety reverse, a 4½ minute light delay, and an emergency release that allows manual door operation during power failure. A 4-foot power cord plugs into a standard grounded outlet. A standard control console allows for operation of the door from inside the garage. The 53491 comes with two remote controls that have a security coding system, which will automatically choose a new entry code from a base of 3.5 billion codes each time the door is opened . This unit can also be used with compact and keypad wireless controls, which are available at an additional cost. An easy-to-follow installation and maintenance manual is included. A 24-hour toll-free number can provide help with any installation problems.

Warranty: 5 years, motor; 1 year, parts; 90 days, labor.

Manufacturer's Suggested Retail Price: $180

Approximate Low Price: $180

SEARS CRAFTSMAN 53535

Recommended

The Sears Craftsman 53535 garage door opener is a dependable ½-horsepower chain/cable-driven unit. Included standard safety features are the infrared safety reversing sensor, which stops the door and reverses it before making contact, and a safety reverse, in which the door automatically reverses when it meets an obstruction. Other safety devices include a 4½ minute light delay, a lock switch that locks out hand-held radio signals to prevent unlawful access, and an emergency release that allows manual door operation during power failure. A 4-foot power cord plugs into a standard grounded outlet. A control console with an independent light switch allows you to operate the door from inside the garage. The unit comes with two remote controls that have a security coding system, which automatically chooses a new entry code from a base of 3.5 billion codes each time the door is opened. This unit can also be used with compact and keypad wireless controls that are available at an additional cost. An easy-to-use installation and maintenance manual is included.

Warranty: 5 years, motor; 1 year, parts; 90 days, labor.

Manufacturer's Suggested Retail Price: $160

Approximate Low Price: $160

STANLEY SD 550

Recommended

The SD 550 is one of Stanley's heavy duty screw-drive garage door openers, which has a ½-horsepower motor for dependable operation. It fits garage doors up to 8 feet high. This unit has the same safety features as the other Stanley models listed here, including an electronic instant reverse system that automatically opens the door if an obstruction is met during the closing cycle, a safety monitor that electronically regulates the force resistance of a door's closing cycle, an infrared reversing system that stops and reverses a closing door when the infrared beam detects something in the threshold, a system that opens the door if it hasn't closed completely in 23 seconds, and a feature that allows the opener to accept the closing signal only from the wall button. This unit comes with two hand-held, two-button transmitters, a lighted wall-mounted push-button opener, and an informative installation booklet.

Warranty: Lifetime on motor; 3 years, parts.

Manufacturer's Suggested Retail Price: $229

Approximate Low Price: $185

STANLEY ST 200

A basic chain-drive garage door opener, the Stanley ST 200 features a ⅓-horsepower motor for dependable operation and fits most doors up to 7½ feet high. The ST 200 has the same safety features as the other Stanley garage door openers listed here, including an electronic instant reverse system, a safety monitor that electronically regulates the force resistance of a door's closing cycle, an infrared reversing system that stops and reverses a closing door when the infrared beam detects something in the threshold, a system that opens the door if it hasn't closed completely in 23 seconds, and a feature that allows the opener to accept the closing signal only from the wall button. The ST 200 is a Budget Buy because of the lack of frills and features. It comes with a wall-mounted push-button opener and an informative installation booklet. A hand-held remote transmitter is available at an additional cost.

Warranty: 5 years, limited on the motor; 1 year, parts.

Manufacturer's Suggested Retail Price: $149

Approximate Low Price: $140

POWER HAND TOOLS

Power drills are the most basic of power tools. The keyed chuck—once a part of all power drills—has fallen by the wayside thanks to the much-improved keyless type, at least on the currently popular ⅜-inch-capacity electric drills. These drills are fast, accurate, and have excellent gripping power—plus, there is no key to lose. Nails and old-fashioned wood screws are passé as fasteners for structural woodwork, cabinetry, decking, and drywall. A high-torque, reversing power tool—as opposed to a hammer—is needed to sink the new self-drilling screws. When we do need a drill, a tool that can both drill and screw is preferable. Welcome to the drill/driver. Battery-powered drilling tools have evolved from 6-volt units in 1.2- and 2.4-volt increments to 14.2-volt pro tools. You may want to choose a drill and a drill/driver, either corded or cordless. Look for cordless drill/drivers that come in a kit with accessory bits, charger, and two batteries for uninterrupted service. Cordless utility screwdrivers are still useful and necessary to assemble modular furniture and to take things apart for repairs.

A circular saw provides the best way to accurately make straight, angle, beveled, and ripping cuts. By selecting the proper blades, you can professionally cut anything from treated deck lumber to paneling and laminates, even masonry and thin metals. Select a jigsaw for drywall and paneling cutouts. A jigsaw is also the best choice for making curving and scrolling cuts. A variety of available blades makes cutting metal and plastic possible.

The single most useful power sander is the random-orbit palm-grip type. With quick-stick prepunched sanding discs, you can quickly change grits to do everything from heavy stock removal to very fine sanding. The random-orbit feature leaves very little surface scratching.

A moderately priced and easy-to-use power plane makes it possible to accurately trim and smooth edges on furniture, shelves, doors, and other surfaces up to 3⅝ inches wide. An edge guide, which is sometimes offered as an accessory, is well worth purchasing.

The final power tool that is a must-have for home improvement projects and repairs is a router for trimming laminate, making attractive edges on furniture and craft items, carving freehand, and making slots, grooves, dados, and rabbets. There are two types of routers, a plunge model and a barrel router. If most of your work is likely to involve plunging into wood for cut starting, consider a plunge router, which plunges from a retracted position to a preset depth and then locks to proceed with the cut. If most of your task involves edge work, a conventional, adjustable barrel router will do the job. Dozens of cutter bits are available to make contour cuts. Though some excellent routers are available that accept ½-inch cutters, ¼-inch collet routers are smaller, lighter, less expensive, and easier to handle for portable work.

Best Buys '97

Our Best Buy, Recommended, and Budget Buy choices follow for power hand tools. This section is divided into drills and electric screwdrivers, saws, and miscellaneous power tools. Remember that a Best Buy, Recommended, or Budget Buy designation applies only to the model listed, not to other models made by the same manufacturer.

Electric Drills, Drill/Drivers, Screwdrivers

RYOBI CTH1202K CORDLESS
DRILL/DRIVER

✔**BEST BUY**

The Ryobi CTH1202K features a soft-grip, center-positioned handle for comfort and balance. This VSR (variable speed, reversing) drill holds a 1-hour battery charge. Other desirable features include an electric brake and six clutch settings that drive the screws into the surface in a controlled manner. The rigid plastic protective carrying case also houses a 1-hour charger, a second battery to ensure virtually continuous operation, and screwdriver bits. The 12 volts of power allow the user to drill with large bits or to drive and remove large, long wood screws. This Ryobi model also drives and removes moderate-sized nuts.

Specifications: ⅜-inch keyless chuck; weight, 3.6 lb. **Warranty:** 2 years, limited.

Manufacturer's Suggested Retail Price: $149

Approximate Low Price: $129

BOSCH 1001VSR CORDED DRILL   ✓**BEST BUY**

The Bosch 1001VSR is a high-quality corded drill that's a good choice for those who do not purchase many tools. It features a hardy 4-amp, variable speed reversing motor and quiet, cut-steel gearing. The fan on this Bosch drill works exceptionally well to dissipate motor-generated heat, making this unit ideal for continuous-duty work. The ⅜-inch keyed chuck is of very good quality. The drill accepts bits up to 1 inch in diameter for drilling in wood, ⅜-inch bits for use in steel, and ½-inch bits for drilling in aluminum. The comfortable grip is big enough for a large hand, and it has a lip at the butt end to keep it from sliding out of your grasp.

Specifications: ⅜-inch keyed chuck; weight, 3.3 lb. **Warranty:** 1 year, limited.

Manufacturer's Suggested Retail Price: $79

Approximate Low Price: $79

RYOBI D18C CORDED DRILL/DRIVER   ✓**BEST BUY**

Here is a corded compact drill/driver you can confidently use for almost any do-it-yourself drilling or screw-driving chore. Pros like this tool for the same reason you will: It is compact and ergonomically designed for prolonged operation and for use in tight places. The D18C is reversible and has six clutch positions for woodworking with screws. It has five easily changed torque settings for driving in screws and one setting for drilling. The drill has one speed, which operates at 540 rpm. A 10-foot power cord is an added convenience.

Specifications: ⅜-inch keyless chuck; weight, 2 lb. **Warranty:** 2 years, limited.

Manufacturer's Suggested Retail Price: $45
Approximate Low Price: $37

MAKITA 6041DWXK
CORDLESS DRILL/DRIVER

Recommended

Compared to heavier, more powerful cordless drill/drivers, this model, which has reversible action, might be considered a Budget Buy. However, because it is a well-made tool from a highly respected manufacturer, this Makita model is a Recommended product. Because of its light weight, and the fact that it is a keyless-chuck model, it is ideal for the home-owner who prefers an easy-to-use, comfortable tool. However, it still has adequate power for most tasks. For added value and convenience, five high-speed steel drill bits, four Phillips power bits, five slotted power bits, and four nut-driver socket bits are stored in the carrying case along with the charger. The battery recharges in 3 hours.

Specifications: ⅜-inch keyless chuck; weight, 1.8 lb. **Warranty:** 1 year, limited against defects in parts and workmanship.

Manufacturer's Suggested Retail Price: $105
Approximate Low Price: $68

SEARS CRAFTSMAN 11169
CORDLESS SCREWDRIVER

Recommended

This tool has less screwdriving power than the drill/drivers discussed above, making it a Recommended prod-uct rather than a Best Buy. However, the Sears 11169 has a def-inite place in any do-it-yourselfer's tool kit. It is extremely handy for everyday household tasks, particularly in close quar-ters. The handle adjusts to a pistol shape for added control, or it can be left as a stick for use in tight places. This screwdriver operates at 130 rpm and 400 rpm no-load speeds, and it has a ¼-inch hex collet to accept standard hex bits. It comes with two double-ended screwdriver bits and a wrist strap. It charges in 3 hours in an LED charger that is also a cradle.

Specifications: weight, 3 lb. **Warranty:** 1 year, repairs.

Manufacturer's Suggested Retail Price: $30

Approximate Low Price: $30

Circular Saws and Jigsaws

PORTER-CABLE 743 OR 347
CIRCULAR SAW

✔**BEST BUY**

   This powerful, highly regarded 7¼-inch circular saw has just about everything you could want in a helical or spur gear-drive saw. It comes in a version for right-handers and a version for left-handers; the 743 is the blade-left model, and the 347 is the mirror-image blade-right model. The desirable features on this saw are strong, weight-reducing magnesium shoes and blade guards, top-of-the-line ball-and-needle bearings, adjustable stops at 90 and 45 degrees, and a 10-foot, flexible rubber cord. It also has a spindle lock for blade changes—a feature not found on many lower-priced circular saws. The blade has carbide tips. The 743/347 is equipped with a dust nozzle for an optional vac hose.

Specifications: 5800 rpm blade speed; 7¼-inch blade; weight, 10¼ lb. **Warranty:** 1 year, limited.

Manufacturer's Suggested Retail Price: $135

Approximate Low Price: $133

SKIL 5350 CIRCULAR SAW

✔**BEST BUY**

   Circular saws are so closely identified with Skil that many refer to any circular saw, regardless of brand, as a Skilsaw. Moderately priced, this saw is at the top end of Skil's consumer line. A 2¾ horsepower, 12-amp motor operates the 5350 saw. Its desirable features include ball-and-sleeve bearings, a remote lower-guard lift lever, and a lateral lock-off switch to prevent accidental starts. The maximum cutting depth is 2⁷⁄₁₆ at 90 degrees and 1⁵⁄₁₆ at 45 degrees. Additional features are onboard wrench storage and truly comfortable rear and front handles. Though this saw does not have an arbor (or, spindle) lock, and it has only a 6-foot plastic power cord, its high quality and reasonable price make it a Best Buy.

Specifications: 5500 rpm blade speed; 7¼-inch blade; weight, 10.1 lb. **Warranty:** 2 years, home use.

Manufacturer's Suggested Retail Price: $148

Approximate Low Price: $92

RYOBI JS45 JIGSAW

✓**BEST BUY**

Variable speed jigsaws such as the JS45 are the preferred tools for plunge cutting and for cutting curves and intricate patterns in wood. With the proper blades, variable speed jigsaws can also cut patterns in plastics and in some metals. They're also suited for ripping and crosscutting wood. Variable speeds (from 0 to 3000 strokes per minute in the case of the JS45) match the speed to the work. The baseplate on the JS45 adjusts from 0° to 45° for right or left bevel cuts. The baseplate reverses to adapt for scrolling or straight cutting. The cutting depth is 2¼ inches for wood and ½ inch for aluminum. It also has a chip shield and sawdust blower.

Specifications: ⅝-inch stroke; weight, 3.1 lb. **Warranty:** 2 years, limited.

Manufacturer's Suggested Retail Price: $45

Approximate Low Price: $40

SKIL 4470 JIGSAW

Recommended

If you plan to do a lot of intricate scroll or orbital cuts, use a scrolling jigsaw, which has a blade that can be steered for better control. For aggressive cutting, the five variable orbit ranges on the Skil 4470 scrolling jigsaw allow the blade to thrust forward as it cuts. Furthermore, this reasonably priced jigsaw with a 3.7-amp motor has a variable speed range of 0 to 3,200 strokes per minute. There is a blade storage compartment in the body, as well as a wrench storage slot. The linear counterbalance reduces vibration. This model features a directed air stream to blow dust away from the cutting line.

Specifications: ⅝-inch stroke; weight, 4 lb. **Warranty:** 2 years.

Manufacturer's Suggested Retail Price: $55

Approximate Low Price: Not available

Miscellaneous Home Improvement Tools

DEWALT DW421
RANDOM-ORBIT SANDER
✔**BEST BUY**

DeWalt's DW421 is one of the best 5-inch, hook-and-loop random-orbit palm sanders. Those who plan to own only one power sander should strongly consider one with an integral dust collection system, such as the DW421. The DW421 features 100 percent ball-bearing construction. Its switch is dust sealed, and it has an excellent finishing system, which keeps the pad at a controllable speed. An effective counterbalance system minimizes vibration.

Specifications: pad has 5-inch diameter; weight, 3 lb. **Warranty:** 30 days, no-risk satisfaction guarantee; 1 year, warranty and free service contract.

Manufacturer's Suggested Retail Price: $144

Approximate Low Price: $76

RYOBI RE175 PLUNGE ROUTER
✔**BEST BUY**

Because of its smooth plunging action and fine depth-adjustment features, a plunge router is the best choice for tasks that require the user to begin cutting in the middle of a workpiece. Plunge routers don't come any better than the RE175, at least in the ¼-inch collet category. This model has an electronic variable speed control, allowing the user to start a plunge cut slowly and to handle large router bits more comfortably. The 9-amp motor rates the tool at 1¾ horsepower. The plunge depth ranges from 0 to 2 inches. The ergonomic grips are well-shaped for confident handling and for easy starting and locking at your fingertips. The polished plunge rods are protected with accordian boots. There is also a transparent chip shield, and the spindle locks for easy bit changes.

Specifications: ¼-inch collet; weight, 8.1 lb. **Warranty:** 2 years, limited.

Manufacturer's Suggested Retail Price: $125

Approximate Low Price: $110

SEARS CRAFTSMAN 17505 ROUTER

`Recommended`

For a solid performance at a reasonable price from this size router, it is hard to beat the Sears 17505. The 17505 is a ¼-inch collet capacity router, which operates at 2 horsepower. It has a dial variable speed control that operates in a range of 15,000 to 25,000 rpm. There is a lock-on trigger in one of the smooth, comfortable grips for continuous use. It also comes with an automatic spindle lock for changing the cutter bits with ease. Additional convenient features include a clear plastic chip shield and a built-in work light. A zero reset ring raises or lowers the depth of the cut incrementally. A threaded lock knob locks the motor housing to the base.

Specifications: weight, 8.1 lb. **Warranty:** 1 year, parts and labor.

Manufacturer's Suggested Retail Price: $80

Approximate Low Price: $60

SKIL 7435 RANDOM-ORBIT SANDER

`Recommended`

The Skil 7435 is a competent, reasonably priced tool for the do-it-yourselfer who is looking for a two-hand grip random-orbit sander. The 7435 uses 5-inch hook-and-loop sanding discs and polishing accessories. Its all ball-bearing construction will help give this tool a long life. In addition, it has the all-important dust bag to keep dirt and dust away from its parts. Cleverly, the front handle folds up for close-quarter work. The integral pad dampening system effectively controls pad speed, which helps prevent gouging and controls vibration.

Specifications: pad has 5-inch diameter; weight, 3.8 lb. **Warranty:** 2 years, home use.

Manufacturer's Suggested Retail Price: $75

Approximate Low Price: $75

SEARS CRAFTSMAN 17371 POWER HAND PLANER

`Recommended`

Every do-it-yourselfer needs a power hand planer to smooth edges, trim sticking doors, and surface wood.

This model planes up to 3⅝-inch wide boards in an easy, controlled manner. The double-edge blade is belt-driven at the no-load speed of 19,000 rpm, which provides a very smooth cut. The blades are reversible to double the cutting life, and they are easily replaced. It is recommended that you purchase an optional $10 planer edge guide to provide edge guidance and to help make square-edged cuts.

Specifications: weight, 3 lb. 14 oz. **Warranty:** 1 year, repairs.

Manufacturer's Suggested Retail Price: $75

Approximate Low Price: $75

SNOW REMOVAL

Gas-engine-powered snow throwers can be divided into three categories, based on size and horsepower: (1) small single-stage throwers, which are under 5 horsepower and generally auger-propelled; (2) medium two-stage throwers, which are 5 to 7 horsepower and predominantly wheel propelled; and (3) large two-stage throwers, which are over 8 horsepower and wheel propelled.

Small snow throwers are for homeowners with relatively small spaces to clear and for areas of the country that usually receive light snowfall—6 inches or so per year. These machines are capable of handling heavier snows, including compacted driveway snow, but it will probably mean more effort for you, and it will take longer. These units are not wheel propelled, although the biting action of the auger blades helps propel the machine, thus the description "auger-propelled." You'll find both two- and four-stroke engines in this category, and the small engine size means they are generally easy to start. These are the simplest snow throwers to store because they are light and in many cases can be hung on the garage wall.

If you live in the snowbelt and have an average-size walk or driveway, any of the medium snow throwers should be adequate for just about anything winter might bring. They're an excellent all-around choice—neither too big nor too expensive. These units have four-cycle engines and can be hard to start under extremely cold conditions. However, the majority of snow throwers now have Tecumseh Snow King engines specially engineered for cold-weather performance, with primers, automatic compression releases for reduced starting effort, shrouding, and moisture-resistant ignition systems. Honda snow thrower engines also have similar cold-weather starting aids. Electric starters are offered as standard equipment or as options on almost all models, and we recommend them. All these models are two-stage, meaning that a slow-speed auger breaks up the snow and feeds it to a high-speed impeller, which then throws it up and out the chute.

If your area of the country measures its winter snowfall in the hundreds of inches, or if you have an especially long walk or drive to clear, consider a large snow thrower. In this category, buy as much power as you can afford. Also, be sure it is an electric-start. Few people can effortlessly pull-start a large snow thrower in frigid weather. An 8-horsepower engine may sound like a lot, but in this situation, more is better. These larger units are self-propelled, and they can cut a 28-inch path.

Best Buys '97
Our Best Buy, Recommended, and Budget Buy snow removal models follow. The reviews are divided into small, medium, and large snow throwers. A Best Buy, Recommended, or Budget Buy designation applies only to the model listed.

SNOW THROWERS UNDER 5 HORSEPOWER

TORO CCR 2400

✔**BEST BUY**

Typical driveways are about two cars wide and three cars long, and for the average driveway, the Toro CCR 2400 is an excellent snow thrower. This single-stage machine, which uses a 4-horsepower, two-cycle engine, clears a path about 20 inches wide. Toro's patented rotor system helps the CCR 2400 remove snow efficiently. This curved rotor, in combination with a high-capacity funnel, scrapes surfaces clean, and propels the snow about 25 feet away—a considerable distance for a single-stage machine. The CCR 2400 features easy-to-use centralized controls and an adjustable chute, which aims snow where you want it. An electric start is optional, but if you store your machine in a reasonably warm place, you will have no need for it.

Warranty: 2 years, full.

Manufacturer's Suggested Retail Price: $550

Approximate Low Price: $516

JOHN DEERE TRS22

Recommended

The TRS22 really does "run like a Deere" on propelled wheels, which is the appeal of this model. It is relatively small, yet it acts like a big snow thrower in that it has six forward and two reverse speeds. A two-stage snow blower, the TRS22 is powered by the Tecumseh Snow King, a well-designed 4-horsepower, four-cycle engine. Tecumseh Snow Kings are specially designed for severe winter service. This machine features a 10-inch-diameter auger, which moves through the snow and ice safely and efficiently. A 9-inch impeller moves snow from the auger and out of the chute. While the TRS22 is high-priced for a thrower with a clearing path of 21 inches, it is a very durable, well-designed machine that is highly maneuverable.

Warranty: 2 years, parts and labor.

Manufacturer's Suggested Retail Price: $849

Approximate Low Price: $780

ARIENS SS322

Budget Buy

The reasonably priced Ariens SS322 has proven to be a great auger-propelled performer. Its 22-inch clearing-width capacity is as large as single-stage snow throwers offer. And like many big snow throwers, it uses a Tecumseh Snow King engine. This particular motor is 3-horsepower. The SS322 has a particularly well-designed auger that helps it perform well, and this machine can discharge snow up to 35 feet with 220-degree directional control. A mitten-grip starter allows you to keep your hands warm while starting the engine, and the gas cap and key are oversized so that you can turn them with your mittens and gloves still on. Because it weighs only 50 pounds, it is easy to move and store. An optional electric start kit is available—a recommended option if any concern exists about the user's ability to manage pull starting.

Warranty: 5 years, limited.

Manufacturer's Suggested Retail Price: $499

Approximate Low Price: $476

SNOW THROWERS
FROM 5 TO 8 HORSEPOWER

TORO 38072 (ALSO CALLED 724)   ✔ BEST BUY

The Toro 38072 also goes by the model name
724, which is the way it is referred to in Toro's literature. This
model—a very popular 7-horsepower, two-stage snow
thrower—features a Tecumseh Snow King engine and cuts a
clearing path 24 inches wide. The 724 is a particularly impressive performer in heavy, wet, and deep snow, thanks in part to
Toro's husky drum-type auger design. This self-propelled unit
has four speeds—three forward and one reverse. The snow
chute adjusts up to 180 degrees. Pneumatic tires provide excellent traction, and the handle levers and starter are easy to use
because of their mitten grips. Available options are an electric
start, chains, a shield, and drift breakers.

Warranty: 2 years, full.

Manufacturer's Suggested Retail Price: $1,050

Approximate Low Price: $966

ARIENS ST 524   Recommended

The Ariens ST 524 is highly regarded because
of its rugged performance. Its 5-horsepower Tecumseh Snow
King engine is coupled with Ariens' highly regarded, dependable, variable-speed drive. There are six forward and two reverse
speeds. The ST 524, which is capable of clearing a 24-inch path,
throws snow up to 35 feet with 220-degree directional control.
Like most wheel-propelled snow throwers, it is equipped with
large, knobby 12-inch tires that provide excellent traction for
clearing all types of snow—no matter how deep or wet. The
adjustable skid shoes allow you to clear gravel driveways without actually clearing away the gravel. A mitten-grip starter handle aids in starting the machine. Electric drift cutters, an electric
start, a tiller, and a broom are optional.

Warranty: 5 years, limited.

Manufacturer's Suggested Retail Price: $1,080

Approximate Low Price: $876

SNAPPER 17242

The popular, dependable Snapper 17242 is a **Recommended** medium-size snow thrower with a 7-horsepower Tecumseh Snow King engine. It can clear a path of snow 24 inches wide, and its chute rotation is 187 degrees. The one reverse and four forward speeds on this wheel-propelled model can be shifted on the go with a single lever. Mitten-grip handles aid in starting the machine. At 6 inches, the tires are a bit smaller than those on some other models, but that does not diminish the performance. The 17242 comes with a set of drift cutters, while an electric start, snow cab, and tire chains are optional.

Warranty: 2 years, limited.

Manufacturer's Suggested Retail Price: $1,125

Approximate Low Price: $1,000

SNOW THROWERS
8 HORSEPOWER AND ABOVE

TROY-BILT 42010

✔ **BEST BUY**

Troy-Bilt has a reputation for building rugged machines, and the 42010 is no exception. This wheel-propelled machine is loaded with smart features, such as an 8-horsepower Tecumseh Snow King engine, five forward and two reverse speeds, and limited slip differential. Also included are electric hand warmers built into the grips and rugged, knobby tires for excellent traction. The 42010 is capable of cutting a path 24 inches wide and can propel snow up to 30 feet. It has a chute rotation of 220 degrees. Attesting to Troy-Bilt's confidence in its product is the 7-year warranty. The wealth of features makes this model a Best Buy. An electric start, a set of chains, a cab, and a headlight are optional.

Warranty: 7 years.

Manufacturer's Suggested Retail Price: $1,339

Approximate Low Price: $1,275

HONDA HS828K1WAS

Recommended

After a price increase this year, Honda's top-of-the-line 8-horsepower snow thrower is more premium-priced than ever. However, aside from Honda's much-admired overhead valve engine, the HS828K1WAS does not have as much going for it as comparable models from other manufacturers. Reasons for the high price include the standard electric start and the hydrostatic drive system, which gives infinitely variable forward and reverse travel speeds and precise control. The unique interconnected drive and auger clutch levers leave one hand free to make chute adjustments as you travel. The self-propelled HS828K1WAS has a 28-inch cutting path, a chute turning radius of 210 degrees, and a maximum snow discharge of 49 feet. An optional light kit is available.

Warranty: 2 years, parts and labor.

Manufacturer's Suggested Retail Price: $1,995

Approximate Low Price: $1,995

YARD-MAN E753F

Budget Buy

The price of the Yard-Man E753F makes it a Budget Buy, but this track-propelled, 9-horsepower snow thrower is also a tremendous value in terms of quality and power. The power is delivered via a rugged chain drive to a power-steered, heavily cleated track drive. This track-propelled machine can handle snow that is 20 inches deep, and it can clear a path 26 inches wide. Weight can be transferred forward in order to plow through hard-packed snow without the machine climbing. If that isn't enough, this model also comes with six forward and two reverse speeds, an electric start, and handles that fold for compact storage.

Warranty: 2 years, repair or replace; 90 days, no fault.

Manufacturer's Suggested Retail Price: $999

Approximate Low Price: $999

LAWN CARE

As you shop for power lawn care equipment these days, you'll see some changes and improvements. You'll find sleeker, more ergonomic designs, an expanded use of tough plastics, and better paint jobs on metal parts. To help you choose large equipment, look for elaborate point-of-sale displays on cartonized items and detailed explanations of features and uses right on the box. As some major chains add in-house service departments or make arrangements for local service, you'll see more high-end, formerly independent, dealer brands there. With the exception of the riding mower category, you'll find more cordless, battery-powered equipment, too. And, more mowers and lawn tractors now feature easy conversion from side-discharge to mulching.

String Trimmers and Blower/Vacs

This pair of exceedingly handy tools can take care of most of the touch-up jobs around your lawn and garden. String trimmers use a spinning nylon line to cut grass, weeds, and even light brush. Power comes from a corded or battery-powered electric motor or a small two-stroke engine, although four-stroke engines made by Ryobi are available on some models. The nylon line must be replaced periodically because it wears out during operation.

Some string trimmers allow the cutting head to rotate 90 degrees so that the trimmer can be used as an edger. Larger models can be fitted with brush-cutting blades (similar to circular saw blades) to remove heavy brush and shrubs.

Hand-held blower/vacs simplify the cleanup of debris, grass clippings, and leaves in yards, driveways, and even gutters, with a powerful blast of air directed from a long tube. You can quickly convert a blower/vac into vac-and-mulch mode in which leaves, small twigs, and debris are picked up, chewed up, and deposited into a shoulder-hung bag. Black & Decker has a model that deposits debris directly into a trash can. Most of these tools are intended for small, soft yard debris. However, a few will also pick up larger debris and beverage cans but will not chew them up.

As with most other tools, engine-powered blower/vacs are generally more powerful and convenient to use than electric models, but since the need for such a tool is usually infrequent, an electric model is a better investment for most consumers.

Best Buys '97

Our Best Buy, Recommended, and Budget Buy lawn care products are listed below. Remember that a Best Buy, Recommended, or Budget Buy designation applies only to the model listed; it does not necessarily apply to other models made by the same manufacturer or to an entire product line.

LAWN MOWERS
Gasoline-Powered Mowers

SEARS CRAFTSMAN 37729 SELF-PROPELLED

✔ **BEST BUY**

This new 22-inch, 6.25-horsepower mower, introduced this year, comes with geared, two-speed, front-wheel drive and a steel deck that makes it an effective mulcher as well as a rear bagger. (A deflector for discharged clippings is optional.) The 2.4-bushel bag releases much less dust than other models do, and the lift top makes it easy to unload. The tires are wider than average, and the handle pivots and folds for easy storage. The Craftsman is also produced in a CARB version for Southern California consumers.

Warranty: 2 years, limited.

Manufacturer's Suggested Retail Price: $330

Approximate Low Price: $288

LAWN-BOY SILVER SERIES 10277 PUSH-TYPE

Recommended

If you want a dependable, easy-to-start, push-type mower, consider this moderately priced Lawn-Boy. The commercial-grade engine has been upgraded to 4.75 horse-power. This design retains its popular staggered front wheels and allows neat and easy mowing around fences and under shrubs, cutting a 21-inch path. Optional features on the 10277 include a rear bagger, a leaf shredder, and even a Lawn-Boy version of Toro's popular mow-and-feed fertilizer attachment that lets you fertilize as you mow.

Warranty: 2 years, full; 5 years, ignition.

Manufacturer's Suggested Retail Price: $270

Approximate Low Price: $251

MURRAY ULTRA 22859
Recommended

This self-propelled mower offers a lot of quality features, not the least of which is a 5.5-horsepower, three-speed Kawasaki OHV (overhead valve) engine, known for easy starting. Other pluses include a steel deck and 8-inch, gear-driven, ball-bearing wheels. The cutting height can be adjusted to any of seven positions with a single handle, and the mower cuts a 22-inch path. The 22859, which doubles as a mulcher, has a bagging attachment equipped for either side or rear bag discharge.

Warranty: 2 years, full; 5 years, engine.

Manufacturer's Suggested Retail Price: $449

Approximate Low Price: Not available

MTD 410A
Budget Buy

MTD says the deep-domed, stamped steel deck on this low-priced mower is designed for optimum performance at mulching, bagging, or discharging. The fingertip height adjusters are easy to use and maximize the mower's performance. The Briggs & Stratton 3.5-horsepower engine performs superbly, and the rear grass catcher is easy to handle. The cutting path is 21 inches wide. Side discharge and mulching functions are optional.

Warranty: 90 days, no-fault; 2 years, supreme, repair or replace.

Manufacturer's Suggested Retail Price: $189

Approximate Low Price: $166

Electric Mowers

BLACK & DECKER CORDED ELECTRIC MM850

✔ BEST BUY

The 13-amp motor that quietly powers this mulching/rear bagging mower is said to develop the equivalent of 4 horsepower. A one-touch, spring-loaded height adjuster adjusts all four wheels simultaneously, and the tough polymer deck makes this push-type mower lightweight. The bag is easy to unload and replace, and an attachment for side discharge is sold separately. The motor switch is safe and easy to use. This electric mower cuts a 19-inch path and weighs 48 pounds.

Warranty: 30 days, no risk; 2 years, full; 5 years, deck.

Manufacturer's Suggested Retail Price: $225

Approximate Low Price: $189

RYOBI BMM2400 MULCHINATOR

✔ BEST BUY

For anyone who mows an average-size lawn, the Mulchinator offers quiet operation and minimal fussing with fuel or cords. With 90 minutes of cutting time per battery charge from its 24-volt rechargeable battery, this mower can cover about half an acre in one walk-through (the cutting path is 18 inches). A full recharge takes 16 hours. This model features one-touch height adjustment, a rigid plastic deck, and a fold-down handle for on-end storage. The charger knows when to top off the charge, so it's best to keep it plugged in all the time. The Mulchinator weighs 75 pounds.

Warranty: 2 years, full; 7 years, deck.

Manufacturer's Suggested Retail Price: $350

Approximate Low Price: $321

Riding Mowers

HONDA HARMONY H1011RSA

✔ BEST BUY

If you want a riding mower with attention-getting good looks, this is it. The H1011RSA offers handy control locations and operation. This model comes with an 11-horsepower OHV engine, recoil start, and in-line manual shifting, but electric-start and hydrostatic-drive models are also available. This 350-pound mower has a 16.5-inch turning radius, and it cuts a 30-inch path. Double grass-baggers and mulching kits are additional options. The mower floor is uncluttered, and the driver has a view of all four tires.

Warranty: 2 years, parts and labor.

Manufacturer's Suggested Retail Price: $1,699

Approximate Low Price: $1,631

JOHN DEERE SRX75

Recommended

The SRX75 is a sturdy rider with a top-quality, 9-horsepower, OHV electric-start engine. The unique foot-controlled, variable-speed drive lets you change speeds with the touch of a pedal, so you can keep both hands on the wheel at all times. The shuttle-shift feature uses simple forward and backward motion to change directions, and this mower's 14-inch turning radius is one of the shortest available. Deere equips this model with a high back seat for added comfort. The manufacturer's renowned mulching attachment is optional on this model, as is a 6½-bushel rear-bagger kit. The mower weighs 365 pounds.

Warranty: 2 years, parts and labor.

Manufacturer's Suggested Retail Price: $2,299

Approximate Low Price: $2,100

SNAPPER 250815B

Budget Buy

Except for electric start, Snapper's rear-engine rider has many features found on the manufacturer's other mowers. It comes with a 25-inch deck and a correspondingly small 8-horsepower engine. It offers Snapper's disc drive and sealed differential, has a 23-inch turning radius, and weighs 307 pounds. Available accessories include a bagger and a dethatcher.

Warranty: 2 years, engine; 5 years, deck and chassis.

Manufacturer's Suggested Retail Price: $1,199

Approximate Low Price: $1,199

Mulching Mowers

TROY-BILT 34322

√BEST BUY

Troy-Bilt builds its machines strong, and this 5-horsepower, 21-inch, self-propelled mulcher is a good example. This model is also backed by the manufacturer's 7-year, limited warranty. The 34322 features a cast-aluminum deck, a single-lever cutting height adjuster, and a self-propel feature that eases operator fatigue and maximizes the effectiveness of the mulching action on grass of varying density and moistness. This mulcher/mower is also available with a 4-horsepower engine and/or an electric starter. A side-discharge grass catcher can be purchased separately.

Warranty: 3 years, engine (by manufacturer); 7 years, limited.

Manufacturer's Suggested Retail Price: $559

Approximate Low Price: $526

TORO SUPER RECYCLER 20462

Recommended

This user-friendly, self-propelled mower is, as its name implies, a super recycler, thanks to the effective design of its blade and its cast-aluminum deck. It has a 5.5-horsepower engine and cuts a 21-inch path. Three-speed rear-wheel drive is a bonus on uneven terrain, and a color-coded wheel-adjustment feature helps you select proper cutting height. Available options include a rear-bag kit, a side discharge, a dethatcher, and a fertilizer spreader that works as you mow.

Warranty: 5 years, full.

Manufacturer's Suggested Retail Price: $590

Approximate Low Price: $512

SNAPPER R21501

Recommended

Most mulching mowers are self-propelled, so if you prefer the push-type mower, consider this Snapper. It's outfitted with a Briggs & Stratton 5-horsepower engine, a standard mulching blade, and a steel deck. This mower has a 21-inch cutting path, and its handle folds down easily for compact storage. Other available options include a rear grass catcher, a side-discharge kit, a high-grade mulching kit, and a leaf shredder.

Warranty: 2 years, engine; 5 years, components; 10 years, transmission and mower deck.

Manufacturer's Suggested Retail Price: $350

Approximate Low Price: $350

LAWN TRACTORS
14 Horsepower or Less

HONDA HARMONY H2013SDA

✔**BEST BUY**

This popular lawn tractor from Honda features a top-quality, 13-horsepower Honda overhead-valve engine and a 38-inch, twin-blade deck. The Harmony H2013SDA is standard as a side-discharge mower but easily converts for mulching or rear bagging. This model features a five-speed, shift-on-the-go transmission, but a hydrostatic-transmission model is also available. Optional add-ons include a snow thrower.

Warranty: 2 years, parts and labor.

Manufacturer's Suggested Retail Price: $2,295

Approximate Low Price: $1,948

CUB CADET 2135

`Recommended`

This tough tractor features a direct drive shaft from the engine to the transmission; cruise control on the hydrostatic drive; a full-length, welded, twin-channel, steel frame; a cast-iron front axle with grease fittings; and a 13-horsepower overhead-valve engine. The Cub Cadet comes with steel fenders, full instrumentation, dual 27-watt halogen headlights, front electric PTO, and a mower deck with a quick attach/detach system. Optional attachments include a front blade, a two-stage snow thrower, and a twin rear bagger.

Warranty: 2 years, limited.

Manufacturer's Suggested Retail Price: $3,199

Approximate Low Price: $3,025

More Than 14 Horsepower

SEARS CRAFTSMAN 25354 ✔BEST BUY
New this year, the Sears 25354 green lawn tractor is powered by a reliable and durable 15-horsepower Kohler engine with a cast-iron cylinder sleeve. This model comes with a conventional six-speed transmission, but the same tractor is also available with hydrostatic drive (model #25355). The 42-inch deck mulches without a blade change, and a front blade and a snow thrower are optional add-ons. This lawn tractor has a 25.5-inch turning radius, which is short considering the tractor's size.

Warranty: 1 year, limited.

Manufacturer's Suggested Retail Price: $1,400

Approximate Low Price: $1,288

MURRAY 42910X92 Budget Buy
This new Murray offers a lot for the money. Its foot-operated hydrostatic drive allows you to control forward and reverse speeds without taking your hands off the steering wheel. It comes fully assembled and features a 42-inch mower deck and a 14.5-horsepower Briggs & Stratton industrial-commercial engine with cast-iron cylinder sleeves. The step-through design makes it easy to get on and off this mower. Optional extras include a bagger and a 46-inch snow blade.

Warranty: 2 years.

Manufacturer's Suggested Retail Price: $999

Approximate Low Price: $895

STRING TRIMMERS
Gasoline Models

RYOBI 990r ✔BEST BUY
Ryobi's powerful 990r trimmer uses the company's 26cc, four-stroke, Pro4Mor engine and comes with a

brush-cutting blade accessory. Well-balanced, easy to handle, and easy to start, this model is a fine performer. To round it out as a lawn-and-garden system, Ryobi offers optional snap-on "Trimmer Plus" accessories, including an edger, a blower, a cultivator, a pruner, and a brand-new snow thrower—all powered by the same engine.

Warranty: 2 years.

Manufacturer's Suggested Retail Price: $229

Approximate Low Price: $219

HOMELITE z725ce
`Recommended`

The Homelite z725ce was introduced last year. This 17-inch, dual-line, gas trimmer features push-button electric start. Homelite's standard 25cc, two-stroke, pull-start engine (found on previous models) started easily, but this one is even easier. With its sleek housing and improved starter, this trimmer still weighs only about 12 pounds.

Warranty: 2 years, parts and labor.

Manufacturer's Suggested Retail Price: $170

Approximate Low Price: $152

Electric Models

RYOBI 132r TRIMMERPLUS
✔BEST BUY

This electric version of Ryobi's popular gas TrimmerPlus mower can be converted to an edger, blower, vac, or light-duty cultivator with some optional snap-on accessories. As a trimmer, it weighs only 9 pounds; has a 5.2-amp, two-speed motor; and cuts a 15-inch swath. The housing and handle are designed to provide balance and control. This same tool is available with a straight shaft (model #137r) for use under fences and bushes.

Warranty: 2 years.

Manufacturer's Suggested Retail Price: $65

Approximate Low Price: $62

BLACK & DECKER ST4000 TRIMMER/EDGER

Recommended

The ST4000 has a 3.5-amp motor, features a push-button edger, and still weighs only 4 pounds. This trimmer/edger can cut a 12-inch path and handle thick weeds and grass without getting bogged down. You simply push a button and the head indexes for use as an edger. Another push of the button and it switches back into a trimmer.

Warranty: 2 years, full.

Manufacturer's Suggested Retail Price: $41

Approximate Low Price: $39

Cordless Models

RYOBI 150R

✔ BEST BUY

Keep this handy trimmer, with its 12-volt battery, plugged into its charging cradle so it will be ready to go whenever you need it. This 10-pound model will trim about a mile of mowed grass and weeds on a single charge, and it cuts a 10-inch path.

Warranty: 2 years.

Manufacturer's Suggested Retail Price: $95

Approximate Low Price: $90

WEED EATER HANDYSTIK

Recommended

The Handystik deserves its name. This 9.4-pound, 12-volt, cordless trimmer cuts a 9-inch swath. It features a specially designed line-advance system and comes with a wall-mount charger bracket. Capable of trimming an average lawn on a single charge, this trimmer features an easy-to-use spool replacement and a foam-covered assist handle.

Warranty: 2 years, limited.

Manufacturer's Suggested Retail Price: $75

Approximate Low Price: $67

BLOWER/VACS

Electric Models

BLACK & DECKER SUPER VAC 'N' MULCH BV1000

✓BEST BUY

The BV1000 does a great job of vacuuming and mulching, thanks to its exclusive mulching blade system. A two-speed switch controls blower air flow (top speed is 180 miles per hour), and switching from blower to vac and back again is easy (no tools needed!). This model has a 12-amp motor and weighs 6.9 pounds. The BV-004 option kit consists of a large hose, a shoulder bag, and a fabric cover that allows leaves to be mulched and deposited directly into a trash can for disposal.

Warranty: 2 years, full.

Manufacturer's Suggested Retail Price: $69

Approximate Low Price: $62

TORO SUPER BLOWERVAC 51582

`Recommended`

Toro's Super BlowerVac 51582 has a shutter in its blower-intake grille. With the movement of the dual air-speed control tab, this shutter causes blower velocity to shift between the unit's two speeds. It has an air-speed rating of 190 miles per hour. Mode change, from blower to vac or vice versa, is easy and requires no tools. This model has a 12-amp motor and weighs 6.1 pounds.

Warranty: 2 years, full.

Manufacturer's Suggested Retail Price: $70

Approximate Low Price: $66

Gasoline Models

WEED EATER BARRACUDA SV 30

✓BEST BUY

Named for the fierce barracuda, with its powerful shredding jaws and voracious appetite, this blower/vac has a 30cc engine, a 16.5:1 reduction rating, and an anti-vibe handle. Top airflow velocity is 180 miles per hour. Optional add-ons include a gutter cleaning kit and a kit that converts the machine to a shop-type vac. Because of the hazards of engine fumes, however, the Barracuda SV 30 must never be used in an enclosed area.

Warranty: 2 years, limited.

Manufacturer's Suggested Retail Price: $150

Approximate Low Price: $136

ECHO SHRED 'N' VAC ES-2100

Recommended

This blower/vac from Echo comes with a quiet 21.2cc engine, a three-speed throttle that optimizes flow control when it's used as a blower, a four-blade mechanism that preshreds debris before it's passed into the vac, a long vac intake tube, and a curved discharge connection. The Shred 'n' Vac weighs 9.44 pounds in its blower mode and 11.35 pounds as a vac. It has an airflow speed of 125 miles per hour (with its fan head nozzle). An optional gutter cleanout kit is available.

Warranty: 2 years, parts and labor; lifetime, electronic ignition module (parts and labor).

Manufacturer's Suggested Retail Price: $200

Approximate Low Price: $189

FOOD PREPARATION

Today, the name of the game in cooking is speed. Few people can make a habit of spending hours in the kitchen turning out magnificent lunches and dinners. Still, no one wants to sacrifice quality and flavor in their daily meals. To respond to this need for efficient, quality food preparation, manufacturers have created a variety of appliances to handle every job.

Food Processors

Today's kitchen is equipped with an array of modern appliances, from staples such as coffeemakers and toasters to the more esoteric pasta and breadmakers. In between are the food processors. Considered a trendy toy or culinary fad for many years, the food processor has proven itself to be a reliable, essential member of the kitchen appliance family. Today, bigger, more powerful machines can knead dough for two loaves of bread, slice and shred a party-size batch of coleslaw, or slice whole fruits or vegetables through an expanded feed tube. The biggest processors are the food preparation centers—machines that not only perform all the functions of the largest processors but also come with added attachments that enable them to function, for example, as stand mixers. Some models also come with fancy disc attachments that can julienne vegetables or slice potatoes for french frying. Smaller models save work space and are perfect for smaller tasks such as processing a single onion, a handful of herbs, or a cup of mayonnaise. Minimincers specialize in chopping small items such as garlic cloves, nuts, or coffee beans. These small units are also handy for making up single servings of baby food.

Because of the differences among the many types of food processors, avid cooks may decide to purchase more than one. However, because some food processors perform the added functions of a mixer, a blender, and a citrus juicer, the average cook can make do with one appliance. And because of their ease of use, versatility, and compact size, minimincers should be in every kitchen.

Depending on how often you cook, and for how many people, you will want to choose a processor that suits your lifestyle. The larger machines offer the most functions and versatility, while carrying a higher price tag. Smaller machines do an admirable job with smaller quantities of food. Compact models may be just right for singles or small families.

The first-time processor owner may want a machine that's as uncomplicated as possible. The single-button or two-speed models offer the most ease of use. Masters of processor techniques may prefer the versatility of a variable-speed model. All models share certain features, including a stainless steel chopping blade, or "S" blade, which is used for chopping, mixing and blending, pureeing, and even kneading bread dough. Some machines, however, do have separate dough blades or hooks. All machines have work bowls, which are usually transparent. Some come with extra bowls as well as blender carafes for added features and convenience. All machines have an on/off/pulse function: "On" is for continuous action, while "pulse" is for short, consecutive rotations of the blade. Finally, every machine has a motor base. In general, the bigger the machine, the more powerful the motor.

Mixers

The electric mixer is both familiar and reliable when it comes to mixing batters, whipping cream, and mashing potatoes. Not only does the mixer eliminate much of the drudgery associated with these tasks, but it also does a faster, more thorough job. This machine is unmatched when it comes to aerating mixtures. Aerating refers to increasing the volume by incorporating air into creams, batters, and egg whites.

Traditional stand mixers, with their supplied work bowl(s), offer the most power, and they have the added advantage of hands-free mixing. Portable mixers are less expensive and can be tucked away in a drawer when not in use. A relatively new option is the stand/hand combination unit, which offers the convenience of both types of mixer, usually at a reduced cost. Many mixers now come with added attachments, such as dough hooks, whisks, or immersion blender rods.

Blenders

The whirlpool design of the traditional blender makes it the perfect choice for thoroughly combining liquids with solids or for crushing ice or other hard food items. The carafe and its added power not only crush the ice but also protect the user from flying ice particles and splashes. Carafe blenders vary by model, which gives consumers a choice between glass and plastic carafes; push-button, dial, and touchpad controls; and such specialty features as ice-crushing and pulse.

Immersion blenders, on the other hand, excel at jobs involving soft food items, such as pureeing cooked vegetables or blending fruit or ice-cream drinks. They also offer the added convenience of being able to go directly into your own drink cup, saucepan, or other container. For versatility, many immersion blenders come with chopping or whipping attachments to help them function as minimincers or hand mixers.

Toasters and Toaster Ovens

Of all the small kitchen appliances available, toasters are arguably the most common. Many manufacturers produce toasters, and it is not difficult to find inexpensive models at any department store—if toasting bread is all you want to do. The models listed here, however, are top-of-the-line toasters that offer a great deal more.

For singles and many small families, toaster ovens conserve precious counter space but offer a convenient combination of functions, such as toasting, broiling, and baking.

Specialty Food Prep

In this category are appliances that handle very specialized jobs. These machines take up valuable counter or cabinet space, so those who do little cooking may not find them useful. Included in this category are pasta makers, juicers, and breadmakers.

Best Buys '97

Our Best Buy, Recommended, and Budget Buy food preparation appliances follow. Products within each category are listed according to quality. The best of the Best Buys is listed first, followed by our second choice, and so on. A Best Buy, Recommended, or Budget Buy designation applies only to the model listed; it does not necessarily apply to other models made by the same manufacturer or to an entire product line.

FOOD PROCESSORS
Large Food Processors

CUISINART PRO FOOD PREP CENTER DLC-7SFP

✓ BEST BUY

The Cuisinart Pro Food Prep Center DLC-7SFP performs all the functions of a processor—from pureeing cooked vegetables to chopping nuts. It also comes with a whisk attachment that lets it function as a high-powered stand mixer. This unit features a 14-cup Lexan work bowl, which is large enough to hold over 2 pounds of ground beef, enough dough for two large bread loaves, or about 12 cups of pureed vegetables. Those who entertain frequently will appreciate the larger capacity, which lets you shred an entire head of cabbage without emptying the work bowl. For all its power, the Pro Food Prep Center is surprisingly quiet. The Pro Food Prep Center comes with a stainless-steel chopping blade, a heavy-duty plastic dough blade, a medium slicing disc, a medium shredding disc, a stainless-steel whisk attachment, and a plastic spatula. Two covers—one compact cover for use with chopping and mixing and one standard cover with both large and small feed tubes—enable you to slice whole fruits and vegetables in addition to long, thin produce. Because of the many options on this model, the feed tube assembly may seem overly complicated at first. A little practice, however, will yield confident results in no time. Also included with the package is a Cuisinart how-to video, which shows the proper techniques for achieving perfect results with your processor. Optional attachments include a fine shredding disc, fine and medium julienne discs, a french-fry disc, and a set of slicing discs of various thicknesses. All parts, except the motor base, are dishwasher safe.

Warranty: 3 years, limited; 5 years, motor.

Manufacturer's Suggested Retail Price: $440

Approximate Low Price: $310

KITCHENAID 11-CUP ULTRA POWER FOOD PROCESSOR KFP600WH

✓**BEST BUY**

The KitchenAid 11-Cup Ultra Power Food Processor is powerful, efficient, and easy to use. The unit comes with a chopping blade, a reversible thin-slicing/shredding disc, a medium slicing disc, a medium shredding disc, a dough blade, a plastic spatula, and a minichopping bowl and blade. The multipurpose chopping blade and minichopping blade are made by Sabatier, the renowned manufacturer of knives. This model also comes with an accessory storage box, which houses all the blades and discs when not in use. The touchpad controls let you switch from on to off or pulse instantly. With this superior unit, you can process up to 6 cups of chopped beef or produce, enough dough for one large pizza, or up to 3 cups of chopped nuts or peanut butter. A handy feature of this machine is the minichopper attachment, which eliminates the need for a second appliance to chop small amounts. The minichopper bowl can handle up to 1 cup of semiliquid ingredients or 2 cups of solids. This unit assembles and disassembles easily for hassle-free operation and wipes clean with a damp cloth. The bowls and blades are dishwasher safe. A variety of accessories and attachments are available at an additional cost.

Warranty: 1 year, total replacement.

Manufacturer's Suggested Retail Price: $250

Approximate Low Price: $229

BRAUN FOOD PREPARATION CENTER 5-IN-1 K1000

Recommended

The Braun K1000 Food Preparation Center combines the functions of five appliances: food processor, kitchen machine, blender, chopper, and ice crusher. It comes with a clear, 11-cup processor work bowl for slicing, shredding, grating, mixing, and chopping. An opaque, 18-cup kitchen machine work bowl allows for heavy kneading, beating, mixing, mashing, and whipping, while a 4-cup, glass blender carafe is included for crushing ice, liquefying, pureeing, and chopping. Also included are a stainless steel chopping blade and a set of discs for slicing, shredding, grating, and making french fries. The blades are made by Sabatier, a renowned knife manufacturer. Other accessories that come with this unit are two whisks for light and heavy mixing, a dough hook, a disc storage box, and a plastic spatula. The motor is powerful but not excessively noisy. A variable-speed dial control requires a bit of practice but yields excellent results. Speeds are designated with numerals ranging from 1 to 5. One dial selects your speed, while another activates the power. A separate button allows manual pulse operation to obtain exact results. Automatic pulse is also provided for convenient hands-free operation. The 5-in-1 is not geared toward the occasional cook, but the avid cook/entertainer will find its many functions and quality parts to be an exceptional value.

Warranty: 1 year.

Manufacturer's Suggested Retail Price: $290
Approximate Low Price: $270

Mid-size Food Processors

CUISINART PRO CLASSIC FOOD PROCESSOR DLC-10S

✔ **BEST BUY**

The Cuisinart Pro Classic Food Processor is a reduced-capacity machine that retains all of the power and performance of the Cuisinart line. Its size and price make it the perfect choice for small households or for those who don't often entertain. This machine comes with a 7-cup Lexan work bowl, which is capable of processing enough dough for two standard loaves of bread or grinding up to 1¼ pounds of meat in a single batch. A three-position lever simplifies operation and lets you switch from off to on or pulse in seconds. Standard equipment includes a cover with both large and small feed tubes, a flat cover for chopping and mixing, a stainless steel chopping/mixing blade, a reinforced plastic dough blade, a serrated slicing disc, a medium shredding disc, and a plastic spatula. You also receive a special how-to video that explains the ins and outs of processor operations. Optional attachments include a fine shredding disc, both fine and medium julienne discs, a french-fry disc, a range of slicing discs, and a citrus juicer attachment. Except for the motor, all parts are dishwasher safe.

Warranty: 3 years, limited; 5 years, motor.

Manufacturer's Suggested Retail Price: $240

Approximate Low Price: $190

BLACK & DECKER POWERPRO PLUS
FP1011

✔**BEST BUY**

The Black & Decker PowerPro Plus is not only very efficient but also extremely easy to use. It does an excellent job with basic tasks, such as chopping an onion or slicing apples for a pie. The "Plus" is a french-fry disc that makes great home fries or carrot sticks. The unit is equipped with a clear, 6-cup work bowl and a chopping blade that is straight on one side and curved on the other for better bowl coverage and more thorough processing. Other features include two reversible discs for thick or thin slicing and shredding, and an exclusive expeditor that helps push food through the chute. The expeditor can also be used to close off the chute. The unit is activated by three touchpad buttons for on, off, and pulse. Assembly and disassembly are a snap on the Black & Decker PowerPro Plus, and cleanup is easy because the bowls and blades can go right into the dishwasher. The PowerPro's ease of use and low price tag make it a good choice for cooks who want the basics plus a little more.

Warranty: 2 years.

Manufacturer's Suggested Retail Price: $87

Approximate Low Price: $62

HAMILTON BEACH CHEFPREP 70700

Budget Buy

The Hamilton Beach ChefPrep is efficient, easy to use, and priced for those who are budget-conscious. A 7-cup work bowl handles chopping, mixing, slicing, and shredding. For slightly liquid ingredients, the capacity is reduced to about 2 cups. For added versatility, the ChefPrep features a continuous feed chute that enables you to slice or shred unlimited quantities into a waiting bowl. This unit comes with a stainless steel chopping blade, a reversible slicer/shredder disc, and a continuous-feed disc. Two fingertip controls are used for selecting the speed (either high or low) and on/off/pulse, making this unit a snap to operate. The bowl, lid, and blades can be hand-cleaned with warm, soapy water or washed in the top rack of your dishwasher.

Warranty: 2 years, limited.

Manufacturer's Suggested Retail Price: $70

Approximate Low Price: $50

Compact Food Processors

CUISINART LITTLE PRO PLUS LPP

✔ **BEST BUY**

The Cuisinart Little Pro Plus compact food processor is an excellent choice for the weekend gourmet or families with limited counter space. Despite its small size, the Little Pro Plus is powerful, quiet, and surprisingly versatile. It comes with a clear, 3-cup Lexan work bowl for chopping and mixing, an opaque bowl with a chute assembly for continuous slicing or shredding into a waiting bowl, a stainless steel chopping/mixing blade, a serrated slicing disc, a medium-fine shredding disc, and a spatula. The "Plus" is a citrus juicer attachment with three stackable reamers for juicing lemons, limes, oranges, and grapefruit. The clear work bowl can hold up to 3 cups of sliced or shredded produce, ½ pound of chopped meat, or enough dough for a 15-inch pizza. A three-position on/off/pulse lever is easy to use. Except for the motor base, all parts are dishwasher safe.

Warranty: 3 years, limited; 5 years, motor.

Manufacturer's Suggested Retail Price: $140

Approximate Low Price: $120

KRUPS MASTERPRO PLUS 704

`Recommended`

This compact processor from Krups has nearly the capacity of a full-size processor. The clear work bowl can handle up to 5 cups of sliced or shredded ingredients, 3 cups of dry batter or light dough, or about 2 cups of heavy dough. This unit comes with a stainless steel chopping blade, a disc with stainless steel inserts for slicing and shredding, and a plastic spatula. For whipping egg whites or cream, there is an emulsifier disc with a superblender crown, which acts like a spatula to produce smooth results. The feed tube/pusher assembly is divided into two parts to handle both large and small food items, and the pusher doubles as a 5-ounce measuring cup. Three large buttons let you select on, off, or pulse, and an electronic variable-speed control slide lever has settings from 1 (low) to 4 (high). The settings can be selected at the start of processing or adjusted as needed while the machine is operating. Also included is a creative cooking booklet that offers step-by-step directions as well as an assortment of recipes. Except for the motor base, the parts can be cleaned with warm, soapy water. The blades are dishwasher safe.

Warranty: 1 year.

Manufacturer's Suggested Retail Price: $95

Approximate Low Price: $77

Minimincers

CUISINART MINI-PREP PROCESSOR DLC-1

✔ **BEST BUY**

The Cuisinart Mini-Prep Processor DLC-1 looks and acts like a full-size processor—in miniature. While it cannot slice or shred, it does an excellent job with chores such as chopping onions or nuts. This unit features a clear, 21-ounce-capacity work bowl, which is the largest in its class, and a patented, reversible, stainless steel chopping blade. It chops and minces onions and garlic, mixes and blends sauces and mayonnaise, purees baby food, grinds coffee beans and spices, and grates chocolate and cheeses. Two push-button controls let you select low and high speeds with pulse control. Use the high speed with the blade's blunt edge for grinding and grating hard foods. Use the low speed and sharp edge for soft or watery foods. The Mini-Prep takes up minimal space, and the hidden wrap-around cord keeps counter clutter to a minimum. The work bowl and lid disassemble easily, and they are dishwasher safe.

Warranty: 18 months, limited.

Manufacturer's Suggested Retail Price: $48

Approximate Low Price: $39

BLACK & DECKER HANDYCHOPPER PLUS HC3000

✓**BEST BUY**

The Black & Decker HandyChopper Plus mincer/chopper is an easy-to-use machine that quickly chops or minces up to 1½ cups of onion, garlic, fresh herbs, or cut-up produce items. The "Plus" is a 12-ounce work bowl—larger than the bowls for most other mincers. This unit comes with a stainless steel chopping blade and cover. A ribbed grip on the lid makes it easy to lock into position. The oversized control button is simple to use in both the on and pulse modes. Simply press and release the fingertip control button for pulse action or hold for continuous processing. Most items are processed in seconds. You can also use your minimincer for grinding nuts or pureeing baby food. A curly, telephone-style cord expands to 3½ feet and retracts to reduce counter clutter. Rubber feet aid stability. Except for the base, the parts are dishwasher safe. The HandyChopper Plus mincer/chopper tucks away easily in a cabinet or deep drawer.

Warranty: 2 years.

Manufacturer's Suggested Retail Price: $34

Approximate Low Price: $24

PROCTOR-SILEX FOOD CHOPPER 72500 `Recommended`

The Proctor-Silex Food Chopper is a no-non-sense, economical minichopper. A single oversized button controls the unit in the on, off, or pulse modes: push and release for pulsing action or hold for continuous processing. You can process up to 1½ cups of onion, parsley, or celery. You can also process small portions of cooked vegetables for baby food. Most items are processed in seconds. The basic unit (bowl, stainless steel chopping blade, and cover) is simple to assemble and easy to clean; wash all parts, except for the motor base, in warm, soapy water. Rubber feet help the unit stay put during processing.

Warranty: 2 years, limited.

Manufacturer's Suggested Retail Price: $25

Approximate Low Price: $15

MIXERS
Portable Mixers

CUISINART SMART POWER 7-SPEED
ELECTRONIC LED HAND MIXER HTM-7L   ✓BEST BUY

Cuisinart's Smart Power 7-Speed Electronic LED Hand Mixer is a sophisticated machine with electronic touchpad controls that let you switch between speeds with a gentle touch on the "+" (increase speed) or "-" (decrease speed) buttons. Depressing the power button activates the mixer on its lowest speed. The mixer starts slowly to prevent splattering even when working with dry ingredients. The lower speeds are perfect for folding or start-up mixing, while the higher speeds are extremely fast and are good for quick whipping and aerating. The sturdy wire beaters have no center posts for the dough to climb, because that can clog mixing action. Made of stainless steel, these beaters can cut through even the heaviest cookie doughs. The unit also comes with an oversize stainless steel whisk for use with whipped cream and egg whites. Other features include a rotating cord that is designed to stay out of the way during mixing and a plastic spatula for scraping the sides of the bowl. The beaters and whisk are dishwasher safe for easy cleanup.

Warranty: 3 years, limited.

Manufacturer's Suggested Retail Price: $70

Approximate Low Price: $55

KITCHENAID CLASSIC PLUS KHM5TBWH ✓BEST BUY

The KitchenAid Classic Plus offers an alternative for those who want a powerful mixer without the added cost or bulk of a stand mixer. This unit comes with stainless steel turbo beaters, which are heavy wire beaters that cut through thick batters and act as efficient whisks for light batters. Because the beaters have no center posts, dough cannot climb them and clog mixing action. A convenient thumb-operated switch adjusts speeds from 1 (low) to 5 (high) in an instant. An electronic sensor automatically adjusts when more power is needed to maintain a consistent speed. The "Plus" is a unique blender rod attachment that converts the mixer to an immersion blender for shakes and other drinks. The mixer's handle is comfortable to grip even during extended mixing.

Warranty: 1 year, total replacement.

Manufacturer's Suggested Retail Price: $66

Approximate Low Price: $57

BRAUN MULTIMIX 4-IN-1 HANDHELD FOOD PREPARATION SYSTEM M880   Recommended

The Braun Multimix 4-in-1 Handheld Food Preparation System offers the ultimate in versatility. It performs the functions of a hand mixer, an immersion blender, a kneader, and a minimincer. Standard accessories include two heavy wire beaters that have a unique angled design for more efficient blending of ingredients, two sturdy dough hooks for tackling bread doughs, an immersion blender rod attachment and beaker, and a chopper attachment with a 10-ounce transparent bowl and plastic cover for storing ingredients. Because of its many attachments, this appliance is a bit complicated to use, so be sure to read the instructions and familiarize yourself with its many functions. Three speeds provide an adequate range for mixing and blending. The pulse option is great for quick mix-ins and for removing any dough clinging to the beaters. Pulse, however, is a little too fast for blending dry ingredients, which can be tossed up and out of the bowl on higher speeds.

Warranty: 1 year.

Manufacturer's Suggested Retail Price: $60

Approximate Low Price: $60

Stand Mixers

KITCHENAID ULTRA POWER STAND MIXER KSM90

✓ **BEST BUY**

The KitchenAid Ultra Power Stand Mixer KSM90 can tackle the most tedious and strenuous chores effortlessly. Then in the next minute it can be ready for all your light mixing. This unit's power comes from its mighty 10-speed motor. Features include a 4½-quart stainless steel mixing bowl with a handle, a flat beater, a dough hook, a stainless steel wire whisk, and a nonsealing bowl cover. Instead of bowl rotation, this mixer has unique planetary mixing action, which spins the beater and rotates it around the stationary bowl for maximum bowl coverage. The bowl locks into the base of the mixer for added stability. The mixer is available in a variety of colors. With several optional accessories, the KSM90 converts to a food grinder, a pasta maker, a fruit/vegetable strainer, a rotor slicer/shredder, a grain mill, a citrus juicer, and even a can opener. A 3-quart bowl, extra bowl covers, a fabric cover, a food tray, a two-piece pouring shield, and a temperature-retaining water jacket are also sold separately.

Warranty: 1 year, total replacement.

Manufacturer's Suggested Retail Price: $299

Approximate Low Price: $265

KRUPS POWERMIX PRO 610

✔ **BEST BUY**

The Krups PowerMix Pro is a combination stand and hand mixer that boasts three speeds, a pulse option, and a turbo speed to satisfy all your mixing needs. This unit consists of a hand mixer that is more powerful than most other hand mixers, a 3½-quart plastic mixing bowl with a grooved rim for automatic gear-driven rotation, a lightweight stand base, two heavy-duty wire whisks, and two dough hooks. A thumb-control lever effortlessly clicks into each of the three speeds. Turbo speed can be activated at any speed by depressing a button located on top of the mixer. To operate in manual pulse, press down and move the lever to the left. This movement may seem unfamiliar on first use, but it is easily mastered. The pulse option is great for slow-stirring dry ingredients or for mixing in last-minute items, such as chips. The mixer also has an oscillating feature that operates when the unit is locked into position: Every 15 seconds the mixer automatically moves from the side of the bowl to the center for more thorough bowl coverage. For all its power, this unit is surprisingly quiet. Its ability to detach and act as a hand mixer makes it extremely versatile and an exceptional value.

Warranty: 1 year, limited.

Manufacturer's Suggested Retail Price: $100

Approximate Low Price: $67

BLENDERS

KRUPS POWERX PLUS 239

✔ **BEST BUY**

The Krups PowerX Plus blender comes equipped with a large glass carafe, a powerful motor to crush ice cubes and other hard food items, and such specialty features as an ice crusher and power burst buttons. The variable-speed dial control lets you choose from any of the 14 speeds. On and off buttons start and stop the motor. The ice crusher and power burst buttons are touch-and-release to afford a pulselike control. With these features, you can crush ice for a frosty daiquiri or

puree tomatoes to a smooth consistency. The 48-ounce glass jar
is extra strong and has angled sides with interior ribs that create a whirling motion to achieve thorough blending. The carafe
lid has a removable center that doubles as a 2-ounce measure,
which makes adding ingredients a snap. The base is extra wide
with rubber feet so it won't rock back and forth on your counter
during tough blending jobs. Other features include a quiet
motor and hidden cord storage.

Warranty: 1 year, limited.

Manufacturer's Suggested Retail Price: $65

Approximate Low Price: $57

BRAUN MULTIPRACTIC HANDBLENDER
MR 550CA

✔**BEST BUY**

The Multipractic Handblender MR 550CA is
part of Braun's new culinary series. This versatile kitchen tool
consists of a blending rod with detachable shaft, a stainless
steel blade, a whisk attachment, a resealable 1-pint mixing/
measuring beaker, a minichopper accessory, and a convenient
wall bracket. To operate, place the shaft into the desired mixing vessel and press the control grip. Releasing the grip shuts
off the motor. The variable-speed regulator on this model lets
you switch from speeds 1 and 2 (for use with the whisk attachment) to 3 (for basic functions, such as blending and mixing)
and 4 (for use with the chopper attachment). The slim design
allows you to blend a milkshake in your own glass or puree soup
right in the pan. Use the whisk attachment for whipping cream,
egg whites, or skim milk. The 7-ounce chopping bowl is perfect for mincing or chopping small quantities of onions, garlic, fruits, nuts, or cheeses. It is not designed for extremely hard
food items, such as ice cubes, coffee beans, or chocolate. The
double-function chopper bowl base/lid seals the bowl to let you
store unused quantities quickly and easily. Except for the motor
base, the parts can be cleaned in hot water with a mild detergent. The shaft, chopper bowl, and mixing/measuring beaker
are also dishwasher safe.

Warranty: 1 year.

Manufacturer's Suggested Retail Price: $50

Approximate Low Price: $32

CUISINART QUICK PREP VARI-SPEED HAND BLENDER CSB-1C

✔BEST BUY

The Cuisinart Quick Prep Vari-Speed Hand Blender is a powerful blending tool with variable-speed control. With this model, you can stir, mix, chop, mince, beat, froth, whip, puree, crush, grind, or liquefy a variety of foods. To operate, select your speed on the variable-control dial, then press the control switch on the hand grip to activate the motor. An up-and-down pulsing motion provides the best results. This unit comes with a stainless steel chopping/mincing blade for pureeing semi-cooked vegetables or making baby food. Other accessories include a stainless steel blending/mixing disc for powdered drinks, sauces, and dressings, and a plastic whipping/beating attachment for making milkshakes, whipped cream, and mashed potatoes. This unit also comes with a 16-ounce Lexan mixing container and a 24-ounce stainless steel container, which retains icy cold temperatures. The whipping attachment can be used to aerate skim milk to three times its volume for nonfat beverages or desserts. To clean the blender, simply rinse the stem and blades under running water. All parts, except for the motor base, are dishwasher safe. Finally, the Cuisinart Quick Prep Vari-Speed Hand Blender comes with a wall bracket for off-the-counter storage.

Warranty: 18 months, limited.

Manufacturer's Suggested Retail Price: $70

Approximate Low Price: $42

WARING NUBLEND NB5VB

Budget Buy

The Waring NuBlend NB5VB features a large 48-ounce carafe with variable-speed control that lets you use just the right amount of power for your particular blending needs. Simply add ingredients to the unbreakable carafe and turn the dial. Then mix, stir, grind, whip, puree, blend, and liquefy to your heart's content. The one-piece plastic lid has a hinged opening for adding ingredients and for pouring. Pouring through the lid is slightly less efficient than pouring through standard spouts, however, and a few drips might occur until you master the new technique. A pulse/crush ice button is provided for quick chopping bursts. The smooth base easily wipes clean, and the carafe, lid, and blade assembly are all dishwasher safe.

Warranty: 5 years, limited on motor; 1 year, other parts.

Manufacturer's Suggested Retail Price: $46

Approximate Low Price: $40

HAMILTON BEACH BLENDMASTER 50188

The Hamilton Beach Blendmaster offers `Budget Buy` specialty features at a very affordable price. Choose from ten speeds using the touchpad control panel. Select high or low speed and any of the five blending options: whip/grate, aerate/grind, puree/beat, crumb/blend, or chop/liquefy. The shatter-resistant plastic jar holds 48 ounces and has a three-position lid that can be closed for blending, opened for pouring, or set to strain so ice and/or other solids remain in the jar. Other features include a powerful ice-breaker function and a timed blending option that can be programmed in 5-second increments for a 5- to 25-second duration. It can also operate as manual pulse, auto-pulse, and timed auto-pulse for hands-free blending.

Warranty: 2 years, limited.

Manufacturer's Suggested Retail Price: $50

Approximate Low Price: $28

TOASTERS & TOASTER OVENS

KRUPS TOASTRONIC AUTOLIFT 455

✓ **BEST BUY**

The Krups Toastronic Autolift is a completely automatic unit that toasts all types of breads and other baked goods. This model features one 1½-inch-wide slot that can accommodate bagels, English muffins, frozen waffles, or two slices of bread. To use, position the bread in the slot, push the toast color button to select the desired degree of toasting, and press the start/stop button. The bread is automatically lowered into the slot. When toasting is complete, a bell signals and the toast is raised for easy removal. The toaster turns itself off automatically. To interrupt toasting at any time, simply press the start/stop button a second time. The Krups Toastronic Autolift also has settings for "keep warm," which keeps already-toasted breads at the desired temperature for up to 10 minutes; "reheat," which rewarms previously toasted breads; and "defrost," which thaws and toasts frozen breads. Other features include a bun warmer rack that rests above the toaster, a slide-out crumb tray, and wrap-around cord storage.

Warranty: 1 year, limited.

Manufacturer's Suggested Retail Price: $95

Approximate Low Price: $52

CUISINART CLASSIC STYLE ELECTRONIC TOASTER CPT-70

✓ **BEST BUY**

The Cuisinart Classic Style Electronic Toaster is reminiscent of the old-fashioned chrome-plated toasters of yesteryear, but with contemporary features such as push-button controls that let you defrost, reheat, or cancel toasting. The two toasting slots are 1½ inches wide to accommodate a variety of bread thicknesses. To use, position bread in the slots, set the desired toast color using a dial control (in six increments ranging from light to dark), and press the carriage lever until it locks into position. When toasting is complete, the carriage lever is released and the toast is raised for easy removal. To interrupt toasting, press the cancel button at any time. The defrost button is designed to first thaw and then toast the bread. The reheat button allows you to reheat previously toasted breads without additional browning. Other features include wrap-around cord storage and a slide-out crumb tray. The carriage lever also has a built-in extra-lift control that lets you lift the carriage up for safe and easy removal of smaller items, such as English muffin halves.

Warranty: 18 months, limited.

Manufacturer's Suggested Retail Price: $70

Approximate Low Price: $55

KRUPS TOASTRONIC ULTRA 4-SLICE TOASTER 119

✔**BEST BUY**

The Krups Toastronic Ultra can handle up to four slices of bread but has a slim design that saves counter space. This unit features two extra-long, wide slots, plus a unique energy-saver switch, which lets the user turn off the rear bread slot when not in use. The shade-selector dial has settings from 1 (light) to 6 (dark). Two additional buttons let you defrost frozen bread prior to toasting or reheat previously toasted items. An automatic bread guide centers thick or thin bread items, and a quartz heating element ensures even toasting without overdrying the food. The Toastronic Ultra has a cool-to-the-touch housing that wipes clean with a damp cloth. Two removable crumb trays make cleanup easy.

Warranty: 1 year, limited.

Manufacturer's Suggested Retail Price: $80

Approximate Low Price: $70

DELONGHI ALFREDO ELITE XU-30

✔**BEST BUY**

The DeLonghi Alfredo Elite toaster oven is a high-quality appliance with many convenient features. An extra-large interior can accommodate up to six slices of bread, a 5-pound roast, a 10-inch pie, or a 2-quart casserole. Three dial controls operate the DeLonghi Alfredo Elite: One dial controls the oven temperature, with settings ranging from "keep warm" to "toast/broil." Another dial controls the "oven on" position and the toast color selection, while the third dial sets the function (toast, broil, or bake). The unit comes with a multipurpose bake and broil pan, a broil grid, and a removable oven rack. One of this unit's best features is the interior light, which lets you view the progress of your foods as they are cooking. Other features include a toast cycle bell timer and automatic shut-off; a full-view glass door; a scratch-resistant, easy-care exterior with the look of stainless steel; a continuous-cleaning interior; a removable crumb tray; cool-touch handles; wrap-around cord storage; and nonslip rubber feet. A pizza stone is available separately for about $20.

Warranty: 1 year, limited.

Manufacturer's Suggested Retail Price: $139

Approximate Low Price: $139

BLACK & DECKER ULTRA OVEN
TOAST-R-OVEN BROILER T670

✔ **BEST BUY**

The Ultra Oven Toast-R-Oven Broiler is the largest of Black & Decker's toaster ovens. For ease of use, this unit features simplified controls. A single dial operates the unit, with bake/broil temperatures ranging from 200 degrees to 500 degrees, and toast color selection ranging from light to dark. An extra-large interior accommodates up to six slices of bread or a 2½-quart casserole. You can bake a standard-size cake or broil up to three medium steaks using the multipurpose bake/broil pan. Of course, the Ultra Oven also toasts, defrosts, top-browns, and reheats foods. This unit has a chrome top with white and gray end panels, a continuous-cleaning interior, a wire rack that slides forward as the door is opened, and a slide-out crumb tray. Other features include a separate on/off switch, a bell that signals when toasting is complete, and a power light that signals when the unit is in use.

Warranty: 2 years, full.

Manufacturer's Suggested Retail Price: $120

Approximate Low Price: $82

BLACK & DECKER TOAST-R-OVEN
BROILER TR0515

Budget Buy

The Black & Decker Toast-R-Oven Broiler TR0515 is a compact model that is well suited for singles, smaller families, or households with infrequent or small-scale toasting needs. This easy-to-use, economical appliance can handle up to four bread slices, a 1½-quart meat loaf or casserole dish, one frozen dinner, or a 6-cup muffin tin. Two independent dials control toast color selection (with settings from light to dark and top brown) and bake/broil temperature settings (from 200 degrees to 500 degrees plus broil). To toast, select the darkness and press the toasting lever down. A signal bell lets you know when the toast is ready. For baking or broiling, turn the dial to the desired temperature; this activates the unit. It will remain on until the dial is returned to the off position. An in-use light signals when the machine is in operation. This model comes with a multipurpose bake/broil pan, a dual-position broiling grid, a continuous-cleaning interior, a swing-open crumb tray, and an easy-care exterior. The oven rack automatically comes forward when the door is opened. An under-the-cabinet heat-guard mounting hood is available separately for about $30.

Warranty: 2 years.

Manufacturer's Suggested Retail Price: $82

Approximate Low Price: $52

SPECIALTY FOOD PREP

SALTON JUICEMAN JR. JM-1
✔ BEST BUY

The Salton Juiceman Jr. JM-1 produces delicious vitamin-rich juice in minutes. It comes with a compact motor base, a large pulp collector, a stainless steel extractor blade/basket with a micromesh screen to separate and strain pulp, a clear dome cover, and a food pusher. To use, prepare fruits or vegetables by washing and trimming away any undesirable parts. Cut into pieces small enough to fit into the feed tube. With the juice cup in position, turn the motor on and feed the fruits/vegetables into the machine using the food pusher with gentle pressure. The pulp will automatically collect in the pulp container. Soft fruits, such as bananas and apricots, are not suitable for juicing and may damage the motor. The JM-1 features a safety switch so that the juicer cannot be activated unless properly assembled. This unit also comes with its own fresh juice recipe book, an audiocassette with tips on juicing, and an instruction book that gives nutritional information and helpful hints for getting the most from your processor. The unit disassembles, and all parts—except for the motor base—rinse clean in warm, soapy water.

Warranty: 1 year, limited.

Manufacturer's Suggested Retail Price: $100

Approximate Low Price: $85

BLACK & DECKER ALL-IN-ONE DELUXE AUTOMATIC BREADMAKER B1600

✔**BEST BUY**

The Black & Decker All-in-One Deluxe Automatic Breadmaker will quickly become a favorite addition to your household as it fills your kitchen with the tempting aroma of home-baked bread. To use, remove the bread pan from the machine, attach the kneading blade, place the ingredients in the pan, and return it to the machine. Close the lid, then select from five settings using the digital control panel, and press "start." Or set the timer for up to a 13-hour delay before breadmaking is completed. The Automatic Breadmaker makes large 2-pound loaves, with regular or dark crust. You can also choose whole grain or sweet bread settings. Finished bread takes about 3 hours. The "Rapid Bake" setting can produce basic white bread in less than 2 hours. The "Dough/Pasta" setting lets you make dough for dinner rolls, pizza, pretzels, and more. A "keep warm" function keeps bread warm for up to 1 hour after baking is completed. An "add ingredient" function signals to let you add fruit or nuts to the dough at the appropriate time during the mixing cycle. The unit also features a viewing window at the top of the machine, which lets you check the progress of your bread without opening the machine, plus an instructional video and cookbook to help you obtain perfect results. This unit's thin profile makes it especially suited for placement on a counter next to the refrigerator or microwave oven.

Warranty: 2 years.

Manufacturer's Suggested Retail Price: $151

Approximate Low Price: $125

SALTON BREADMAN PLUS BREADMAKER TR600

✓**BEST BUY**

The Salton Breadman Plus features seven settings for bread, plus a setting for dough only. Basic bread takes about 2 hours and 40 minutes from start to finish. Darker crust, sweet, French, or whole wheat breads take a bit longer—up to 4½ hours. The delay timer lets you add ingredients and set the machine up to 12 hours in advance so hot, fresh bread can be waiting for you when you come home from work or awaken in the morning. Include whole grain breads as part of a healthy diet or sweeten a dinner with a fruit bread. Since you make it yourself, you control the ingredient list, resulting in the freshest, most wholesome bread for you and your family. The Breadman Plus can prepare 1-pound, 1½-pound, or 2-pound loaf sizes. A digital control panel lets you select the setting, and a clock displays the time remaining in the cycle. A viewing window lets you monitor the progress as the Breadman Plus preheats, kneads the dough, lets it rise, shapes a loaf, and bakes it automatically. Cleanup is simple: Wash the bread pan and kneading paddle in warm, soapy water. Wipe the outside of the machine with a damp cloth, and wipe the inside to remove any flour or crumbs from the baking chamber. An instructional video is included.

Warranty: 1 year.

Manufacturer's Suggested Retail Price: $230

Approximate Low Price: $175

SALTON POPEIL PASTA MAKER PM400

Recommended

The Salton Popeil Pasta Maker is so simple to use, you'll want to make batch after batch of fresh, delicious pasta. This unit comes with 24 pasta dies, an automatic pasta cutter, a four-way ravioli cutter, a pasta measuring cup, a pasta fork, a recipe booklet, and an instructional videotape. To operate: First, assemble the machine by fitting the mixing blades together, inserting them into the mixing bin, attaching a pasta die, and screwing on the locking ring. Next, measure the flour and place it in the mixing bin. Close the lid. Then measure the liquids and (optional) flavorings, switch the machine on, and slowly add the liquids to the machine through the slots in the lid. The mixing bin is clear, so it allows you to watch the progress of the dough as it mixes and kneads. When the dough is the correct consistency, you are ready to extrude. Mixing takes only a few minutes. Extrusion takes a bit longer and requires constant supervision since the pasta must be cut into desired lengths as it comes out of machine. Getting the right consistency is a matter of practice, but this machine accommodates beginners beautifully. To clean, disassemble the unit and remove the excess dough. Let the machine parts dry overnight, so the dried dough falls off. Except for the base, all the parts can be washed in the dishwasher. This machine is powerful, so it is expensive and a bit noisy, but it saves time and energy compared to rolling the dough by hand. Dies are included to make spaghetti, linguine, fettuccine, angel hair, vermicelli, tagliatelle, macaroni, rigatoni, and lasagne. Specialty dies are also included for penne, rotini, shells, fusilli, and more. You can also use your Popeil Pasta Maker to mix dough for cookies or bagels.

Warranty: 1 year, limited.

Manufacturer's Suggested Retail Price: $350

Approximate Low Price: $120

TOASTMASTER BREAD & BUTTER MAKER 1195

Recommended

The Toastmaster Bread & Butter Maker is unique because in addition to making fresh bread it also has a butter cycle that churns fresh butter from cream in 30 minutes. The nine bread settings are: basic light, medium, and dark; whole wheat light, medium, and dark; French; sweet breads; and a dough-only program for making dinner rolls or other fancy-shaped breads in your conventional oven. The unit makes a 1- to 2-pound loaf. Cycles take anywhere from just under 3 hours to 4½ hours. The dough can be made in 1 to 1½ hours. The machine uses a variety of steps: reheating, mixing, kneading, rising, punching down, shaping, and baking. The mixing steps tend to be a bit noisy, but during rising and baking the machine is virtually silent. Other features include a delay timer, a viewing window that lets you check on bread without opening the lid, digital push-button controls, a bread warming feature that keeps bread warm for up to 1 hour after baking, and a nonstick loaf pan.

Warranty: 3 years, parts and labor.

Manufacturer's Suggested Retail Price: $149

Approximate Low Price: $134

TOASTMASTER JUICER 1106

Budget Buy

The Toastmaster Juicer is a compact, economical choice for individuals or families who prefer the taste of fresh citrus juices. This unit consists of a compact motor base, a clear, 32-ounce juice container with pouring spout, a pulp and seed strainer, a grooved juice cone, and a clear dust cover. Downward pressure on the cone activates the machine. You can juice oranges, grapefruit, lemons, or limes directly into the juice container. Other features include a pulp collector built into the strainer and rubber feet for stability. The pitcher, cone, and strainer disassemble easily for cleaning in warm, sudsy water or on the top rack of the dishwasher.

Warranty: 3 years, parts and labor.

Manufacturer's Suggested Retail Price: $18

Approximate Low Price: Not available

COFFEEMAKERS AND TEAMAKERS

Automatic-drip coffeemakers consist of a power base, a water reservoir, a filter holder, a carafe, and a built-in warming plate or carafe stand. Optional features include permanent gold-tone or screen filters, which replace the standard disposable paper

FOOD PREPARATION

filters; digital clocks with timers to preset the start of coffee making; an automatic shutoff; and a pause-to-serve feature that lets you halt brewing long enough to pour a cup of coffee. Larger machines make up to 12 cups, but they can usually be set for smaller servings. Personal-size machines make up to 4 cups at a time and save counter space. Auto-drip coffeemakers require periodic cleaning or decalcifying to remove mineral deposits. This is accomplished by brewing a cycle with a special cleaning solution or a mixture of vinegar and water.

Electric percolators are self-contained carafes with built-in brewing mechanisms, permanent filter baskets, and lids. Many have detachable cords. These units brew coffee by pumping hot water over and through coarse grounds at an incredibly fast (a cup-a-minute) speed. Sizes range from 4 to 12 cups for standard percolators, anywhere from 12 to 30 cups for larger units, and up to 100 cups for the largest percolator urns.

Espresso/cappuccino makers, the newest addition to the coffee market, are quickly becoming an American household standard. This type of coffeemaker operates by heating water and using steam or pump pressure to force the water quickly through fine grounds for maximum flavor extraction. Steam can then be diverted through a nozzle to foam milk for cappuccino. There are two types of espresso/cappuccino makers—steam machines and pump machines. Pump machines are more powerful, heating water to the optimal temperature (190 to 197 degrees as recommended by the Specialty Coffee Association of America), then propelling it through fine-ground beans in about 20 to 30 seconds. The fast rate of expulsion produces a rich layer of foam, known as crema. Crema is the standard for judging espresso. Though steam machines do not possess the power of pump machines, they do produce a good strong cup of espresso and are generally smaller and less expensive than pump models. Combination units, which make regular brew coffee as well as espresso and cappuccino, are also available.

A recent development in kitchen appliances is the combination iced coffeemaker and iced teamaker. These machines can be set for steeping tea or for brewing coffee, which then drips into an ice-filled pitcher for a refreshing summertime drink.

Automatic-Drip Coffeemakers

BLACK & DECKER BREW 'N GO SMALL DRIP DCM17

✔**BEST BUY**

The Black & Decker Brew 'n Go Small Drip coffeemaker is ideal for the busy executive, commuter, college student, or parent on the go. This unit consists of a compact base with a water reservoir, a filter basket, a permanent plastic and mesh filter, a 16-ounce thermal travel mug, and a lid. Simple to use, this unit brews directly into the travel mug in about 8 minutes. A shower-head water spreader distributes water evenly over grounds for good saturation and full flavor. For a quick cup of tea or cocoa to go, add a tea bag or instant cocoa to the travel mug and run the machine without adding coffee grounds to the filter. Other features include automatic shutoff and a power indicator light. To clean this coffeemaker, wait until the unit has cooled down, then empty the grounds and wipe the base with a damp cloth. The filter basket, travel mug, and lid can be washed in warm, soapy water or in the top rack of your dishwasher. Extra mugs and filters are available separately.

Warranty: 2 years.

Manufacturer's Suggested Retail Price: $26

Approximate Low Price: $23

MR. COFFEE ACCEL SMALL DRIP PR5

✔**BEST BUY**

The Mr. Coffee Accel has a 1- to 4-cup capacity and is well suited for singles or families who consume a smaller amount of coffee. An accelerated brewing feature produces up to 4 cups in just 4 minutes. Easy to use, this unit also has a lighted on/off switch, a "pause 'n serve" feature that lets you sneak a cup before brewing has finished, a swing-out filter holder with a removable basket, and a flip-back water-tank lid with convenient cup markings for easy filling.

Warranty: 1 year, limited.

Manufacturer's Suggested Retail Price: $25

Approximate Low Price: $25

CUISINART PROGRAMMABLE 10-CUP COFFEEMAKER DCC-140

✓ BEST BUY

The Cuisinart Programmable 10-Cup Coffee-maker is a large automatic-drip machine with a digital clock/timer. When you set the dial for the number of cups to be brewed, the coffee-bar flavor system goes to work. The correct amount of water is distributed through the grounds for maximum extraction and flavor without bitter undertones. Available in black or white, this unit uses paper filters and brews from 2 to 10 cups of coffee. Some of its convenient features include a flip-back reservoir lid for easy filling, a large water-level indicator window, a removable swing-out filter holder, and a comfort-grip handle for controlled pouring with fewer drips. Specialty features include brew pause, which lets you sneak a cup while brewing is in progress; a 1- to 4-cup setting that adjusts brewing for fuller flavor with smaller quantities; and a 2-hour auto shutoff. The carafe, lid, and filter basket and holder are dishwasher safe for easy cleaning. Cord storage saves counter space.

Warranty: 3 years, limited.

Manufacturer's Suggested Retail Price: $70

Approximate Low Price: $57

HAMILTON BEACH AROMA ELITE LARGE DRIP 47264

Recommended

The Hamilton Beach Aroma Elite Large Drip coffeemaker delivers 2 to 12 cups of coffee using an accelerated brewing process that is complete in about 10 minutes. Available in black or white (model #47261), this unit also features a digital clock and a 24-hour programmable timer, an automatic "pause 'n serve" function that interrupts the brew cycle when the carafe is removed from the warming plate, and a 2-hour automatic shutoff. The filter cover rotates out to provide access to the filter basket. The removable cone-shaped basket uses paper filters and has a swing-up handle for convenient emptying and cleaning. Other features include a flip-up reservoir lid, a nonstick warming plate, interior water-level markings, and hideaway cord storage. This unit also comes without the clock (#47104, black; #47101, white).

Warranty: 2 years, limited.

Manufacturer's Suggested Retail Price: $70

Approximate Low Price: $45

BRAUN FLAVORSELECT LARGE DRIP KF157

The Braun FlavorSelect Large Drip KF157 **Budget Buy** coffeemaker features a multipath brewing system that distributes water evenly throughout the cone-shaped filter for full extraction of flavor. Specialty features include a flavor selector dial that lets you adjust coffee flavor from mild to robust and a self-monitoring water filter that reduces chlorine taste and prevents calcification. Available in black or white, this unit has a filter basket that swings out for easy filling and removes for cleaning. The convenient "pause and serve" function prevents dripping on the warming plate when the 12-cup carafe is removed to pour a cup during brewing. Other features include a 1- to 3-cup switch that adjusts brewing for smaller quantities, a lighted on/off switch, a water level indicator, a flip-back tank lid for easy filling and cleaning, and cord storage. A permanent gold plate or long-lasting gold screen filter is available separately for about $50.

Warranty: 1 year, limited.

Manufacturer's Suggested Retail Price: $50

Approximate Low Price: $50

Percolators

WEST BEND STAINLESS STEEL PERCOLATOR URN 59005

The West Bend Percolator Urn is a large, hand-✔ **BEST BUY** some percolator suitable for household or commercial gatherings. This unit brews from 25 to 55 cups of fresh coffee and keeps it warm in a polished stainless steel urn. Brewing is

FOOD PREPARATION

quick—1 minute per cup. The Percolator Urn comes with its own permanent filter basket that removes for easy cleaning, a twist-lock cover, a two-position dripless faucet spout for quick, convenient dispensing into cups or a coffee server, and a ready light. The heat-resistant base, handles, and knob provide safe handling. The West Bend Percolator Urn can also be used to heat water for tea or other instant beverages.

Warranty: 1 year.

Manufacturer's Suggested Retail Price: $198

Approximate Low Price: $125

WEST BEND PARTY PERK 58030
Recommended

The West Bend Party Perk is an economical alternative to the higher-priced stainless steel percolator urns. Available in polished aluminum or antique white plastic for a cooler exterior surface, this unit features a 12- to 30-cup brewing capacity, an automatic temperature control to maintain a consistent serving temperature after brewing is completed, a two-way dripless faucet, a twist-lock lid, heat-resistant handles and lid, a heat-resistant base, a detachable cordset, and a ready light. It can also be used to heat water.

Warranty: 1 year.

Manufacturer's Suggested Retail Price: $45

Approximate Low Price: $28

WEST BEND AUTOMATIC COFFEEMAKER 54129
Budget Buy

The West Bend 54129 is a medium-sized percolator with a 5- to 9-cup capacity. Made of polished aluminum, this unit features automatic temperature control. It comes with a permanent cool-tip filter basket, a pump assembly, a twist-lock cover, and a detachable cordset. The heat-resistant handle and base provide safe handling.

Warranty: 1 year.

Manufacturer's Suggested Retail Price: $31

Approximate Low Price: $18

Espresso/Cappuccino Machines

DELONGHI CAFFE VENEZIA BAR-29

✔**BEST BUY**

Designed and manufactured in Italy, the DeLonghi Caffe Venezia is a pump-driven machine that delivers cup after cup of rich espresso or cappuccino. Convenient features include an easy-to-operate on/off switch, an "OK" light that indicates when the desired temperature has been reached, a pump switch, and a steam switch. The pump is quiet and efficient. The swiveling jet frother utilizes dry steam to produce thick foam for cappuccino. Other features include a warming area on top of the machine to preheat cups, a removable 1.3-liter (approx. 45-ounce) water tank with water-level markings, a removable drip tray, and built-in storage for two stainless steel filter holders and a measuring spoon. This unit carries a higher price tag than most, but the quality construction, including a stainless steel boiler and chromed brass filter for better heat retention, make it both durable and desirable. An instructional video is included.

Warranty: 1 year.

Manufacturer's Suggested Retail Price: $250

Approximate Low Price: $250

BRAUN BARISTAMASTER KFE750

✔**BEST BUY**

The Braun BaristaMaster combination unit is unique because it can brew four types of coffee: espresso, cappuccino, automatic-drip, and French-press style. The pump-driven brewing system delivers up to 4 cups of espresso with a rich crema. This unit comes with a 16-ounce capacity water tank/boiler; a tank cover with steam vents for preheating cups; a swing-out filter basket; three filters for 1 to 2 cups or 3 to 4 cups of espresso, or 1 to 4 cups of specialty coffee; a 4-cup glass carafe with lid; an easy-froth attachment; an adjustable-drip tray/stand for cups or the carafe; and a measuring spoon with tamper. The four-position function selector lets you choose espresso/coffee specialties, steam, neutral (for use during preheating or in between servings), or water (for dispensing hot water for tea or for emptying the boiler tank). Other features include a coffee selector switch, a ready-to-brew light and audible signal, an easy-to-use on/off button, a 2-hour auto shutoff, and cord storage.

Warranty: 1 year, limited.

Manufacturer's Suggested Retail Price: $180

Approximate Low Price: $160

SALTON THREE FOR ALL PLUS EX-30 VHSWHT

The Salton Three for All Plus combination `Recommended` coffeemaker and espresso machine offers an 8-cup capacity for automatic-drip coffee, or up to 4 cups of espresso or cappuccino, with its easy-to-use steam-operated brewing system. Drip coffee features include a glass carafe with a lid, a swing-out filter basket, an automatic "pause and serve" function, a water reservoir with water level indicator, and a hinged lid for easy filling. Espresso/cappuccino features include a cappuccino-only valve, which regulates the strength of the espresso (light, medium, or dark) and the steam for frothing milk. The espresso part of the unit is equipped with an easy-to-use steam jet, a 4-cup glass espresso carafe with lid, an espresso filter, and a filter holder. Other features include lighted on/off switches for espresso/cappuccino and for automatic-drip coffee, a how-to video with step-by-step instructions, and convenient cord storage. This unit is available in black or white.

Warranty: 1 year, limited.

Manufacturer's Suggested Retail Price: $140

Approximate Low Price: $85

Coffee Grinders and Mills

KRUPS FAST-TOUCH COFFEE GRINDER 203

The Krups Fast-Touch Coffee Grinder has a **✓ BEST BUY** 3-ounce capacity (sufficient for up to 15 cups of coffee). Its oval shape helps attain a uniform grind and facilitates pouring grounds directly into a coffee filter. The quality stainless steel cutting blades process beans from coarse to ultrafine in seconds. Operation is simple: Just press "on" to activate the motor. Since the motor cannot be engaged without the lid in place, this acts as a safety mechanism. Available in black, white, or red, the Krups Fast-Touch is compact and tucks away easily in a drawer or cabinet.

Warranty: 1 year, limited.

Manufacturer's Suggested Retail Price: $28

Approximate Low Price: $20

DELONGHI ELECTRONIC COFFEE GRINDER DCG-1
✔**BEST BUY**

The DeLonghi DCG-1 has electronic programming to ensure the perfect grind for all types of coffee preparations. This unique grinder eliminates the guesswork by calculating the optimal time for achieving coarse-, medium-, or fine-ground coffee. It can grind 4 to 12 cups of coffee. Made of high-impact plastic with a stainless steel inner bowl and blade, the DCG-1 features a clear plastic cover that doubles as a measuring cup, a cover tab, and a safety switch slot. The thumb-activated control button starts the grinder. Signal lights indicate the grind (red for coarse, amber for medium, and green for fine). To stop the motor when the desired grind is achieved, just release pressure on the switch.

Warranty: 1 year, limited.

Manufacturer's Suggested Retail Price: $25

Approximate Low Price: $22

BRAUN COFFEE MILL KMM30
✔**BEST BUY**

The Braun Coffee Mill KMM30 uses a unique precision milling system to grind coffee beans to the exact texture indicated for all types of coffee preparations. Available in white or black, this unit features an adjustable fineness control dial (with 24 settings from coarse to very fine) and an automatic quantity selector with timer, which determines the grinding time based on the number of cups of coffee desired. To shorten or stop the grinding process, return the timer to the off position. The conical bean container has a lid and holds up to 8 ounces of coffee beans (enough for up to 60 cups of coffee). Ground coffee is dispensed into a separate container with a rounded bottom to allow easier removal with a measuring spoon. This unit comes with wraparound cord storage. The coffee bean container, lid, and ground-coffee container remove for easy cleaning in warm, soapy water or in a dishwasher.

Warranty: 1 year, limited.

Manufacturer's Suggested Retail Price: $60

Approximate Low Price: $57

MAXIM COFFEE MILL GC 30 ✓BEST BUY

The Maxim Coffee Mill is both compact and efficient for producing uniform coffee grounds no matter what type of coffeemaker you use. Choose from 10 degrees of fineness along the thumb-operated dial control. The bean chamber holds up to 4 ounces (enough for about 18 cups of coffee). An automatic portion timer can be set for the number of cups you wish to brew—from 1 to 12 cups per batch. Press the on button to activate the motor. This coffee mill will process the set number of cups then switch off automatically. The grounds are dispensed into a separate storage container. To turn off the unit during grinding, return the portion timer to the off position. The bean chamber lid and ground coffee chamber can be removed for easy cleaning in warm, soapy water or in a dishwasher.

Warranty: 1 year, limited.

Manufacturer's Suggested Retail Price: $50

Approximate Low Price: Not available

TOASTMASTER COFFEE GRINDER 1112 Budget Buy

The Toastmaster Coffee Grinder is an economical, easy-to-use grinder with a 2½-ounce capacity (sufficient for up to 12 cups of coffee). Don't let the low price tag fool you. This unit offers quality stainless steel blades, a clear cover that locks in the "on" position for safe operation, an easy-to-use pulse-action control button, and convenient wrap-around cord storage. Approximate grinding times are given in the enclosed manual for coarse-, medium-, or fine-ground coffee; most beans require only 10 to 20 seconds of grinding.

Warranty: 3 years, parts and labor.

Manufacturer's Suggested Retail Price: $18

Approximate Low Price: $10

Teamakers

MRS. TEA HTM1

✔**BEST BUY**

Using Mrs. Tea by Mr. Coffee is a delightful way to enjoy a relaxing pot of tea. This unit includes a power base with warming plate, a lighted "on" switch, a swing-out steeping filter basket, a wide-mouth water reservoir, and a 6-cup ceramic teapot with lid. Select a stronger or weaker brew by adjusting the steeping lever on the filter basket. The brewing cycle takes from 8 to 11 minutes, depending on the length of steeping. The tea is kept warm as long as the teapot remains on the warmer plate. Or place the lid on the teapot to keep the tea warm while serving. To make a second pot of tea, you must wait until the ceramic pot cools down.

Warranty: 1 year, limited.

Manufacturer's Suggested Retail Price: $36

Approximate Low Price: $36

SALTON ICED COFFEE/ICED TEA MAKER KM-44

Recommended

The Salton Iced Coffee/Iced Tea Maker is similar to an auto-drip coffeemaker but with a special two-position filter basket that can be set for steeping tea as well as brewing coffee into an ice-filled pitcher for a delicious cold beverage in about 10 minutes. This unit comes with a clear, 2-liter plastic pitcher, a power base with an easy-to-use "on" button and power indicator light, a water reservoir with a hinged lid and a clear water-level indicator, and a removable filter basket. Insert a paper filter and measure coffee grounds or loose tea into the filter basket. (Tea bags don't require a filter). Fill the tank with cold water to the desired level and press the "on" button. The water is heated and then distributed through the filter to extract the coffee or tea flavor. You can also make flavored blends by combining different teas. The unit shuts itself off automatically once brewing is completed.

Warranty: 1 year, limited.

Manufacturer's Suggested Retail Price: $40

Approximate Low Price: $20

MICROWAVE OVENS

What size microwave do you need? That depends on whether you plan to cook entire family-size casseroles or just warm up meals for one. Most microwave recipes and cookbooks require an oven with at least 650 watts of power. Compact/subcompact ovens have capacities of up to 0.7 cubic feet and usually have 700 watts of power or less. Medium-size microwaves range from 0.8 to 1.0 cubic feet in capacity and usually have about 900 watts. Full-size microwaves, recommended for larger families, are over 1.0 cubic foot in capacity and are rated at 1,000 watts and up.

Features and Terminology

Convection ovens are most valuable when the microwave has a combination convection/microwave setting. The marriage of the microwave's quick-cooking abilities and the convection oven's browning and crisping abilities is very useful. Convection ovens work by circulating air heated by an electric element. Microwave/convection ovens often contain metal interiors, which can slow microwave cooking time and make the unit harder to clean. Another disadvantage of metal interiors is that, unlike plastic, the metal becomes very hot to the touch.

Browning dishes/trays/elements help the microwave turn out crispy, browned foods. Browning dishes are special utensils with a metal content on the bottom that allow the microwave to crisp potatoes and other foods. Browning trays generally need to be preheated several minutes before using and do not perform as well as traditional ovens. Browning elements are similar to broilers in traditional ovens and can help the microwave crisp foods better and more evenly. Automatic sensors determine when the food is heated by the amount of steam in the microwave. These sensors are not foolproof, however, and it may still be necessary to stop the oven and check the food's temperature.

Temperature probes work continuously to determine when a food reaches a preset temperature and are often included in microwave/convection models. Like a sensor, a temperature probe will automatically turn off the microwave oven when it finishes cooking the food.

One-button cooking allows you to press one button for cooking items such as popcorn, potatoes, pizza, or beverages. If you frequently prepare one certain food, consider this feature when purchasing a microwave. Another one-button feature is something called minute plus, which gives you the ability to add an extra minute to a food's cooking time without turning off the oven.

Automatic defrost/automatic reheat/automatic start are programmable functions that allow you to reheat or defrost a food, often with the single push of a button. Automatic defrost takes the work out of defrosting foods. This feature generally works at several different power levels for a length of time based on the weight of the food: Program in the weight of the food, and the oven selects the correct time. A timed or manual defrost feature lets you program the defrost time and power levels yourself. Automatic start is a feature that allows you to program the oven up to 12 hours in advance to turn on at a specific time.

Interactive displays are now available on the higher-end models. These guide you through the microwave's use and tell you when and how to reset the clock or remind you to specify a weight when defrosting a food.

Best Buys '97

Our Best Buy, Recommended, and Budget Buy choices follow. Remember that a Best Buy, Recommended, or Budget Buy designation applies only to the model listed. It does not necessarily apply to other models made by the same manufacturer.

FULL-SIZE MICROWAVES

GENERAL ELECTRIC JE1540GW ✓BEST BUY

The JE1540GW is a 1.5-cubic-foot unit with all the basic one-touch features that make microwave cooking flexible and easy. This oven has 1,000 watts and ten power levels. Valuable features include a delay start/reminder feature, an add-30-seconds pad, two timed cooking settings, and a child-lockout feature. This unit also has convenient cooking controls with beverage, cook, popcorn, snack, and reheat pads. Instant-on controls, a cooking complete reminder, and a kitchen timer add to this model's versatility. The greystone cabinet with black front adds a contemporary look to any kitchen. A kit to convert it to a built-in oven is available at an additional cost. This unit also comes in almond or white.

Specifications: Overall dimensions: height, 13⁵⁄₁₆″; width, 23²¹⁄₃₂″; depth, 17²¹⁄₃₂″; capacity, 1.5 cubic feet. Cavity dimensions: height, 9³⁄₁₆″; width, 16½″; depth, 16²⁷⁄₃₂″. Cooking power: 1,000 watts. **Warranty:** 1 year, parts and labor; 10 years, parts only on magnetron tube.

Manufacturer's Suggested Retail Price: $239
Approximate Low Price: $196

SHARP R-5H08

✓BEST BUY

   This family-size microwave includes a Sharp innovation called Tactile Control, which means the unit uses rounded and raised keys to improve fingertip control and assist those who are sight-challenged. A handsome, stone-gray unit, the R-5H08 boasts an interior capacity of 1.6 cubic feet, with a 16-inch turntable for large dishes. The Custom Help key guides the user through programming and includes a demonstration mode. This feature-laden model includes automatic defrost and automatic cook functions, which calculate cooking times for favorite foods. Sensor reheat and sensor cook controls automatically determine reheating and cooking times and power levels. Additional features include a programmable four-stage cooking mode, a timer, and a minute-plus key. The latter sets the oven for 1 minute on high with one touch. This model is an excellent choice for consumers who want a state-of-the-art microwave. A kit to convert this oven to a built-in unit is available at an additional cost.

Specifications: Overall dimensions: height, 13¼″; width, 24″; depth, 19″; capacity, 1.6 cubic feet. Cavity dimensions: height, 9¼″; width, 16⅞″; depth, 17⅜″. Cooking power: 1,000 watts.

Warranty: 1 year, parts; 1 year, related labor and carry-in service; 5 years, magnetron tube.

Manufacturer's Suggested Retail Price: $329

Approximate Low Price: $230

KITCHENAID KCMS125Y   ✔ BEST BUY

KitchenAid's top-of-the-line cooking appliances include their microwave ovens. A stylish countertop microwave, the KCMS125Y has a 1.2-foot capacity and 800 watts of power. A sensor cook control automatically calculates cooking and reheating times. Other convenient features include a custom defrost cycle, an automatic start feature, and easy minute cycles. The KCMS125Y boasts a 99-minute, 99-second electronic touch control along with a ten-level variable power control. This model is available in white, almond, black, or stainless steel styling. Optional built-in kits are available, and trim kits can be purchased separately to install the microwave in cabinetry above any cooking appliance.

Specifications: Overall dimensions: height, 12¼"; width, 21⅝"; depth, 16¾"; capacity, 1.2 cubic feet. Cavity dimensions: height, 8¼"; width, 15"; depth, 16⅛". Cooking power: 800 watts. **Warranty:** 1 year, parts and labor; 5 years, parts only on electronic controls and magnetron tube.

Manufacturer's Suggested Retail Price: $389

Approximate Low Price: Not available

PANASONIC NN-S776WA   ✔ BEST BUY

A full-powered, 1,000-watt microwave, this white Panasonic model boasts a multilingual menu-action screen, which displays operating instructions in English, French, or Spanish. One-touch sensor cooking allows you to cook favorite foods from 15 categories without knowing the quantity or having to select the cooking time. This model also includes one-touch sensor reheat so you can reheat leftovers automatically, without programming in a time or quantity. The defrost sensor automatically calculates the time and power level for consistent defrosting. The more/less control allows fine-tuning of the cooking time without having to reprogram. Auto-cooking keys include pasta, rice, casserole, stew, fish fillets, shellfish, whole chicken, chicken pieces, beef, and pork. This model is also available in black (NN-S776BA).

Specifications: Overall dimensions: height, 14"; width, 23⁷⁄₁₆"; depth, 16⁵⁄₁₆"; capacity, 1.5 cubic feet. Cavity dimensions: height, 10³⁄₁₆"; width, 16⁵⁄₁₆"; depth, 15⅛". Cooking power: 1,000 watts. **Warranty:** 1 year, carry-in service on parts and labor; 5 years, carry-in service on magnetron tube.

Manufacturer's Suggested Retail Price: $200

Approximate Low Price: $184

MEDIUM-SIZE MICROWAVES

SHARP R-3A98
✔ **BEST BUY**

Sharp is quickly becoming the industry leader in providing versatile microwaves for a good value. A sleek-looking white unit, the R-3A98 provides the most features for the lowest price of all the medium-sized models reviewed here. An advanced seven-digit interactive display helps the user with cooking hints and information on programming with full word prompts that roll vertically. A defrost function quickly defrosts meats and poultry: Users can enter weight in 0.1-pound increments for superb results. This model also includes a child lock, an audible signal elimination, a one-touch popcorn key, and a programmable four-stage cooking mode. A 12¾-inch glass turntable is included. This model is also available in stone gray.

Specifications: Overall dimensions: height, 12"; width, 20½"; depth, 15⅜"; capacity, 0.9 cubic foot. Cavity dimensions: height, 7¾"; width, 13¾"; depth, 14½". Cooking power: 900 watts. **Warranty:** 1 year, parts; 1 year, related labor and carry-in service; 5 years, magnetron tube.

Manufacturer's Suggested Retail Price: $250

Approximate Low Price: Not available

PANASONIC NN-S576

✓ BEST BUY

Panasonic has increased the oven capacity of its midsize microwaves to 1.0 cubic foot, which is the largest size available in this category from any manufacturer. The menu-action screen, which offers operating instructions in French, English, or Spanish, makes this microwave user-friendly. A major convenience is one-touch sensor cooking, which offers the one-touch function in 15 categories, including potatoes, vegetables, rice, pasta, frozen foods, seafood, casserole, stew, poultry, and meats. This model also has a one-touch sensor reheat that takes the guesswork out of warming leftovers. The NN-S576 also includes an automatic defrost mode, a popcorn key, a quick-minute control, a more/less control button, and an easy-to-open door handle. This model is available in white (NN-S576WA) or black (NN-S576BA).

Specifications: Overall dimensions: height, 12"; width, 20"; depth, 14³⁄₁₆"; capacity, 1.0 cubic foot. Cavity dimensions: height, 9"; width, 13⅞"; depth, 13⁵⁄₁₆". Cooking power: 1,000 watts. **Warranty:** 1 year, limited on parts and labor; 5 years, magnetron tube.

Manufacturer's Suggested Retail Price: $180

Approximate Low Price: Not available

PANASONIC NN-S566WA

Budget Buy

The NN-S566WA is similar to the NN-S576WA but doesn't have the sensor heat mode, making it Panasonic's most economical microwave oven. It does have many of Panasonic's standard microwave features, such as the multilingual menu-action screen, the easy-to-open door handle, six power levels, and automatic reheat and defrost. Special keys are included for bacon, frozen bagels, potatoes, popcorn, hot dogs, oatmeal, frozen foods, and vegetables. A quick-minute feature is also included. It is also available in black (NN-S566BA).

Specifications: Overall dimensions: height, 12"; width, 20"; depth, 14³⁄₁₆"; capacity, 1.0 cubic feet. Cavity dimensions: height, 9"; width, 13⅞"; depth, 13⁵⁄₁₆". Cooking power: 1,000 watts. **Warranty:** 1 year, parts and labor; 5 years, magnetron tube.

Manufacturer's Suggested Retail Price: $160
Approximate Low Price: Not available

COMPACT MICROWAVES

SHARP R-2A98

✔**BEST BUY**

Consumers who have limited kitchen space but don't want to be short-changed on features will find that this model answers their needs perfectly. The Sharp R-2A98 has only 700 watts and 0.7 cubic foot of oven space, but it includes an automatic defrost, five snack and reheat settings, a one-touch popcorn key, a dinner plate key for convenient reheating of leftovers, and a minute-plus feature. The latter sets the oven for 1 minute on high with one touch. There are three automatic defrost settings (ground meat, steaks/chops, and chicken pieces) and five automatic cook settings (baked potatoes, fresh vegetables, frozen vegetables, rice, and ground meat). Additional features include ten variable power levels, audible signal elimination, a child lock, and a 10¾-inch turntable. The R-2A98 is white; the R-2A88 is the same oven with a stone gray cabinet.

Specifications: Overall dimensions: height, 11¼"; width, 19⅞"; depth, 13"; capacity, 0.7 cubic feet. Cavity dimensions: height, 7⅛"; width, 13⅜"; depth, 11⅞". Cooking power: 700 watts.
Warranty: 1 year, parts; 1 year, related labor and carry-in service; 5 years, magnetron tube.

Manufacturer's Suggested Retail Price: $190
Approximate Low Price: Not available

OVER-THE-RANGE MICROWAVES AND MICROWAVE/CONVECTION OVENS

GENERAL ELECTRIC JVM1350WW

✔**BEST BUY**

The JVM1350WW is a stylish, white-on-white, over-the-range microwave oven, with a capacity of 1.3 cubic

MICROWAVE OVENS

feet. It features GE's SmartControl system, which is an easy-to-read horizontal scrolling display that offers step-by-step instructions at the touch of a pad. The versatile sensor-cooking control has separate pads for popcorn, beverages, automatic reheat, ground meats, fish fillets, chicken pieces, potatoes, and three different vegetable settings. Other features include a programmable night-light, start delay, and a roast setting that uses a temperature probe. Some of GE's standard microwave features, such as instant-on controls, a beeper sound-level control, and child lockout, are also included. It is also available in black-on-black (JVM1350BW) and in almond-on-almond (JVM1350AW).

Specifications: Overall dimensions: height, 16½"; width, 29⅞"; depth, 14"; capacity, 1.3 cubic feet. Cavity dimensions: height, 9⅛"; width, 19"; depth, 12½". Cooking power: 900 watts. **Warranty:** 1 year, in-home parts and labor; 10 years, magnetron tube.

Manufacturer's Suggested Retail Price: $479

Approximate Low Price: $434

GENERAL ELECTRIC PROFILE SERIES
JVM1090

✓ BEST BUY

The JVM1090 is an over-the-range, combination microwave/convection model, with a 1.0-cubic-foot capacity and 825 watts of power. A wonderful feature in many of GE's microwaves is the SmartControl system—an easy-to-read horizontal scrolling display designed to make cooking easier. Step-by-step instructions are displayed at the touch of a keypad to guide cooks through all of this oven's functions. Features included on the JVM1090 are a broil pan/rack, electronic touch controls, a sensor cook pad, variable beeper volume, and a two-speed exhaust fan with a cooktop and programmable night light. This oven's controls include a button that allows you to add 30 seconds, an express-cook control, a minute pad, and a delay start feature. The oven's selections include combination cook, combination roast (probe), and convection broil/cook. This model comes in white, almond, or black.

Specifications: Overall dimensions: height, 15½"; width, 29¹⁵⁄₁₆"; depth, 14¼"; capacity, 1.0 cubic feet. Cavity dimensions: height, 8¹⁄₁₆"; width, 18"; depth, 12½". Cooking power: 825 watts. **Warranty:** 1 year, parts and labor; 10 years, parts only on the magnetron tube.

Manufacturer's Suggested Retail Price: $769

Approximate Low Price: Not available

KITCHENAID KHMS105E

Recommended

This sleek-looking over-the-range microwave oven is available in black, white, or almond stylings. (The white and almond cost an extra $30.) The KHMS105E is a full-featured microwave with 1.1 cubic feet of space and 850 watts of power. Its best features include an easy-to-understand electronic touch control timer, a delay start option, an automatic sensor feature, a convenient custom defrost option, and an electronic temperature probe. For extra versatility, the two-speed exhaust system with a light can be installed to be either vented or nonvented. The high price makes this microwave a Recommended product.

Specifications: Overall dimensions: height, 16"; width, 29⅞"; depth, 13⅞"; capacity, 1.1 cubic feet. Cavity dimensions: height, 8⅞"; width, 13"; depth, 12⁹⁄₁₆". Cooking power: 850 watts. **Warranty:** 1 year, parts and labor; 5 years, electronic control and magnetron tube.

Manufacturer's Suggested Retail Price: $599

Approximate Low Price: $509

MICROWAVE/CONVECTION OVENS

SHARP R-9H66

✓BEST BUY

The R-9H66 offers both convection and microwave cooking for a surprisingly low price. The oven has a stainless steel interior and a porcelain enamel turntable. A broiling trivet and a baking rack are also included. The four-way cooking system browns, bakes, broils, or crisps. The broil key preheats the oven and signals when it is ready. This full-featured oven also includes a sensor with eight food choices. Other convenient features are an automatic start function; a minute-plus option to set the oven on high for 1 minute with one touch; cook, simmer, and slow-cook levels; and a programmable four-stage memory. The R-9H66 is white; the R-9H76 is the same model in metallic charcoal. With an optional trim kit, this model can be transformed into a built-in oven.

Specifications: Overall dimensions: height, 14⅞"; width, 24⅝"; depth, 18¾"; capacity, 1.5 cubic feet. Cavity dimensions: height, 9⅝"; width, 16⅛"; depth, 16⅛". Cooking power: 900 watts. **Warranty:** 1 year, parts; 1 year, labor and carry-in service; 5 years, magnetron tube.

Manufacturer's Suggested Retail Price: $550

Approximate Low Price: $499

SHARP R-7A95 ✔BEST BUY

This high-quality microwave/convection model offers brown, bake, broil, or crisp settings with convection, microwave, and broiling capabilities—plus two combination settings ideal for roasting and baking. The R-7A95 has a capacity of 0.9 cubic foot and 850 watts of power. Among the convenient features are an automatic defrost, programmable four-stage cooking, a popcorn key, a child lock, a demonstration mode, and a minute-plus feature. The slow-cook feature expands the timer up to 4 hours for soups, stews, or chili. A broiling/roasting trivet and a baking rack are also included in this feature-packed model. The R-7A95 is white; the R-7A85 is the same model in a stone gray finish. An optional built-in kit is available.

Specifications: Overall dimensions: height, 12"; width, 20½"; depth, 18¼"; capacity, 0.9 cubic foot. Cavity dimensions: height, 8⅛"; width, 13¾"; depth, 13½". Cooking power: 850 watts. **Warranty:** 1 year, parts; 1 year, labor and carry-in service; 5 years, magnetron tube.

Manufacturer's Suggested Retail Price: $400

Approximate Low Price: $249

RANGES

Today's cooking appliances provide more choices than ever before. Modern ranges, cooktops, and ovens are powerful and easy to clean.

Gas or Electric?

Unless you plan to undertake a costly remodeling job, your present kitchen setup may dictate your choice of a gas or electric range. Electric ranges require a 208- or 240-volt line. Gas ranges need to be hooked up to a gas line and also to a 115-volt outlet for the lights, clock, and burner-ignition system.

Some people prefer cooking with gas because of its instant response time and the visible flame. Gas ranges are slightly more expensive than electric. A traditional burner on a gas range produces about 9,000 Btu (British Thermal Units).

People who use electric ranges prefer the even heat of electric ovens, the slow simmering that is possible with electric burners, and the variety of burner styles currently available. Electric coils represent the most typical burner style, but radiant smoothtop cooktops—in which a flat ceramic-glass surface is placed above an electric coil—are quite popular. Smoothtop cooktops are easy to clean and can be used only with flat-bottomed metal cookware. Halogen burners are often added to smoothtop cooktops because they heat up somewhat faster than other burners. Magnetic induction cooktops require special cookware but heat up instantly and heat only the pot, not the cooktop surface.

Range Designs

Freestanding ranges have a cooktop and an oven, and they can stand on the floor between two base cabinets, at the end of a line of cabinets, or alone. The most common size of freestanding range is 30 inches wide.

Slide-in and drop-in ranges fit between two cabinets or into a space in a cooking island. The sides of these ranges are usually unfinished. A slide-in range sits on the floor; a drop-in range may hang from the countertop or sit on a low base. The advantages of slide-in and drop-in ranges are that they are a bit less expensive, and they help provide a seamless transition between your cabinets and your range.

Built-in wall ovens and their corresponding cooktops are divided into separate units for flexibility in kitchen design. A built-in oven may contain one or two ovens and possibly a microwave or a combination electric/convection oven.

Cooktops

Traditional cooktops have four cooking elements. On most gas models, the burners are all the same size. There are two 6-inch and two 8-inch burners on traditional electric coil ranges. The traditional cooktop design allows for a work space in the center of two rows of burners, but some newer cooktops may have a grill/griddle in the center, additional burners in the center, or even a totally different design with the burners arranged in an inverted U. Modular or convertible cooktops are the ultimate in flexibility. Each burner is an interchangeable, plug-in unit. Some cooktops include a grill or griddle, and separate units such as a wok-ring, a rotisserie, or a deep-fat fryer can also be purchased.

Ovens

Separate wall ovens can be found in either conventional electric or gas models. Convection and microwave ovens are also available as built-in wall models. Convection electric ovens bake with a fan that moves heated air throughout the oven. Many convection ovens have a separate heating element that surrounds the convection fan to improve performance. Convection ovens are also available in combination with microwave ovens.

Commercial-Style Ranges

The latest trend in kitchen design is commercial-style ranges. Stainless steel with an industrial look, these ranges are now specifically engineered for home use. The advantage to using a commercial-style gas range is that it can produce more heat than a traditional range—almost 15,000 Btu per burner. Because of this extra heat, these ranges require high-powered range hoods. Some models also include a built-in grill or griddle in the center of the cooktop. Commercial-style gas ranges manufactured specifically for domestic use generally do not require special clearance or a special gas hook-up to operate. However, many manufacturers recommend adding stainless steel backsplashes between the cooktop and the hood.

Cleaning Your Range

A self-cleaning oven is rapidly becoming a standard feature on both gas and electric ranges. Temperatures above 800 degrees Fahrenheit burn spills to a powdery ash that can be easily wiped clean after the self-cleaning cycle has ended. Continuous-cleaning ovens have a rough-textured interior that absorbs dirt, and soils gradually burn off with continued use. This cleaning method is not as efficient as the self-cleaning cycle and will still involve a certain degree of manual cleaning of the oven's interior. Manual-clean ovens need to be cleaned regularly using abrasive cleaners and/or harsh chemicals.

Smoothtop electric ranges and sealed gas burners are cooktops designed for minimal cleaning. Spills wipe clean and the design eliminates the need to lift up the entire cooktop surface to clean below the burner trays. Most cooktops today are made from porcelain enamel and have upswept backsplashes and slightly upturned edges to prevent spills from running over the edge of the cooktop.

Range Hoods

A range hood is a very important item. Using a poor or non-vented range hood can be dangerous, especially with a gas range. A cooktop burning natural or bottled gas can leave left-over fumes. Both fumes and cooking odors need to be eliminated by a ventilation system. Nonvented range hoods are available but are not recommended.

The traditional type of range hood is either a horizontal model (vents through a hole in the wall) or a vertical model (vents through the ceiling). Downdraft or proximity ventilation systems are sometimes included with certain types of modular cooktops. These ventilation systems are recommended only for those who do not use pots or pans taller than 4 inches or for those who do not frequently fry foods.

All ventilation systems have a "cfm" rating that details the amount of cubic feet per minute of air moved. The amount of noise they make is measured in sones. Generally, the more cfms, the more sound the hood motor makes. The depth of the hood should be determined by how high it is mounted above the cooktop. Most traditional wall-mounted range hoods have from 200 to 300 cfm. Island hoods and hoods over open grills should have a minimum of 600 cfm. Always check with your cooktop manufacturer for more details before you choose a range hood.

Best Buys '97

Our Best Buy, Recommended, and Budget Buy ranges and range hoods follow. The ranges are divided into categories of gas and electric, each with several subcategories. Remember that a Best Buy, Recommended, or Budget Buy designation refers only to the model listed and not necessarily to other models made by the same manufacturer.

GAS RANGES

Freestanding Gas Ranges

GENERAL ELECTRIC JGBP24BEW

✓BEST BUY

With a capacity of 4.4 cubic feet, General Electric's JGBP24BEW boasts the largest oven of all the standard gas ranges. Available in white or almond with a black oven door, this model has four standard 9,000-Btu burners with black porcelain enamel drip pans and porcelain-on-steel grates. The upswept cooktop is porcelain-enameled. While this model does not have the convenience of sealed burners, the size of the oven and the attractive price make it a Best Buy. The self-cleaning oven has two racks that can slide into six different positions.

Other convenient features include an in-oven broiler, an extra-large broiler pan/grid, and an electronic pilotless ignition.

Specifications: Overall dimensions: height, 45¾"; width, 30"; depth, 28¼". Oven dimensions: height, 17"; width, 24"; depth, 19". **Warranty:** 1 year, parts and labor.

Manufacturer's Suggested Retail Price: $599

Approximate Low Price: $582

MAGIC CHEF 3468

✔**BEST BUY**

At 30 inches wide, with an oven capacity of 4.0 cubic feet, the Magic Chef 3468 is a nice standard-size range with several convenient features. The four burners on this model are sealed to keep spills from getting under the cooktop, and they also feature ignition protection to keep the flames from going out. Two of the burners have been designated "Super-Speed" burners because they offer a 12,000-Btu setting for 30 percent more cooking power. This self-cleaning model has an electronic thermostat and electronic controls. The 3468 also sports a spill-catching porcelain cooktop, a waist-high broiler, and an electronic pilotless ignition. This versatile model comes in several colors: designer white, white with a black glass door, almond with a black glass door, or designer almond.

Specifications: Overall dimensions: height, 46¼"; width, 30"; depth 26⁵⁄₃₂". Oven dimensions: height, 16½"; width, 23"; depth, 18⅛". **Warranty:** 1 year, parts and labor; 5 years, limited on sealed burner parts.

Manufacturer's Suggested Retail Price: $789

Approximate Low Price: $721

MAYTAG CRG9700

✔**BEST BUY**

The Maytag CRG9700 is a gas range that has all of the desirable features a consumer might want, yet it is offered at a reasonable price. It is a sleek, 30-inch-wide range with four sealed surface burners; two of the burners offer a 12,000-Btu setting, while the remaining two have the normal 9,000 Btu. The cooktop is porcelain enamel with a drip-retainer around the edges and a back upsweep to catch spills and drips. The large 4.0-cubic-foot oven is self-cleaning and programmable. It features a waist-high broiler, an oven light, and two heavy-duty racks. This model also has a solid-state pilotless ignition, a deluxe electronic clock with timer, a storage drawer, and precision burner controls. It is available in a white or almond exterior with a glass front oven door.

Specifications: Overall dimensions: height, 44⅞"; width, 29⅞"; depth, 28⅛". Oven dimensions: height, 16½"; width, 23"; depth, 18⅛". **Warranty:** 1 year, labor; 2 years, parts; 5 years, electronic clock parts; 10 years, sealed gas burner replacements.

Manufacturer's Suggested Retail Price: $729

Approximate Low Price: $660

Drop-in/Slide-in Gas Ranges

MAYTAG CHG9800
✔**BEST BUY**

This 30-inch-wide slide-in range offers many extra features for its relatively high price. The large-capacity oven is 4.0 cubic feet and includes two heavy-duty racks and five rack positions. A major convenience with this model is that it offers many features to aid in cleaning. The oven is self-cleaning, and the oven door lifts off. The drip-retainer cooktop and sealed surface burners make the cooktop easy to clean as well. One of the burners is a power burner at 12,000 Btu, and this range can be adjusted to use LP gas. The CHG9800 also includes a storage drawer with a removable liner and an electronic clock with a timer. This model comes in deco white or black.

Specifications: Overall dimensions: height, 37"; width, 30¾"; depth, 28⅛". Oven dimensions: height, 16½"; width, 23"; depth, 18⅛". **Warranty:** 1 year, labor; 2 years, parts; 5 years, electronic clock parts; 10 years, sealed burners.

Manufacturer's Suggested Retail Price: $870

Approximate Low Price: $753

MAGIC CHEF 6498

✔**BEST BUY**

This 30-inch slide-in gas range with a one-touch self-cleaning oven is a good value. The 4.0-cubic-foot oven has five rack positions, a porcelainized broiler pan, anti-tilt oven racks, and an electronic thermostat. The front control panel is tilted back to make it easier to see from above, and two of the sealed burners are high speed, at 12,000 Btu, for more cooking power. This model is available in almond (VTA), designer white (VTV), and designer almond (VVD).

Specifications: Overall dimensions: height, 35⅞"; width, 30¾"; depth, 26⁵⁄₁₆". Oven dimensions: height, 16½"; width, 23"; depth, 18⅛". **Warranty:** 1 year, parts and labor; 5 years, limited on sealed burners.

Manufacturer's Suggested Retail Price: $949

Approximate Low Price: $732

Gas Cooktops and Modular Gas Cooktops

KITCHENAID KGCT305B

✔**BEST BUY**

This 30-inch-wide black glass cooktop is quite attractive and will spice up the decor of most kitchens. It is also available in white or almond for an additional $60. Four sealed, high-efficiency burners are arranged in an inverted U design; two of these are power burners that offer significantly more cooking power. Also included are power track guides and color-coordinated cast iron grates. This cooktop can be converted to LP gas.

Specifications: height, not available; width, 30¾"; depth, 21¾". **Warranty:** 1 year, parts and labor; 5 years, gas burner parts and ceramic glass cooktop.

Manufacturer's Suggested Retail Price: $589

Approximate Low Price: $505

KITCHENAID KGCT025A

✔**BEST BUY**

The KGCT025A, a modular gas cooktop, is one unit in KitchenAid's Create-A-Cooktop System. This cooktop includes two raised, high-efficiency, sealed burners. This model has pilotless electric ignition and automatic reignition. The front burner has 6,000 Btu, and the rear burner has 10,000 Btu for significantly increased cooking power. This quality cooktop is available in white, almond, or black.

Specifications: height, $4\frac{1}{4}''$; width, $11\frac{15}{16}''$; depth, $21\frac{3}{4}''$. **Warranty:** 1 year, parts and labor; 5 years, gas burners and ceramic glass cooktop.

Manufacturer's Suggested Retail Price: $429

Approximate Low Price: $343

JENN-AIR CVG 4280 ✔BEST BUY

The Jenn-Air CVG 4280 is a 30-inch-wide modular cooktop, which comes in black, white, or with a stainless steel perimeter. It offers two gas burners, one at 8,000 Btu and one at 10,000 Btu, and an even-heat grill element. Other convenient features on the CVG 4280 include an electronic pilotless ignition and downdraft ventilation with a two-speed fan. This model accepts an optional two-burner module and gas grill accessories.

Specifications: height, not available; width, $28\frac{7}{8}''$; depth, $20\frac{15}{16}''$. **Warranty:** 1 year, labor; 2 years, parts.

Manufacturer's Suggested Retail Price: $820

Approximate Low Price: $785

Built-in Gas Ovens

WHIRLPOOL SB160PED ✔BEST BUY

The SB160PED is a 24-inch, built-in, self-cleaning gas oven. Two adjustable oven racks, a porcelain broiler pan, and a chrome grid are included with this oven. The SB160PED is black, though the same model also exists in white with a slightly different model number. The door is removable, and there is a blanket-o-flame broiler at the top. An electronic clock, with oven controls and a minute timer, is also included.

Specifications: Overall dimensions: height, 40"; width, 23⅞"; depth, 23⅝". Oven dimensions: height, 16"; width, 17"; depth, 18½". **Warranty:** 1 year, parts and labor.

Manufacturer's Suggested Retail Price: $859

Approximate Low Price: $732

Commercial-Style Gas Ranges and Cooktops

VIKING VGSS300-4B

✓ **BEST BUY**

Viking was the first manufacturer of commercial-style ranges for home kitchens. These ranges are high-performance kitchen appliances certified by the AGA (American Gas Association) for residential installation. The VGSS300-4B is a standard 30-inch gas range with versatile burner settings ranging from 1,000 to 15,000 Btu. The infrared broiler reaches broiling temperatures in approximately 30 seconds, and the spacious 4.2-cubic-foot oven has a porcelain interior with a removable bottom, door, and sides. Like many commercial-style ranges, the VGSS300-4B does not have a self-cleaning oven. The large knobs have childproof, push-to-turn safety features. Other features of this attractive range include an oven light, a broiler pan/grid, two heavy-duty five-position oven racks, and dishwasher safe porcelain burner bowls. All ranges in the Viking VGSS series are available in stainless steel, black, white, or almond exteriors. (The black, white, and almond models are about $175 less.) Installation accessories included with the range are a 6-inch-high stainless steel backguard and a curb base front to conceal the range legs. Optional accessories available separately are a wok grate, a wok-ring, a portable griddle, and a hardwood cover to fit over surface grates.

Specifications: Overall dimensions: height, 37⅝"; width, 29⅞"; depth, 26¼". Oven dimensions: height, 16¼"; width, 24"; depth, 18¾". **Warranty:** 1 year, parts and labor; 5 years, limited on surface and tube burners; 10 years, porcelain oven.

Manufacturer's Suggested Retail Price: $2,550

Approximate Low Price: $2,198

FIVE STAR TTM325-B

✓BEST BUY

The Five Star TTM325-B offers consumers the best of both worlds, with commercial-style 14,000-Btu gas burners and an electric oven and broiler. With a flip of the switch on the control panel, you can turn on the convection system, which uses forced air for even baking. The oven is self-cleaning, and the burners have the lowest simmer available in commercial ranges—4,000 Btu. Other desirable features on the TTM325-B include an electronic pilotless ignition, an exclusive pull-out broiler tray, and a stainless steel backguard for extra wall protection. A handy barbecue grill accessory is available for an additional cost.

Specifications: Overall dimensions: height (with backguard), 47"; width, 36"; depth, 24". Oven dimensions: height, 14"; width, 24"; depth, 19". **Warranty:** 1 year, parts and labor; 2 years, electronic ignition module; 5 years, stainless steel surface burner.

Manufacturer's Suggested Retail Price: $4,800

Approximate Low Price: $3,947

DYNASTY DCT36-6

✓BEST BUY

An attractive addition to a hard-working kitchen, the Dynasty commercial-style gas cooktop is 36 inches wide. This model has six side-by-side gas burners with black, heavy duty, cast iron grates. (Traditional cooktops have four cooking elements.) The rear burner is a special simmer burner, with a Btu range of 500 to 10,000. The other burners are 1,000 to 15,000 Btu. This model includes removable stainless steel drip trays, which are a convenience when cleaning. The cooktop is stainless steel with black accents on the stay-cool, pull-off knobs. Options for this cooktop include an 11-inch backguard and a butcher block cutting board.

Specifications: height, 9½"; width, 36"; depth, 24". **Warranty:** 1 year, parts and labor; 5 years, burners.

Manufacturer's Suggested Retail Price: $1,460

Approximate Low Price: $1,443

ELECTRIC RANGES

Freestanding Electric Ranges

MAGIC CHEF 3868

✔**BEST BUY**

The Magic Chef 3868 is a 30-inch, self-cleaning, smoothtop electric range priced to sell. It is available in white, almond, or black, with a color-matching or black glass door. The smoothtop is available in a white stipple design for the white models or a textured design for the black and almond models. The 3868 has two 8-inch burners, two 6-inch burners, and an oven capacity of 4.0 cubic feet. The smoothtop elements are as fast as electric coil elements. A spill-catching cooktop and a one-touch self-cleaning oven cycle make this range easy to clean. This model also has an electronic thermostat, a removable oven door, and a deep, porcelainized broiler pan.

Specifications: Overall dimensions: height, 46¼"; width, 30"; depth, 26⅝₂". Oven dimensions: height, 16½"; width, 23"; depth, 18⅛". **Warranty:** 1 year, parts and labor; 5 years, limited on smoothtop surface and radiant heating element.

Manufacturer's Suggested Retail Price: $810

Approximate Low Price: $766

GENERAL ELECTRIC JBP25GV

✔**BEST BUY**

This 30-inch electric-coil range has the standard two 6-inch and two 8-inch electric coil elements and removable one-piece chrome-drip bowls. The cooktop lifts up for easy cleaning, and the oven is self-cleaning. This unit offers GE's QuickSet III oven controls, an audible preheated signal, an electric clock and minute timer, a storage drawer, and an automatic oven shutoff. It is available in white.

Specifications: Overall dimensions: height, 45⅛"; width, 29⅞"; depth, 27½". Oven dimensions: height, 16"; width, 23"; depth, 17¾". **Warranty:** 1 year, parts and labor.

Manufacturer's Suggested Retail Price: $559

Approximate Low Price: $536

KITCHENAID KERI500Y

Recommended

The KERI500Y is 24½ inches deep, which will make it flush with standard kitchen cabinets. It has two 8-inch, 2,600-watt coils and two 6-inch, 1,500-watt coils. This range offers convenient features that make it easy to clean, including a self-cleaning oven and a lift-up cooktop with dual support rods. Other notable features include a power "on" light and automatic-time baking. This model, which is available in white or almond, is a Recommended product because of its high price.

Specifications: Overall dimensions: height, 46¹³⁄₁₆"; width, 29¹⁵⁄₁₆"; depth, 24½". Oven dimensions: height, 15¾"; width, 23¹⁄₁₆"; depth, 18¼". **Warranty:** 1 year, parts and labor; 5 years, limited on electric elements and electronic controls; 10 years, porcelain liner and inner door.

Manufacturer's Suggested Retail Price: $799

Approximate Low Price: $765

Drop-in/Slide-in Electric Ranges

GENERAL ELECTRIC JSP34BW

✔BEST BUY

The JSP34BW takes the basic 30-inch electric slide-in range into the future, with a sleek black exterior and a lift-up, overhanging, porcelain-enameled cooktop. It also includes an oven timer, a self-cleaning oven with electronic controls and a delay-clean option, an automatic oven shutoff and oven timer, and modern-style touchpad controls. There are two plug-in heating elements and porcelain-enameled one-piece drip bowls. Extra conveniences include a storage drawer, a lift-off oven door, an electronic clock, and a kitchen timer. This model is available in almond or white.

Specifications: Overall dimensions: height, 35⅞"; width, 30"; depth, 28½". Oven dimensions: height, 15¾"; width, 22¾"; depth, 17". **Warranty:** 1 year, parts and labor.

Manufacturer's Suggested Retail Price: $789

Approximate Low Price: $745

JENN-AIR SVE47500

✔**BEST BUY**

This 30-inch slide-in range has enough versatility for all your cooking needs. The range has a two-speed fan and comes with downdraft ventilation that can vent up to 60 equivalent feet. The self-cleaning bake/broil oven is 3.8 cubic feet and includes two heavy-gauge, nickel-finish oven racks. The cooktop includes two elements and a grill that's coated with a nonstick coating. You can have your choice of elements—either smoothtop, electric coil, radiant, or halogen. Other features include an electronic clock with two timers, a child lockout control, an optional backsplash, and an optional color side panel. Other optional accessories include a griddle, a wok, a cooker-steamer, a rotiss-kebab, a big pot element, and an energy-saver grill assembly. This model comes in black or white.

Specifications: height, 35½"; width, 29⅞"; depth, 26⅜". Oven dimensions: height, 15¼"; width, 23½"; depth, 18½". **Warranty:** 1 year, labor; 2 years, parts; 5 years, electronic control panel and solid elements.

Manufacturer's Suggested Retail Price: $1,150

Approximate Low Price: $1,084

Conventional, Modular, and Smoothtop Electric Cooktops

WHIRLPOOL RC8536XTH

✔**BEST BUY**

A conventional electric coil cooktop, the RC8536XTH is 36 inches wide and has a spillguard cooktop in brushed chrome. There are two 6-inch and two 8-inch plug-in surface elements, and the reflector pans are removable. There are three indicator lights and lift-off control knobs. A nice feature of this cooktop is the built-in griddle with removable cover.

Specifications: width, 36"; depth, 21¾". **Warranty:** 1 year, parts and labor.

Manufacturer's Suggested Retail Price: $409

Approximate Low Price: $409

JENN-AIR CVE 4270W

✔ BEST BUY

This 30-inch modular electric cooktop has a ceramic-glass surface in black, white, or stainless steel. It comes with an energy-saver grill module. The CVE 4270W offers dual convertible bays, with your choice of smoothtop, electric coil, radiant, or halogen bays. There is a downdraft vent in the center of the cooktop with a two-speed fan. This model has a nonstick grill-grate finish. The two convertible bays on this versatile cooktop have many accessories available for an additional cost, including a solid disc element, a wok, a griddle, a rotisserie, and a 2,100-watt big pot canning element.

Specifications: width, 28⅞"; depth, 20¹⁵⁄₁₆". **Warranty:** 1 year, labor; 2 years, parts; 5 years, limited on selected parts.

Manufacturer's Suggested Retail Price: $599

Approximate Low Price: $539

KITCHENAID KECC501B

✔ BEST BUY

A smoothtop electric cooktop, the KECC501B is made of easy-to-clean glass-ceramic that has a 5-year warranty against breakage. There are four single-circuit radiant elements. Among this model's best features are the built-in overheat protection, the hot-surface indicators, and the infinite-heat controls. Other conveniences on this model include the power "on" light. The KECC501B is black..

Specifications: width, 30"; depth, 21". **Warranty:** 1 year, parts and labor; 5 years, ceramic glass cooktop and electric element parts.

Manufacturer's Suggested Retail Price: $589

Approximate Low Price: $562

Built-in Electric Ovens

JENN-AIR WW27430

✔ BEST BUY

The WW27430 is from Jenn-Air's impressive Expressions Collection. This 27-inch-wide double-wall oven has a sleek flush design with a large oven window. Both ovens are self-cleaning, with an automatic lock. The upper oven has two dual convection settings—convect roast and convect broil—along with a temperature probe. Among this oven's high-quality features are a high-grade porcelain oven interior, variable temperature-controlled broiling, and clock-controlled baking and cleaning. Both ovens are an extra-large 3.3 cubic feet and are operated by separate electronic timers. This model is available in black or white.

Specifications: height, 49¹⁵⁄₁₆"; width, 26¾"; depth, 24⁷⁄₁₆". Oven dimensions: height, 14¾"; width, 21"; depth, 18⁹⁄₁₆". **Warranty:** 1 year, labor; 2 years, parts; 5 years, electronic control panel.

Manufacturer's Suggested Retail Price: $1,600

Approximate Low Price: $1,480

GENERAL ELECTRIC JKP69BW
Recommended

General Electric's JKP69BW is a built-in electric oven and microwave. This 27-inch-wide unit offers almost every feature available in ovens today. The 800-watt microwave is a spacious 1.4 cubic feet, and it has ten power levels and a temperature probe. The oven has electronic touchpad controls, an audible preheat signal, and a broiler pan with grid. The JKP69BW is a Recommended product because of its high price.

Specifications: Overall dimensions: height, 43"; width, 26¾"; depth, 23½". Upper oven dimensions: height, 11⅛"; width, 16"; depth, 13⅜". Lower oven dimensions: height, 15"; width, 19"; depth, 18". **Warranty:** 1 year, parts and labor.

Manufacturer's Suggested Retail Price: $1,399

Approximate Low Price: $1,263

Conventional Range Hoods

GENERAL ELECTRIC JV376V
✔BEST BUY

The JV376V is GE's high-performance range hood, and is a standard 30 inches wide. It is designed with an easy-to-clean continuous surface and two large filters that can be cleaned at the sink or dishwasher. This product is recommended for use with indoor grills and griddles and has a 410-cfm vertical exhaust rating and a 380-cfm rear exhaust rating. One unique feature of this range hood is the two cooktop lights that can help illuminate the cooking area. A night-light and a variable-speed fan control are also included. This model is available in white or black.

Specifications: height, 7"; width, 29⅞"; depth, 19¾". **Warranty:** 1 year, parts and labor.

Manufacturer's Suggested Retail Price: $279

Approximate Low Price: $275

BROAN 412401

Recommended

This versatile, economy-model range hood comes in black, white, almond, harvest, avocado, and coffee baked enamel finish, as well as stainless steel. The duct-free, nonvented system filter, which is called Microteck, has two speeds. The Broan 412401 has two-speed fan control and the capability to hold a 75-watt lightbulb.

Specifications: height, 6"; width, 24"; depth, 17½". **Warranty:** 1 year, parts.

Manufacturer's Suggested Retail Price: $96

Approximate Low Price: $63

REFRIGERATORS AND FREEZERS

Today's refrigerators and freezers offer more features and choices than ever before. With these attractive new sizes and finishes, your refrigerator/freezer can be a decorator item in your kitchen. For your convenience, the refrigerators reviewed here are categorized as side-by-side, top-freezer, bottom-freezer, built-in, and compact. The freezers are categorized as upright or chest.

Best Buys '97

Our Best Buy, Recommended, and Budget Buy refrigerators and freezers follow. They were evaluated for quality, price, efficiency, and energy use. Remember that a Best Buy, Recommended, or Budget Buy designation refers only to the model listed and not necessarily to other models made by the same manufacturer.

REFRIGERATORS

Refrigerators consume more energy than most appliances in your home, so replacing an old unit may save you money in the long run. New refrigerators use as much as 50 percent less energy than refrigerators built just a few years ago. Any refrigerator manufactured after the end of 1995 should be CFC (chlorofluorocarbon) free.

Which Model?

Side-by-side refrigerators have become the most popular style even though they are less energy-efficient and more costly than other models. Their modern look, along with the increased freezer space, make them the choice of many buyers. Most side-by-sides offer through-the-door ice and water as either a standard feature or a factory option. While this is a popular feature, it is one that increases repair needs and costs.

Top-freezer refrigerators are the most energy efficient and the freezer is conveniently located at eye-level, but the lower refrigerator compartment is less convenient. Top-freezers come in a wide variety of sizes and with a large range of styles and features. Bottom-freezer refrigerators offer a larger freezer than top-freezer models, and fresh foods are available without stooping, but few bottom-freezer models are on the market.

"Built-in" has a new meaning with today's refrigerators. Several manufacturers offer shallow refrigerators that can function either as built-ins or as free-standing models, because they are finished on the sides. Many of them protrude less than 2 inches past normal counter depth. Trim kits help customize the look. Compact refrigerators are small enough to fit into college dorms, offices, family rooms, and other limited spaces, yet large enough to hold snacks, drinks, or even a moderate supply of groceries.

Which Features?

Glass shelves with sealed edges are the easiest to clean. Cantilever shelves, which attach to hangers at the back of the refrigerator compartment, adjust more easily than shelves fixed to the sides, but slide-out shelves provide easy access to items toward the back. Adjustable, half-width shelves offer the most flexibility, allowing you to arrange your refrigerator interior to most efficiently hold its contents. Many new refrigerators include gallon storage in adjustable door shelves and bins, which is a real convenience. Meat keepers with a separate temperature control will keep meat fresh longer than standard storage compartments. Carefully consider whether snack pans, beverage chillers, wine racks, miniserve dishes, and other convenient features fit your family's needs. Ice makers and dispensers are handy features, but you should consider whether the added cost and potential repairs justify the convenience. With careful consideration of your family's refrigerator needs and a close look at the features, benefits, and prices of today's models, you can choose a refrigerator within your budget that will serve your family well for many years.

Side-by-Side Refrigerators

AMANA SRD25S5

✔ **BEST BUY**

This large refrigerator offers 24.6 cubic feet of storage. The two full and two half-width slide-out, adjustable, spill-saver glass shelves make clean-up and item location easy. A deli drawer with an adjustable temperature control keeps meat and cheese fresh, while two clear crispers on rollers keep fruits and vegetables at their peak of freshness. The door adds four shelves of storage, one with gallon and tall container capacity and two that are closed compartments. This unit also has a wine rack and temperature-controlled beverage chiller. The freezer features three glide-out baskets, one compartment shelf, and five shallow door shelves. The through-the-door ice and water dispenser is equipped with a handy night-light. This refrigerator exceeds federal energy standards by 25 percent, and it operates quietly. It is available in white, almond, or ebony. Trim kits are also available.

Specifications: height, 67½"; width, 35¾"; depth (with handle), 35¼"; shelf area, 26.1 square feet. **Warranty:** 1 year, full; 5 years, full on sealed system and food compartment liner; 10 years, limited on sealed system components.

Manufacturer's Suggested Retail Price: $1,749

Approximate Low Price: $1,320

FRIGIDAIRE FRS22WRC

✔ **BEST BUY**

This 22.3-cubic-foot refrigerator offers many features for the price and sufficient storage for an average-size family. The three adjustable, cantilever spill-saver glass shelves; the see-through, adjustable-temperature deli drawer; the clear utility bin; and the clear, adjustable-humidity crisper with glass cover will hold lots of groceries. Interior storage also includes an egg bucket. The door offers a dairy keeper, two adjustable gallon-plus bins, and two fixed bins. The freezer in this unit contains two compartment shelves, two sliding baskets, and four door shelves. The clear plastic and glass surfaces on some of these storage units make cleaning up easy. To help keep the temperature constant, the Frigidaire FRS22WRC uses an automatic air-flow system. A through-the-door ice and water dispenser keeps ice and cold water handy. An energy-saver loop helps reduce energy usage. This refrigerator is available in white or almond.

Specifications: height, 67"; width, 35¼"; depth (with handle), 32"; shelf area, 20.3 square feet. **Warranty:** 1 year, parts and labor; 2 years, full on ice dispenser; 5 years, cabinet liner and sealed system; 10 years, compressor.

Manufacturer's Suggested Retail Price: $1,399

Approximate Low Price: $1,329

GENERAL ELECTRIC PROFILE TFX25PRY ✔BEST BUY

The 25.2 cubic feet of storage will keep a substantial amount of food fresh and organized for a large family. The spill-saver shelves include three adjustable shelves, plus two adjustable, slide-back glass shelves for tall bottle storage. Other features include a temperature-controlled meat pan, a humidity-controlled crisper, a beverage rack, a humidity-controlled snack pan, and a utility bin. Door storage on this refrigerator includes four shelves and a dairy compartment with a glass butter dish. The through-the-door ice and water dispenser is standard equipment. The freezer features one clear sliding bin, three slide-out baskets, and five door shelves. The TFX25PRY has an automatic energy saver, operates quietly, and is available in white, almond, or black. Trim kits are available.

Specifications: height, 68¾"; width, 35¾"; depth (with handle), 32½"; shelf area, 25.2 square feet. **Warranty:** 1 year, full; 5 years, parts and labor on the sealed system; lifetime, limited on polycarbonate resin pans, drawers, and bins.

Manufacturer's Suggested Retail Price: $1,699

Approximate Low Price: $1,248

GENERAL ELECTRIC TFX22ZRX ✔BEST BUY

This 21.7-cubic-foot refrigerator offers good value for the cost. Storage features include three adjustable, spill-proof glass shelves, an adjustable-temperature meat pan, an adjustable-humidity crisper, a utility bin, and a sealed snack pack. Door storage includes two fixed door shelves, two adjustable shelves with gallon storage, and a dairy compartment with a butter trivet. The freezer contains three adjustable shelves, one sliding bin, and five door shelves. Ice and water are conveniently available from the through-the-door dispenser. This refrigerator includes an automatic energy saver and is available in white or almond.

Specifications: height, 66⅝"; width, 33½"; depth (with handle), 32½"; shelf area, 24.1 square feet. **Warranty:** 1 year, full; 5 years, full on the sealed system; lifetime, limited on polycarbonate resin pans, drawers, or bins (covers not included).

Manufacturer's Suggested Retail Price: $1,299

Approximate Low Price: Not available

HOTPOINT CSX22GRX
✓**BEST BUY**

The capacity of this refrigerator is 21.7 cubic feet, making it a lot of refrigerator for the price. It includes three adjustable glass shelves, an adjustable-temperature meat pan, an adjustable-humidity fruit and vegetable crisper, and a utility bin. Door storage includes four shelves (two with gallon storage) and a dairy compartment. The freezer offers one sliding storage bin, three adjustable shelves, and five door shelves. It comes with a through-the-door ice and water dispenser. An automatic energy saver helps reduce power usage. The unit is available in white or almond.

Specifications: height, 66⅝"; width, 33½"; depth (with handle), 32½"; shelf area, 22.4 square feet. **Warranty:** 1 year, full; 5 years, full on the sealed system.

Manufacturer's Suggested Retail Price: $1,059

Approximate Low Price: $950

MAYTAG RSD2000
✓**BEST BUY**

This 20.3-cubic-foot refrigerator is the smallest side-by-side that Maytag offers. It has three adjustable glass shelves in the refrigerator compartment, a meat drawer with temperature adjustment, two sealed crispers with moisture control, and a beverage rack. The door storage includes four adjustable bins capable of holding gallon containers, a covered dairy compartment, and a removable egg crate. The freezer features five adjustable shelves, one slide-out wire basket, and six deep-fixed door bins. An automatic ice maker is optional. An automatic energy-saver switch helps reduce power usage. This refrigerator comes in white or almond.

Specifications: height, 67½"; width, 31"; depth (with handle), 32⅛"; shelf area, 24.4 square feet. **Warranty:** 1 year, parts and labor; 2 years, parts only; 5 years, parts and labor on the sealed system and cabinet liner.

Manufacturer's Suggested Retail Price: $1,149

Approximate Low Price: Not available

WHIRLPOOL ED20TKXD   ✔BEST BUY

This small, economical side-by-side still offers 19.9 cubic feet of food storage space. It has three full-width, cantilever glass shelves, a temperature-controlled meat drawer, a see-through fruit and vegetable crisper, and an egg bin. The door adds four shelves, including gallon storage and a dairy compartment. This unit has up-front temperature controls. The freezer has one slide-out bin, four fixed shelves, and five fixed door shelves. An ice maker is optional. This refrigerator meets federal energy standards and is available in white or almond.

Specifications: height, 65⅞"; width, 32¾"; depth (with handle), 30⅜"; shelf area, 20.5 square feet. **Warranty:** 1 year, full; 5 years, parts and labor on the sealed system.

Manufacturer's Suggested Retail Price: $929

Approximate Low Price: $749

WHITE-WESTINGHOUSE MRS22WNE   ✔BEST BUY

The MRS22WNE, with its capacity of 22.3 cubic feet, fits the needs of an average-size family in terms of space and features. The refrigerator compartment includes three adjustable, cantilever glass shelves; a clear, adjustable-temperature meat keeper; and one clear crisper with a glass cover. The door has five fixed shelves and a clear dairy compartment. An automatic air flow system helps maintain a constant temperature throughout the entire refrigerator compartment. The freezer features three compartment shelves, four door shelves, and one sliding basket. A handy through-the-door ice and water dispenser keeps ice and chilled water readily available. An energy-saver loop helps keep energy costs down. Color choices for this unit are white and almond.

Specifications: height, 67"; width, 35¼"; depth (with handle), 32"; shelf area, 22 square feet. **Warranty:** 1 year, full; 5 years, parts and labor on the sealed system.

Manufacturer's Suggested Retail Price: $1,079

Approximate Low Price: Not available

KITCHENAID SUPERBA KSRS22QD

Recommended

This high-end KitchenAid Superba refrigerator, with a capacity of 21.6 cubic feet, has a hefty price tag, making it a Recommended selection. However, it offers many amenities, including one cantilever, spill-saver glass shelf and two adjustable spill-saver glass shelves on rollers. The temperature-controlled meat locker circulates air from the freezer for safe meat storage, and a sealed, humidity-controlled crisper on rollers keeps fruits and vegetables fresh. A beverage rack holds two-liter bottles, and a covered egg bucket is included. The door offers four adjustable gallon bins, a dairy compartment, and one can rack. A clear, covered carousel pan with an adjustable divider rotates 360 degrees, providing easy access for often-used foods. This unit circulates freezer air through the refrigerator compartment for fast temperature adjustment. The freezer features two slide-out baskets, two shelves, and five door bins. Ice and water are always available from the through-the-door dispenser. This refrigerator, which is available in white or almond, operates at 30 percent above federal energy standards.

Specifications: height, 65⅞"; width, 32¾"; depth (with handle), 31"; shelf area, 23.9 square feet. **Warranty:** 1 year, parts and labor; 5 years, parts and labor on the sealed system; 10 years, parts only on the sealed system.

Manufacturer's Suggested Retail Price: $1,679

Approximate Low Price: $1,409

HOTPOINT CSX20EAY

Budget Buy

This model is a good choice for the budget-minded consumer interested in a side-by-side refrigerator. It offers some of the features of higher-priced models at a reduced price. However, at 19.7 cubic feet, it has a smaller capacity than our Best Buy and Recommended units. And its three adjustable shelves are made of wire instead of glass, which makes cleaning more of a chore. Still, this model includes several desirable features, such as an adjustable-temperature meat pan, one sealed crisper, and one utility bin. The door has four shelves, two of them offering gallon storage, and a dairy compartment. The freezer offers one storage bin, three adjustable shelves, one fixed shelf, and six door shelves. This unit is equipped so that an ice maker can be added. The automatic energy saver is another economy feature. Available in white or almond.

Specifications: height, 66⅝"; width, 31½"; depth (with handle), 32½"; shelf area, 20.6 square feet. **Warranty:** 1 year, parts and labor; 5 years, parts and labor on the sealed system.

Manufacturer's Suggested Retail Price: $799

Approximate Low Price: $750

Top-Freezer Refrigerators

FRIGIDAIRE GALLERY COLLECTION FRT22TGC

✔**BEST BUY**

This full-featured refrigerator offers 21.6 cubic feet of food storage. The five half-width, cantilever, spill-saver glass shelves are adjustable. A clear, adjustable-temperature meat keeper and two lighted, adjustable-humidity crispers on rollers help keep perishables fresh for a maximum amount of time. A wine rack keeps a favorite beverage accessible. The door offers one fixed shelf, four adjustable gallon bins with adjustable dividers, and two clear dairy compartments. Door space also includes two microserve dishes for handy leftover or snack storage. This refrigerator offers easily accessible up-front temperature controls. The freezer features three half-width adjustable shelves and four adjustable door bins. A factory ice maker keeps fresh ice on hand. An electricity-saver switch reduces energy consumption. This unit comes in white, almond, or black, and the doors are reversible.

Specifications: height, 67"; width, 32"; depth (with handle), 32"; shelf area, 30.1 square feet. **Warranty:** 2 years, parts and labor; 5 years, cabinet liner and refrigerator systems; 10 years, compressor.

Manufacturer's Suggested Retail Price: $1,039

Approximate Low Price: $963

GENERAL ELECTRIC PROFILE TBX19PAY   ✓ BEST BUY

This 19-cubic-foot-capacity refrigerator offers many features at a moderate cost. The four adjustable, spill-saver, slide-out, split glass shelves can be arranged to take maximum advantage of shelf space. An adjustable-temperature meat pan, two adjustable-humidity crispers, a utility bin, and a beverage rack will hold enough groceries for the average family. The door offers gallon storage and includes four adjustable bins, one fixed bin, and a dairy compartment with a butter trivet. The freezer features a two-position rack and three door bins, including one that is adjustable. A factory ice maker is optional. The doors reverse for installation in any kitchen floorplan, and the unit promises quiet operation. An energy-saver switch conserves electricity. Color choices are white, almond, and black.

Specifications: height, 64"; width, 29⅜"; depth (with handle), 32¾"; shelf area, 24.8 square feet. **Warranty:** 1 year, parts and labor; 5 years, parts and labor on the sealed system.

Manufacturer's Suggested Retail Price: $899

Approximate Low Price: Not available

HOTPOINT CTX18GAX ✔**BEST BUY**

A very reasonable price combined with the solid features on this 18.2-cubic-foot-capacity refrigerator make it a smart choice. Two full-width, adjustable glass shelves, a snack pan, and two clear crispers comprise the refrigerator compartment. Door storage includes two shelves with gallon storage and a dairy compartment. The freezer has one adjustable, full-width shelf and two door shelves. A factory ice maker is optional. Electricity usage can be minimized with use of the energy-saver switch. This refrigerator is available in white or almond. The unit doors reverse to open conveniently in any kitchen layout.

Specifications: height, 64"; width, 29⅜"; depth (with handle), 31½"; shelf area, 23.2 square feet. **Warranty:** 1 year, parts and labor; 5 years, parts and labor on the sealed system.

Manufacturer's Suggested Retail Price: $649

Approximate Low Price: $501

KITCHENAID PRESTIGE KTRP18KD ✔**BEST BUY**

This 18.1-cubic-foot-capacity refrigerator in the KitchenAid Prestige line offers excellent value and performance. Four adjustable, spill-saver glass shelves and one flip-up shelf store plenty of groceries and clean up easily. The clear meat locker, which is on rollers, circulates air from the freezer to keep meat extra fresh. The beverage rack can hold a two-liter bottle. The two clear, sealed crispers are also on rollers. Door storage offers four adjustable gallon bins and a dairy keeper. This unit circulates freezer air through the refrigerator automatically for instant temperature control and offers automatic moisture control. The freezer features two door bins and one shelf. An optional factory-installed ice maker can be added for extra convenience. This refrigerator operates at 20 percent better energy efficiency than federal standards require. The doors are reversible, and the refrigerator comes in white or almond. A door trim kit is available.

Specifications: height, 65⅞"; width, 29½"; depth (with handle), 30⅛"; shelf area, 24.8 square feet. **Warranty:** 1 year, parts and labor; 5 years, parts and labor on the sealed system; 10 years, parts only on the sealed system.

Manufacturer's Suggested Retail Price: $799

Approximate Low Price: $668

WHIRLPOOL ET25DKXD ✔**BEST BUY**

This large, full-featured refrigerator offers 25.1 cubic feet of storage space. The four half-width, adjustable, spill-saver, cantilever glass shelves include one handy lateral sliding shelf for tall container storage. A clear meat keeper and two clear, humidity-controlled crispers keep meats and produce fresh and at-hand. A three-piece egg bin is included. Gallon storage is available in the door, which includes one full-width and four half-width gallon bins, as well as two covered dairy compartments. Cabinet temperature controls are located up-front in this model. The freezer features adjustable door bins and two compartment shelves. This unit is available with an ice maker as model ET25DMXD. Color choices are white, almond, and black, and the doors are reversible. This refrigerator meets federal energy standards.

Specifications: height, 68⅞"; width, 35½"; depth (with handle), 33"; shelf area, 34.9 square feet. **Warranty:** 1 year, parts and labor; 5 years, parts and labor on sealed system.

Manufacturer's Suggested Retail Price: $1,119

Approximate Low Price: $1,037

WHITE-WESTINGHOUSE MRT21GNE `Recommended`

This basic refrigerator offers 20.7 cubic feet of storage space. That storage area includes two full-width, adjustable, cantilever, epoxy wire shelves, plus a tinted meat drawer and two tinted crispers with glass covers. Its price for the size makes it a good choice for a family on a budget. Storage in the door includes two shelves and a tinted dairy compartment. An automatic air-flow system helps keep temperatures stable throughout the refrigerator. Compartment temperature is easy to adjust with the up-front controls. The freezer offers one adjustable compartment shelf and two door shelves. A factory-installed ice maker is optional. The unit includes an energy-saver switch and is available in white or almond. The doors are reversible.

Specifications: height, 66¾"; width, 31"; depth (with handle), 31¼"; shelf area, 23 square feet. **Warranty:** 1 year, parts and labor; 5 years, parts and labor on the sealed system.

Manufacturer's Suggested Retail Price: $669

Approximate Low Price: Not available

WHITE-WESTINGHOUSE MRT13CRE

`Budget Buy`

The capacity of this refrigerator is 12.6 cubic feet. It is a good choice for shoppers on a budget who need only a small refrigerator. There are two adjustable, sliding, full-width, epoxy wire shelves and one white crisper with a plastic cover. Door storage includes two shelves and a white dairy compartment. Temperature controls are up front in this unit. The freezer features one half-width compartment shelf and two door shelves. This refrigerator does not include an option for a factory ice maker. An energy-saver switch economizes on energy use. Available colors are white and almond. The doors are reversible to open conveniently in any kitchen arrangement.

Specifications: height, 60"; width, 28"; depth (with handle), 27¾"; shelf area, 12.8 square feet. **Warranty:** 1 year, parts and labor; 5 years, parts and labor on the sealed system.

Manufacturer's Suggested Retail Price: $479

Approximate Low Price: $424

Bottom-Freezer Refrigerators

AMANA BR22S6

✔**BEST BUY**

This 21.7-cubic-foot refrigerator offers the convenience of fresh food storage on the top with freezer items on the bottom. The refrigerator compartment includes four adjustable, half-width, glass spill-saver shelves that slide out. An adjustable-temperature deli drawer keeps meat and cheese at the correct temperatures. Two clear crispers with glass tops hold produce, and a beverage rack keeps a favorite beverage handy. Door storage offers space for gallon containers in the bottom shelf, along with three open and two closed bins. The freezer features a slide-out basket and four door shelves. A factory ice maker is optional. This unit operates quietly, exceeds energy standards by 30 percent, and is available in white, almond, or ebony. A trim kit is available.

Specifications: height, 67⅝"; width, 32⅝"; depth (with handle), 34⅞"; shelf area, 29.2 square feet. **Warranty:** 1 year, parts and labor; 5 years, parts and labor on the sealed system.

Manufacturer's Suggested Retail Price: $1,279

Approximate Low Price: $908

GENERAL ELECTRIC TCX22ZAX   ✓BEST BUY

The capacity of this refrigerator is 21.7 cubic feet. Its four adjustable, split, spill-saver cantilever glass shelves offer convenience and easy clean-up for messy spills. A sealed snack keeper, one sealed crisper, and one adjustable-humidity crisper keep perishables fresh. A beverage rack lets wine bottles rest on their sides. The door offers one fixed and four adjustable bins, gallon-container storage, and two dairy compartments. The freezer features include an interior light, one full-width shelf, one sliding basket, and four door bins. This unit is equipped for an optional factory ice maker. An energy-saver switch helps keep electricity costs down. This unit comes in white or almond.

Specifications: height, 67⅝"; width, 32¾"; depth, (with handle), 33¾"; shelf area, 28.6 square feet. **Warranty:** 1 year, parts and labor; 5 years, parts and labor on the sealed system.

Manufacturer's Suggested Retail Price: $1,099

Approximate Low Price: $967

WHIRLPOOL EB21DKXD   ✓BEST BUY

This 21-foot-capacity refrigerator features half-width, spill-saver glass shelves, including one lateral sliding shelf for tall container storage. There is a see-through meat drawer as well as two clear, humidity-controlled crispers, and an egg bin. The door offers gallon and tall-container storage in the one full-width shelf and four half-width bins. Two dairy compartments are also located in the door. The freezer features two slide-out baskets and two full-width door shelves. An ice maker is a factory option on this model. This refrigerator meets current federal energy standards. It is available in white, almond, or black.

Specifications: height, 65⅞"; width, 32¾"; depth (with handle), 33"; shelf area, 28.6 square feet. **Warranty:** 1 year, parts; 5 years, parts and labor on the sealed system.

Manufacturer's Suggested Retail Price: $1,029

Approximate Low Price: $952

Built-in Refrigerators

AMANA BRF20T

✔ BEST BUY

This unique refrigerator, with a capacity of 19.7 cubic feet, is a built-in model with the freezer on the bottom. Among its features are four half-width, adjustable, spill-saver glass shelves. Also included is a temperature-adjustable deli port and an adjustable-humidity-and-temperature drawer. The door storage includes four half-width shelves and one full-width, gallon-capacity shelf. The freezer features a slide-out basket, one full-width shelf, and shallow door storage to hold flat packages upright. Factory options include an ice maker. The Amana BRF20T refrigerator meets federal energy standards, and its quiet operation is a plus. Available colors are white, almond, and ebony.

Specifications: height, 68⅝"; width, 35⅝"; depth, 26¾"; shelf area, 25.3 square feet. **Warranty:** 1 year, parts and labor; 5 years, parts and labor on the sealed system; 10 years, limited on sealed system components.

Manufacturer's Suggested Retail Price: $1,649

Approximate Low Price: $1,409

AMANA SRD20S4

Recommended

Though this well-appointed side-by-side refrigerator offers 19.6 cubic feet of efficiently laid-out storage space, its higher price makes it a Recommended choice. Two full-width, spill-saver, slide-out glass shelves and two similar half-width shelves are adjustable for your convenience. An adjustable-temperature deli drawer and two clear crispers with glass tops, all on rollers, hold ample supplies of meat and produce. The door has a temperature-controlled beverage rack with gallon-container capacity, four shelves, and two dairy compartments. The freezer features three slide-out baskets and five door shelves, plus an extra, shallow holder behind the ice and water dispenser. The through-the-door ice and water dispenser comes equipped with a night-light. With all its amenities, this refrigerator still exceeds federal energy standards by 20 percent and operates quietly. Most new refrigerators use much less energy than those made just a few years ago, and this model is a prime example. You can choose it in white, almond, or ebony.

Specifications: height, 67½"; width, 35¾"; depth (with handle), 29"; shelf area, 20.4 square feet. **Warranty:** 1 year, parts and labor; 5 years, parts and labor on the sealed system; 10 years, limited on sealed system components.

Manufacturer's Suggested Retail Price: $1,949

Approximate Low Price: Not available

GENERAL ELECTRIC PROFILE
TPX24SIYBS

Recommended

The capacity of this side-by-side built-in is 23.7 cubic feet. The high price tag makes it a Recommended purchase rather than a Best Buy. Three adjustable glass shelves, two of which are spill-saver and slide-out, hold a great deal of food. There is also an adjustable-temperature meat pan, an adjustable-humidity crisper, an adjustable-humidity snack pan, and a beverage rack. The door has four shelves, including two that are adjustable for gallon storage. The freezer features three slide-out baskets, one shelf, and five door shelves. This unit comes with a factory ice maker, an automatic energy saver, and factory-installed stainless steel exterior panels. Stainless steel collar trim is optional.

Specifications: height, 68¾"; width, 35¾"; depth, (with handle), 28¼"; shelf area, 24 square feet. **Warranty:** 1 year, parts and labor; 5 years, full on the sealed system.

Manufacturer's Suggested Retail Price: $2,399

Approximate Low Price: $2,154

WHIRLPOOL ED20DBXE

Recommended

The interior capacity of this side-by-side refrigerator is 19.7 cubic feet. Because of its high price tag it is a Recommended buy. The cantilever, spill-saver glass shelves adjust to meet your storage needs. The clear, temperature-controlled meat drawer and the two clear, humidity-controlled crispers will hold a variety of meats and produce. An out-of-the-way yet handy beverage rack keeps a favorite drink easy to reach. An egg bin is included. The door offers five bins—two with gallon storage—and a dairy compartment. The freezer features three adjustable slide-out shelves, one slide-out basket, one adjustable and three fixed door shelves, and a quick-freeze compartment. The through-the-door ice and water dispenser comes with its own night-light. This refrigerator exceeds federal energy standards by 20 percent and comes in white, almond, and black.

Specifications: height, 67½"; width, 35¾"; depth (with handles), 27⅞"; shelf area, 21.3 square feet. **Warranty:** 1 year, parts and labor; 5 years, parts and labor on the sealed system.

Manufacturer's Suggested Retail Price: $1,849

Approximate Low Price: $1,719

Compact Refrigerators

GENERAL ELECTRIC TAX6SNXWN

✔BEST BUY

This compact refrigerator offers 6 cubic feet of space. It has two adjustable wire shelves and a dairy compartment. The door has three shallow shelves. The 0.49-cubic-feet freezer includes two miniature ice trays. The unit is available in white or woodgrain. It has manual defrost and the doors are reversible so it will fit anywhere. An optional trim kit is available.

Specifications: height, 34¼"; width, 23⅝"; depth (with handle), 25⅞"; shelf area, 8.8 square feet. **Warranty:** 1 year, limited; 4 years, limited on the compressor.

Manufacturer's Suggested Retail Price: $349

Approximate Low Price: $338

GENERAL ELECTRIC TAX2SNXWN ✔BEST BUY
This 1.7-cubic-foot-capacity refrigerator serves as a terrific snack holder. It has one fixed compartment shelf. The door has one full-width shelf and one half-width shelf. The freezer space is 0.21 cubic feet and contains two miniature ice trays. This refrigerator is available in woodgrain only.

Specifications: height, 18⅞"; width, 18⅝"; depth (with handle), 26⅛"; shelf area, 2.9 square feet. **Warranty:** 1 year, limited; 4 years, limited on the compressor.

Manufacturer's Suggested Retail Price: $169

Approximate Low Price: Not available

WHIRLPOOL EL03CCXDW ✔BEST BUY
The capacity of this refrigerator is 2.8 cubic feet. It has one full-width, removable, slide-out wire shelf and one full-width tray. The door has one half-width and two full-width shelves. Temperature is adjustable. The freezer compartment includes an ice cube tray. This small refrigerator comes in white only.

Specifications: height, 24.3"; width, 18.7"; depth, 20.7". **Warranty:** 1 year, parts and labor; 4 years, parts and labor on the compressor.

Manufacturer's Suggested Retail Price: $199

Approximate Low Price: $199

FREEZERS

Freezers are a necessity for large families, those who grow their own food, and those who cook in large quantities. For those consumers, refrigerators simply do not offer enough frozen food space. However, home freezers can assist any consumer in saving money. A freezer can pay for itself over the years by storing bulk items, garden produce, or meat supplies.

Upright or Chest?

Some facts about upright versus chest freezers can help you decide which model will best suit your needs. Upright freezers keep food more accessible but are less energy-efficient than chest models. Chest freezers maintain a more stable internal temperature than upright freezers, but they take up more floor space. All chest freezers need to be defrosted manually, while some upright freezers offer automatic defrost cycles.

Which Features?

Defrosting is a dreaded word for many freezer owners. Some new manual-defrosting freezers offer a power defrost, which can cut the defrost cycle to as little as 20 minutes by circulating heat through the cooling coils. Another desirable feature is a power-freeze or quick-freeze setting, which puts the freezer in a maximum cooling mode for freezing large quantities of food at one time. A fast-freezing shelf has an extra cooling coil and is useful when adding new foods to be frozen. Many models come with a power cord retainer to prevent accidental unplugging of the freezer or audible temperature alarms to notify you if the temperature inside the freezer is too warm.

Upright Freezers

AMANA ESU15JW

✔**BEST BUY**

This 15.2-cubic-foot upright cabinet freezer includes three evaporator shelves as well as a slide-out basket at the bottom. The door offers four shelves. Other handy features include a lock and key, adjustable-temperature control, defrost drain, and leveling legs. This model defrosts manually. It is available in white. A frost-free model (ESUF15JW) with similar features is also available.

Specifications: height, 60½"; width, 30"; depth, 27¹³⁄₃₂".
Warranty: 1 year, parts and labor; 10 years, parts and labor on the sealed system; 10 years, food loss.

Manufacturer's Suggested Retail Price: $569

Approximate Low Price: $477

FRIGIDAIRE FFU20F9C

✔**BEST BUY**

With a storage capacity of 20.3 cubic feet, this freezer will hold food for an average-size family for a long period of time. The four cabinet shelves adjust to accommodate your specific needs. The two baskets at the bottom of the cabinet slide out. The door offers six additional shelves. Other desirable features on this well-appointed freezer include an adjustable-temperature control, a lock with a pop-out key, leveling legs, a power cord retainer to prevent the unit from accidentally being unplugged, a door closer, and a temperature alarm system. This frost-free unit comes in white only.

Specifications: height, 70"; width, 32"; depth, 28½"; shelf area, 23.07 square feet. **Warranty:** 1 year, parts and labor; 5 years, limited on the sealed system; 10 years, limited on the compressor.

Manufacturer's Suggested Retail Price: $699

Approximate Low Price: $607

GENERAL ELECTRIC FF16DX

✔**BEST BUY**

This freezer has a capacity of 15.7 cubic feet. The cabinet offers four shelves and one slide-out basket. Five more shelves are located in the door. Adding to the convenience of this unit are an audible temperature alarm, an adjustable-temperature control, a lock with a self-ejecting key, and leveling legs. This frost-free freezer is available in white only.

Specifications: height, 61½"; width, 32"; depth, 26½"; shelf area, 18.2 square feet. **Warranty:** 1 year, parts and labor; 5 years, limited on the sealed system; limited food coverage.

Manufacturer's Suggested Retail Price: $629

Approximate Low Price: $578

Chest Freezers

FRIGIDAIRE FFC15D9C
✔**BEST BUY**

This 14.8-cubic-foot-capacity freezer has two removable baskets for items that are frequently used. A particularly desirable feature on this unit is a power freeze, which allows the temperature to be manually lowered for quick freezing. Also included are an audible temperature alarm, a lock with a pop-out key, an adjustable temperature control, a defrost drain, and a power cord retainer. This manual-defrost freezer includes a 20-minute power defrost that significantly reduces maintenance time. White is the only color available.

Specifications: height, 35"; width, 48"; depth, 29½". **Warranty:** 1 year, parts and labor; 5 years, limited on the sealed system; 10 years, limited on the compressor.

Manufacturer's Suggested Retail Price: $499

Approximate Low Price: $441

GENERAL ELECTRIC FH10DX
✔**BEST BUY**

This high-quality GE model has a capacity of 10 cubic feet. It includes one removable, sliding basket. Other desirable features include a temperature monitor with an audible alarm, a built-in lock with a self-ejecting key, and an up-front defrost drain. This manual-defrost freezer is available in white. Similar models are available in several sizes, from 5.3 cubic feet to more than 24 cubic feet.

Specifications: height, 35"; width, 42⅛"; depth, 24¼". **Warranty:** 1 year, parts and labor; 5 years, limited on the sealed system; limited food spoilage.

Manufacturer's Suggested Retail Price: $369
Approximate Low Price: $347

WHITE-WESTINGHOUSE MFC23M4BW `Recommended`
   This large freezer has a capacity of 22.7 cubic
feet, with two removable baskets. It is a Recommended selection because of the cost. It features an adjustable temperature
control, a lock with pop-out key, a power cord retainer, a defrost
drain, and a divider/drain pan. This manual-defrost freezer
exceeds federal energy standards by 8 percent. It comes in white
only.

Specifications: height, 35"; width, 69"; depth, 29½". **Warranty:**
1 year, parts and labor; 3 years, limited for food spoilage;
5 years, limited on the sealed system.

Manufacturer's Suggested Retail Price: $499
Approximate Low Price: $490

DISHWASHERS

Dishwashers range in price from about $200 to over $2,000. Buying a model at the low end can be a mistake because evidence of inferior materials, faulty construction techniques, or a poor engineering design won't show up until years after you've purchased the unit. High-end dishwashers, on the other hand, tend to have seldom-used features that often pose problems during installation and servicing. As a rule, brand-name dishwashers that are priced in the middle range and include commonly used features make the best investment.

Built-in dishwashers remain the most popular type, and they are the easiest to use. Built-in dishwashers are typically located in a convenient place under the countertop and are hooked up to a hot-water line, a drain, and electrical lines.

Portable dishwashers have a finished exterior, wheels, a plug-in cord, and a hose that connects to your kitchen faucet during use. Most portables are mechanically the same as built-in units and can later be converted to built-ins (except for top-loading portables). Though sales of portable units have declined steadily over the past few years, they are still popular with renters who plan to purchase a home.

Features and Terminology

Controls: Push-button or dial controls are the most economical and reliable. Electronic touch controls can add up to $150 to the cost of the machine, but they offer a contemporary, high-tech look. Electronic controls may also include features such as indicator lights that tell you when a drain is clogged, when the wash arms are stuck, or how much time is remaining in the cycle. A child lock-out feature, which prevents children from playing with the controls, may also prove convenient for many households.

Cycles: Three basic cycles—normal wash, light wash or water saver, and pots and pans—handle most loads. Quick rinse, or rinse and hold, allows you to rinse a partial load and wait until you load more dirty dishes before adding detergent and washing a full load. As a rule, most units do a better job of washing on a normal or heavy cycle.

Rinse Aid Dispenser: Many units have a feature that dispenses a special conditioner during the final rinse cycle. This aids in eliminating water spots and speeds up drying.

Sound Insulation: The more noise-dampening features, the quieter the operation. All units have at least a fiberglass blanket on the top and on two sides of the tub and at least two inches of fiberglass insulation in the door and kickplate. High-priced models have a fully insulated tub and four inches of insulation in the door and kickplate. A quiet-running electric motor and pump, usually mounted on rubber grommets, will make the dishwasher even more quiet during operation.

Time Delay: Time delay is a worthwhile feature that delays operation up to 12 hours. This allows you to take advantage of off-peak electric rates and to use hot water at a time when it is not being used by other household members.

Tub and Inner Door Materials: Stainless steel is the most durable and expensive tub and inner door material. Triple-coated porcelain enamel on steel is durable, widely used, and the most cost-effective. Polypropylene is durable, the least expensive, and used most frequently because it tends to be quieter than steel.

Washing Action: The best cleaning results are obtained with a three-way mechanism, though good results can be obtained with two-way action. One-way action may not provide satisfactory cleaning.

Water Heating: Many dishwashers have an automatic water-temperature booster system that ensures consistently hot water (140°F) during the wash and rinse cycles. This feature reduces the cost of operating your hot water heater by lowering the thermostat to as low as 120°F. Some models also have an extra hot rinse option that heats water to about 160°F. Water at this temperature may be effective at killing germs.

Best Buys '97

Our Best Buy and Recommended dishwashers follow. They are divided into categories of built-in and portable models.

Within each category, the units we consider to be Best Buys are listed first, followed by our Recommended models. Remember that a Best Buy or Recommended designation applies only to the model listed. It does not apply to other models made by the same manufacturer.

BUILT-IN DISHWASHERS

FRIGIDAIRE GALLERY FDB878GC ✓BEST BUY

Quiet and convenient, the Frigidaire Gallery FDB878GC dishwasher features a dynamic cleaning system called Ultra-Power that includes a solid food disposer, a fine-mesh self-cleaning filter, and a power pump. The system helps eliminate the need to rinse or prewash dishes. A fixed tower wash system circulates water at three levels for maximum efficiency. The normal wash cycle uses only 7.7 gallons of water (9 gallons is typical). The rotary control operates five wash cycles: normal, heavy, power scrub, water saver, and rinse and hold. Easy-to-use touchpads control such options as start/cancel, 6-hour delay, high-temperature (140°F) wash, and no-heat drying. The effective sound insulation system includes asphaltic-based sound-dampening sheets on the top and sides of the tub, a tub and inner door liner, 1-inch sound-absorbing acoustic foam pads in the door, 1-inch foil-covered fiberglass tub wrap on the top, back, and sides, and fiberglass insulation behind the service and toe panels. Other features include a fan-drying system, a child-lock safety latch, nylon-coated racks, a removable silverware basket, and a separate utensil basket with a closed compartment to contain small items during washing. This dishwasher has a ⅓-horsepower motor and is available in white, almond, or black.

Specifications: height, 34" to 35"; width, 24"; depth, 24¼"; water use, normal cycle, 7.7 gallons. **Warranty:** 2 years, full; 5 years, electronic controls and racks; 20 years, tub and door.

Manufacturer's Suggested Retail Price: $469

Approximate Low Price: $397

SEARS KENMORE 15925   ✔ BEST BUY

The Sears Kenmore 15925 dishwasher is a top-of-the-line unit with a ⅓-horsepower motor. Its cleaning system washes off dried-on food, separates food particles from the circulating water (through the use of a microfilter), grinds food particles and small bones with a heavy-duty food grinder, and drains these particles to leave dishes sparkling. This unit has two spray arms and three water levels. An electronic keypad controls six cycles: pots and pans, normal, water miser, china and light dishware, quick rinse, and favorite cycle. For finishing dishes, this unit includes a heated water option, a sanitary rinse option, and a no-heat drying option for saving energy. Other features include a detergent dispenser, a rinse dispenser with a signal eye, a child lock-out, and an electronic-cycle status read-out. A 12-hour start delay allows the user to take advantage of off-hour electricity rates. The 4 inches of insulation behind the toe panel and 4 inches behind the access panel, together with a fully fiberglass tub and sound-dampening material, help make this unit operate quietly. The lower rack contains a large silverware basket with cover, small-items basket and one fold down tine row. The upper rack is high sided with four cup shelves and two fold-down tine rows, and it is both adjustable and removable. This dishwasher is available in black, white, almond, or with an almond door and access panel. The different colors are denoted by slightly different model numbers.

Specifications: height, 33"; width, 24"; depth, 24"; water use, normal cycle, 6.5 gallons. **Warranty:** 3 years, full; lifetime, tub and door liner.

Manufacturer's Suggested Retail Price: $600

Approximate Low Price: $592

KITCHENAID SUPERBA KUDR24SE   ✔ BEST BUY

The Superba KUDR24SE, a top-of-the-line dishwasher, features a ⅓-horsepower motor. A notable feature about this unit is the durable, stainless steel interior, which is resistant to staining, spotting, and streaking. This interior also offers heat retention and transfer, and it protects against rust-through for the life of the dishwasher. The Superba has electronic controls, which operate four cycles: pots and pans, normal, light dishware and china, and rinse only. An LED display indicates cycles. This model offers 2-, 4-, and 6-hour delay starts, which will allow you to take advantage of off-peak electric rates. A self-cleaning filtration system keeps loosened debris from recirculating in the wash chamber. Standard features include high-temperature wash, an energy-efficient drying option, a four-way wash-arm system that reaches every corner of the wash chamber, and effective sound insulation for quiet operation. The racks are nylon-coated, and the high-sided lower rack holds a one-piece utensil basket. A direct water feed to the upper spray arm assures that the items in the upper rack are always washed in clean water. This dishwasher is available in black, white, or almond.

Specifications: height, 33⁷⁄₁₆"; width, 23⁷⁄₈"; depth, 26"; water use, normal cycle, 6.5 to 7 gallons. **Warranty:** 1 year, parts and labor; 5 years, motor, electronic controls, and nylon rack finish; lifetime, stainless steel tank against leaks.

Manufacturer's Suggested Retail Price: $649

Approximate Low Price: $578

MAYTAG DEPENDABLY QUIET PLUS DWU9202

✔**BEST BUY**

The Dependably Quiet Plus DWU9202 features a ⅓-horsepower motor. This Maytag unit has push-button controls with indicator lights to designate what cycle the machine is in. The machine has six cycles: normal, pots and pans, light china, sani-rinse, rinse and hold, and quick cycle. The number of additional features on the DWU9202 make this a best buy. Additional options include a 6-hour start delay, no-heat drying, an automatic water-temperature booster system to ensure consistently hot water, a three-level jetspray washing system for greater scrubbing action, a self-cleaning micromesh filter and food disposer, and sound-absorbing insulation for quiet operation. This unit has deluxe, nylon-coated racks with several desirable features, including an extra large removable silverware basket, convertible bowl tines for loading flexibility, and lock systems to support stemware and odd-shaped items. Color options are white, almond, and black.

Specifications: height, 33¾" to 35¼"; width, 23⅞"; depth, 23½"; water use, normal cycle, 9 gallons. **Warranty:** 1 year, parts and labor; 2 years, parts; 5 years, wash system, controls, racks, and exterior cabinet; 20 years, tub and door liner.

Manufacturer's Suggested Retail Price: $499

Approximate Low Price: $482

GENERAL ELECTRIC PROFILE 4900 SERIES

Recommended

The dishwashers that make up the Profile 4900 series are the same basic machine but in different colors. The color options are black, almond, white, and stainless steel with a black control panel; the product number for each color begins with "49." The design of the 4900 series offers a pleasing, clean appearance. The touchpad controls have no crevices to catch dirt, which enhances the contemporary design. This dishwasher is a state-of-the-art machine with four cycles: normal, pots and pans, china and crystal, and rinse and hold. Other quality features include a three-level, multi-orbital washing system, a sensor system that adjusts water level and temperatures according to wash load, and a self-cleaning filter. A digital system monitor displays information about the dishwasher's functionings. A 14-hour delay start, reset options, and an energy-saving drying option add to this unit's appeal. The flexible rack system includes a utensil basket with two sections that can be further divided into three compartments. A slotted compartment can be used to contain knives or loose items. A lock-out touchpad prevents accidental starting by children.

Specifications: height, 34" to 35"; width, 24"; depth, 24¾"; water use, normal cycle, 6.5 gallons (light normal) to 9.3 gallons (heavy normal). **Warranty:** 1 year, full; 2 years, parts; 5 years, electronic controls and racks; 20 years, tub and inner door liner.

Manufacturer's Suggested Retail Price: $599–$629

Approximate Low Price: $548

PORTABLE DISHWASHERS

GENERAL ELECTRIC GSC 1200X
✓BEST BUY

The GSC 1200X has all of the features of a built-in unit with the added versatility of a portable. This unit can easily be converted to a built-in dishwasher by removing the top and wheels and making electrical, water, and drain hook-ups. The GSC 1200X, with its ⅓-horsepower motor, features three wash levels. Its touchpad and rotary controls operate seven cycles: normal, potscrubber, light wash, short wash, water saver, rinse and hold, and plate warmer. Other desirable features include a 6-hour delay start, temperature boost, a self-cleaning filter, a no-heat drying option, and a rinse-aid dispenser with an indicator light. Extra deep racks accommodate tall items, with the deluxe upper rack containing a split shelf for cups. The lift-out silverware basket divides into two sections with three compartments each. This model comes in black with white sides.

Specifications: height, 36¼"; width, 24¾"; depth, 27"; water use, normal cycle, 8.5 gallons. **Warranty:** 1 year, full; 2 years, limited, parts; 5 years, limited, rack and electronic parts; 20 years, tub and door liner.

Manufacturer's Suggested Retail Price: $499–$529

Approximate Low Price: $443

SEARS KENMORE 17625/1
✓BEST BUY

The Sears Kenmore 17625/1 portable dish-washer, which has a ⅓-horsepower motor, is an easily convertible unit with a butcher block top and wheels. Its three-way wash system uses two spray arms. Eight push buttons and a dial control five cycles: pots and pans, normal, water miser, china and light dishware, and quick rinse. There are also three heat options: water heat, no heat rinse, and no heat dry. Other desirable features include a rinse dispenser with a signal eye and a detergent dispenser. The adjustable, removable upper rack has two cup shelves. The lower rack contains a large silverware basket and a small-items compartment. A quality sound insulation system ensures quiet operation. This portable is available in black or white, with black or almond reversible panels.

Specifications: height, 36"; width, 24"; depth, 25"; water use, normal cycle, 6.5 gallons. **Warranty:** 1 year, full; 2 years, parts; lifetime, tub and door liner.

Manufacturer's Suggested Retail Price: $480
Approximate Low Price: $480

FRIGIDAIRE FDP652RBR

The FDP652RBR stands out because of its **Recommended** attractive cherry wood-veneer top. For ease of use, it slides smoothly on its four wheels. In terms of performance, this unit has a ⅓-horsepower motor and a three-level washing system. Its push-button and rotary controls operate five wash cycles: normal, heavy, power scrub, water saver, and rinse and hold. Other features include a no-heat drying option, high-temperature (140°F) wash, a rinse-aid dispenser, a soft food disposer, and adequate insulation for quiet operation. The racks are vinyl coated. This model comes in black on black, or with reversible color panels in almond and black, with almond side panels.

Specifications: height, 36"; width, 24½"; depth, 26⅞"; water use, normal cycle, 7.6 gallons. **Warranty:** 1 year, full; 10 years, limited, poly tub and door liner.

Manufacturer's Suggested Retail Price: $440
Approximate Low Price: $392

FLOOR CARE

The era of the one-vacuum-cleaner household is fast becoming a thing of the past. The reason? Over the years, the vacuum cleaner has been refined and improved, giving rise to a new generation of specialized floor-care appliances.

Upright, Canister, or Powerhead Vacuum Cleaner?

An upright works best for rug and carpet cleaning. Its agitator—essentially a beater bar outfitted with bristles—digs out embedded dirt and grit even from high-pile carpeting. The newer uprights are more lightweight than earlier models, so they're easier to handle on stairs but still not as maneuverable as canisters. The upright is also usually less efficient than the canister at above-the-floor cleaning (upholstery, windowsills, and draperies, for example) because the attachments needed to tackle these jobs are often less accessible, and the upright doesn't roll along as easily as the canister. A new generation of upright cleaners, however, stores cleaning tools on the unit, and some come with a permanently attached hose for greater convenience on those above-the-floor jobs.

Canister vacuum cleaners eliminate some of the shortcomings of uprights. They are usually quieter than uprights and do a fine job of cleaning bare floors and low-pile carpets. The canister nozzle's low profile permits better access under furniture, in tight spaces, and on stair treads. Easy-to-change attachments remove dust from walls, curtains, and lampshades. Because it lacks the upright's agitator, the canister is less effective than the upright at removing dirt that has sifted down into the carpet pile. Most new canister models are extremely lightweight and maneuverable, but their suction is generally less powerful than the uprights'.

A strong canister vacuum cleaner with a powerhead offers the best features of the upright and the standard canister. It has the canister's rolling tank (usually equipped with a tool caddy), hose, and nozzle, combined with a powerhead outfitted with an agitator similar to an upright's. When you shop for a powerhead canister, examine its brush roll carefully. Some units have independent motors that allow them to dig deeper into thick-pile carpet. Others have turbo- or suction-driven brush rolls, which have less strength but may still be adequate for your particular needs. Remember, try it before you buy it.

Mini Vacuum Cleaners and Brooms

Compact vacuum cleaners and brooms are available in many shapes and sizes. These scaled-down units, designed for quick spot clean-ups or dry spills, can be a great convenience as long as you remember that they are intended for smaller jobs. The motors on these minis and brooms have less power, and the dust bags or cups must be emptied often. Cordless minis are supremely portable and ideal for room-to-room touch-ups and for car care. Corded models are more powerful and won't run out of juice, but they have the same outlet limitations as regular vacuum cleaners.

All-Purpose Cleaning Machines

Sometimes an ordinary vacuum cleaner just won't do the job, and you need a specialized cleaning machine. There are plenty of options on the market, some of which incorporate features that were once found only on industrial-strength vacuums. Once available only through rental services, carpet steam cleaners are now a significant presence at retail outlets. Typically, these vacuums are bigger-ticket items than their conventional counterparts, but they offer a lot of added cleaning capability. Also known as spray extraction machines, these units dispense a cleaning solution into the carpet; then a brush connected to the head of the nozzle agitates the carpet pile to loosen the dirt before the dirt and water are sucked back into the machine.

Wet/dry vacuum cleaners handle messy chores, indoors and out, that conventional vacuums can't. They can clean a muddy garage floor, suck up soapy washing-machine overflow, and gobble up whole chunks of dirt. These units, however, are noisy and lack many of the convenient features of standard vacuums. For ease of use, you'll want an easy-to-maneuver machine with widely spaced wheels (for stability) and one that changes from wet to dry pick-up with the flip of a switch. Also check to see how difficult it is to remove the tank lid, and look for a long power cord, detachable blowers, and an extra-wide hose.

Best Buys '97

Our Best Buy, Recommended, and Budget Buy floor-care appliances follow. These appliances have been selected on the basis of convenience, performance, and overall value. Within each category, the item we consider the best of the Best Buys is listed first, followed by our second choice, and so on. Remember that a Best Buy, Recommended, or Budget Buy designation applies only to the model listed; it does not apply to other models made by the same manufacturer or to an entire product line.

UPRIGHT VACUUM CLEANERS

HOOVER POWER DRIVE DIRT FINDER
U6331-930

The Hoover Power Drive Dirt Finder merits its **✔ BEST BUY** price, which is higher than other upright models', because of its superior cleaning capacity, loads of special features, and solid construction. It does a remarkable job of picking up dust and dirt, thanks to an energy-efficient motor that actually uses only 7.8 amps of power and to a special dirt-finder feature: When the red light is on, the machine is in the process of removing dirt; when the light turns green, the carpet is clean. This vacuum is billed as "self-propelled" based on its power-drive feature, which makes the unit exceptionally easy to maneuver despite its substantial size. The other features on the Dirt Finder are also well thought out and sensibly designed: an on/off switch in the hand grip (no need for bending); a five-piece tool kit (including a super-stretch hose, crevice tool, dusting brush, extension wand, and upholstery nozzle) placed at the top of the unit in an on-board storage box covered with clear plastic; uncomplicated slide-button controls located on the unit's base; a durable, snap-open bag compartment for easy changing; and a powerful headlight. The unit has a built-in handle for carrying it between floors, an extra-long, 35-foot power cord for added flexibility, and on-board storage for an extra dust bag and motor belt. Made of high impact ABS thermoplastic, this unit is extremely sturdy and a great performer.

Warranty: 1 year, parts and labor.

Manufacturer's Suggested Retail Price: $500

Approximate Low Price: $337

SHARP BIG WHEEL EC-S2620

✔**BEST BUY**

The Sharp EC-S2620 is part of the new, high-performance Big Wheel series, which measures up admirably on all fronts. Its larger wheels keep the unit stable and easy to move on thick plush carpets or bare floors. Its quiet and efficient 11-amp motor does a fine job of picking up dust and dirt, and the "Edge Eater" feature—with a front shutter that opens as the unit moves forward—allows thorough cleaning all the way to the baseboards. The motor has a triple filtering system, which Sharp claims captures over 99 percent of fine dust and pollen particles, and the unit's protective bypass system keeps coins and other hard objects from damaging the motor. Tools (a combination upholstery tool and detachable brush, two plastic extension wands, a crevice tool, and an extendable vacuum hose) are stored on board. This Big Wheel also offers automatic carpet height adjustment, a headlight, a wrap-around bumper (to protect moldings and furniture while vacuuming), and an 18-foot power cord. Although it lacks a few desirable extras (such as a longer cord and a full-bag indicator), this sleekly designed premium unit performs very well overall.

Warranty: 1 year, limited on parts and labor.

Manufacturer's Suggested Retail Price: $230

Approximate Low Price: $149

EUREKA BRAVO II THE BOSS PLUS 7640AT

✔**BEST BUY**

If you can sacrifice the solid construction of a sturdier vacuum (the more expensive models cover their dust bags with hard plastic casings instead of this unit's cloth **bag**), this is a superb choice. The efficacy of the 12-amp motor, which has a high-efficiency Direct Air Flow System for deep carpet cleaning, makes Bravo an apt name. This no-frills vac does a great job and offers an on-board assortment of tools, including a crush-resistant hose, two extension wands, a crevice tool, and a combination upholstery nozzle/dusting brush. It also has seven-position carpet height adjustment, a three-position handle that can lie flat for cleaning under coffee tables and beds, a wrap-around furniture guard, an automatic dual edge-cleaning function, and a carrying handle. The whole package weighs only 13 pounds. It's impossible to go wrong with this vacuum cleaner, especially considering its price.

Warranty: 1 year, limited.

Manufacturer's Suggested Retail Price: $180

Approximate Low Price: $100

HOOVER PREFERRED U5095-930

Recommended

The Preferred U5095-930 offers many of the attributes Hoover is known for, such as outstanding cleaning capabilities and a solid, sensible design, at a more moderate price. The very efficient 7.2-amp motor does an admirable job of sucking up dust and dirt, and a number of special features make cleaning easier. The front of the unit snaps wide open for easy dust-bag changes: A tool kit (with a super-stretch hose, crevice tool, dusting brush, extension wand, and upholstery nozzle) and an extra belt are stored on board. This vacuum has a headlight for working under furniture and a three-position handle that allows it to lie flat for cleaning under beds and other low-clearance furnishings. Other nice touches include a 31-foot quick-release cord and uncomplicated slide-button controls located at the base of the unit. A special built-in handle at the front of the vacuum is helpful for cleaning stairs.

Warranty: 1 year.

Manufacturer's Suggested Retail Price: $240

Approximate Low Price: $160

ROYAL DIRT DEVIL ULTRA MVP 089200 `Recommended`

This brand-new addition to the Dirt Devil line is even better looking than the company's Dirt Devil MVP (and it's the same bold shade of red). But the long list of "Ultra features" offered by Royal gives it more than just good looks. The 12-amp motor does a fine job of picking up dirt, and the unit is exceptionally flexible. The Ultra features include an attached Hide-a-Hose that provides over 20 feet of extended reach; a four-position height adjustment; an extra-long 32-foot cord; a 5-piece set of on-board cleaning tools; a full-bag indicator; a touchless bag-change system; and dual headlights. A motor-guard system prevents damage to the fan and motor from hidden debris in sofas and chairs, and the Ultra MVP offers a high-quality filtration system and a relatively quiet motor. Its sensible price and stylish design, coupled with all these extras, make this a good all-around unit you won't want to put away.

Warranty: 30 days money-back; 3 years, product; 6 years, motor.

Manufacturer's Suggested Retail Price: $250

Approximate Low Price: $200

COMPACT CANISTERS

SHARP EC-7311 ✔BEST BUY

The Sharp EC-7311, a sleek, futuristic compact canister, is a bit pricey, but it is such an effective performer that it merits its cost. For a canister vac, it has an extremely efficient motor, which features a triple-filter system that Sharp claims traps over 99 percent of all fine dust and pollen. The unit is small (9¾ inches wide and 14 inches long), lightweight (just over 10 pounds), and equipped with built-in tools (a crevice tool and a combination upholstery tool with a detachable brush). With extra-large wheels and a low center of gravity, the EC-7311 moves smoothly and is extremely stable. Best of all, a simple one-touch release makes it easy to change the bag on this unit, and an automatic feature quickly rewinds the 16-foot cord.

Warranty: 1 year, limited on parts and labor.
Manufacturer's Suggested Retail Price: $170
Approximate Low Price: $117

ROYAL DIRT DEVIL CAN VAC 082023 Recommended

This good-looking, bright-red compact canister has many features that make it worth recommending. The 9.2-amp motor offers good cleaning power on bare floors and moderately strong suction on carpets. This vac's best points include its small size (the main body is 13 inches long and the canister weighs only 8 pounds), an eight-piece on-board tool set (including a hose, carpet and crevice tools, bare floor and dusting brushes, two locking extension wands, and a shoulder strap), and an optional (separately purchased) power nozzle that vastly improves the unit's performance on carpets. Large, easy-roll wheels and a good-sized handle on its back make it extremely maneuverable and round out the Dirt Devil Can Vac's appeal.

Warranty: 1 year.
Manufacturer's Suggested Retail Price: $100
Approximate Low Price: $75

EUREKA THE BOSS MIGHTY MITE II 3621A Budget Buy

The name "Mighty Mite" fits this unit, which looks like a sturdy little creature ready to pounce on dirt. Thanks to its low weight (just over 10 pounds, including hose and attachments) and clever design (oversized wheels and a large handle right on its back), it can do just that. It has relatively good suction, but works much better on bare floors than on carpets. The ingeniously concealed on-board attachments (a crevice tool, dusting brush, upholstery tool, carpet nozzle, crush-resistant hose, and two wands) are designed to work on a variety of household surfaces; the dust bag is very easy to change; and the 20-foot power cord wraps around the cleaner for easy storage. Another nice touch is the triple-filtration bag system. The oversized wheels make this a great multipurpose vacuum that can complement an upright for cleaning carpets or suffice on its own in a residence with mostly bare floors.

Warranty: 1 year, limited.

Manufacturer's Suggested Retail Price: $120

Approximate Low Price: $80

POWERHEAD CANISTERS

EUREKA WORLD VAC 6856B

✔ BEST BUY

Don't be fooled by the "precious" appearance of this powerhead vac: It delivers superior performance. The 12-amp motor provides sufficient suction for cleaning both carpets and bare floors, and Eureka asserts that the filtered bag system retains 99 percent of the dirt, dust, and pollen the World Vac picks up. The motorized carpet nozzle, complete with a headlight for working under furniture, has a double-sweep bristle brush roll that provides dual-edge cleaning. The World Vac is easy to maneuver thanks to a swivel joint at the base of its hose. Large easy-glide wheels, a 7-foot hose, a 25-foot power cord, and a comprehensive tool set (with two chrome steel wands, an upholstery nozzle, dusting and bare-floor brushes, and a crevice tool) conveniently stored on top of the unit also contribute to this vacuum's ease of use. Extra touches—a full-bag indicator, automatic carpet height adjustment, and a sturdy carrying handle for transporting the 12-pound vac (the hose and attachments weigh an additional 8.5 pounds)—add to the unit's efficiency. This is a value-priced buy considering its superior performance, outstanding features, and attractive appearance.

Warranty: 1 year, limited.

Manufacturer's Suggested Retail Price: $320

Approximate Low Price: $160

HOOVER FUTURA S3567

Recommended

The Hoover Futura is priced to make an effective entry into the powerhead canister vacuum market. Its sleek styling gives it an aerodynamic look, and its efficient 9.8-amp motor does a superior job of picking up dust and dirt. In addition, the Futura is loaded with features characteristic of more expensive models, including a 6-foot swivel hose, a 25-foot retractable cord with pedal rewind, a full-bag indicator, a carrying handle, and on-board molded storage space for its tool set (two chrome extension wands, a crevice tool, a dusting brush, a furniture nozzle, and a wall/floor brush). The motorized power nozzle has a two-brush agitator, brushed-edge cleaning on both sides, and a powerful headlight. Although this unit isn't cheap, the price is fair, considering all it has to offer.

Warranty: 1 year.

Manufacturer's Suggested Retail Price: $290

Approximate Low Price: $199

ROYAL DIRT DEVIL POWER PAK 082123 | Budget Buy

This bright-red compact powerhead canister, very similar to the 082023 model can vac reviewed earlier, has chunky good looks, weighs in at only 16 pounds, and has a 10-amp motor. It offers adequate cleaning power on bare floors (only moderate suction on carpets), and its low price and weight make it a good option for consumers with wood floors or low-pile carpets. The Power Pak's best points include its small size, 20-foot cord, and on-board tool set (including a 7-foot flexible hose, a crevice tool, a dusting brush, two extension wands, and a shoulder strap). Easy-roll wheels and a good-sized handle on its back make it extremely maneuverable.

Warranty: 1 year.

Manufacturer's Suggested Retail Price: $150

Approximate Low Price: $110

MINI VACUUM CLEANERS AND BROOMS

EUREKA POWERLINE SUPERBROOM 296A

✔ BEST BUY

Most electric brooms are not very powerful, but the Powerline Superbroom is stronger and quieter than the others. Its efficient 6-amp motor makes it suitable for light tasks (spills or quick cleanups), and electronic speed-control dials adjust and regulate its power for specific cleaning tasks. A floor nozzle with a two-position adjustable brush and an edge cleaner make the unit easier to use on both carpet and bare floors, and its light weight (about 6⅓ pounds), 20-foot cord, and built-in carrying handle make cleaning stairs a breeze. But a 1.8-quart dust cup is the best feature of this electric broom—no need to change bags, although you do have to empty the cup frequently.

Warranty: 1 year, limited.

Manufacturer's Suggested Retail Price: $80

Approximate Low Price: $60

EUREKA CORVETTE VAC 52A ✔BEST BUY

Don't be fooled by the Eureka Corvette Vac's slick styling: It's a real workhorse. The 2-amp motor that directly drives the brush roll is efficient at sucking up dirt and dust, and the front visor that houses the brush can be placed in a horizontal or vertical position to reach nooks, crannies, and crevices. A long cord (25 feet) and low weight (4 pounds) give the unit maximum mobility. One of the Corvette Vac's most appealing features is the easy-to-empty clear plastic dust cup that takes the place of a dust bag. The bright red unit comes with no additional tools, but two different accessory sets (the Corvette Attachment Set with three tools for cars or the Mini-Tool Attachment set with seven tools for the home and for electronic equipment) are available separately and greatly increase the vac's versatility.

Warranty: 1 year, limited.

Manufacturer's Suggested Retail Price: $50

Approximate Low Price: $30

ROYAL DIRT DEVIL BROOM VAC BV2000 ✔BEST BUY

This newly released product looks like a high-tech broom—and that's exactly what it is: a cordless, rechargeable stick vac that sweeps and vacuums at the same time. It's shaped like its old-fashioned kin, but the base that holds the two rows of sweeping bristles is much larger since it also houses the motor (which is in the center of the unit's bristles where it can suck up dirt and dust as you sweep). The unit is almost as lightweight as a real broom (3.5 pounds) and has a telescoping handle that adjusts to its user's preferred position, a toe-push switch on top of the base, and a dirt compartment and filter instead of a vacuum bag. Four nickel-cadmium battery cells provide a full 10 minutes of suction power for sweeping, and the unit includes a wall-mounted charging base. This truly innovative vacuum is especially helpful for anyone with a bad back, because it totally eliminates any need for bending. It's also an ideal tool for cleaning dry spills from bare floors.

Warranty: 2 years.

Manufacturer's Suggested Retail Price: $50

Approximate Low Price: $50

ALL-PURPOSE CLEANING MACHINES

HOOVER STEAMVAC DELUXE F5861-900 ✔BEST BUY

The Hoover SteamVac is configured as an upright, which brings the ease and convenience of upright vacuuming to deep steam cleaning for carpets and upholstery (these units have traditionally resembled canister vacs). This machine also features a unique configuration, which enables it to clean in forward and reverse motion, and a five-brush agitator for removing embedded dirt. A two-tank design (the upper tank for cleaning solution and the bottom tank for dirty-water recovery) eliminates the need for faucet hook-ups (use hot tap water and cleaning fluid), while a handle with a trigger controls how much hot cleaning solution is sprayed into the carpet. At 21.7 pounds (with hose and cord), the SteamVac is lightweight enough to carry and has several outstanding features that make it easy to use: large, simple latches to empty the recovery tank; easy-roll wheels for maneuverability; an 8-foot hose-and-nozzle attachment that quickly converts the unit for cleaning carpeted stairs and upholstery; see-through tanks; a built-in measuring cup; a toe-pedal handle release; a brush-speed selector; and a 33-foot, quick-release power cord.

Warranty: 1 year.

Manufacturer's Suggested Retail Price: $290

Approximate Low Price: $227

ROYAL DIRT DEVIL WET-DRY PLUS
081600

✓ **BEST BUY**

Royal's Wet-Dry Plus units are superb performers that incorporate all the essential features of a good all-purpose cleaning machine. They handle chores above and beyond the scope of the typical vacuum, such as picking up chunks of dirt or sucking up large spills—or small floods. The 081600 model offers on-board tool storage and useful accessories—a long power cord, an exceptionally stable design, a wide hose, and a detachable blower—and is relatively easy to use. Nevertheless, wet-drys are noisier, heavier, and harder to maneuver than regular vacs, and this unit is no exception. They do a very good job, however, at the special tasks they are intended for. The 081600 has a 20-foot cord, a 16-gallon capacity, and a 5.0-peak-horsepower motor, and is equipped with two wands, two extra-wide 7-foot hoses, and tools for floors, crevices, and upholstery. This model also has a removable tool caddy, an extra-wide wheel base (thanks to its "outboard" design), and an easy-to-use tank drainage system.

Warranty: 2 years.

Manufacturer's Suggested Retail Price: $120

Approximate Low Price: Not available

BISSELL BIG GREEN CLEAN MACHINE
1671-Y

Recommended

Bissell calls its Big Green Clean Machine "the one for all," which it may very well be. This three-function cleaning system takes the wet-dry vac to a new level: use it for both wet and dry vacuuming as well as for heavy-duty deep cleaning. With a 2-gallon capacity, it's much smaller than other wet vacs, but it's also much more maneuverable thanks to its small size and easy-to-lift design (a huge handle sits right on top). It can be used for dry vacuuming (unlike other deep-cleaning units); it contains a washable, reusable dry filter, which eliminates the need for bags; and it is equipped with a high-pressure pump for deep cleaning. A built-in brush can be used to tackle stubborn stains, and a varied supply of tools enables the user to clean upholstery, stairs, and crevices (and even to unclog sinks). The extra-long cord (18 feet) and flex hose (8 feet) are a big bonus.

Warranty: 2 years.

Manufacturer's Suggested Retail Price: $190

Approximate Low Price: $190

BISSELL LITTLE GREEN DELUXE 1653-6 | Recommended

Bissell's Little Green Deluxe is a portable home cleaner just about the size of a cosmetics case. It has a small handle right on top because it's actually meant to be carried from task to task. Given its size, range of features, and reasonable price, it's an extremely attractive buy for household maintenance, useful for deep cleaning carpet and upholstery or cleaning glass surfaces and leaving them streak-free. To those ends, it has a high-pressure spray to loosen dirt; a built-in brush to scrub spots and stains; powerful suction to extract dirt and moisture; and special tools for cleaning glass, stairs, and crevices. The unit is self-contained (no faucet hook-ups necessary), compact, and lightweight (under 10 pounds).

Warranty: 1 year.

Manufacturer's Suggested Retail Price: $120

Approximate Low Price: $98

LAUNDRY CARE

Like so many other industries, the laundry care business changes quickly. Despite any changes the industry has already made, saving energy is still a major issue for consumers in 1997. Therefore, one of the most important pieces of information about a washer or dryer is how much energy it uses. Look closely at any machine and you'll quickly discover its energy-saving features, which are usually built around an eye-catching name or phrase.

Which machine is right for you? Price point and personal needs figure into the buying process. Prices range from $250 for a low-end machine to over $1,800 for a designer-style washer with every conceivable feature. In addition to price, you should consider the type of clothing you own. If you favor permanent press fabrics, buy a dryer with a permanent press cycle. If you prefer delicate materials, consider a washer with a hand-wash option.

Counting Cycles

Determining how many cycles a specific washer actually has is akin to doing higher math. Total washer cycles are counted as the number of time-settings labeled normal, heavy, and permanent press multiplied by the number of speed combinations available for each setting. If there are no time-settings labeled, it counts as one cycle multiplied by the speeds. To this is added one cycle each for prewash, soak, manual second rinse, and automatic second rinse, regardless of the number of speeds available. Using this system to determine the number of cycles can yield a surprisingly high number, and this type of information is basically a marketing tool conceived by the manufacturers. For consumers, the best policy may be to look for what types of cycles a machine has, rather than for the actual number.

Gas or Electric Machines

Whether you buy an electric or gas unit depends on which energy source you have in your home. Both gas and electric dryers come in full-size and compact models. Small-capacity, portable, electric units are also available. Gas dryers must be permanently installed because they require attachment to a gas line and must be vented to the outside. Most gas models include an energy-saving electronic-ignition system, so there is no pilot light. In general, gas dryers cost up to $50 more than electric models.

Washer Features and Terminology

Capacity: Tub sizes range from 1½ to 3½ cubic feet. Machines with extra-large capacity boast over 3 cubic feet; large capacity, 2½ to 3 cubic feet; regular or standard capacity, 2 cubic feet; and compact, 1½ cubic feet.

Controls: The new wave in appliances is digital controls. You'll find them on radios, televisions, audio units, and even washers and dryers. While the appearance is upscale, the performance can be below that of more traditional push-button and rotary dial units. The best advice may come from appliance repair service technicians. Most agree that reliability still favors push-button or rotary dial machines.

Cycles: Commonly found cycles are heavy, regular, permanent press, delicate, and soak. Cycles can be automatic or set prior to washing.

Lint filter: All units have lint filters. Their primary purpose is to strain lint out of the rinse water and keep it off your clothes. Many machines have self-cleaning filters. Others catch lint in a basket, which must be cleaned manually. Which is best? Both work well, but consider whether your wash water empties into a home septic or sewer system. If it goes into a septic system, you may not want the extra material flowing into it.

Load balance stabilizer: When a load becomes unbalanced, some washers sound a warning, others shut off, and still others slow down and automatically correct the problem. A buzzer is generally the most effective warning, provided you are able to hear it.

Speed: Most washers have two speeds: high and low. Others offer combinations such as normal agitate/normal spin, and slow agitate/slow spin.

Water temperature: All machines carry a number of wash-rinse water temperature settings based on combining hot, warm, and cold water. The most energy efficient is a cold water cycle. Warm water rinse is better for clothes than hot water, which is best for soaking heavily soiled white clothes.

Dryer Features and Terminology

Air fluff: This feature, which is commonly used for pillows, blankets, and towels, tumbles the load without heat to make items soft.

Controls: There are three types of controls. Timed controls permit you to run the machine for an hour or longer. Automatic controls can be set for the desired degree of dryness. Electronic controls sense when the load is dry and shut off the machine.

Drying cycles: The three basic cycles are regular, permanent press, and delicate. Permanent press has a cool-down period of about 5 minutes, during which time the drum rotates with the heat off. This cycle minimizes wrinkles and brings the load to room temperature. The delicate cycle runs on low heat and offers the least amount of wear and tear on clothing.

Drying rack: This feature has limited uses, but you'll be glad to have one when you're drying sneakers. If you dry these items without a rack, you will risk damaging the inside of your machine.

Drying sensor: This feature prevents overdrying, but the sensor also detects moisture content in the clothes or in the dryer's exhaust and shuts off the unit when the humidity reaches a specific level.

Lint filter: This feature catches lint as the load is drying. The filter should be accessible and easy to clean. Some dryers signal when the filter needs cleaning. The most common locations for filter screens are in the front around the dryer opening or on top of the dryer.

Wrinkle prevention: Ever unload your dryer long after it stopped only to find wrinkles in the clothes? If so, then you may want to invest in this feature, which continues to tumble the load intermittently without heat for up to 2½ hours. On some models, a buzzer sounds at intervals during this period.

Irons

Today's easy-care clothing and modern dryers almost eliminate wrinkles. However, from time to time you will probably find
yourself touching up some articles of clothing with an iron. Fortunately, modern irons are equipped with several features that
make ironing easier than ever before. Fingertip controls regulate features such as heat settings, mist, and steam. All irons in
this section offer automatic shutoff if the iron is left unmoved
for more than about 8 to 10 minutes, or if the iron is tipped
over. Factors to consider when purchasing an iron are soleplate
choices, steam options, and cord storing facilities. Other desirable features include a clear water reservoir so you can monitor the water level, a spray button, and a smooth stick-free
glide. Modern irons are user-friendly and are available in a variety of sizes, shapes, and weights to meet the varied demands
of busy people.

Best Buys '97

Our Best Buy, Recommended, and Budget Buy washers, dryers, and irons follow. For washers and dryers, we've arranged
our selections in subcategories according to size, including
extra-large, large, standard, and compact capacity. Another
section covers an over-and-under combination. Remember that
a Best Buy, Recommended, or Budget Buy designation does not
necessarily apply to other models made by the same manufacturer.

WASHERS

Extra-Large-Capacity Washers

GENERAL ELECTRIC WWSR3090T
✔**BEST BUY**

The General Electric WWSR3090T is a high-
quality, extra-large-capacity washer with a spacious 3.2-cubic-
foot basket. This model has three wash/spin speed
combinations, four water-level settings, and four wash/rinse
temperature combinations. It offers seven automatic cycles:

power wash, heavy soil, medium soil, light soil, permanent press, knits, and auto soak. Other useful features include an automatic load-balance compensation, a self-cleaning lint filter, dispensers for bleach and fabric softener, and an extra-rinse option. It is available in white-on-white or almond-on-almond.

Specifications: height, 42"; width, 27"; depth, 25½"; volts/amps, 115/9.5. **Warranty:** 1 year, full on the auto-balance suspension system, transmission, lid and cover; 5 years, limited on outer tub; 10 years, limited on basket; 20 years, limited overall.

Manufacturer's Suggested Retail Price: $489

Approximate Low Price: Not available

SEARS KENMORE 26952   ✔BEST BUY

A popular clothes washer, the Sears 26952 is an extra-large-capacity machine. This model has three intermittent motor speeds, electronic water levels, an electronic speed switch, and electronic touch controls. To meet all your laundry needs, the 26952 offers an amazing 23 automatic cycles and options, including regular, permanent press, heavy duty, six automatic soak cycles, handwash, delicate, six automatic prewash cycles, soak, second rinse, spin, and a handy wrinkle-guard cycle. Other useful features include automatic temperature control, a triple action agitator, an end-of-cycle signal, a self-cleaning lint filter, automatic dispensers for detergent, bleach and fabric softener, and a double-coated porcelain steel wash tub. A bag for your delicates comes with this machine, which is available in white-on-white, almond-on-almond, or black-on-black.

Specifications: height, 43⅛"; width, 26⅞"; depth, 25½"; volts/amps 120/10. **Warranty:** 1 year, full.

Manufacturer's Suggested Retail Price: $750

Approximate Low Price: $750

SEARS KENMORE 26842   ✔BEST BUY

A reliable extra-large-capacity washer, the Sears Kenmore 26842 offers a basket capacity of 3.0 cubic feet. An exclusive feature on this model is Sears' trademarked dual-action agitator, which moves the clothes twice around the tub. The agitator pushes the clothes to the surface and then pulls them down again, gently lifting out soil. The machine's wash-action cycle includes regular, heavy duty, delicate, hand wash-able, and hang dry settings. The ultra-clean cycle includes prewash, soak, normal, and permanent press settings. The ultra clean cycle works in conjunction with the wash-action cycle to let you select your preferred wash option based on the fabric type. There are 16 cycle combinations altogether. This model also has variable water-level settings and automatic tempera-ture control. Other notable features on the 26842 include an effective insulation package for quieter operation, a self-cleaning lint filter, dispensers for bleach and fabric softener, and a double-coated porcelain wash tub. It is available in white-on-white or almond-on-almond.

Specifications: height, 43⅛"; width, 27"; depth, 25½"; volts/amps 120/10. **Warranty:** 1 year, full.

Manufacturer's Suggested Retail Price: $560

Approximate Low Price: $560

ADMIRAL LATA200

Recommended

A fine quality, extra-large-capacity clothes washer, the LATA200 offers a 3.1-cubic-foot tub. Admiral describes this size washer as a "super capacity" machine. With its two-speed, ¾-horsepower motor, it can wash 20 pounds in one load, and the solid-base design, motor mountings, and one-piece agitator make for quiet operation. Admiral's washers use a turbo-power agitator, which moves in a 202-degree arc to create effective washing action as clothes are moved back and forth as well as up and down. The LATA200 has variable water level settings and four wash/rinse temperature combinations. This model offers three automatic cycles: cotton & linen, per-manent press, and knits & delicates. Its rotary control dials are durable and easy to use. Other useful features include a self-cleaning lint filter, dispensers for bleach and fabric softener, and self-leveling legs. The LATA200 is available in white or almond.

Specifications: height, 44"; width, 27"; depth, 27"; volts/amps, 120/11.5. **Warranty:** 1 year, parts and labor; 10 years, transmission (parts); 20 years, inner wash basket and tub (parts).

Manufacturer's Suggested Retail Price: $399

Approximate Low Price: $399

Large-Capacity Washers

AMANA LW8201

The Amana LW8201, a reliable large-capacity ✔**BEST BUY** clothes washer, sports a basket capacity of 2.68 cubic feet. This model has two wash/spin speeds, variable water-level settings, and three wash/rinse temperature combinations (hot/cold, warm/cold, and cold/cold). The seven automatic cycle options featured on this machine are regular-heavy, regular-normal, regular-light, permanent press-normal, permanent press-light, delicate-normal, and delicate-light. The rotary controls may not be as contemporary looking as digital controls, but they will be more durable. Other notable features include a self-cleaning lint filter, self-adjusting rear leveling legs, dispensers for detergent and fabric softener, and a stainless steel tub. This washer is available in white or almond.

Specifications: height, 43¼"; width, 25⅝"; depth, 28"; volts/amps, 120/15. **Warranty:** 2 years, full; 5 years, full on transmission; 5 years, limited against rust on entire cabinet; 10 years, limited on transmission; 20 years, limited on stainless steel tub.

Manufacturer's Suggested Retail Price: $479

Approximate Low Price: Not available

Standard-Capacity Washers

MAGIC CHEF W225

For a top-quality standard-capacity washer, you ✔**BEST BUY** could do little better than the Magic Chef W225. With a range of basic features, this model should suit the needs of a single person or small family. The W225, which has a two-speed motor, offers three speed settings, three water-level settings, and three wash/rinse temperature combinations. This model offers eight automatic cycles: cotton/linen—heavy, normal, and light; permanent press—heavy, normal, and light; and delicate—normal and light. Other notable features include an automatic load-balance compensation, a self-cleaning lint filter, and a dispenser for bleach. The tub is made of a durable co-polymer. The Magic Chef W225 standard-capacity washer is available in white or almond.

Specifications: height, 44"; width, 27"; depth, 27"; volts/amps, 120/15. **Warranty:** 1 year, parts and labor; 10 years, replacement on parts related to transmission; 22 years, parts on tub.

Manufacturer's Suggested Retail Price: $465

Approximate Low Price: $426

Compact Washers

SANYO ASW36NP

✔BEST BUY

For a quality compact washer, the Sanyo ASW36NP offers several features for a reasonable price. This model features two wash/spin speeds (normal and gentle), four water-level settings, and two wash/rinse temperature combinations. There are three automatic cycles: fully automatic, drip dry, and wash only. This model offers several useful features, including automatic load-balance compensation, a lint filter, and a dispenser for fabric softener. The poly washtub is durable. The Sanyo ASW36NP does not require plumbing: Simply attach the water supply line to the sink faucet and drain the waste water into a sink. This model comes in white only.

Specifications: height, 23¹¹⁄₁₆"; width, 27⁹⁄₁₆"; depth, 23⁷⁄₁₆"; volts/amps, 120/15. **Warranty:** 1 year, parts and labor.

Manufacturer's Suggested Retail Price: $420

Approximate Low Price: $417

Over/Under Combinations

FRIGIDAIRE FLSG 72GC (GAS)/
FLSE 72GC (ELECTRIC)

✓**BEST BUY**

Frigidaire's FLSG 72GC/FLSE 72GC represents a high-quality washer/dryer system. This unit contains a ¾-horsepower, 2-speed motor. The washer offers three wash/spin speed combinations, four wash/rinse temperature combinations, and variable water-level settings. The ten automatic wash cycles cover most washing needs: There are four regular cycles, three permanent-press cycles, a knits/delicate cycle, a soak cycle, and prewash. This machine offers several desirable features, including automatic load-balance compensation, a self-cleaning lint filter, dispensers for bleach and fabric softener, and a helpful safety lid lock. The tub and basket are made of durable polypropylene. The dryer has four timed dry cycles, three automatic dry cycles, and four temperature settings. You'll find the wrinkle-prevention feature a handy addition to this model. For added convenience, the dryer boasts an interior drum light, a drying rack, and an end-of-cycle signal. This unit is available in white or almond.

Specifications: height, 75½"; width, 27"; depth, 30¹³⁄₁₆"; volts/amps (gas), 120/20; watts/volts/amps (electric), 4,500/240/30; gas dryer heating element, 20,000 Btu. **Warranty:** 2 years, parts and labor; 25 years, tub.

Manufacturer's Suggested Retail Price: $1,090 (gas); $1,030 (electric)

Approximate Low Price: $1,090 (gas); $1,016 (electric)

WHIRLPOOL LTG5243D (GAS)/
LTE5243D (ELECTRIC)

Budget Buy

For those in search of an economical over/under combination washer/dryer, Whirlpool's LTG5243D/LTE5243D should fit the bill. The washer has a 1.5-cubic-foot-capacity polypropylene wash tub and offers two wash/spin speed combinations. It has four wash/rinse temperature combinations and three water-level settings. This model offers five automatic wash cycles: super wash, regular/heavy, permanent press, delicate, and soak. Other notable features include an easy-to-clean lint filter and a corrugated drain hose. The clothes dryer features a 3.4-cubic-foot-capacity drum, five timed dry cycles, a push-to-start button, and a 180-degree side-swing door. The dryer also has an end-of-cycle signal and an easy-to-clean lint screen. This system is available in white or almond.

Specifications: height, 71¾"; width, 23⅞"; depth, 27¼"; volts/amps (gas), 120/15; watts/volts/amps (electric), 3,600/240/30; gas dryer heating element, 10,500 Btu. **Warranty:** 1 year, parts and labor; 5 years, replacement parts related to top rust and gearcase assembly; 10 years, parts on the outer tub.

Manufacturer's Suggested Retail Price: $899

Approximate Low Price: $881

DRYERS

Large-Capacity Dryers

SEARS KENMORE 66902 (ELECTRIC)/ 76902 (GAS)

✓**BEST BUY**

The Sears Kenmore 66902/76902 has a capacity of 7.0 cubic feet. This dryer offers 12 cycles, including such convenient choices as air dry, soft heat, and wrinkle prevention. These models have five temperature settings, including air only. An end-of-cycle alarm with a variable volume control alerts you when the cycle is complete. The lint filter has an audible alarm, which goes off when the front-mounted screen requires cleaning. Extra frills on this model include an interior drum light and a heated drying rack. These units feature four-way rear venting (up, down, left, or right) and an insulation package for quieter operation. Available colors are white-on-white, almond-on-almond, and black-on-white.

Specifications: height, 43⅛"; width, 27"; depth, 27¾"; volts/amps (gas), 120/6; watts/volts/amps (electric), 5,600/240/27; gas heating element, 22,000 Btu. **Warranty:** 1 year, parts and labor.

Manufacturer's Suggested Retail Price: $500
Approximate Low Price: $399 (electric); $449 (gas)

FRIGIDAIRE GALLERY FDG847GE (GAS)/ FDE847GE (ELECTRIC)

✔BEST BUY

The top-quality Frigidaire Gallery FDG847GE/ FDE847GE is a 5.5-cubic-foot-capacity model that offers two-way tumble drying. Six automatic cycles, including permanent press, extended cool-down, and refresher, should satisfy most of your drying needs. The FDG847GE/FDE847GE has four timed drying cycles: regular, permanent press, knits/delicate, and air fluff. There are four basic temperature options: high, medium, low, and air fluff/no heat. In addition to such useful features as a drying rack, an internal drum light, and an easy-to-clean lint screen, this model boasts an end-of-cycle signal with adjustable volume and a safety start button. There are three venting options for the gas model and four for the electric unit. Both models are available in white-on-white or almond-on-almond.

Specifications: height, 44"; width, 26⅞"; depth, 27"; volts/amps (gas), 115/15; watts/volts/amps (electric), 4,500/240/30; gas heating element, 25,500 Btu. **Warranty:** 2 years, full.

Manufacturer's Suggested Retail Price: $480 (gas); $420 (electric)

Approximate Low Price: $421 (gas); $379 (electric)

KITCHENAID SUPERBA KGYW770B (GAS)/ KEYW770B (ELECTRIC)

✔BEST BUY

The KitchenAid Superba KGYW770B/ KEYW770B is a reliable clothes dryer with a basket capacity of 6.8 cubic feet. The automatic cycles available on this machine are regular/heavy, permanent press (with cool-down), air tumble, and quick press. A time-dry feature, with a range of 0 to 70 minutes, is a bonus. There are five temperature selections. Other useful features include a drying rack, an end-of-cycle signal with adjustable volume, an internal drum light, a top-mounted lint screen with an audible signal, and a safety start button.

There are three venting options for the gas model and four for the electric unit. An optional fabric softener sheet dispenser is available as an accessory. The KGYW770B/KEYW770B is available in white-on-white, black-on-white, and almond-on-almond.

Specifications: height, 42"; width, 29"; depth, 27¾"; volts/amps (gas), 120/6; watts/volts/amps (electric), 5,400/240/30; gas heating element, 22,000 Btu. **Warranty:** 1 year, parts and labor.

Manufacturer's Suggested Retail Price: $589 (gas); $539 (electric)

Approximate Low Price: $515 (gas); $466 (electric)

WHIRLPOOL LGR8858E (GAS)/ LER88588E (ELECTRIC)

✔ **BEST BUY**

The super-capacity LGR8858E/LER8858E by Whirlpool offers 6.8 cubic feet of space. A moisture sensor detects the amount of moisture in the load and shuts the dryer down when the preset level of moisture is reached, thus conserving energy. This model boasts eight drying cycles, including such convenient cycles as timed drying, damp dry, and fluff air. The temperature settings are high, medium, low, delicate, and air dry. Other desirable features include an on/off end-of-cycle signal, an extra-large top-mounted lint screen, and durable rotary controls. The LGR8858E/LER8858E is available in white-on-white and almond-on-almond.

Specifications: height, 42⅜"; width, 29"; depth (gas), 28³⁄₁₆", (electric) 27¹³⁄₁₆"; volts/amps (gas), 120/6; watts/volts/amps (electric), 5,400/240/30; gas heating element, 22,000 Btu. **Warranty:** 1 year, parts and labor.

Manufacturer's Suggested Retail Price: $399

Approximate Low Price: $389

WHIRLPOOL LGR5636E (GAS)/ LER5636E (ELECTRIC)

✔ **BEST BUY**

Slightly lower-priced than Whirlpool's LGR8858E/LER8858E, the LGR5636E/LER5636E is a quality dryer with a 6.5-cubic-foot-capacity basket. It offers a moisture sensor that will assess the amount of moisture in a load and shut the dryer down when a preset level of moisture is reached. This machine features five drying cycles and three temperature settings. Other notable features include an extra-large top-mounted lint screen and durable rotary controls. This dryer is available in white-on-white and almond-on-almond.

Specifications: height, 42⅜"; width, 29"; depth (gas), 28³⁄₁₆", (electric)27¹³⁄₁₆"; volts/amps (gas), 115/15; watts/volts/amps (electric), 5,400/240/30; gas heating element, 22,000 Btu. **Warranty:** 1 year, parts and labor.

Manufacturer's Suggested Retail Price: $339

Approximate Low Price: $339

Standard-Capacity Dryers

HOTPOINT NJLR473GT (GAS)/
NJLR473ET (ELECTRIC)

✔**BEST BUY**

An enticing feature of Hotpoint's NJLR473GT/ NJLR473ET is the automatic dry control, which monitors the moisture level and ends the cycle when the clothes are properly dried. This feature saves you time and energy. This top-quality dryer offers seven automatic cycles, including optional cotton press guard, timed dry (up to 80 minutes), and dewrinkle. There are four temperature selections. Other desirable features on the NJLR473GT/NJLR473ET include an interior light and a removable lint screen on the front. An optional press-guard feature helps to prevent wrinkles. There are three venting options for the gas model and four for the electric unit. Available in white or almond with a black backsplash.

Specifications: height, 42"; width, 27"; depth 25¾"; volts/amps (gas), 120/15; watts/volts/amps (electric), 5,600/240/30; gas heating element, 22,000 Btu. **Warranty:** 1 year, full.

**Manufacturer's Suggested Retail Price: $329 (gas);
$299 (electric)**

Approximate Low Price: $329 (gas); $299 (electric)

ASKO 7705

Recommended

The Asko 7705 is a high-quality standard-capacity electric dryer that features a condenser to collect moisture, so conventional venting is not required. This well-made machine offers drying cycles that are controlled by moisture sensors. There are four drying cycles: extra dry, normal dry, damp dry, and iron dry. In addition, anticrease, low heat, and timed drying (5 to 90 minutes) programs are also available. Other notable features on the 7705 include a nonvariable volume end-of-cycle signal, a large door-mounted lint screen, a lint screen cleaning alarm, wrinkle prevention, air fluff drying, and a delay start (up to 12 hours). The 7705 features a stainless steel drum and electronic controls, and is available in white only. The hefty price makes this a Recommended selection rather than a Best Buy. Vented units are available at a lower cost.

Specifications: height, 33½"; width, 23½"; depth 23¾"; watts/volts/amps, 3,150/220/30. **Warranty:** 1 year, full; 5 years, solid state controls, pumps, and motors; 25 years, stainless steel drum tank from rust.

Manufacturer's Suggested Retail Price: $1,199

Approximate Low Price: $1,167

FRIGIDAIRE FDG336RE (GAS)/
FDE336RE (ELECTRIC)

Budget Buy

The Frigidaire FDG336RE/FDE336RE is a reliable standard-capacity dryer. It has one automatic cycle and three timed drying cycles. In addition, there are four temperature options: high, medium, low, and air fluff/no heat. Other notable features include a quick-clean lint screen and a safety start button. There are three venting options for the gas model and four for the electric unit. The FDG336RE/FDE336RE is available in white-on-white and almond-on-almond.

Specifications: height, 44"; width, 26⅞"; depth, 25¾"; volts/amps (gas), 110/15; watts/volts/amps (electric), 4,500/240/30; gas heating element, 20,000 Btu. **Warranty:** 1 year, parts and labor.

Manufacturer's Suggested Retail Price: $364 (gas); $320 (electric)

Approximate Low Price: $340 (gas); $298 (electric)

Compact Dryer

SANYO CD25UT

✔**BEST BUY**

The Sanyo CD25UT is a dependable, compact, electric clothes dryer that is well-suited for locations where venting is not possible, because it is duct-free. This model features semiconductor-controlled heating with automatic temperature control. There is a setting for air fluff drying, and a postcycle automatic cool-down feature to minimize wrinkles. Other notable features include a removable rack for drying sneakers, a door-mounted lint filter, an adjustable (forward/reverse) 2-hour timer, and a poly drum. This unit can be stacked on top of the Sanyo ASW36NP washer with the help of an accessory steel rack (Sanyo SDS926).

Specifications: height, 25³⁄₁₆"; width, 25³⁄₁₆"; depth 13¹¹⁄₁₆"; watts/volts/amps, 1,450/120/15. **Warranty:** 1 year, parts and labor.

Manufacturer's Suggested Retail Price: $300

Approximate Low Price: $300

IRONS

ROWENTA DE-283 CLIP-UP

✔**BEST BUY**

The Rowenta DE-283 Clip-Up is a well-constructed, easy-to-use, self-cleaning iron with many features not found on other irons. The most notable is a stainless steel soleplate that improves the appliance's ability to glide by 50 percent when compared with coated soleplates. Another feature unique to the Clip-Up is a detachable, transparent water tank. This popular feature allows you to remove the water-fill compartment and then reattach it after filling, to prevent you from spilling water on the rest of the iron. This feature also keeps water from leaking and scalding clothing and hands. An extendable heel provides convenient cord storage and offers greater stability. The power cord extends from the rear center of the handle rather than from the right as with many irons, which helps to prevent the cord from tangling. Fingertip controls allow the user to spray a cool mist or a powerful burst of steam to remove stubborn wrinkles. Steam and heat settings can be set for different types of fabrics. A unique dual-time, multiposition automatic-off feature shuts off the iron in 8 minutes if it is left upright, or in 30 seconds if it is tipped over. The many convenient features on this ultramodern iron will meet the varied demands of even the busiest people.

Warranty: 1 year.

Manufacturer's Suggested Retail Price: $90

Approximate Low Price: Not available

ROWENTA PROFESSIONAL DE-871

Recommended

The Rowenta Professional DE-871 is capable of almost any ironing task you can imagine. This well-balanced, self-cleaning iron has a ten-step variable steam feature that allows you to dial settings from light steam for delicate fabrics to constant steam for heavy fabrics. There is even a vertical steam setting for special pressing needs. In addition, a button can be pressed for a burst of steam to remove stubborn wrinkles. Another button can be pressed to spray a cool mist. A wide, stainless steel soleplate improves the iron's ability to glide by up to 50 percent when compared with coated soleplates. A wide, stable heel provides cord storage. There is a large transparent water tank, which provides a clear view of the water level. A unique dual-time, multiposition, automatic-off feature shuts off the iron in 8 minutes if it is left vertical, or in 30 seconds if it is tipped over. The automatic shutoff feature is an important safety consideration for any home, but it is essential in a home with small children. Only the hefty price tag makes the Rowenta Professional DE-871 a Recommended product rather than a Best Buy.

Warranty: 1 year.

Manufacturer's Suggested Retail Price: $120

Approximate Low Price: $104

BLACK & DECKER SURGEXPRESS X690 ~~Recommended~~

The SurgeXpress X690 is a lightweight, easy-to-use iron with several convenient features. Fingertip buttons are included for spraying mist, activating a surge of steam, and cleaning. The SurgeXpress X690 also boasts automatic shutoff if the iron is not moved in 10 minutes, and adjustable steam control. This iron is filled or emptied through a convenient slot in the face, and a clear plastic tank makes it easy to check the water level. The Silverstone, nonstick, coated soleplate has a full-length button groove. When the surge button is pressed, water is quickly heated and surges from the soleplate steam holes to remove even the most stubborn wrinkles. This same button can be adjusted for a spray of mist. The 8-foot, pivoting electrical cord is an added convenience.

Warranty: 2 years, full.

Manufacturer's Suggested Retail Price: $67

Approximate Low Price: $42

BLACK & DECKER QUICK 'N EASY 480 ~~Budget Buy~~

The Quick 'N Easy 480 is a lightweight, easy-to-use iron with several popular features usually found on more expensive units. These include fingertip buttons for a spray of mist or a surge of steam, and automatic shutoff if the iron is not moved within an hour. When the control dial is turned to the off position, an exclusive valve feature automatically clears the steam valve of any microscopic water and fiber deposits. This adds life to the iron by eliminating clogged valves, the most common cause of iron failure. This iron is filled or emptied through a convenient slot in the nose, and a small, clear plastic window makes it easy to check the water level. The soleplate is Silverstone-coated and has a full-length button groove. When you press the surge button, heated water surges from the soleplate steam holes to quickly remove wrinkles. A separate button can be pressed for a spray of mist. A colorful rhubarb trim color is used for the buttons, dial, and logo on a shiny white base.

Warranty: 2 years.

Manufacturer's Suggested Retail Price: $48

Approximate Low Price: $32

SEWING MACHINES

Basic machine-stitch formation hasn't changed in the 150 years since Elias Howe patented the sewing machine. What has changed are the machine's capabilities beyond the basic straight stitch and the ease with which it can accomplish an ever-increasing variety of sewing techniques on a wide range of fabrics.

Even if you'll never use half the stitches available on today's models, you will appreciate their time- and effort-saving features: electronic control, stronger motors, improved feeding systems, jam-free hooks, and more consistent thread tension. Easier operation often expands the fabric choices and techniques you're able to try. If you've avoided sewing silky fabric, for example, or garments with buttonholes because your machine can't handle them, it's time for an upgrade. At the upper price range, hobbyists are discovering new pleasure in elaborate hooped embroidery, previously possible only on professional equipment but now standard on several top-of-the-line home models.

Before you buy, spend time alone at various machines sewing with your preferred fabrics. How does each machine feel and sound? Does it sew balanced stitches without skipping or jamming, even on hard-to-sew fabrics? How easily and well does it stitch a buttonhole? Examine the owner's manual for readability. Compare any problems and suggested solutions of the various machines you test. Perform the same tests on all machines for a fair comparison.

As you shop, assess dealers' knowledge, services, and reputation as well. After all, few appliances involve as many variables for proper operation—thread, fabric, needle, technique—as sewing machines. What kind of lessons do dealers offer? Will they be able to help you with sewing problems? Do they have on-site parts and repair services? Will they keep you up-to-date on new accessories and techniques? Will they stand behind the product if you're not satisfied? Ask about their trade-in policy should you decide to upgrade.

Prices may be enticing at discount and mail-order outlets, but information and service can vary greatly or be nonexistent. That's why it's worth the additional expense to buy the machine from a dealer that guarantees continued satisfaction. Otherwise, the warranty can be meaningless when the machine needs service.

Best Buys '97

Our Best Buy, Recommended, and Budget Buy sewing machines follow. They are categorized into two sections: computerized and noncomputerized. Within these categories the product we consider to be the best of the Best Buys is listed first, followed by our second choice, and so on. At the end of the categories, we list some products as Budget Buys. These are products that may not have all the features of a Best Buy or Recommended product but that offer a solid value in terms of performance, features, and price. Remember that a Best Buy, Recommended, or Budget Buy designation applies only to the model listed. It does not necessarily apply to other models made by the same manufacturer.

COMPUTERIZED

Computerized machines feature electronic operation plus a "memory." Select a stitch at the push of a button, and the machine automatically adjusts for the ideal settings (though you can change those settings if you wish). Most models include memory buttonholes, so you can repeat as many identical buttonholes as desired.

Increased computer memory is responsible for the tremendous expansion of the sewing machine's creative capabilities. The excitement began when it became possible to combine, or "program," stitches into elaborate borders or patterns and to "write" with a machine's built-in alphabet and numerals. The latest technology is enabling machines to interface with a personal computer for customizing designs and converting them into stitchery.

VIKING HUSQVARNA #1+

✓BEST BUY

The Viking #1+ is a multipurpose sewing machine that offers professional-quality machine embroidery, an optional computer interface, and efficient features. The embroidery unit and electronically-guided hoop allow for accurate stitching. Insert an embroidery card and its companion cassette to create decorative stitches, combine patterns, enlarge or reduce motifs, or repeat and rotate designs. Optional customizing software, easily installed in your computer, gives you even more embroidery capabilities with three lettering styles and 53 shapes. The optional digitizing software enables you to scan designs in other media to create original embroidery. When you remove the embroidery mechanism from the machine, the #1+ is ready for traditional sewing. Select a stitch with one touch of a button. Enter the weight and type of fabric being sewn, then the technique, and an "advisor" feature automatically sets the correct stitch, length, width, tension, and sewing speed. The display window provides even more sewing guidance to help eliminate guesswork. Five cassettes featuring utility and decorative stitches are included with this model. With 10 buttonhole styles plus special stitches for quilting, heirloom work, appliqué, and more, this machine offers virtually unlimited creativity.

Warranty: 20 years, manufacturer's defective parts; 5 years, electrical; 1 year, parts and labor (original owner only).

Manufacturer's Suggested Retail Price: $3,799

Approximate Low Price: $3,066

BABY LOCK BL9500

✓BEST BUY

Even without hooped embroidery or computer interface, the Baby Lock BL9500 is loaded with creative potential at an affordable price. With 294 built-in stitch patterns, the machine includes two alphabet styles, automatic darning, and automatic basting. The BL9500's stitch patterns are grouped for convenience on the LCD readout screen; just touch to select the category, then scroll through and touch-select the stitch. The extensive selection includes satin stitches, picture motifs, cross stitches, and more. Buttonholes come in three styles and are stitched and sized to the button automatically with the one-step buttonhole foot. Other convenient features include automatic thread-tension control, variable speed, and the "quick-set" bobbin, which simplifies the bobbin and thread setup. The automatic thread cutter cuts both upper and lower threads after stitching and raises the needle to its highest position so that the fabric is ready for removal.

Warranty: 25 years, limited; 1 year, electrical.

Manufacturer's Suggested Retail Price: $1,999

Approximate Low Price: $1,481

PFAFF CREATIVE 7570

Recommended

The Pfaff Creative 7570 may "have it all," but it comes at a price. Pay the price, though, and you have a model of sewing sophistication and versatility. The optional computerized embroidery hoop system allows you to create detailed embroidery patterns up to 120mm wide. This program works with Pfaff's new memory card system to create elaborate monograms, cross-stitches, Richelieu, appliqué, quilting, and hemstitches. Hook up your home computer with the optional stitch design software and custom designing is at your fingertips. For traditional sewing, stitch selection involves a combination of scrolling through menus and pushing buttons. Then the display screen shows you the preprogrammed settings and other sewing facts. An info button, when pressed, displays a help menu. The 7570 also includes a Pfaff exclusive—a built-in dual feed system. This feature promotes even fabric feeding from the top and bottom at the same time. On the creative side, the machine offers more than 500 decorative stitch programs, including 10 buttonhole types, six alphabet styles, and 30 maxi-stitch designs up to 60mm wide.

Warranty: 25 years, mechanical; 2 years, electrical; 1 year, labor.

Manufacturer's Suggested Retail Price: $3,499

Approximate Low Price: $2,766

NEW HOME MEMORY CRAFT 4000 `Recommended`

Only a few years ago, the Memory Craft 4000 would have qualified for top-of-the-line status, but today it has to settle for a few notches down in the New Home line because it has *only* 167 patterns. Still, that's plenty of creative potential for most home sewers, especially at such an affordable price. Besides utility and decorative stitches, the machine includes a block and script alphabet, and most patterns can be memorized consecutively with up to 31 in a combination. The pattern selector panel allows easy push-button stitch selection. The desired stitch appears on the LCD message screen, which indicates the suitable presser foot to use for the stitch. Press the "?" key and the screen shows additional sewing information. The sensor buttonhole foot enables the machine to stitch buttonholes automatically to the right length for the button. You can choose from five styles of standard buttonholes and two styles of elastic buttonholes. Other features include a convenient one-hand thread cutter and automatic tension.

Warranty: 25 years, limited.

Manufacturer's Suggested Retail Price: $1,399

Approximate Low Price: $1,166

VIKING HUSQVARNA 400 LE `Budget Buy`

If you're more interested in the efficient performance of computerized sewing—at a low price—than in an extensive array of stitches, the Viking Husqvarna 400 LE is an excellent choice. Although it features just 30 stitches, they're all you'll need if you work with more traditional sewing. Among the utility stitches is the one-touch mending capability; the decorative options include entredeux and other heirloom stitches. A one-step overlock stitch feature is also included. The 400 LE offers bartack and keyhole buttonholes, both of which can be stitched in one step and memorized for repeat stitching. Stitch selection with this model couldn't be simpler: Just touch the button for the stitch you want and begin sewing. The display window shows you the recommended presser foot and thread tension as well as the preset stitch width and length. These settings can be modified to suit your own sewing needs—the stitch width and length are each adjustable up to 6mm. For customized sewing, you can program a combination of decorative stitches, using the display window to review the design before stitching.

Warranty: 20 years, manufacturer's defective parts; 5 years, electrical; 1 year, parts and labor (original owner only).

Manufacturer's Suggested Retail Price: $999

Approximate Low Price: $799

NONCOMPUTERIZED

Since noncomputerized machines have no memory their stitches are usually less complex than computerized machines, and you have to adjust the stitch length and width manually. But some of these models have electronic circuitry. The most common electronic element is the speed control, which allows full needle penetration power of any fabric weight even at the slowest speed. Electronic control also allows more precise reaction during the start and stop of motion, enabling the machine to make one stitch at a time for precise accuracy.

A mechanical foot control, by contrast, loses power as it loses speed, so it can be difficult to pierce heavy fabrics without "flooring" the foot pedal. Electronic regulation allows constant speed changes without the foot control heating up, thus prolonging sewing machine life. In general, electronic machines are more reliable and quicker to repair than mechanical models since electronic circuitry replaces so many parts.

BABY LOCK PRO LINE BL6600 ✔ BEST BUY

With its LCD information screen, the BL6600 reduces guesswork for the less-experienced home sewer. Select a stitch by turning a dial, then touch the message button and the screen instantly displays the function of the stitch selected. The machine's 21 stitches can be varied with separate stitch width and length controls—a feature not always found at this price range. The built-in buttonholer stitches the buttonhole in one step, sizing it to the button automatically. A variable speed lever makes it possible to limit the speed, while electronics help maintain power at the slower speeds. An electronic needle-stop automatically raises the needle to its highest position for easy fabric removal once sewing stops. As on more advanced Baby Lock models, the BL6600 features the quick-set bobbin system for easy bobbin setup.

Warranty: 25 years, limited on parts; 1 year, electrical.

Manufacturer's Suggested Retail Price: $799

Approximate Low Price: $599

ELNA 3007

Recommended

You'll pay a little more for the Elna 3007, but its appealing assortment of 25 stitches and some surprising features (for this price range) will make it worth the cost. All stitches are not only adjustable in width and length, but the width can be increased up to 6.5mm. This is noticeably larger than most machines offer at this price, and that extra width allows for more attractive decorative stitches. Speed control is electronic and variable via a horizontal sliding lever marked with Elna's trademark settings: tortoise (for slow) and hare (for fast). Besides the electronic needle-up feature, which stops the needle in a high position when sewing is completed, the 3007 also includes an additional button to lower the needle without turning the handwheel. This prevents excess pivoting when sewing decorative work or stitching appliqués. Another unexpected convenience is the automatic needle threader. The one-step automatic buttonhole rounds out this machine's pleasing marriage of convenience and utility.

Warranty: 25 years; 2 years, electrical.

Manufacturer's Suggested Retail Price: $899

Approximate Low Price: $719

NEW HOME JD-1818

Budget Buy

Every household needs a sewing machine for the occasional mending job, Halloween costume, or set of garage curtains. The New Home JD-1818 gives you more features and reliability than most machines at this price. With 18 stitches and a one-step automatic buttonhole, this mechanical machine performs all the most basic sewing operations. The stitch width is preset when you select the stitch with the pattern selector dial, but the length is variable from 0 to 4mm by turning another dial. Other features include a one-hand thread cutter and a hidden tension dial. With upscale lines and contemporary graphics, the JD-1818's pleasing appearance belies its unquestionable economy.

Warranty: 25 years, limited.

Manufacturer's Suggested Retail Price: $569

Approximate Low Price: $418

ENVIRONMENTAL APPLIANCES

Making our home environments comfortable and healthy has become a priority in this modern era of air pollutants, heat indexes, and high pollen counts. These environmental control appliances can help ensure that your house is a clean, comfortable place for you and your family.

Ceiling Fans

Ceiling fans are wonderful for creating a soft breeze in a stuffy room. They come in a great variety of styles and models, from the very elegant to the very functional.

Most fans come with five blades, although four-blade versions are still available. The more blades there are and the longer each blade is, the more air will be circulated. The more air that is circulated, the cooler it will be. The downside is that a ceiling fan can get very noisy in a small room. Check to see how noisy the fan is before you purchase it; try it out in the store and imagine how it will sound in a smaller room.

Most fans have a light kit option. If you decide to add a light afterwards, make sure that you will be able to control the fan and the light independently. This way you can run the fan with or without the light being on. Some fans come with remote controls, which are great for bedroom fans or fans on high ceilings.

An important concern with ceiling fans is how low they hang in a room. If you have low ceilings but would like a ceiling fan, look for one that mounts flush to the ceiling or has blades that extend from the sides of the motor rather than below it.

If you want to use the fan during the winter to redistribute warm air, be sure that it has a reverse operation switch. These are often located on the motor casing, which makes them difficult to access if the fan is on a high ceiling. However, the effectiveness of this feature is questionable. In theory, the reverse speed is supposed to redistribute warm air by pulling up the cold air from the center of the room and circulating the warm air that rises to the ceiling. In practice, too many other factors—including insulation, the outside temperature, and the quality of the fan—affect the unit's ability to do this.

Room Air Conditioners

Do you have just one room that gets unbearably hot? Is your bedroom so hot and stuffy that you can't sleep? A room air conditioner is a fast, easy way to spot-cool your house. Even if you have central air conditioning, a room air conditioner can make a difference. Maybe you have one room that gets hot long before the rest of the house. Why cool the whole house? Just cool that room and save money.

The goal in purchasing a room air conditioner is to buy one with enough cooling capacity for your needs without getting one that is too big. A too-small unit won't cool the room enough. A too-large unit will waste energy and won't dehumidify the room properly. It's better to buy several small units than to use one large air conditioner to cool several rooms.

Areas to be cooled (in square feet)	Cooling capacity needed (in Btu)
up to 150	4,000–5,000
150–250	5,000–6,000
250–450	6,000–8,500
450–600	8,500–11,000
600–900	11,000–14,000
900–1,200	15,000–19,000

Most models are designed for casement-style windows (which open up and down), though models are also available for sliding windows (which open side to side). Be sure to take the measurements of your window opening with you when you shop for a room air conditioner.

When you are shopping, pay close attention to the big yellow Energy Efficiency Ratio (EER) stickers on the front of the units. Since January 1, 1990, the federal government has required all room (window) air conditioners to have an EER of at least 8.0. The EER is computed by dividing cooling capacity, measured in British Thermal Units per hour, or Btu, by the watts of electricity used. The higher the EER, the more efficient the unit, and the less it will cost to operate.

Installation is similar on all window air conditioners. First, you need to install a lightweight case by attaching it to the window frame, and then slide in and secure the heavy cooling unit. Finally, snap on the front cover. When you are installing the unit, be careful not to push together the thin cooling vanes behind the front panel. These are the heat exchangers, and they are very soft. If they do get pushed together, gently separate them with your fingernail or a piece of plastic such as a driver's license or library card.

Instead of installing the air conditioner in a window, you might opt for through-the-wall installation. In a room with only one window, this might be the only way you can retain the use of the window. Through-the-wall installation means cutting a hole in the wall and siding, but it provides a much quieter and more secure installation. There is also less air leakage from through-the-wall installation. Your unit will be more effective in the summertime and will keep the warm air in during the winter. Most units provide instructions for this type of installation. Be sure to check for any additional hardware requirements.

To reduce operating costs and improve the efficiency of your air conditioner, you can cover the outside of the unit with an awning. You could strap a sun shade to it, but a standard window awning will do the trick. Keeping the air conditioner in the shade will make it run less while keeping the room just as cool.

You can extend the life and efficiency of your purchase with just a few minutes of work each month. Maintenance on a room air conditioner is pretty simple. There is a removable air filter hidden in the front panel. Simply pull out the filter, rinse it under running water, let it dry, and put it back. This should be done at the beginning of the air-conditioning season and at least once a month when the unit is in use.

The cooling vanes or coils behind the front cover should be checked for dust at the beginning of each season. These do the actual heat exchange and should be kept as clean as possible. They are very soft and fragile, so be extra careful when dusting them. Separate any vanes or coils that are pushed together with your fingernail or a soft piece of plastic.

Rinse off vents on the exterior of the air conditioner with a hose or bucket of water. This will remove any spider webs and accumulated debris and allow the unit to vent properly. Do check first for any bird or wasp nests.

During the off-season, you may want to cover the exterior of the air conditioner. This will protect the case and reduce the amount of debris that can collect around the unit. In a window installation, this can also reduce the amount of air leakage into the house.

Finally, a word of warning. When the humidity is extra high, you will find a large amount of water dripping from your air conditioner, but don't be alarmed. An air conditioner pushes the heat and humidity from the inside of your house to the outside. Most of the time, the humidity becomes water, which cools the exterior coil of the air conditioner. When the unit takes out humidity faster than it can evaporate off the outside coils, the extra water drips off.

Air Care Appliances

Keeping your home clean and odor-free doesn't just mean dusting the furniture and mopping the floors. It's keeping the air we breathe clean, too. If you live near a high-traffic road or somewhere that is dusty or wet, or if you have allergies or health problems, consider installing an air filter in your home.

Air filters come in several different types, the most common being a HEPA-type room or area filter. HEPA (High Efficiency Particulate Air) filters remove the smallest of pollutants and pollen from the air. A HEPA-type filter looks like a true HEPA filter but is not as densely packed with glass fibers. Both do a good job of cleaning the air, but the true HEPA filter will remove more and smaller particles, up to 99.97 percent of all particulates in the air. If you have asthma or allergies, consider getting a HEPA filter. If you just want to breathe cleaner air, then a HEPA-type filter will perform adequately and cost less.

In addition to cleaning the air, you might want to adjust the humidity in your home, which may be too humid in the summer or too dry in the winter. Two different appliances, humidifiers and dehumidifiers, are available in both room and whole house models.

Do you walk across a room in the winter and get a static electricity snap when you touch a doorknob? Or do you wake up in the morning with a sore throat and dry mouth? If so, then consider purchasing a humidifier. Most are simple to use and maintain and will pay back their cost in reduced health problems.

Dehumidifiers are not just for keeping a basement dry year-round. In the summer, they can help keep your house cool by reducing the amount of moisture in the air. Most room models have "quiet" or "nighttime" settings that do an effective job while letting you sleep comfortably.

Portable Heaters
Portable heaters have come a long way in terms of efficiency, safety, and variety since they were first introduced. You can choose from a selection of different fuels including propane gas, kerosene, and electricity. If you choose a gas or kerosene model, be sure to follow the manufacturer's directions for adequate ventilation. If you choose an electric heater, make sure that you have enough power available so that it doesn't blow a fuse each time it goes on.

Heaters range in size from small models suitable for keeping your feet warm to large units that will warm a two-car garage. Important features to look for are tip-over switches, which shut off the unit if it is knocked over, and hard-to-reach or concealed heating elements. Choose the unit that is easiest for you to move and to fuel.

Keep any heater away from flammable materials, especially curtains, blankets, and other fabrics. Heaters should be used only on firm, flat surfaces.

Best Buys '97
Our Best Buy and Recommended environmental appliances follow. Remember that a Best Buy or Recommended designation applies only to the model listed; it does not apply to other

models made by the same manufacturer or to an entire product line.

CEILING FANS

HUNTER SOJOURN 25874

✔BEST BUY

A high-performance fan, the Hunter Sojourn offers excellent air movement and a variety of color options. Like other Hunter fans, this one has five 52-inch blades and a quiet motor. A special feature of this fan is the midbody blade design; the switchblades are attached to the middle of the motor instead of below it. This allows the fan more head clearance than most models have. Installation is easy and includes three position options: flush to the ceiling, standard height, and extra long or angled. The reversible blades make it easy to coordinate with your decor because the blades are walnut on one side and oak on the other. The motor has a bright brass finish. Four other models are available with different combinations of motor and blade finishes, including white, black, or brass motors with rosewood or white blades. All the wood finish blades are reversible.

Warranty: 25 years, motor parts.

Manufacturer's Suggested Retail Price: $189

Approximate Low Price: $170

BEVERLY HILLS RIO OUTDOOR 12500

✔BEST BUY

Just as the name implies, the Beverly Hills Rio Outdoor fan is designed for use outdoors in damp locations, which makes it an excellent way to increase your use of a porch or covered deck. The motor is a sealed unit, and the blades are made of acrylic for long life in wet conditions. The entire unit is UL-rated for outdoor use. The interior of the motor housing has four small 4-watt light bulbs, which provide a soft, gentle light that's comfortable for nighttime lighting. Bulbs can be changed by loosening the motor casing. The motor casing and the four 52-inch blades are white. The motor is three-speed and reversible. Installation is straightforward and includes two position options: low ceiling and standard hang. The fan adjusts to ceiling slopes of up to 35 degrees. There are many option kits available including an acrylic light kit, wall-mounted fan speed control, and downrods in six lengths.

Warranty: Lifetime, limited.

Manufacturer's Suggested Retail Price: $295

Approximate Low Price: $231

ENCON GEORGIAN 5GN52PBC

✓**BEST BUY**

The Georgian ceiling fan by Encon is an elegant solution to your cooling needs. It has a polished brass finish and a Georgian-style four-light fixture. Detailing in the brass on the motor housing, mount, blades, and light fixture adds to its beauty. One of the advantages of this fan is that you can adjust it in many ways to suit your needs. The 52-inch fan blades can be reversed for either a white or a walnut finish. The fan housing can be mounted flush with the ceiling, or you can use a standard drop mount. Even the motor has knock-out plugs so that you can use four blades instead of five. The fan has three speeds and reverses for heating in the winter. Separate cords control the lighting and fan blades. Along with its low price and quality construction, its 10-year warranty makes it a good value.

Warranty: 10 years, limited.

Manufacturer's Suggested Retail Price: $100

Approximate Low Price: $84

HUNTER MASTER SUITE 21909

Recommended

The Hunter Master Suite ceiling fan is ideal for those who want a high-quality, durable, remote control fan. The fan has five 52-inch blades and a high-performance, quiet motor. The remote control unit is easy to operate even in the dark, making it ideal for bedrooms. From the remote control you can change the one reverse and three forward speeds and the six light levels. Installation is straightforward and simple to adjust to fit your needs. The fan can be installed flush to the ceiling, at standard hanging height, or extra long or angled for vaulted ceilings. The integrated light kit is also easy to assemble. In addition to this model with a white and brass motor and white blades, the Master Suite is available with a brass motor and rosewood/dark walnut blades (21904) and with a white motor and white blades (21906). Hunter's 25-year warranty is one of the best available.

Warranty: 25 years, motor parts.

Manufacturer's Suggested Retail Price: $349

Approximate Low Price: $271

KING OF FANS ASTRO DELUXE 53590 `Recommended`

The Astro Deluxe by King of Fans is a sleek, glossy, quiet ceiling fan. Its black 52-inch blades and bright brass spotlights make it both beautiful and functional. The blades are electronically weighted and pitched for maximum air movement. With its four spotlights, this fan works well in large rooms or stairways, and it provides maximum cooling in smaller rooms. It is easy to adjust the spotlights to provide general lighting or to highlight a specific area—just tilt them into position. The spotlights stay aligned and balanced even under the highest fan speed. There are three forward and reverse speeds. Installation is easy, and an all-angle mounting system is included for flush mount, standard hang, or cathedral mounting. The brass finish is corrosion resistant, as is the black motor housing. The motor unit is sealed and never needs oiling or maintenance.

Warranty: 5 years, limited.

Manufacturer's Suggested Retail Price: $60

Approximate Low Price: $60

AIR CONDITIONERS

CARRIER TCA081P ✓ **BEST BUY**

At the top of the Siesta series of lightweight air conditioners by Carrier are the Siesta II Premium models. This model, TCA081P, has all the features of the other Siesta models plus several extras. It has three fan speeds instead of two, six-way air flow control, exhaust controls, and an energy-saver switch. Like the other models in the Siesta line, it has a one-piece fixed chassis that makes it easy to install. The TCA081P's slightly larger size and weight (63 pounds) make it less transportable than many fans, but its 8,600-Btu capacity makes it suitable for cooling large rooms. It will also fit in large windows (up to 36 inches). This model includes an easy-to-remove filter, built-in sound reducers, rust-proof fan and blower wheels, and a high-efficiency fan motor. Security features, such as special locking screws, make it hard for intruders to remove the air conditioner. Its EER rating of 10.0 makes this an efficient air conditioner in the 8,000- to 10,000-Btu range. The higher the EER, the more efficient the unit.

Specifications: height, 15½"; width, 22"; depth, 14½"; weight, 63 lb.; watts, 875; volts, 115; Btu, 8,500; EER, 10.0. **Warranty:** 1 year, full in-home; 5 years, sealed refrigeration system.

Manufacturer's Suggested Retail Price: $ 449

Approximate Low Price: $449

SHARP AF-T1106X

✔**BEST BUY**

If you have a big room to cool, or one that receives a lot of sunlight, this Sharp air conditioner may be just what you need. It has a powerful compressor which generates plenty of cooling power. And despite its power, it still fits in a window only 20¹⁵⁄₃₂ inches wide and is only 14¾ inches high. To make installation easy, you install the cabinet first, then slide in the chassis. The fully installed unit is 22⁷⁄₁₆ inches deep and weighs 75 pounds. The window-mounting kit is standard. An optional, through-the-wall kit is also available. The one-touch filter pops out for cleaning with little effort. User-friendly buttons, three cooling speeds, exhaust lever, and four-way air direction make it convenient. An energy-saver switch, a fan-only mode, and a 12-hour timer make it efficient. Best of all, it has an EER rating of 9.5.

Specifications: height, 14¾"; width, 20¹⁵⁄₃₂"; depth, 22⁷⁄₁₆"; weight, 75 lbs.; watts, 1,105; volts, information not available;

Btu, 10,5000; EER, 9.5. **Warranty:** 1 year, full in-home service; 5 years, limited on sealed cooling system.

Manufacturer's Suggested Retail Price: $550

Approximate Low Price: $424

PANASONIC CW-806TU

✔**BEST BUY**

One of the best midsize window air conditioners, Panasonic's CW-806TU is a "3 in One" window air conditioner. It is designed to be installed in a double-hung window, sliding window, or through the wall. It has an extra-slim design—only 17²³⁄₃₂ inches wide—so it will fit almost anywhere, and it has a separate, slide-in chassis for easy installation. A double-layered top panel adds strength and reduces vibration noise. Along with extra sound-absorbing material, the compressor is in the part of the air conditioner that extends outside the window. All this results in a very quiet unit. Other features of the CW-806TU include a one-touch air filter, a four-way air deflection system, two cooling speeds, a separate thermostat, ventilation control, two fan speeds, and an economy operation mode. It has a high EER rating of 10.0.

Specifications: height, 13⅝"; width, 17²³⁄₃₂"; depth, 20⅞"; weight, 66 lb.; watts, information not available; volts, 115; Btu, 7,800; EER, 10.0. **Warranty:** 1 year, parts and labor in-house; 5 years, limited on the compressor.

Manufacturer's Suggested Retail Price: $500

Approximate Low Price: $444

CARRIER TCA051B

Recommended

Part of the Siesta series of lightweight air conditioners by Carrier, this model is extra quiet and great for bedrooms or living rooms. Its light weight, only 46 pounds, makes it easy to install, and a retractable handle makes it simple to move, if necessary. The unit also has factory-installed wing panels. Combining these three features makes installation much simpler than it is for most window air conditioners. The filter is easy to remove and replace—just pull up the insert on the front panel. An automatic thermostat maintains the desired temperature. Built-in sound reducers that isolate moving parts, a rust-proof fan and blower wheels, and a high-efficiency fan motor contribute to this model's quiet operation. Extra corrosion protection, which adds to the life of the air conditioner, makes this a reliable choice. The Carrier TCA051B has an EER rating of 8.0.

Specifications: height, 14"; width, 19"; depth, 11"; weight, 46 lb.; watts, 630; volts, 115; Btu, 5,000; EER, 8.0. **Warranty:** 1 year, parts and labor in-home; 5 years, limited on sealed system parts and labor.

Manufacturer's Suggested Retail Price: $279

Approximate Low Price: $279

SHARP AF-806X

Recommended

This Sharp window air conditioner makes an excellent choice for medium size (up to 450 square feet) rooms. It has many of the same features as those in Sharp's Comfort Touch line but at a lower price. The controls are mechanical and there are three cooling speeds, a thermostat control, and a fan-only mode. Installation is simple since this is a fixed-chassis air conditioner in which the cabinet and chassis are in one piece. The unit weighs just 49 pounds and will fit in a small window. Even the depth of this unit is small, which makes it especially useful in locations where a bigger unit might protrude into a path or walkway outdoors. A window mounting kit is standard with this model. The filter easily slides out of the front of the unit for quick cleaning. Other features include two-way air direction and a rotary compressor. This model has an EER rating of 9.0.

Specifications: height, 14⁹⁄₁₆"; width, 19¹¹⁄₁₆"; depth, 16¹⁷⁄₃₂"; weight, 49 lb.; watts, 889; volts, information not available; Btu, 8,000; EER, 9.0. **Warranty:** 1 year, full in-house service; 5 years, limited on sealed cooling system.

Manufacturer's Suggested Retail Price: $450

Approximate Low Price: $347

AIR CARE

HONEYWELL ENVIRACAIRE 12520 AIR CLEANER

✔**BEST BUY**

The Enviracaire 12520 Air Cleaner by Honeywell is a high-efficiency particulate HEPA air filter that is especially quiet. It has a 360-degree air intake and output, making it very efficient at cleaning: It can clean and recirculate the air in a 16-by-20-foot room six times an hour. The cleaner uses a true HEPA air filter to remove 99.97 percent of all the particles in the air, including the most common allergens and pollutants. A prefilter extends the life of the more expensive HEPA filter. The prefilter should be replaced every 3 months, and the HEPA filter every 3 to 5 years. The unit is light (less than 14 pounds) and has a convenient carry handle. It's also small—only 12 inches high by 16 inches in diameter—making it easy to move from room to room. You could set it up in the family room while you watch TV, then move it to the bedroom for nighttime comfort. The controls are located on the front of the unit and are easy to read.

Warranty: 2 years, limited.

Manufacturer's Suggested Retail Price: $220

Approximate Low Price: $184

EMERSON QUIET KOOL DEHUMIDIFIER DG50G

✔**BEST BUY**

The Emerson Quiet Kool is a high-capacity dehumidifier that works very well, especially in tight situations. Its small size, 13½×17¼×21⅜ inches, and front tank access make it easy to use, even in small rooms. With the holding tank in the front of the unit, you can empty the tank without moving the dehumidifier. The holding tank has two hand grips on the sides. If you prefer, the humidifier can be connected to a hose, instead of to the tank, for automatic draining. A slide-out washable filter helps clean the air and allows the unit to run more efficiently. Access to the filter is available from the front of the dehumidifier. To clean the filter, just rinse it in a sink. The dehumidifier also has a top-mounted control panel, making it easy to see and adjust the controls. Basic features include automatic shutoff when the tank is full or removed, a special de-icing control, easy-glide casters, and an automatic humidistat.

Warranty: 1 year, parts and labor; 5 years, limited on sealed refrigeration system.

Manufacturer's Suggested Retail Price: $250

Approximate Low Price: $232

TOASTMASTER COMFORT CONDITIONER HUMIDIFIER 3425

✓ BEST BUY

This Toastmaster Humidifier is an attractive console model that will add up to 10 gallons of moisture to the air every day. This should humidify a medium-size house (up to 2,250 square feet). Its water tank is actually two simple-to-clean 3-gallon tanks, which each have a handle for easy filling and carrying. Water is filtered through a cotton wick to keep impurities from getting into the air. Filters may be cleaned by soaking in a cleaning solution, or they can simply be replaced. Even the streamlined appearance makes for easy cleaning. Its light grey cabinet is textured and the controls are concealed. The unit is quiet, with two-speed operation. The higher speed is useful for raising the humidity rapidly while the quieter, lower speed is comfortable for continuous operation. Other handy features include an automatic humidistat, automatic shutoff, a safety interlock, and a water reservoir refill light.

Warranty: 3 years, parts and labor.

Manufacturer's Suggested Retail Price: $132

Approximate Low Price: $110

WHITE WESTINGHOUSE MDH40FW

Recommended

The White Westinghouse dehumidifier will keep things dry even in extremely wet conditions. It has an adjustable humidistat: At the higher, normal speed, the unit will dry the air quickly, but it is noisier. Once the humidity is lowered to a comfortable level, the lower, quiet speed will keep the air dry. The holding bucket is in the back of the unit. To empty it, pull on the handle and remove the bucket. A convenient pour spout minimizes spills. A larger, separate opening makes it easy to clean the inside of the bucket. An automatic shutoff light signals when the bucket is full, missing, or seated incorrectly. The condensation coils are at the back of the unit and simple to keep clean. Other features include an 18-pint-capacity bucket, casters, frost control, and direct drain hookup.

Warranty: 1 year, parts and labor; 5 years, limited on the sealed system.

Manufacturer's Suggested Retail Price: $229

Approximate Low Price: $184

HEATERS

LAKEWOOD 7096

✓BEST BUY

The Lakewood electric heater is an efficient, clean source of heat. Its heating element warms a sealed diathermic oil that radiates an even, gentle heat. The oil never needs replacing or refilling and there are no fumes or flames. The heating element itself is enclosed in the unit, making it safer than a heater with an open element. With its choice of three wattages (600, 900, or 1500), the 7096 can be used in many locations without tripping a circuit breaker. It has a separate thermostat for constant temperature and automatic on/off cycling. All controls are easy to read and reach. The heater has seven steel fins to disperse the heat quickly, and there is a thermal fuse that shuts off the unit to prevent overheating internally. Even at 28 pounds, the unit moves easily because of its casters.

Warranty: 1 year.

Manufacturer's Suggested Retail Price: $55

Approximate Low Price: $50

DURACRAFT EUROSTYLE CZ-2100

✓BEST BUY

The Duracraft Eurostyle heater fan is a stylish and safe heater. A child-resistant selector switch prevents young children from turning it on. If the heater is knocked over, a tip-over switch shuts it off. There are two separate circuit breakers to detect overheating. Even the cabinet stays cool to the touch. The heater has two settings, drawing 1,000 or 1,500 watts, respectively. A separate, adjustable thermostat maintains the room-temperature you prefer. There is a power-on light and a caution indicator. One advantage of this unit is that it can be used as a fan in the summer and a heater in the winter. At 4.42 pounds, with a built-in handle, the CZ-2100 can easily be carried from room to room. The heating and fan unit tilts to direct the air flow. The controls are easy to read and use.

Warranty: 5 years.

Manufacturer's Suggested Retail Price: $40

Approximate Low Price: $40

KERO-SUN OMNI 105

Recommended

The Kero-Sun Omni 105 by Toyotumi is a kerosene heater for use outdoors or in shop areas. It is a sturdy, well-made unit, designed for easy maintenance. No tools are required—not even to change the wick, which has a mechanical stop that controls its movement for proper heat output without adding pollutants to the air. It's also treated for water resistance, is specially woven for improved combustion, and has a turnoff knob, which reduces noxious odors when the heater is turned off. At only 26 inches high, the heater is a compact unit with the fuel tank integrated into it. The tank itself holds just under 2 gallons of fuel, and its double wall prevents fuel from leaking, even when the unit is tipped over. A separate tip-over safety device shuts off the heater when it is jarred or knocked over.

Warranty: 1 year, parts and labor.

Manufacturer's Suggested Retail Price: $189

Approximate Low Price: $189

BABY EQUIPMENT

Choosing the best baby products can be overwhelming for new parents. These days, the baby equipment industry is more innovative than ever, with companies racing to develop the most advanced products at the most competitive prices. That's great news, but it means the market can be very confusing for the inexperienced shopper. In shopping for baby equipment, keep in mind that your first considerations are safety and comfort; looks are a fringe benefit.

Safety Tips

Several organizations monitor juvenile products. The Juvenile Products Manufacturers Association (JPMA) rigorously tests and certifies products in categories not covered by government regulations. Products that pass the JPMA test may state this on their labels, so look for the JPMA seal of approval.

Make sure all hinges and rough parts are covered so that they cannot pinch or scratch your baby's fingers or toes. Look for baby-safe materials such as plastic and rubber; avoid metals because they can heat up in the sun. Also look for soft, comfortable fabrics, such as cotton.

Make sure that all small parts are firmly secured. Small objects that could come loose represent a choking hazard for your baby.

Any product meant to hold your baby should have a sturdy frame that won't tip over. Look for a high chair with a wide base and for a stroller with large wheels and a substantial body that won't tip when you hang your bag on the handlebars.

Look for straps on car seats, changing tables, and high chairs, and check to see that these will hold your baby securely.

Once you've made your purchase, it's important to stay on top of recall information in case the product turns out to be faulty. The U.S. Consumer Product Safety Commission keeps track of most children's products that have been recalled. The National Highway Traffic Safety Administration tracks recalled car seats.

Portable Cribs and Play Yards

Play yards (or playpens) and portable cribs are similar, and they are often considered to be the same thing. Sometimes they can be used interchangeably, but it's better to use each of these products exactly as specified by its manufacturer. A piece of equipment intended only for use as a portable crib should not be used as a play yard, and vice versa. It's also important to stop using these units when your baby outgrows them; for the most part, they are intended for children less than 34 inches tall or weighing less than 30 pounds.

A portable crib is a handy piece of equipment for travel or for overnight visits to friends and relatives, but it should not be used on a permanent basis in place of a full-size crib. Most portable cribs are rectangular and have sturdy metal or plastic frames, hard bottoms covered with padding, and fabric sides with mesh panels. Generally, these cribs fold down into a compact package that fits inside a carrying case.

Some play yards closely resemble portable cribs, while others are a bit roomier and have mesh sides that allow parents a full view of the child inside. Some also have drop-down sides that make it easier to fold the unit away. These sides, however, should always be raised when the play yard is in use.

When purchasing either a portable crib or a play yard, first make sure that it's sturdy. Give it a shake to see whether it will tip over or collapse accidentally. Look for tightly woven mesh, so small fingers or the buttons on baby clothing can't get caught. Also be sure that the mesh is securely attached to the top rail and floor of the unit and that any vinyl on the unit is sufficiently thick. Otherwise, when a baby sucks on it—or chews it when he or she is teething—small pieces can get stuck in the child's throat. For this same reason, make sure no foam is exposed for tiny fingers to pick at. As with all baby furnishings, watch for sharp points or edges and exposed seams or hardware.

Swings

When you shop for a swing for your baby, stability is the most important concern. After that, you want to consider the ease of setting it up and taking it down, the padding and comfort of the seat, the winding mechanism or motor, and possibly the portability or adaptability of the swing. Some swings double as car seats and/or car beds. This may be a deciding factor for you, or you may decide not to pay for features you don't need.

Nursery Monitors

Nursery monitors help put your mind at ease when you're not in the same room as your baby. The monitor's transmitter stays in the baby's room and relays noise—from soft cooing to loud crying—to your receiver. Most transmitters pick up sounds within a 6- to 10-foot radius and can relay them as far as 150–200 feet, depending on the environment. Modern monitors come with extra features: some come with night-lights; others are cordless for greater mobility; and some very expensive ones feature video display units. One highly desirable feature is a range finder that beeps when the transmitter is too far from its monitor (so there's no more guessing about whether you'll be able to hear your baby if you're in the back yard). Keep in mind that monitor systems are sensitive to interference from other environmental sources (such as physical obstructions or cordless phones), so they are no substitute for periodic in-person checks on your baby.

Car Seats

Car seats for infants and young children are mandatory in all states, and newborns may not be released from hospitals unless a parent has an appropriate restraint system to use on the trip home. All car seats are required to conform to Federal Motor Vehicle Safety Standards, but this does not mean that all seats are suitable for all children. It is important to be aware of the many varieties on the market so you can choose the appropriate car seat for your child. Options include infant-only, convertible, and booster car seats.

Infant Car Seats

Infant car seats, which can also be put to good use outside the car, are intended for newborn babies up to about 20 pounds (a weight usually reached between 9 months and 1 year of age). These car seats are used only in a rear-facing position in the car and must not be used in the front seat if the car is equipped with an air bag. If an air bag deployed, it would strike the back of the infant's car seat at over 200 miles per hour (the base speed for such devices), and the impact of this violent blow to the baby's head could cause brain damage or death. Outside the car, however, these seats can double as carriers, feeding seats, or even rockers. This type of seat is also the best choice for low-birth-weight babies, because the convertible car seats that also accommodate older infants or toddlers are likely to be too large—even in the infant position—for smaller newborns. Remember, if the child does not fit correctly in the seat, the seat cannot provide optimum protection.

Convertible Infant Car Seat/Strollers

These products can come in handy as car seats, strollers, and infant carriers. Many parents enjoy the convenience of being able to take the baby from the car to the stroller without undoing and refastening complicated harnesses. If you're shopping for a convertible infant car seat/stroller, first read our introductions on infant car seats and on strollers to make sure the model you're considering has all the safety and comfort features recommended for a car seat or a stroller. In addition, check the fasteners that hold the car seat to the stroller—they should be sturdy and secure—and try it out to see whether conversion from car seat to stroller and back is quick and easy enough to suit your needs.

Strollers

Many parents tend to buy infant carriages or standard strollers in addition to the umbrella strollers that can be carried around easily in the car. Today, however, the best strollers grow with your baby, combining the luxury of a carriage and the practicality of an umbrella stroller.

Look for a lightweight, easy-to-fold stroller with removable padded seats, reversible handles, and large, durable wheels. Certain extra features can be important, too. Many strollers come with seat inserts to keep a tiny baby's head secure, two shopping baskets, and/or a removable canopy with a sun strip.

A safe stroller has a wide base to prevent tipping; wide wheels and shock absorbers for smooth, straight steering; seat and crotch belts securely attached to the frame; straps that are easy to fasten and unfasten; and secure brakes. (It is important to test the brakes before purchasing a stroller.) Shopping baskets should be located directly over or in front of the rear wheels. Always fasten the seatbelt, and keep your child's hands away when you fold or unfold the stroller.

Best Buys '97

Our Best Buy, Recommended, and Budget Buy baby equipment follows. Within each category, products are rated according to quality and safety. The item we consider the best of the Best Buys is listed first, followed by our second choice, and so on. Remember that a Best Buy, Recommended, or Budget Buy designation applies only to the model listed. It does not necessarily apply to other models produced by the same manufacturer or to an entire product line.

PORTABLE CRIBS AND PLAY YARDS

EVENFLO HAPPY CAMPER BASSINET
TRAVEL PLAY YARD 344811
✓ BEST BUY

Thanks to a special attachment that elevates the mattress and support board of this unit to a position suitable for newborns (about 9 inches down from the top rail of the crib instead of the full 21 inches), this colorful travel play yard can be used from birth as a bassinet and a bit later as a small play yard/travel crib. The sturdy Happy Camper Bassinet comes in royal blue with a contrasting fabric in a teddy-bear pattern. It has smooth corners and padded rails, is lightweight and extremely portable, and can be set up or collapsed in a few minutes. Large wheels (with locks) on one end of the unit make it mobile when it's set up, and you can transport the play yard in its zippered carry bag when it's collapsed (it collapses to a

10×10×30-inch package). A mattress, a fitted sheet, and a removable toy bag are included with the unit. One special feature of the Happy Camper is the new cabana attachment (Cabana 639711, $20) that can be purchased along with it. This separate cover shields your baby from the elements and makes the crib/play yard more versatile outdoors. The cabana includes a shade that can be rolled down on one side, covering the see-through panels and acting as a draft guard when the baby naps. Both the cabana cover and the toy bag are washable.

Warranty: 1 year, parts and labor.

Manufacturer's Suggested Retail Price: $100

Approximate Low Price: $95

EVENFLO HAPPY CABANA TRAVEL PLAY YARD 346185

✔**BEST BUY**

Clean-lined nautical looks brighten this green-and-white-striped travel crib, which can double as a small play yard. The sturdy Happy Cabana Travel Play Yard has smooth corners and padded rails. The separate cabana can be fitted to the top of the assembled crib to provide shelter from damp or breezy weather. This cover comes with a shade that can be rolled down one side of the crib, covering the see-through panels and keeping out drafts or bright sunlight when the baby dozes. This shade matches the removable toy bag and sheet included with this crib. This model is lightweight and fits into a zippered 10×10×30-inch carrying bag. When it's set up, the crib can be moved by means of large wheels on two of its legs; for safety and stability, these wheels lock. The Happy Cabana is also available in blue and white.

Warranty: 1 year, parts and labor.

Manufacturer's Suggested Retail Price: $100

Approximate Low Price: $100

CENTURY FOLD 'N' GO 10-830

✔**BEST BUY**

This play yard is portable, so you can travel with it, but it's also an ideal size for use at home. All its corners are covered with sturdy plastic. The strong steel frame and the floor-board are covered with padded nylon in a variety of patterns. Mesh panels on all four sides allow you and your baby to keep each other in view. One end of the unit holds the large removable matching toy bag, and the other end offers a roll-down draft guard for protection during naps. One special feature is the Fold 'n' Go's easy-to-use "micro-fold" system with a lock mechanism on the top rail. It's simple to set the play yard up and take it down, and it folds into a package roughly 1×1×3 feet. Folded down, it's enclosed in its comfort pad and can be carried (it weighs just 25 pounds) in a tote bag with a handle strap (included). Set up, it measures 28×41 inches long.

Warranty: 1 year, limited.

Manufacturer's Suggested Retail Price: $80

Approximate Low Price: $80

KOLCRAFT OCTAGON PLAYARD
18503

✔**BEST BUY**

This roomy "playard" is 27.5 inches high, 38.5 inches long, and 38.5 inches wide. In spite of its ample size, it's relatively easy to set up and take down (the double-drop sides have sturdy stay-locked hinges). The Kolcraft Octagon Playard folds to a manageable size for storage or travel, weighs only 24 pounds, and includes carrying handles. The strong steel frame and floorboard are covered with padded nylon casings and mats in a variety of patterns and colors, and the sides of the unit are made of a strong but see-through mesh. Instead of a post at each corner, the frame features center support legs that extend diagonally to the unit's outside edges.

Warranty: 1 year, repair or replace.

Manufacturer's Suggested Retail Price: $70

Approximate Low Price: $70

GRACO PACK 'N' PLAY 9046CN

Recommended

This model offers the standard features of a good travel crib, plus a bassinet attachment that elevates the mattress and support board to a position suitable for newborns (about 10 inches down from the top rail of the crib instead of the full 22.5 inches). The Pack 'n' Play's lightweight construction incorporates smooth corners, and it can be assembled in less than 1 minute. There is strong nylon mesh on two of the panels and a roll-down flap on one side. The basic fabric is an attractive, easy-to-clean, navy-blue nylon. The Pack 'n' Play comes with a unique attached carrying case—the support board actually folds up to encase the unit—and it has swivel casters with brakes on one end for added mobility.

Warranty: Not available

Manufacturer's Suggested Retail Price: $130

Approximate Low Price: $100

COSCO ZIP 'N' GO 05-361

Budget Buy

This model, which is 28 inches wide and 40 inches long, features rounded molded-plastic corners, a strong steel frame and floorboard (both covered with nylon padding), and mesh panels on all four sides. The padded floorboard becomes a carrying case for the unit when it's folded, and folding the Zip 'n' Go is very easy. If space is at a premium in your home, this is a play yard to consider.

Warranty: 1 year, conditional.

Manufacturer's Suggested Retail Price: $60

Approximate Low Price: $55

SWINGS

COSCO DREAM RIDE PLUS 08-980

✔**BEST BUY**

This classic wind-up swing from Cosco offers several special features. The swing seat is also a combination rear-facing car seat or side-facing car bed, and this seat can be used in a sideways cradle position on the swing or in the car. When it's attached to the swing frame, you can switch it from this cradle position to the conventional forward-facing position with a simple rotating motion—you don't have to remove and reattach the seat. This deluxe baby swing operates on a winding mechanism instead of on batteries, but its crank is unusually quiet to operate, the swing runs for a full 30 minutes, and a Minute-Minder times the mechanism as it winds down. As a car bed, this is the only infant restraint that can be used in a seat equipped with an air bag. (If you don't need the car seat/cradle option and just want a long-running, quiet, wind-up swing, consider Cosco's Quiet Time Elite, model 08-989, for $60.) This swing is available primarily through hospitals.

Warranty: 1 year, conditional.

Manufacturer's Suggested Retail Price: $100

Approximate Low Price: $100

GRACO ADVANTAGE SWING 1434NF `Recommended`

The Advantage Swing's seat doesn't turn into a car seat or a carrier, but the swing itself is a fine product. The "A"-shaped frame forms a stable base for the unit. The seat, which can be set in four positions from sitting to reclining, is covered in a handsome, thickly padded, navy blue cloth. This cover can be removed and washed, and the seat itself features a head support and a tray with a toy bar. A simple push-button control panel on the side operates the swing. The motor allows three speed variations and should run for up to 200 hours on four alkaline D cell batteries.

Warranty: Not available

Manufacturer's Suggested Retail Price: $90

Approximate Low Price: $85

NURSERY MONITORS

GERRY RANGE CHECK NURSERY MONITOR 610

✔ **BEST BUY**

This monitor offers the exclusive Range Check device that assures parents the unit is actually working and alerts them if they go outside its technical limits. This model also features a low-battery indicator, adapters for outlet use, and two channels to ensure clear reception. The nursery unit comes with a built-in night-light, and the transmitter actually fits inside the receiver for compact, go-anywhere convenience. The transmitter and receiver each run on four AAA batteries.

Warranty: 1 year, repair or replace.

Manufacturer's Suggested Retail Price: $35

Approximate Low Price: $35

FISHER PRICE CORDLESS NURSERY MONITOR 1562

✔**BEST BUY**

The concept of the cordless phone is applied here to the nursery monitor. This Fisher-Price receiver is designed to be portable during the day and can be recharged at night. (The charging base and rechargeable batteries are included with the unit.) The monitor remains operational while it is charging. This feature eliminates the need for frequent and expensive battery changes, and the receiver's charging indicator ensures optimal battery performance. Two separate channels assure parents of good reception, and both the receiver and the transmitter come with an AC adapter and a durable, rubberized antenna.

Warranty: 1 year, limited.

Manufacturer's Suggested Retail Price: $53

Approximate Low Price: $50

FISHER PRICE SUPER-SENSITIVE NURSERY MONITOR 1555

Budget Buy

This basic monitor is sensitive enough to pick up most sounds a baby makes while in its crib. The receiver offers two channels to minimize interference. There is a power light and a flexible antenna on both the transmitter and the receiver. The receiver can be plugged in or powered by a 9-volt battery, but the transmitter must be plugged in.

Warranty: 1 year.

Manufacturer's Suggested Retail Price: $33
Approximate Low Price: $30

CAR SEATS

Infant Car Seats

CENTURY SMARTFIT 4525

✔**BEST BUY**

Century designed the SmartFit infant car seat with compatibility in mind. The unit's sculpted base is contoured to fit more of today's vehicle seats, and the slots on this base are placed higher to accommodate both the raised seatbelts found in most newer cars and the older-model seatbelts. The seat also features a handle that adapts to a variety of comfortable positions (for carrying, rocking, feeding, and play), a one-handed car-seat release, a built-in level indicator to ensure proper installation, and a two-piece harness tie that facilitates securing and removing infants quickly. This car seat, which accommodates children from birth to 20 pounds, must be used in the rear-facing position only and never in an air-bag-equipped seat.

Warranty: 1 year, limited.

Manufacturer's Suggested Retail Price: $70

Approximate Low Price: $65

KOLCRAFT INFANT RIDER WITH SMART HANDLE 13832

Budget Buy

This car seat's ergonomically designed foam-grip handle pivots when the seat is carried, thereby minimizing strain on a parent's wrist and forearm. The Infant Rider also features a three-point harness system with an easy-to-operate push-button release; a removable contoured sunshade that can be pulled up or down; a full-length rocking base; an extra-wide interior for growing babies; and removable, washable, quilted padding. This easy-to-install model accommodates babies up to 20 pounds and can be used only in a rear-facing position. Its handle adjusts so the seat can be used for feeding or rocking outside the car.

Warranty: 1 year, repair or replace.

Manufacturer's Suggested Retail Price: $55

Approximate Low Price: $55

Convertible Car Seats

CENTURY SMART MOVE 4710

✔**BEST BUY**

Parents who wish to buy only one car seat should consider this model. Thanks to a Smart Move feature, this is the first and only child car seat approved by the government that positions infants in a developmentally appropriate rear-facing reclined position while traveling, but shifts them to an upright position (considered more protective in a collision) at the moment of impact. This change of position spreads the force of the impact across the baby's back and shoulders instead of concentrating it in the more vulnerable head and neck areas. Immediately after impact, the infant seat returns to its reclined position. The unit also includes a removable infant head-support cushion. Several features make this car seat worth recommending, whether it's used facing rear (babies under 20 pounds) or forward (under 40 pounds): a quick-release, five-point harness-system; easy-access seat-positioning handles located in the front and back; hourglass contoured seat design for better infant and toddler support; and an easy-to-adjust, six-position growth harness that comes with a front-pull strap.

Warranty: 1 year, limited.

Manufacturer's Suggested Retail Price: $110

Approximate Low Price: $110

EVENFLO ULTARA V PREMIER
234119/234140/234186

✔**BEST BUY**

Removable pillow-like cushions (complete with sturdy fasteners consisting of clips, elastic, and Velcro) and a three-position recline make this Evenflo car seat uncommonly comfortable. The five-point harness system can be adjusted to accommodate a growing child, making this car seat both practical and safe. Use the seat in a rear-facing position for infants from 5 to 20 pounds and in a forward-facing position for toddlers up to 40 pounds. A front strap can be pulled to tighten the harness system, and the luxurious wrap-around plush pad is removable and washable. The Ultara V Premier is available in three colors: hunter green (234119), accent onyx (234186), and blue velvet (234140).

Warranty: 1 year.

Manufacturer's Suggested Retail Price: $109

Approximate Low Price: $87

CENTURY 1000 STE

Budget Buy

This convertible car seat comes with a five-point harness system with a soft anchor for the buckle. The six-position growth harness accommodates growth and/or bulky clothing; the two-position recliner stand is adjustable for stability on different types of upholstery; and the fabric pads are machine washable. The unit accommodates children from birth to 40 pounds, and can be used in a rear- or forward-facing position.

Warranty: 1 year, limited.

Manufacturer's Suggested Retail Price: $60

Approximate Low Price: $55

Convertible Car Seats/Strollers

KOLCRAFT PLUS 5 ULTRA WITH SMART HANDLE 36845

✓**BEST BUY**

Moving a sleeping baby from a car seat to a stroller is easier with this combination unit. The Plus 5 Ultra infant car seat/carrier has an ergonomic handle with a pivoting hand grip, a sunshade canopy, and a three-point harness with a push-button release. It functions as an infant car seat with or without its base. The easy-to-fold, two-position reclining stroller has an adjustable canopy for extra sun protection, a large storage bin, and an extra stroller seat pad. It also features an ergonomic stroller and car-seat handle and an extra padded insert in the seat. As an added bonus, the Plus 5 Ultra can be assembled or adjusted without a screwdriver.

Warranty: 1 year, repair or replace.

Manufacturer's Suggested Retail Price: $150

Approximate Low Price: $150

CENTURY 4-IN-1 SYSTEM PRO SPORT 11-650

✔**BEST BUY**

Century's 4-in-1 System Pro Sport, featuring Century's new SmartFit car seat with the TraveLite Sport Stroller, offers both versatility and convenience. It includes an "All-Ways" handle with a soft grip; a sculptured base designed to fit many cars; an easy one-hand release for removing the carrier from the base; and a new, easy-to-use, two-piece harness design. The stroller folds easily, has a reclining seat-back with a peek-a-boo window, and includes an extended canopy for extra sunshade protection and an extra-large storage bin.

Warranty: 1 year, limited.

Manufacturer's Suggested Retail Price: $150

Approximate Low Price: $150

STROLLERS

GRACO FULL-SIZE STROLLER 7775

✔**BEST BUY**

This Graco stroller offers several practical features at a sensible price. An easy-fold mechanism collapses the stroller in one step; an extra-wide frame provides stability; and a well-padded, three-position reclining seat assures comfort. This stroller comes with a height-adjustable, reversible handle to convert the stroller into a carriage, a pad for infant head support, an adjustable canopy that has a peek-a-boo window with flap, a padded guard rail, and a footrest. There's an extra-large storage basket on the bottom of the stroller and a storage bag built into the canopy, as well as balloon tires for a smooth ride. The Full-Size Stroller weighs 23 pounds.

Warranty: Not available

Manufacturer's Suggested Retail Price: $146

Approximate Low Price: $125

COMBI SAVVY IV 262/263/264

✔**BEST BUY**

Thanks to the use of aircraft aluminum in its frame, this sturdy stroller weighs only 7 pounds. It collapses with a single movement and reclines to any position up to a 140-degree angle, which is good for young infants. The Combi Savvy IV also features an adjustable and removable canopy, a storage bin under the seat, a footrest, and an optional shoulder strap attached to the unit for carrying it when it's collapsed. This model is not JPMA-certified.

Warranty: 1 year, parts and labor.

Manufacturer's Suggested Retail Price: $169

Approximate Low Price: $160

KOLCRAFT MONACO SE DELUXE CARRIAGE STROLLER 46531

✔**BEST BUY**

The Monaco SE Deluxe has reversible handles, which are not essential on a stroller, but are certainly a plus with a baby who wants to see you. This 22-pound stroller features a multiposition reclining seat, an extra-large storage basket, an adjustable sun canopy (with a see-through window), a padded handle, dual rear brakes, Kolcraft's new "Hugger" wheels for smoother maneuverability, a padded napper bar, and a removable and washable seat pad. This stroller collapses with a single motion.

Warranty: 1 year, repair or replace.

Manufacturer's Suggested Retail Price: $90

Approximate Low Price: $90

CENTURY ADVENTURE 11-281

Recommended

This stroller offers a fine suspension system, quick and easy folding, a washable comfort pad, a reclining seat, a sun canopy with a peek-a-boo window, a storage pouch on the back, and an oversized storage basket. It also comes with a removable napper bar and a higher handle for comfortable pushing. The oversized all-terrain wheels (front wheels are 8.5 inches in diameter and rear wheels are 10 inches in diameter) have front-swivel locks and single-action rear brakes.

Warranty: 1 year, limited.

Manufacturer's Suggested Retail Price: $100

Approximate Low Price: $100

BOOSTER

CENTURY BREVERRA PREMIERE 4885

✔**BEST BUY**

This seat, which can be used for children weighing between 30 and 60 pounds, offers a special five-point transitional harness system for lower-weight children (between 30 and 45 pounds). Century equips this booster with a thick, blow-molded, seat-shaped pad that surrounds the back and bottom of a child's body and lifts them several inches off the seat of the car. This makes a child the perfect height for the three-point (lap and shoulder belts) harness system found in newer model cars. Consequently, this booster seat cannot be used for larger children in an older-model car that has only lap belts.

Warranty: 1 year, limited.

Manufacturer's Suggested Retail Price: $60

Approximate Low Price: $59